CARIBBEAN OFFICE PROCEDURE FOR CXC AND SIMILAR EXAMINATIONS

CARIBBEAN OFFICE PROCEDURE FOR CXC AND SIMILAR EXAMINATIONS

FOURTH EDITION

VELMA JARDINE FSCT, MFTCom

*Principal, The Stenotype College, Woodbrook,
The Republic of Trinidad and Tobago*

and

JOSEPHINE SHAW MIPD, FIMgt, FInstD

Josephine Shaw Associates, Lymington, Hampshire, UK

A member of the Hodder Headline Group
LONDON

First published in Great Britain in 1984 as
Office Procedure for CXC or Similar Examinations
Second edition 1995 by Edward Arnold
Third edition 1998 by Arnold
Fourth edition by Arnold,
a member of the Hodder Headline Group,
338 Euston Road, London NW1 3BH

http://www.arnoldpublishers.com

©1984, 1995, 1998, 2002 Velma Jardine, Josephine Shaw

All rights reserved. No part of this publication may be reproduced or transmitted in any form or by any means, electronically or mechanically, including photocopying, recording or any information storage or retrieval system, without either prior permission in writing from the publisher or a licence permitting restricted copying. In the United Kingdom such licences are issued by the Copyright Licensing Agency: 90 Tottenham Court Road, London W1T 4LP.

The advice and information in this book are believed to be true and accurate at the date of going to press, but neither the authors nor the publisher can accept any legal responsibility or liability for any errors or omissions.

British Library Cataloguing in Publication Data
A catalogue record for this book is available from the British Library

ISBN 0 340 76364 7 (pb)

1 2 3 4 5 6 7 8 9 10

Production Editor: Wendy Rooke
Production Controller: Bryan Eccleshall
Cover Design: Meusemat

Typeset in 10 on 14 pt Garamond Book by Charon Tec Pvt. Ltd, India
Printed and bound in Great Britain by The Bath Press

> What do you think about this book? Or any other Arnold title?
> Please send your comments to feedback.arnold@hodder.co.uk

CONTENTS

List of activities   *xiii*
Preface   *xv*
Acknowledgements   *xvii*

1. The organisation   1
- Types of business organisation   1
- Business management   4
- Functions   6
- Departments   9
- Administration   15
- Organisation charts   16
- Questions   17

2. Systems and procedures   21
- Systems   21
- Procedures   22
- Types of office   22
- Furniture   25
- Care for the individual worker   26
- Safety in the office   28
- Security   32
- Rights and obligations of the employee   35
- Interpersonal skills   36
- Specimen job descriptions   37
- Questions   38

3. Information processing   43
- What is information processing?   43
- Who are the people?   44
- Computer equipment   47

	Software	52
	Databases	53
	Security	53
	Consumables	53
	Transmission of data	54
	Internet	55
	Accessing the Internet	56
	E-mail addresses	56
	Using the Internet	57
	E-commerce and e-business	59
	Hacking and corruption	59
	Computerised presentation	60
	Questions	60
4.	**Receiving visitors and using telephone equipment**	**64**
	Reception	65
	Telephone equipment	73
	Telephone services	84
	Using telephone equipment	88
	Creating a professional image	100
	Questions	103
5.	**Written communications**	**108**
	Advantages of written communication	109
	Disadvantages of written communication	109
	Types of written communication	110
	Composing written documents	110
	Planning and preparing to write	116
	Desk notes	116
	File notes	117
	Internal memoranda	118
	Letters	120
	Invitations	125
	Reports	126
	Notes, minutes and reports of meetings	127
	Forms	128
	Legal documents	130
	Transmission	130
	Telegrams	131
	Telex	134
	Facsimile transmission	135
	Electronic mail (e-mail) transmission	138

	Choosing the type of communication to use	139
	Proofreading	140
	Reading	142
	Questions	143
6.	**Document production and reproduction**	**149**
	Documents	149
	Recording equipment	151
	Supplies for typewriters and printers	154
	Typewriters	161
	Word processors	164
	Computer word-processing software	166
	Printers	166
	Copiers	168
	Computerised image copier/printer	172
	Copy printers	172
	Offset lithography and offset-litho machines	173
	Collators and joggers	175
	Guillotines	176
	Punches	176
	Fastenings	177
	Binding	181
	The importance of presentation	182
	Questions	183
7.	**Document storage and retrieval**	**188**
	What filing is	189
	What a filing system comprises	189
	What is filed	190
	Who files	190
	Where information is stored	190
	What equipment is used	193
	How files are arranged	198
	When filing is done	206
	How filing is done	207
	Why filing is a vital task	209
	Security	210
	Retention policy	213
	Archiving	214
	The essential elements of a good filing system	216
	Microcopy	216
	Document destruction	220

	Working files	221
	Bring-forward systems	222
	Electronic storage and retrieval of computer files	223
	Questions	224
8.	**Mailing**	**230**
	Incoming mail	231
	Outgoing mail	236
	Internal mail	242
	Methods of mailing	243
	The mail room	244
	Questions	245
9.	**Post Office services**	**248**
	The seven stages of the postal collection and delivery service	249
	Addressing format	250
	Postcodes/zipcodes	251
	Recommended envelopes and cards	252
	Postage rates	253
	Collection services	256
	Receiving mail	256
	General postal services	259
	Business postal services	262
	Choice of service	265
	Other services	265
	Service standards	266
	Advice, information and complaints	267
	Postal authorities	267
	Questions	268
10.	**Commercial documents for buying and selling**	**271**
	Documents used in a business transaction	272
	Home trade	273
	Requisition	273
	Enquiry	273
	Quotation, estimate, tender	276
	Order	278
	Acknowledgement of order	280
	Processing the order	280
	Pro-forma invoice	281
	Advice note	281

	Packing, despatch, delivery, consignment notes	283
	Goods received note	285
	Invoice	286
	Debit note	287
	Credit note	287
	Statement of account	287
	Receipt	289
	Overseas trade	289
	Bill of lading	289
	Air waybill	290
	Certificate of insurance	290
	Certificate of origin	290
	Application for licence to import goods	294
	Entry ex ship for goods liable to duty	296
	Customs bill of sight	296
	Terms used in trading	296
	Units of measurement	300
	Questions	301
11.	**Methods of payment**	**313**
	Types of bank account	314
	Making payments	317
	Payment by cheque	318
	Payment by bank draft	322
	Payment by crediting	322
	Payment by standing order	322
	Payment by direct debit	323
	Payment by credit card	324
	Payment by Switch card	324
	Payment by money order	325
	Payment by postal order	325
	Payment by documentary credit	325
	Payment by electronic transfer	326
	Payment by travellers' cheques	326
	Withdrawing money from a bank account	327
	Paying money into an account	328
	Bank statements	330
	The banks' clearing system	333
	Borrowing money	334
	Development of banking services	335
	Questions	336

12. Business records — 341

- Purpose of records — 342
- Personnel — 342
- Salaries and wages — 349
- Factory — 373
- Stock — 378
- Credit sales — 381
- Petty cash — 384
- Presentation of statistics — 388
- Questions — 398

13. Meetings — 407

- Purposes of meetings — 407
- Types of meeting — 408
- Arranging a meeting — 410
- Documents — 414
- Minute file — 419
- Committee files — 420
- Presentations — 420
- Meeting room — 421
- Teleconferencing — 422
- Structure of formal committees — 423
- Procedure — 424
- Preparing to take notes at a meeting — 425
- Taking notes at a meeting — 425
- Drafting the record of the meeting — 427
- Numbering minutes — 431
- Presentation of minutes — 431
- Preparing an 'action sheet' — 432
- Indexing minutes — 433
- Role of the chairperson — 433
- Role of the 'committee' secretary — 434
- Role of a member — 435
- Committee terms — 435
- Questions — 437

14. Travel arrangements — 443

- Handling a request — 444
- Travel — 444
- Accommodation — 446
- Documents — 447

	Money and methods of payment	447
	Carriage of equipment and materials	448
	Insurance	449
	General information	449
	Scheduling appointments	450
	Itinerary	450
	Reservations	452
	Checking documents	454
	Electronic airline booking	454
	Travel pack	454
	Checklist	456
	In the absence of the traveller	459
	Sources of information	460
	Questions	461
15.	**Sources of information**	**467**
	Sources of information	467
	Types of information from each source	468
	Reference books	471
	How to use a reference book	475
	How to use a dictionary	476
	The best approach to the process of research	480
	Questions	480
16.	**Obtaining employment**	**483**
	Where to start looking	484
	Applying for a job	489
	Interviews	494
	Being offered employment	499
	Starting work	502
	Appraisals	503
	Resigning	504
	Sex discrimination	504
	Career development	505
	Questions	506
Appendix 1	*Common grammatical errors*	*508*
Appendix 2	*Tips on punctuation*	*512*
Appendix 3	*Part 1 Countries in the Caribbean, their capitals, official languages and currencies*	*516*
	Part 2 Countries of the Commonwealth	*518*

Appendix 4	*Part 1 Caribbean Association of Industry and Commerce Membership listing*	*519*
	Part 2 Caribbean Congress of Labour trades unions mailing list	*526*
Appendix 5	*Answers to activities*	*531*
Appendix 6	*Suggested answers to questions*	*557*
Appendix 7	*Study notes*	*610*
Index		*613*

LIST OF ACTIVITIES

1.1	Functions	9
1.2	Departments	15
1.3	Organisation chart	17
2.1	Procedure	22
2.2	Office layouts – disadvantages	23
2.3	Interpersonal skills	36
3.1	Steps in a project plan	47
4.1	Visitors' register	68
4.2	Telephone calls and services	87
4.3	Telephone message	96
4.4	Outgoing message on answerphone/voicemail	99
4.5	Receptionist – personal presentation	102
5.1	Precise expressions	113
5.2	Desk note	116
5.3	Internal memorandum	120
5.4	Letter	125
5.5	Form for receipt of registered mail	130
5.6	Telegram	133
5.7	Errors	141
5.8	Key points of a letter	143
6.1	Paper sizes	161
6.2	Electronic typewriter facilities	168
6.3	Office equipment and stationery	183
7.1	Alphabetical filing by name	201
7.2	Alphabetical index	202
7.3	Numerical file list	202
7.4	Subject file index cards	203
7.5	Substitution note	213

7.6	'Out' cards	213
7.7	Archiving files	215
8.1	Incoming mail register	235
9.1	Postage	256
9.2	National postage rates and postal services	267
10.1	Letter of enquiry	276
10.2	Order form	279
10.3	Delivery note	284
11.1	Cheque with counterfoil	321
11.2	Paying-in slip	329
11.3	Bank reconciliation statement	332
12.1	Accident form	347
12.2	Wage calculation	371
12.3	Cash requisition	372
12.4	Cost schedule	376
12.5	Stock record card	380
12.6	Petty cash items	384
12.7	Petty cash analysis records	387
12.8	Line graph	390
12.9	Multi-line graph	391
12.10	Pie chart	396
13.1	Arranging a meeting	411
13.2	Notice and agenda	419
14.1	Itinerary and letters	460
15.1	English-language books	473
15.2	Using reference books	475
15.3	Using an English dictionary	479
16.1	Curriculum vitae	489
16.2	Application form	494

PREFACE

Caribbean Office Procedure has been completely rewritten for this fourth edition. The style has been adapted to blend its content with the changing circumstances of the office and to cater for a wider readership in the Caribbean islands. There is more emphasis on technology than in previous editions but manual systems are still common in smaller businesses so have been covered in detail as a means of setting out the basic principles.

The objectives the writers set themselves were to enable students to:

- gain a thorough understanding of the fundamental procedures that form the bedrock of administration
- be guided in how to carry out these procedures
- cover the learning required for CXC Office Procedure examinations, Pitman Qualifications in Office Procedures Levels 1 and 2, and the London Chamber of Commerce Examinations Board Business Administration Levels 1 and 2.

It is also the intention to provide a reference book for students' future working life and for those already working.

In order that students may enjoy their learning, activities have been introduced into each chapter so that they will 'learn by doing'. Understanding will develop by applying the learning to relevant tasks. Suggested answers to the activities are given in Appendix 5. (In some cases it is not possible to give an answer as it depends on the particular territory in which the student is studying.)

In some chapters students are asked to find things out for themselves, e.g. the cost of Post Office services. Charges are constantly being updated and are different in each island in the Caribbean; this provides real-life experience as it occurs in offices.

At the end of each chapter, there are usually three sets of questions to be attempted. The first of these, practice questions, based on the content of the chapters they follow, form a good basis for revision. It is suggested that if time is limited, students could work in groups, each group discussing a few of the questions and giving their answers to the class.

Short answer questions follow the practice questions, while each chapter ends with relevant past examination questions.

Suggested answers to these questions are provided in Appendix 6. In many cases a reference to the text is given. It is thought that this will encourage students to identify their weak areas and to revise appropriately.

For further practice in examination questions it is suggested that students could usefully work through *Past papers 1993-1996 Office Procedures Basic and General Proficiencies*, published by the Caribbean Examinations Council (ISBN 0 333 74443 8).

It should be noted that to avoid the 'gender problem', and the constant use of 'he or she', the pronoun 'they' has been used throughout.

The authors wish to express their sincere appreciation of the help and advice given by many individuals during the preparation of this book. They are also grateful to the many organisations that have allowed their staff to check facts and give guidance on future trends. All, including the organisations that have provided photographs, are listed in the Acknowledgements on pages xvii to xviii.

It is hoped that students and teachers will enjoy learning and teaching, using *Caribbean Office Procedure*, and will achieve success both in their examinations and in their work.

Velma Jardine
Josephine Shaw
London 2002

ACKNOWLEDGEMENTS

The authors wish to express their thanks to the following individuals, who took an interest in the development of this new edition and offered valuable advice.

Mr Hubert Alleyne and Mr David Martin, former Chief Executive Officers of the Trinidad and Tobago Chamber of Industry and Commerce

Mrs Linda Besson, Executive Director, and Mr Gabriel Yates, Industrial Relations Adviser, of The Employers' Consultative Association of Trinidad and Tobago

Mr Paul Dalton, former Managing Director, and Mr Dave Curtis Gunn, Marketing Manager, of Trinidad & Tobago Postal Corporation

Mr James H Gunderson, External Communication Programme Manager of the Universal Postal Union, for the list of postal authorities in the Caribbean

Mr Ernest King, Assistant General Manager, Human Resources, of the Royal Bank of Trinidad and Tobago Limited

Mr Carlos Chan Qui, Payroll Administrator of PricewaterhouseCoopers

Mr Dewan Singh, Marketing Development Manager, Telecommunications Services of Trinidad and Tobago Limited

Mrs Eurica Neckles, Manager, Cellular Marketing of Telecommunications Services of Trinidad and Tobago Limited

Mr Patrick Flook of 3M Interamerica Inc.

The authors wish to thank the organisations that have provided photographs for reproduction.

BWIA British West Indies Airways Limited   Fig. 14.7
Brother UK Ltd   Fig. 6.12
Cambridge Consultants Limited   Fig. 4.7
Canon UK Limited   Figs 5.10, 6.13, 6.14
Citibank (Trinidad and Tobago) Limited   Fig. 11.6
Fellowes Manufacturing (UK) Limited   7.17
Kodak Limited   Fig. 7.15
NRG Group Marketing   Fig. 6.15
Philips Speech Processing   Figs 6.1a, 6.1b

Pitney Bowes plc   Figs 8.12, 8.14
Silver Reed Office Supplies Ltd   Fig. 6.7
Universal Metal Co. Ltd   Fig. 4.11

Thanks are also due to the organisations that allowed reproduction of forms.

BWIA British West Indian Airways Limited
Government of the Republic of Trinidad and Tobago – Board of Inland Revenue Department
Ministry of Trade and Industry and Consumer Affairs
The National Insurance Board of Trinidad and Tobago
The Royal Bank of Trinidad and Tobago Limited
Trinidad & Tobago Postal Corporation

Pitman Qualifications are thanked for permission to reproduce questions from past examination papers. The suggested answers given in Appendix 6 are provided by the authors and are not the work of Pitman Qualifications.

CHAPTER 1

THE ORGANISATION

OBJECTIVES When you have studied this chapter you should have acquired the knowledge and understanding to be able to:

1. differentiate between the different types of business organisation
2. explain how organisations are structured
3. explain the difference between functions and departments
4. explain why administrative tasks have to be carried out in all departments
5. list the functions and the key activities they involve
6. list the activities usually carried out in each department
7. explain the reasons for having organisation charts
8. prepare a simple organisation chart.

Business is conducted by all types and sizes of organisation from sole traders to multinational corporations. The various types of organisation, their structures and who manages them, are explained in this chapter.

TYPES OF BUSINESS ORGANISATION

The main types of organisation, from the smallest to the largest, are:

- sole trader
- partnership
- private limited company
- public limited company.

SOLE TRADER

A sole trader is someone who owns a small business. The owner may run the business alone, e.g. a plumber, electrician or small shop. The business may be conducted under the owner's name or a name that indicates the business, e.g. The Fabric Shop. As the business grows the owner will employ staff. Day-to-day working decisions are made by the owner, who is in sole control and is responsible for paying all debts. Should the owner ever be unable to pay the debts, the assets of the business, e.g. property, machines, have to be sold. If there is still insufficient money to pay the debts the owner must sell their personal possessions and if that does not raise sufficient money the owner is declared **bankrupt**. In most countries this means that the trader is not allowed to trade again until the debts are paid or until a certain number of years have passed since the declaration of bankruptcy.

PARTNERSHIP

A business is called a partnership when two or more people pool their financial resources and run the business jointly. For example, an accountant may start a practice alone and then, as the business develops, employ staff. As the practice grows still further, either one of the staff is promoted to be a partner or someone is recruited as a partner. Sometimes the partner brings money into the business and shares the profits.

Professional partnerships such as solicitors usually do business under the names of the senior partners. Business partnerships may be, e.g. John Smith & Partners (or Company) or a business name such as The Furniture Design Company.

If two or more people start a business together they would all contribute money, called capital, though not necessarily the same amount in each case. For example, Paul, Emily and Ben decide to start a small engineering factory. They each contribute money – Paul 30 per cent, Emily 50 per cent and Ben 20 per cent. They will probably pay themselves a weekly or monthly wage and then, at the end of the year, share the profits in the same ratio as they contributed capital.

A person who contributes capital to a new or developing business, but does not work in it, is known as a 'sleeping partner'. Major decisions, e.g. about the development of the business, are normally taken by all the partners. Everyday decisions about the running of the business are taken by the working partners.

If the business is not successful and accumulates debts, the partners are responsible for paying them. They can be forced to sell their personal belongings in order to pay the debts.

PRIVATE LIMITED COMPANY

When two or more people want to start a business, or when a very small business has grown, the owners may want to limit their responsibility for the payment of debts. They do this by registering the company as a **limited company**, each of the two or more people involved receiving **shares** for the capital they contribute. A **Memorandum and Articles of Association** are drawn up setting out how the business is to be conducted. The company's name is followed by 'Limited' or 'Ltd', e.g. Caribbean Drinks Ltd. In the event of the business being financially unsuccessful the shareholders will lose some or all of the money they invested but are not liable for debts that cannot be paid.

There are other advantages to working as a limited liability company. It is often easier to borrow money from banks to develop the business than it is for a sole trader. They may have access to various government services as a **corporate** body, i.e. a company.

The company has a **Board of Directors**, some or all of whom normally work in the business. The shareholders may or may not work in the business. Those who do are usually paid a salary and share the profits, called **dividends**, according to the number of shares they hold. Those who do not work receive dividends on the same basis.

If a shareholder does not wish to continue holding shares, they can be sold to other shareholders or to someone else. This is a private arrangement, not advertised publicly. The maximum number of shareholders is set out in law in each country. A limited company must produce **annual accounts**, a copy of which has to be sent to the Registrar of Companies, and hold an **annual general meeting** (AGM), which all the shareholders are entitled to attend.

PUBLIC LIMITED COMPANY

The difference between a private and a public limited company is that the shares of the latter can be bought and sold on the Stock Exchange by members of the public and other organisations. A limited company adds 'Company Limited' (Co. Ltd) or 'Limited' (Ltd) after its name.

A public company has a Board of Directors headed by a **President**. Large companies have vice-presidents who are each responsible for a **business unit**, which is a particular function of the organisation. Business units operate as specialist companies, which have to be profitable and meet pre-determined objectives.

As a public limited company grows it may be divided into smaller companies. For example, a company producing food products decides to divide into two small companies, one to produce processed food, the other to buy and sell fresh foods. Additional smaller companies may be added to produce new types of product. These smaller companies each have to be successful within the **group**, which is owned by the same shareholders as those who owned the original company.

As the number of companies in a group increases there is often a **holding company**, which is the financial **parent company** of the group. Each small, or **subsidiary**, company has to be successful. All public companies have to conduct business in accordance with the Companies Acts, and with the regulations instituted by the Security and Exchange Commission or its equivalent regulatory body in each territory. They must produce audited annual accounts and hold an annual general meeting, which shareholders are entitled to attend.

The terms **SMLEs** and **multinationals** are often used. SMLEs are small, medium and large enterprises – sole traders, partnerships and private companies of any size. Many governments make special arrangements in their business legislation to help these businesses to develop and employ more people.

Multinationals are very large companies that have developed by establishing companies overseas. Examples of multinational businesses are AmocoBP (oil), ICI (pharmaceuticals) and Unilever (food and household products).

There are also **corporations**, established to provide government services such as electricity, national banks, telecommunications, tourism and water. Government services can also be provided by privately owned companies, but they are controlled by one or more appropriate government departments and have to adhere to government policy.

Co-operatives are owned by the members, usually owners of very small businesses, who form a group in order to share costs such as transport.

BUSINESS MANAGEMENT

Where a number of people are working together there must be a means of organising the work. There must be a structure and there must be company aims and objectives.

COMPANY STRUCTURE

The shareholders choose the **president** and **directors** who are to be in charge of the company and responsible for its success. People are needed to do the work involved in producing and selling goods/services. A pyramid is the simplest structure. The most senior person, often a **General Manager**, is alone at the top. As we move down the pyramid there are more staff at each level of management and most at the bottom of the pyramid. This is illustrated in Fig. 1.1.

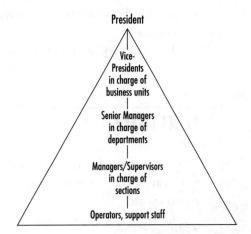

Fig. 1.1 *Pyramid structure of an organisation.*

In many companies there are now fewer levels of management than there used to be. This means that each manager has more responsibility. Also, staff at lower levels are expected to take more responsibility for their own work. This has lead to the development of **team working**.

CORPORATE AIMS AND OBJECTIVES

Whatever the size of the organisation it must have business, or corporate, aims and objectives. The general aim of any business is to make a profit in order to survive and grow. Even non-profit-making organisations have to make a profit in order to develop their products and services, but they do not make profit for distribution.

Corporate objectives are more specific than aims. They are decided by the board of directors for a number of years ahead. They have to be reviewed frequently because changing circumstances in a trading area such as the Caribbean, in an individual territory or in the world, affect individual organisations. For example, if one year the weather is bad for citrus fruits or a disease affects citrus plantations, a company that produces citrus juices will be affected because supplies will be short and what is available will therefore cost more than it did before.

Examples of corporate objectives include:

- increase profits by a certain percentage
- increase turnover (the value of sales) by a certain percentage
- develop one or more new products
- increase or decrease expenditure on research
- establish a new area of activity, e.g. a bank decides to offer insurance services
- close a factory or build a new one.

FUNCTIONS

In order to carry on a business there are certain functions that have to be carried out, most of them in even the smallest business. These functions are:

- finance
- personnel
- marketing
- production
- administration
- information processing.

These functions are carried out in a specific department or group of departments and also partly in the departments of other functions. For example, all senior managers have to deal with budgets and budgetary control (finance), with recruiting staff (personnel) and receiving, processing and transmitting information (administration).

FINANCE

Finance includes:

- ensuring that the organisation complies with the laws on company finance
- obtaining funds needed for expansion of the business, usually from a bank

- setting budgets, i.e. the amount that may be spent on plant, equipment, furniture, vehicles (capital budget), salaries and wages, marketing (advertising, etc.) and all the other expenses of running a business
- budgetary control to ensure that the budgets are not overspent
- paying bills for goods and services bought
- credit control to ensure that the organisation does not have 'bad debts' (money owing that customers cannot afford to pay)
- payment of salaries and wages, including statutory deductions
- cash office to reimburse staff who spend their own money on the organisation's behalf
- internal audit, which involves checking documents, cash and stock to ensure that there is no fraud, pilfering or waste (of money or stock).

PERSONNEL

Personnel includes:

- manpower planning to determine the number and type of staff and skills required over the next few years
- recruiting staff, from the point of producing job descriptions to selecting the best applicants and offering them appointments
- ensuring that conditions of service, including salary scales, are regularly reviewed, and that staff welfare and benefits are made available as appropriate
- ensuring that grievances and disciplinary matters are dealt with effectively
- carrying out industrial relations negotiations with representatives of staff associations and trades unions
- providing induction for new employees, developing training plans and ensuring that individual staff are given the training they need
- administering appraisals or personnel development reviews, and ensuring that they are carried out regularly in order to identify the training needed to help staff improve and develop their potential
- ensuring compliance with national employment legislation.

MARKETING

Marketing includes:

- market research to find out what customers and the public at large want
- liaising with Production (see below) to ensure that the right type of products and/or services can be provided at the right time

- advertising products and services
- public relations to create and maintain the right company image, which will attract new customers and retain existing customers
- maximising sales to existing and new clients, both at home and overseas
- providing after-sales service to customers
- customer relations to deal with complaints quickly and efficiently.

PRODUCTION

Production includes:

- research and development for new products/services
- design of new products and modification of existing products
- purchasing of materials and/or 'bought in' parts to be made into products
- work study to find the most efficient way of producing products
- making standard products and/or individually designed products
- storage of materials and finished goods
- transport for delivering finished goods to wholesalers or retailers, or to individual customers.

ADMINISTRATION

Administration includes:

- legal aspects of the company's business
- office services – reception and telephone, mail, filing, reprography, clerical/secretarial services, maintenance of premises, furniture and equipment
- security – of the site, the building, access control, identification cards/access cards.

INFORMATION PROCESSING

Information processing includes:

- systems development
- programming
- data input
- operations
- communications.

These activities will be explained in detail in Chapter 3.

ACTIVITY 1.1   Look at the tasks listed below. Decide which **function** each task belongs to and write the task number and the function beside it. Example:

1. Buying electric plugs to put on electric kettles to be sold.

   You will write: '1 production'.

   Now continue for numbers 2 to 10.

2. Researching the effect of putting additives in food.
3. Finding the best way to operate a new machine in a factory.
4. Deciding how much money will be needed in the forthcoming year.
5. Printing 20 000 instruction leaflets for a product.
6. Recruiting a manager for the production department.
7. Dealing with a customer's complaint.
8. Contacting a bank for a reference for a new customer.
9. Arranging the route for a delivery van driver.
10. Organising an exhibition.

You will find the answers to all activities in Appendix 5.

DEPARTMENTS

We have said that various aspects of the functions outlined above are carried out across the organisation. Certain tasks are performed by certain departments but many tasks involve two or more departments. We will now look at the departments that carry out specific tasks. (Note that departments are sometimes called 'divisions' or 'units'.)

ACCOUNTS DEPARTMENT

Staff working in an accounts department may be divided into sections to deal with purchase accounts, sales accounts, budgetary control, credit control (see Chapter 10, page 281), or salaries and wages (see Chapter 12, page 349).

The head of the department is the **Chief Accountant**. There will be other qualified accountants in a big organisation, each responsible for one of the sections. There will also be accounts assistants.

Every organisation has a **financial year**. The government's financial year is 1 January to 31 December and all government departments work on that basis. Companies may work on different dates, e.g. 1 April to 31 March or 1 July to 30 June. At the end of the financial year every trader and organisation must produce accounts to show how much money has been spent and received during the year, how much profit has been made and what the financial situation is at year end. These are known as **year end accounts** and include a **trading and profit and loss account**, and a **balance sheet**. Copies of these accounts are sent to shareholders before the annual general meeting of the organisation.

PERSONNEL DEPARTMENT

Depending on the size of the organisation, the personnel function may be carried out by one person or it may be a large department with several staff members each covering an individual activity.

The head of the department is the Personnel Manager who, in a large organisation, is assisted by personnel officers. They may be specialists in recruitment, employment, industrial relations, human resource planning, or welfare and training.

In some organisations there is a separate training department headed by a training manager. There may also be training officers and instructors who are specialists in certain areas such as management development.

In territories where there is employment legislation, the personnel department may have a staff member who is in charge of ensuring that new laws are implemented throughout the organisation. This may include completing returns for the appropriate government department(s).

SALES DEPARTMENT

This department is headed by a **sales manager** who is responsible for ensuring that sales targets are met. There may be two main sections, one dealing with home sales, the other with overseas sales. Each of these sections would be headed by a manager reporting to the sales manager.

Market research may be carried out by the sales staff or by specialist staff. This is an essential pre-requisite to establishing what customers want, how much they will pay for products, what type of advertising produces the best results, and so on.

Many companies, especially those selling plant, machinery and equipment of any kind, have an **after sales service** to ensure that customers are satisfied, to service the equipment, etc., and to investigate complaints.

PURCHASING DEPARTMENT

Finding sources from which to obtain goods required by any department, and the process of ordering goods (see Chapter 10, page 272) is the responsibility of this department.

PUBLIC RELATIONS (PR) DEPARTMENT

The creation and maintenance of a good corporate image – the impression the public has of the organisation – is the responsibility of the **public relations manager** or PR officer. An image is created by many factors. The PR department is responsible for various specialist activities, including:

- advertising in all appropriate media, e.g. newspapers, magazines, TV, radio
- publicity literature
- promotion campaigns involving advertising, mail shots, special or free offers, coupons, etc.
- design of packaging for products
- design of livery for delivery vans
- design of letter headings and commercial documents
- design of house styles, i.e. the layout of documents, which should be followed by all staff
- press releases.

In a large organisation there may be a separate section in the PR department for advertising with an **advertising manager** in charge of this.

Smaller companies often employ public relations and/or advertising **agencies** to undertake the activities outlined above; there may be insufficient work to justify employing a person in-house to do the work.

CUSTOMER SERVICES DEPARTMENT

Sometimes called the 'customer relations' or 'customer care' department, this department is headed by a **customer services manager**. The role of customer services staff is to answer customers' queries, explain how to order goods, in some organisations actually take orders, give telephone numbers of staff in other departments or other branches of the organisation, and deal with complaints.

PRODUCTION DEPARTMENT

A production department is structured in many different ways, depending on the type of product being made. There may be:

- several different types of workshop on various sections within the plant (factory)
- research workshops where prototype, i.e. new, products and updated products are tested
- a design office where products are designed and modified
- a drawing office where working designs are drawn from which the workshop employees can make the products
- stores where materials and 'bought in' parts are kept until needed on the shop floor
- quality control, which involves checking the completed products to ensure that they meet the required standards
- a warehouse where finished products are kept ready for despatch
- a factory office where records of production (the number of products made), machine faults and **down time** (time when machines are out of action), and **wastage** (products that do not meet required standards), are kept.

There is usually a **production manager** or **works manager** who is responsible for all the departments and sections related to production. Each major section has a manager to whom supervisors report.

TRANSPORT DEPARTMENT

This is a separate department in a large organisation but may be integrated into the production department in a small organisation. The **transport manager** is responsible for choosing the means of transport for the various products to be sent abroad as well as within the country of origin (the country where the goods are produced).

Goods may be transported by road, rail (in some countries), sea or air. Many small organisations have their own transport for local delivery, and large companies may have their own fleet of container lorries for trans-continental delivery.

Lorries, trucks and vans must be loaded in order of delivery of the items. Special arrangements may have to be made for packing heavy plant and machinery for which lifting gear may be needed.

LEGAL DEPARTMENT

The **company secretary**, or in a large firm, the **company solicitor** is in charge of the legal department. Here legal matters relating to the business of the organisation are dealt with. These matters can include:

- agreements and guarantees relating to products sold or rented
- contracts, e.g. for building work
- hire purchase and other financial agreements
- insurance
- employees' compensation and motor accidents
- employment legislation and other statutory requirements relating to employees
- statutory requirements under company legislation including holding the minimum number of board meetings, production of the annual report and accounts, and holding an annual general meeting for shareholders to attend, ensuring that the company complies with its Memorandum and Articles of Association, i.e. the documents that established the company at its outset.

TELECOMMUNICATIONS DEPARTMENT

This department may be integrated into the information processing department or may be called the communications department. It is managed by a **telecommunications** or **communications manager**, whose responsibilities include ensuring that all telecommunications equipment functions correctly and that faults are dealt with promptly. The equipment may include the internal network, see Chapter 3 page 54, that links the telephone system, fax machines and centralised dictation systems to the computers. It will also include regular checking of telephone lines linking the computer to the Internet.

It is essential that staff use this equipment properly. To ensure that this can happen, instruction manuals may have to be written, and training given to individuals and/or groups of staff.

MAIL ROOM

The procedures for handling incoming and outgoing mail, including letters, telegraphic communications and faxes are discussed in Chapter 8. There is usually a mail room supervisor, assisted by staff and/or messengers who deliver and collect mail from the departments.

CENTRAL FILING REGISTRY

The procedures for storing and retrieving documents are discussed in detail in Chapter 7. Large organisations may have a central filing registry so that records are available to any member of staff who needs, and is authorised, to see them. The archiving of files that are non-active, i.e. not currently in use, is carried out annually. Records of archived files are updated each year.

PRINTING DEPARTMENT

The printing, or reprographics, department is headed by a **print manager** or supervisor. The various ways of printing documents are discussed in detail in Chapter 6. All kinds of documents, including letterheads and commercial documents, product literature, equipment manuals, posters and bound books may be produced in the printing department.

INFORMATION PROCESSING DEPARTMENT

The work of this department is discussed in detail in Chapter 3. In some organisations it may be called the computer or data processing department. It is headed by an **information processing manager** who is assisted by managers/section heads, whose roles are explained in Chapter 3.

The department staff usually includes:

- a projects manager, responsible for directing and supervising the implementation of computer projects
- systems designers
- systems analysts
- programmers

> **ACTIVITY 1.2** Write down the number of each of the following job titles and beside it write the department in which the person doing this job would be found.
>
> 1. typist
> 2. operator working on a lathe
> 3. van driver
> 4. designer for packaging
> 5. recruitment officer
> 6. packer of goods for distribution
> 7. purchase accounts clerk
> 8. storeman
> 9. sales representative
> 10. clerk preparing contract documents

- operations controller and machine operators
- data input operators
- technical support staff.

ADMINISTRATION

You now know that the main functions are carried out in specialist departments. Administrative tasks are carried out in all departments and may include:

- extracting, collecting, analysing and collating data and information
- recording data and information, manually and electronically
- preparation of correspondence, reports, etc., in manuscript, by dictation and/or by keyboard input to the computer
- production of correspondence, reports and other documents
- checking, comparing and authorising commercial documents, e.g. invoices
- reproduction of documents by copying or printing
- transmission and receipt of information by a variety of media
- sorting, storage and retrieval of documents, manually and electronically
- handling money.

These activities are often referred to as 'office work' but they have to be done in places other than offices. For example, a lorry/truck/van driver has to complete a form showing his mileage and places, times and duration of stops. Staff in all departments have to complete forms for different purposes, send information either internally and, in most departments, externally. It is important to understand that nothing can be done without administrative procedures being carried out accurately and efficiently.

ORGANISATION CHARTS

We have seen that all organisations have five main functions that have to be carried out to make a business successful. In small organisations some of the activities will not be necessary. In medium and large organisations there are so many activities involved that there must be departments to carry out different groups of activities. Within large departments there are usually sections, each section being responsible for some specific activities.

No two organisations work exactly alike. In order to see how a particular organisation is structured it is usual to have an organisation chart. This shows the departments in the organisation, and the numbers and types of staff in each department. In Fig. 1.2a we see a chart that shows the

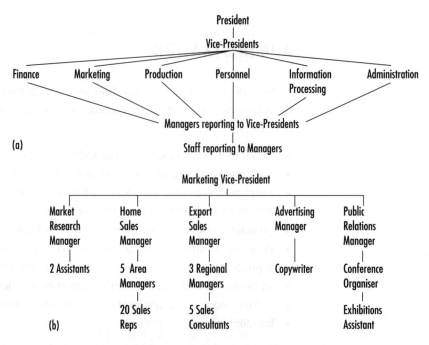

Fig. 1.2 (a) Overview of an organisation chart;
(b) organisation chart of a department.

president at the top, vice-presidents who report to the president, managers who report to the vice-presidents and staff who report to the managers. Fig. 1.2b shows a departmental organisation chart.

ACTIVITY 1.3 Copy out the organisation chart below. Then insert the various job titles, listed below it, in the correct positions. (Make sure you give yourself enough space to write in the job titles.)

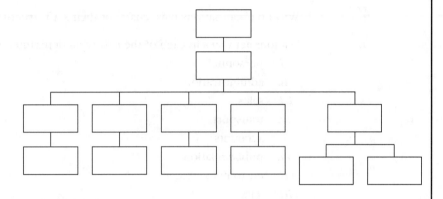

Job titles

Marketing Manager
Systems Analyst
Vice-President
Recruitment Officer
Chief Accountant
Training Officer
Production Manager

Personnel and Training Manager
President
Public Relations Officer
Research & Development Supervisor
Credit Control Clerk
Information Processing Manager

PRACTICE QUESTIONS

1. In which departments would you find staff doing the following tasks:
    i. dealing with a complaint
    ii. operating a computer console
    iii. budgetary control
    iv. delivering mail to departments
    v. security

   vi. ordering bought in parts
   vii. staff welfare
   viii. writing copy for a brochure
   ix. designing a new product
   x. explaining to a potential customer how to order goods?

2. In Fig. 1.1 you see a 'pyramid' staff structure. Why is it described in this way?

3. Who has the greatest amount of responsibility in an organisation?

4. Why do organisations have charts of their staff structure?

5. List four activities in each of the following departments:
   i. personnel
   ii. administration
   iii. sales
   iv. transport
   v. accounts
   vi. public relations
   vii. customer services
   viii. legal
   ix. production
   x. telecommunications.

6. Explain the following words and phrases:
   i. induction course
   ii. organisation chart
   iii. a personnel officer
   iv. home sales
   v. employment legislation

7. What is the difference between a 'sole trader' and a 'partner'?

8. Who is responsible for the debts in a partnership?

9. Give five examples of corporate objectives.

10. What is the difference between a 'function' and a 'department'?

11. State five kinds of work that are done under the heading 'office services'.

12. Name five documents that staff working in a legal department might deal with.

13. Administrative tasks are carried out in all departments. State five activities that administration involves and give an example of each activity.

SHORT ANSWER QUESTIONS

Complete the following sentences.

1. A person who owns a business on his own is a ....

2. People who cannot pay their debts after all their business and personal possessions have been sold are ....

3. The money needed to start a business is called ....

4. When a group of people start a limited company a .... are drawn up setting out how the business is to be conducted.

5. A public company is managed by a .... headed by a ....

Choose the most appropriate ending for each of the following sentences.

6. A multinational company is:
    a. a group of companies in the home country
    b. a group of companies in an overseas country
    c. a group of companies with one or more companies in several countries
    d. a lot of individual companies in various parts of the world.

7. Corporations provide:
    a. free services to the public
    b. government services to the public
    c. specialist services to private individuals
    d. free services to private individuals.

8. A bad debt is:
    a. not being able to pay your creditor
    b. being owed money by someone who cannot pay
    c. having made a mistake in an invoice
    d. being late paying a bill.

9. Which of the following tasks are carried out in the personnel department?
    a. designing advertisements
    b. recruiting staff
    c. dealing with complaints from customers
    d. induction for new employees
    e. secretarial services

10. Organisation charts show:
    a. how the organisation works
    b. the structure of the organisation
    c. the most important people in the organisation
    d. the people who are working in the organisation.

EXAMINATION QUESTIONS

1. State THREE functions of an office.

a. ....

b. ....

c. ....

(Pitman Office Procedures Level 1 1998 Pt 1A)

2. Read the scenario below carefully and then draw an organisation chart to show the new structure of Mr Land's office.

> Scribesworld Ltd is a company distributing speciality writing equipment. Its head office is in London with branch offices in several continents.
>
> You are personal assistant to Mr John Land, general manager at head office. Mr Land controls four departments – administration, finance, sales and shipping – each with a manager and a secretary. Other staff include an accounts clerk, credit control assistants, export/import clerks, a receptionist, representatives, a telephonist and shipping accounts clerks.
>
> New posts of messenger and transport clerk have recently been created.

(Pitman Office Procedures Level 2 1998 Pt 1)

CHAPTER 2

SYSTEMS AND PROCEDURES

> **OBJECTIVES** When you have studied this chapter you should have acquired the knowledge and understanding to be able to:
>
> 1. differentiate between a system and a procedure
> 2. explain the three main types of office layout, their advantages and disadvantages
> 3. explain the importance of being safety-conscious and state the general rules for safe working
> 4. recognise the essential skills, knowledge and personal attributes needed to perform administrative roles effectively
> 5. explain the rights and obligations of the employee, and the importance of interpersonal skills in the work situation.

SYSTEMS

All organisations have systems and procedures. A system is the way in which functions are carried out. For example, a telephone system involves much more than just the telephone on the desk. It involves:

- the types of equipment used – switchboard, extension telephones, etc.
- the location of equipment
- the types of cables used and speed of transmission required
- the facilities available when using the equipment
- the services provided by the telephone company

- the provision of equipment to overcome physical limitations of individuals, e.g. blindness, deafness
- the need for confidentiality
- people's ability to use the equipment and facilities available.

Another example of a system is given in Chapter 7, page 189 (filing).

PROCEDURES

When a system has been designed, the next step is to establish the procedures needed to operate it successfully.

All administrative tasks have to be carried out in accordance with stated procedures. This includes the operation of equipment such as copiers, fax machines and telephones. Procedures are the individual 'steps' involved in carrying out a task.

Procedures for making and receiving telephone calls are set out in Chapter 4. Study these and see how important it is to give all the details.

> **ACTIVITY 2.1** Consider a simple task, e.g. stapling or punching a document. Think what steps you take in doing this task and write a procedure that a newly recruited school-leaver could follow. Number each step.

TYPES OF OFFICE

There are three types of office:

- cellular
- open plan
- landscaped.

CELLULAR OFFICES

A cellular office is a room provided for one person and sometimes two people. The main advantages of this type of office are:

- some people find it easier to concentrate when they are on their own and there are no noises going on around them

- there is no problem when confidential work is being done, since there is no one else to see it
- people vary in liking/not liking windows open, heating/air conditioning levels, etc.
- the door can be locked when the person who works in the office leaves it for a time during the day and at night.

OPEN-PLAN OFFICES

Open-plan offices are large areas in which many people can work. Desks are arranged in rows, and equipment such as filing cabinets, copiers and fax machines are located either centrally in the room or at the sides.

The advantages of open-plan offices are:

- a large room is cheaper to build and maintain than a lot of small rooms
- the layout of the room can be changed easily when necessary
- less equipment is needed as one of each type of machine can be used by everyone in the room
- staff can easily consult each other when the need arises
- it is easier for supervisors to work with their staff and show new staff how to do their jobs.

LANDSCAPED OFFICES

Nicer to work in than open-plan offices, landscaped offices are very large but are divided into individual areas by screens, which provide some privacy. Plants are arranged to contribute to a more pleasant atmosphere. The advantages of landscaped offices are:

- people who are doing the same kind of work can be located together in a section surrounded by screens
- the layout of the desks is less formal than in an open-plan office
- there is better security than in an open-plan office as people doing confidential work can be given an individual area surrounded by screens.

Figs 2.1a, b and c show the three types of office layout.

> **ACTIVITY 2.2** The advantages of each type of office have been suggested. Now consider the disadvantages of each type of office. Make a list for each type.

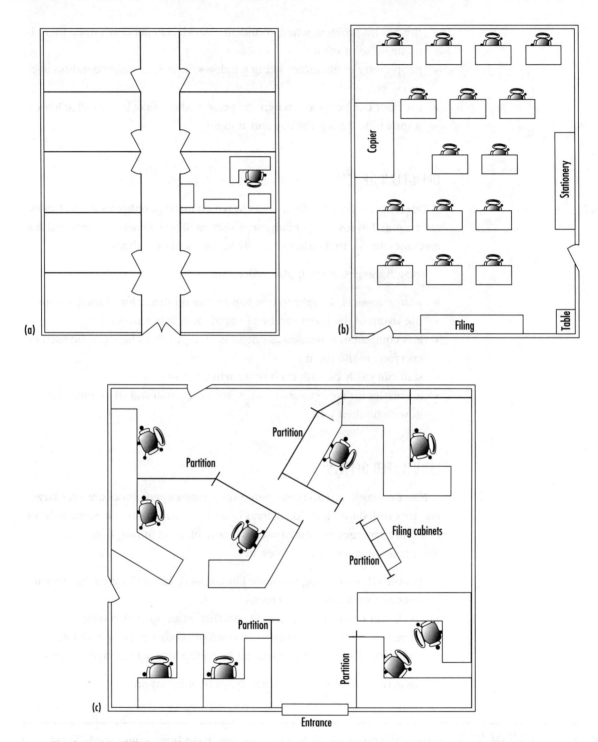

Fig. 2.1 (a) Cellular office layout; (b) open-plan office layout; (c) landscaped office layout.

FURNITURE

Whatever job a person is doing in an office they should be supplied with appropriate furniture and machines. It is important that furniture is **ergonomically** designed. This means that the design of the furniture takes account of the shape of the human body and eliminates strain on any part of it. There are many medical problems associated with such strain, which can be caused by desks not being of the right height and chairs that cannot be adjusted properly.

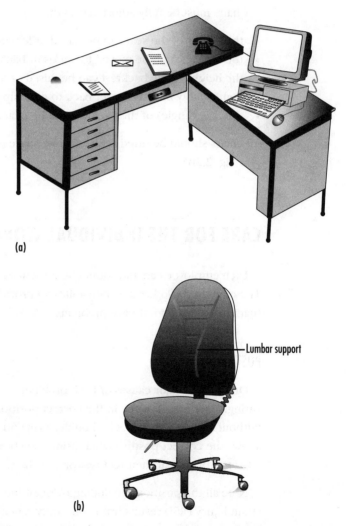

Fig. 2.2 (a) Desk with work surfaces at two levels; (b) ergonomically designed typist's chair.

DESKS

Different heights of work surface are needed for different activities, e.g. writing, operating a particular machine such as a computer keyboard, and drawing, for which a tilted surface is needed.

People commonly carry out more than one activity, e.g. writing and operating a keyboard. There are desks that have two levels of work surface (see Fig. 2.2a) so that each activity can be carried out comfortably, without strain.

CHAIRS

Chairs must be fully adjustable so that:

- the height of the seat can be raised or lowered
- the backrest can be moved forwards or backwards
- the height of the backrest can be raised or lowered so that it fits comfortably into the lower back to give support
- the rake (angle) of the backrest can be changed.

All chairs should be fitted with a five-star base to avoid them tipping over (see Fig. 2.2b).

CARE FOR THE INDIVIDUAL WORKER

Each employee can and should help themselves to avoid some problems. The employer also has a responsibility to provide some services to ensure that employees do not have problems.

POSTURE

One of the major causes of back problems is incorrect posture when sitting. Machines must be in the correct position for the individual to work without straining their neck, shoulder, arm and wrist muscles. Fig. 2.3 shows the correct posture when using a keyboard. Short people should have a **footstool** so that their feet rest on a surface.

Note all the positions, including those of the arms and wrists. Repetitive strain injury (RSI) results from constantly repeated movement of particular ligaments and muscles in a difficult position. The keys on a keyboard should be tapped with the cushions of the fingertips. The line from the second

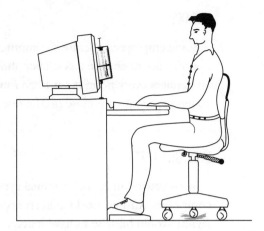

Fig. 2.3 Correct posture for keyboard operation.

joint of the fingers to the elbow should be straight. When the wrists are dropped the strain on neck and shoulder muscles is felt immediately. A **wrist rest** can be used if necessary. The elbows should be held slightly away from the sides of the body.

Copyholders should be used to avoid constantly having to look down to the copy laid flat on the desk. The copyholder should be placed in a position where it is comfortably in view for reading. The angle can be adjusted on some types of copyholder.

KEYBOARD OPERATING

All employees who have to operate a keyboard should be taught the correct posture as explained above. They should also be taught to operate the keyboard with all fingers to avoid the necessity for too much movement of the hands.

When operating a keyboard the following points should be checked.

- Is the keyboard placed where it can be operated comfortably?
- Is the visual display unit in the correct position for reading with the screen tilted at an appropriate angle?
- Is there light reflection from the screen? A **shield** should be placed over the screen to avoid glare. Ideally the screen should be placed where the light does not reflect from it, but this is not always possible.
- Is the density of the text displayed on the screen adjusted so that it is clear but not too bright?

BREAKS

Some employees operate a computer for long periods with little opportunity to change tasks. They should have regular breaks. The ideal is 10 minutes every hour. It has been found that employees who take regular 10-minute breaks are more productive than those who do not.

EYESIGHT TESTS

Many organisations offer annual eyesight tests to staff who operate computers. Anyone working in an organisation that does not offer this facility would be wise to have regular checks themselves, at least every two years. Most people do not have a problem but some find that their sight deteriorates when they operate a computer regularly for long periods.

SAFETY IN THE OFFICE

One hears about accidents in factories but it should be remembered that although there are not many fatal accidents in offices, there are a great many less serious accidents. There should be two types of safety guidance in the office: general procedures to follow at all times, and procedures to follow when using machines and equipment.

GENERAL SAFETY GUIDELINES

Do not:

- block fire exits
- leave cabinet drawers/doors and desk drawers open
- put machines/equipment too close to the edge of a desk
- stack cupboards so full that things fall out when the doors are opened
- leave chairs, waste bins, packages, etc. close to doors
- put packages down in the aisles between desks or in corridors
- open more than one filing cabinet drawer at a time – close one before opening another
- cover scissors, drawing pins, etc. with papers on the desk
- leave spilt liquid on the floor – wipe it up immediately
- stand on a swivel chair to reach to high shelves
- lift heavy items or even reasonable weights without bending the knees
- ignore danger/hazard signs (see Fig. 2.4).

SAFE USE OF MACHINES AND EQUIPMENT

Do not:

- use broken plugs or sockets, or overload plug sockets
- use a machine or extension lead that has a frayed cable
- allow a kettle to boil dry
- remove the plug from the socket or insert a plug into the socket when a machine is switched on
- leave a fault without reporting it
- carry machines incorrectly – DO carry them with the weight against you
- place machines too close to a wall or block off cooling vents
- touch electric equipment with wet hands
- use the wrong equipment for the job
- open a machine, e.g. a printer or copier, without switching it off, unless it is automatically switched off when opened
- touch hot parts of a machine
- remove safety guards from machines such as paper cutters
- ignore danger/hazard signs on equipment.

ACCIDENTS

In spite of following such guidelines, accidents do sometimes happen. It is important to inform someone – a manager, personnel officer, first aider – of the accident. A record must be made of the accident and certain information must be included in the report (see Chapter 12, page 346).

DANGER/HAZARD SIGNS

Various signs are found around an organisation and on machines. Make sure you can recognise them. The most common ones in use are shown in Fig. 2.4.

SAFETY LEGISLATION

Legislation has been enacted in a number of Caribbean territories covering safety in the workplace. Under various Acts of Parliament employers have certain legal obligations to their employees. Employers in each individual territory have to comply with specific laws, as outlined below.

Barbados	Factories Act 1984
Jamaica	Workmen's Compensation Act, applies only to employees under 18 years of age, women over 65 years of age and men over 70 years of age

Fig. 2.4 Hazard signs.

	National Insurance Act Revised Laws of Jamaica 1973 covers female employees between the ages of 18 and 65, and male employees to 70 years of age
Trinidad and Tobago	Factories Ordinance 18 December 1948 Workmen's Compensation Act Chap. 8801 Occupational Safety and Health Bill 2001

Although the requirements of legislation in different territories vary, in general they indicate that the **employer** must ensure that:

- there is a safe and healthy working environment
- equipment/machines are safe, are equipped with guards and are serviced regularly
- safe working practices are maintained and reviewed regularly
- employees are trained to know and follow safety guidelines, and to handle goods and machines correctly
- supervisors refer for disciplinary action those employees who do not comply with safety rules
- employees have adequate working space (minimum 8.5 cubic metres per person)
- there are adequate toilets, washing and drying facilities, accommodation for clothing, and safe drinking water
- there is adequate lighting
- there is adequate ventilation, i.e. windows that can be opened or air conditioning
- eating facilities are available
- rest rooms are available for anyone taken ill
- there are a first-aid box and trained first aiders
- forms are available for reporting accidents
- there is a consultation process for discussing health and safety matters
- there are regular fire alarm tests and fire drills at least annually.

The **employees** are expected to:

- work in a safe manner so as not to put colleagues at risk
- follow safe working practices and safety guidelines
- participate in fire drills
- co-operate on all safety issues.

It is very important that all employees read notices setting out the procedure to follow in the event of fire or bomb threats. Every employee should know what to do, where to go and how to get there. A specimen procedure is shown in Fig. 2.5.

> **FIRE EMERGENCY PROCEDURE**
>
> **If you see smoke or signs of a fire**
>
> - Operate the nearest alarm
> - Go to the nearest telephone and contact security, reception or the police
> - IF IT IS SAFE TO DO SO, operate the nearest fire extinguisher, checking that it is the correct one to use
> - Never put yourself at risk
> - Never attempt to move burning objects
>
> **If you hear the fire alarm**
>
> - Switch off machinery
> - IF IT IS SAFE TO DO SO, close windows and doors, secure cash and confidential documents
> - Leave your workstation, ensuring that any visitors with you follow you
> - DO NOT STOP TO PICK UP PERSONAL BELONGINGS
> - Close doors as you go if there is no one else behind you
> - Follow the signs to the nearest fire exit – WALK QUICKLY BUT CALMLY, DO NOT RUN
> - DO NOT USE THE LIFT
> - Go to your allocated assembly point
> - Report to the fire warden
> - DO NOT RETURN TO THE BUILDING UNTIL TOLD IT IS SAFE TO DO SO

Fig. 2.5 Fire/evacuation procedure.

SECURITY

There is no such thing as 100 per cent security. Nevertheless each individual has an obligation to be constantly aware of the need for security. There are several aspects to security, including:

- access to car parks, buildings and individual rooms
- access to information
- machines, equipment, etc. belonging to the organisation
- personal belongings
- personal safety, especially at night.

ACCESS TO CAR PARKS, BUILDINGS AND INDIVIDUAL ROOMS

Many companies do not have open access to car parks and buildings. Access control can be maintained by authorised people being required to:

- use a swipe card, i.e. a plastic card with a magnetic strip that raises a barrier at the entrance to a car park or opens a door to a building
- key in a code on a keypad affixed to a door
- press a buzzer and, when it is answered, say who they are so that the person they speak to can open the door by remote control
- show their identity (ID) card on entering the building
- wear a visitor's ID card if they are not permanently employed in the building.

There may also be security and/or reception staff on duty at the entrance to the building.

ACCESS TO INFORMATION

Access to information held on computer is discussed in Chapter 3. There is also a great deal of information in documents on desks, in cabinets, and being distributed internally and externally. Every individual has a responsibility to ensure the confidentiality of the organisation's information. This can be done by:

- putting files away as soon as they are no longer needed
- keeping filing cabinets containing confidential documents locked
- never leaving confidential documents on the desk when away from it
- using a 'screensaver' when interrupted while working on confidential documents
- locating a visual display unit (VDU) where it is difficult for other people to see it
- never discussing confidential matters with anyone inside or outside the organisation, except those authorised to know.

MACHINES AND EQUIPMENT BELONGING TO THE ORGANISATION

Ways of ensuring that the organisation's property is as secure as possible include:

- making sure that small items of equipment, such as staplers, are put away in a drawer, especially at night
- marking all movable equipment such as computers, training visual aids, e.g. overhead projectors, with the organisation's/department's name, and either locking everything away or keeping rooms locked overnight.

PERSONAL BELONGINGS

Each individual must take responsibility for the safety of their own personal belongings, such as purses, cheque books, etc. Make sure that:

- you do not leave money lying around
- you do not leave a purse, cheque book, credit card, etc. in a drawer, or in a handbag/shopping bag, which can be seen by people passing your desk
- you lock personal items in a locker if one is provided, or in a locked drawer or cabinet
- you have only a small amount of money with you
- you do not tell people when you are going to the bank to withdraw money
- you do not tell people where you put personal belongings.

PERSONAL SAFETY

There are certain basic steps you can take to help ensure your own safety:

- when you are working late make sure that someone in the building knows you are there, preferably security staff
- do not go along unlit corridors – find the light switch and switch on the lights
- do not go into a room where the light switch does not work – you could fall over something in the dark
- when leaving a building at night keep to well-lit streets if possible but have a torch to use in dark areas and also carry a whistle
- walk with at least one other person if possible
- never walk with anyone you do not know who offers to accompany you
- unless you live alone always tell someone at home what time to expect you and, if possible, let them know if you are delayed.

These safety procedures apply equally to men and women. We all think that nothing untoward will happen to us – until it does!

Finally if you see anything, anywhere – at work, in the street, in a shop – that seems strange or unusual, report it to a security officer or the police. You will not be thought foolish if it turns out that there is nothing wrong.

RIGHTS AND OBLIGATIONS OF THE EMPLOYEE

All employees have rights and obligations. There are statutory rights that are enforceable by law, and these include the right:

- to be paid a wage or salary regularly for the work you do
- to be allowed a certain number of days' paid holiday each year
- to join a trades union or staff association if you wish.

You also have obligations. Your employer can expect you to:

- work a certain number of hours a day at stated times, or for a certain number of days a week or month with some latitude for start and finish times (i.e. flexitime)
- work conscientiously, i.e. accurately and at a reasonable pace
- be punctual at work and take sick leave only when necessary
- carry out your supervisor's/manager's instructions
- obey the organisation's regulations
- always be courteous and considerate to colleagues and help them when you are able to do so
- always dress appropriately and behave in a dignified manner.

Some of the rights above are not stated in law but an employer has the right to terminate your employment if you do not meet your obligations.

In addition everyone has moral rights and obligations. Moral rights are not enforceable by law but if employers and employees fulfil their obligations (see Table 2.1), the working environment will be a good one in which to work.

Table 2.1 *Employer's and employee's obligations*

Employer's obligation	Employee's obligation
Provide a job description	Carry out the duties agreed
Provide training	Do a better job as a result of training
Consider staff for promotion	Prove that you are capable of accepting greater responsibility
Provide appropriate equipment	Use the equipment correctly, keep it in good condition and report faults when they occur
Be loyal to staff	Be loyal to employer and absolutely discreet, i.e. never talk about confidential matters outside work
Criticise constructively	Accept constructive criticism as a means of learning
Conduct regular appraisals (see Chapter 16 page 503)	Contribute constructively to the appraisal process

An employee also has a right to know details of disciplinary and grievance procedures, what constitutes misconduct and gross misconduct, and what the penalties might be. The employer must state and provide evidence of misconduct before implementing a penalty. The employee has a right to appeal against a penalty. They can also be assisted in their case by a representative of the staff association or trades union of which they are a member.

All employees have a right to know what is expected of them. Specimen job descriptions for a receptionist, telephonist, general clerk, secretary and administrative assistant are given on pages 37–8.

INTERPERSONAL SKILLS

When you work in an office you will be in contact with immediate colleagues in the same office, other people in the organisation and people outside the organisation. Some of these people will have the same status in the organisation as you; others will be senior to you; and eventually you may have junior staff working with you. If you are to enjoy your work and do a good job it is essential that you get on with everyone.

Good interpersonal skills enable you to work with a wide variety of people. You need to like and be interested in people. Although every individual is different, few people fail to respond pleasantly when approached in a welcoming manner. A smile makes you a warmer person and indicates a helpful, courteous attitude. Everyone wants to be liked. Courtesy shows respect and, regardless of status, everyone is entitled to respect.

There may be occasions when people are discourteous or unpleasant to you. Try to remember that they perhaps are not well, are worried or feel insecure. Never retaliate by being rude or unhelpful in return. By taking no notice, remaining unperturbed and continuing to be pleasant yourself you will avoid a scene. If you acquire a reputation for always being calm, cheerful and co-operative you will find that people will readily co-operate with you. The effect of this will be that you will do your work more efficiently and gain a sense of satisfaction by overcoming another person's antagonism.

ACTIVITY 2.3 Discuss with fellow students/colleagues/friends the knowledge, skills and personal attributes you think you need to get on well with people. Bear in mind the question of status, of people being under pressure, and think how you like to be treated by others.

SPECIMEN JOB DESCRIPTIONS

Job title: Receptionist
Responsible to: Office Manager
Role: To provide a courteous and efficient reception service to all visitors

Duties
a. receiving visitors
b. directing visitors to appropriate location or person
c. making appointments for visitors who do not have them
d. noting enquiries and providing relevant information
e. dealing with telephone requests for information or appointments
f. supplying information pamphlets, brochures or forms
g. arranging taxis
h. receiving letters, packets, parcels from couriers, etc.
i. arranging collection of letters, etc.
j. keeping the reception area tidy
k. performing other related tasks

Job title: Telephonist
Responsible to: Office Manager
Role: To provide a courteous and efficient switchboard service to both staff and external callers

Duties
a. establishing contact between caller and person called, or other appropriate person
b. when appropriate, paging person wanted
c. dealing with telephone enquiries and recording messages
d. making connections for outgoing calls and routing long-distance calls
e. operating answerphone
f. recording and reporting faults
g. recording charges
h. performing related tasks

Job title: General Clerk
Responsible to: Office Manager
Role: To provide a reliable clerical support service within a specific section or department

Duties
a. stenography and typing
b. operating word processors/personal computers for document production and data entry
c. carrying out basic secretarial duties
d. updating records
e. operating office machines, e.g. copier, fax, binding
f. filing documents
g. dealing with incoming and outgoing mail
h. preparing and checking material for printing
i. writing on behalf of illiterate persons
j. performing a range of general clerical duties

Job title:	Stenographer/typist
Responsible to:	Secretarial Supervisor
Role:	To provide a fast and accurate stenographic service to managers

Duties
a. taking dictation and recording other matter in shorthand
b. making transcripts in typewritten form
c. performing limited clerical duties, such as filing and using copying machines
d. performing related tasks

Job title:	Secretary
Responsible to:	Head of Department
Role:	To provide a reliable secretarial support service to the head of department and his/her team

Duties
a. checking and transcribing correspondence, minutes and reports from dictation or written drafts to conform to office standards, using typewriter or word-processing equipment
b. dealing with incoming and outgoing mail
c. scanning, recording and distributing mail, correspondence and documents
d. screening requests for meetings or appointments, and helping to organise meetings
e. screening and recording leave and other staff member entitlements
f. organising and supervising filing systems
g. dealing with routine correspondence on own initiative
h. performing related tasks

Job title:	Administrative Assistant
Responsible to:	Head of Department
Role:	To provide a reliable administrative support service within a department

Duties
a. drafting administrative correspondence and minutes
b. obtaining, proposing and monitoring deadlines and follow-up dates
c. screening requests for meetings, scheduling and organising meetings and travel arrangements
d. assisting in the preparation of budgets, monitoring of expenditure, drafting of contracts and purchasing or acquisition orders
e. assisting with enquiries of an administrative or organisational nature
f. assisting in organising and hosting hospitality functions for outside visitors or members of staff
g. making verbatim reports of proceedings in legislative assemblies, courts of law and other places, in shorthand or by other means
h. writing and answering business or technical letters and other similar correspondence
i. performing related tasks
j. supervising junior staff

PRACTICE QUESTIONS

1. Describe the kind of office in which you would like to work and give reasons for your choice.

2. With every right there is always an obligation. As an employee you have certain rights. List six such rights, three of them statutory and three of them moral, and state the corresponding obligation in each case.

3. List five things you can do that will help you to get on with people. Say why you think they will help you.

4.
   a. State four ways in which you can contribute to safety in the office.
   b. Suggest ten safety hazards that could arise in the office.

5. Explain the difference between a system and a procedure.

6. Explain the following terms:
   i. ergonomic
   ii. rake of a backrest
   iii. RSI
   iv. copyholder
   v. shield (over a computer screen).

7. List five points that you should check when sitting at a computer.

8. What should be done when someone has an accident in the office?

9. Give the meaning of the danger signs shown below.

10.
    a. State 10 requirements of most health and safety legislation with which employers should comply.
    b. Why is it necessary for full-time computer operators to have regular breaks?

11. State five ways in which you can help to ensure the security of each of the following:
    i. personal belongings
    ii. information
    iii. personal safety.

SHORT ANSWER QUESTIONS

Complete the following sentences.

1. All administrative tasks have to be carried out in accordance with ....

2. In order to avoid strain, all office workers should have .... designed chairs.

3. No one should remove a .... from a machine when operating it.

4. All employees should have job .... in order to know what is expected of them.

5. To avoid accidents, ensure that filing cabinet drawers are .... when not in use.

Choose the most appropriate ending for each of the following sentences.

6. Copyholders should be used so that:
   a. the person operating a keyboard does not suffer neck strain by having to keep looking down at the desk to read the copy
   b. several pages can be secured together
   c. anyone standing in front of the desk cannot read the copy
   d. the operator can key in faster.

7. Fires can be caused in the office by:
   a. blocked fire exits
   b. touching equipment with wet hands
   c. ignoring danger signs
   d. overloading electrical plug sockets.

8. Security of information can be maintained by:
   a. closing files and stacking them so that the contents cannot be seen
   b. taking confidential papers home
   c. discussing confidential matters outside the organisation in a very quiet voice
   d. ensuring that files and disks are stored in locked cabinets when they are not being used.

9. All employees have a right to be paid:
   a. every week
   b. when the employer can afford to pay
   c. in cash, or have their bank account credited on pre-determined dates
   d. partly in cash and partly in kind, i.e. goods.

10. Everyone needs to develop good interpersonal skills in order to:
  a. indicate to a manager that they are willing to work well
  b. enjoy being with people
  c. get on comfortably with other people no matter who or what they are
  d. be liked.

EXAMINATION QUESTIONS

1. Badly stored cleaning fluids are an example of a safety ....

2. Always .... faulty electrical equipment.
(Pitman Office Procedures Level 1 1998 Pt 1A)

3. An office worker should be able to .... legibly.
(Pitman Office Procedures Level 1 1999 Pt 1A)

4. Name THREE personal qualities of a good telephonist.
  a. ....
  b. ....
  c. ....
(Pitman Office Procedures Level 1 1999 Pt 1B)

5. A new junior clerk has just started work in your office. List the safe working practices you would advise him/her to follow regarding:
  a. using the office copier
  b. using filing cabinets
  c. carrying heavy or bulky loads.
(Pitman Office Procedures Level 1 1999 Pt 2A)

6. Prepare a job description, along the lines of the examples on pages 37 and 38, for the administrative assistant as set out in the scenario below.

> You are based at the offices of the Spa Health & Fitness Club, 22–32 Queens Avenue, London NE2 7SP. The club is owned and managed by Mr Joseph Patten.
>
> You are employed as administrator and are in charge of one part-time clerk, who deals with the incoming mail, and two full-time receptionists.
>
> The club is expanding rapidly and Mr Patten has agreed that you may employ an administrative assistant who will act as relief receptionist when necessary.

(Pitman Office Procedures Level 2 1998 Pt 1)

7. Employees have a duty to take reasonable care for their own health and safety and that of others. List 10 ways in which employees can help to prevent accidents to themselves and their colleagues in an office, stating the types of accident that could occur if these precautions were not taken.

(Pitman Office Procedures Level 2 1998 Pt 2)

CHAPTER 3

INFORMATION PROCESSING

> **OBJECTIVES** When you have studied this chapter you should have acquired the knowledge and understanding to be able to:
>
> 1. explain what information processing is
> 2. explain the roles of the people involved in information processing
> 3. recognise the uses of the various components of a computer system
> 4. explain the differences between the main types of computer
> 5. explain the importance of security of data and how it is achieved
> 6. recognise different methods of data transmission
> 7. explain how the Internet is operated and the facilities available, including e-business and e-commerce.

WHAT IS INFORMATION PROCESSING?

Information processing is the term used to include a wide range of activities carried out either manually or with the help of computers and all the related equipment. It is important to understand that computers cannot do anything that the human brain cannot do. They can work very much more quickly and, generally, though not always, more accurately. Computers are machines and can go wrong as can any other type of machine. The major reason for faults in computer operation is **human error**. Never forget that. The information we get out of a computer is only accurate and relevant if we put in the right information for it to work on.

There are two kinds of information that have to be processed: numerical or statistical information, called **data**, and verbal information.

Data, or 'raw data', is useless on its own. It is just a series of figures. For example, the data input when a customer has bought goods has to be processed in a certain way so that an invoice is produced.

A typical example of information processing is the input and printing out of text, i.e. words. (Word processing will be discussed in Chapter 6.) Other kinds of information, such as lines to create drawings and figures to create charts and graphs, can also be input and printed out in the format we want.

A system includes people, the machines and where they are located, the type of work being done and why it is being done, confidentiality and security. (Examples of systems are given in Chapters 2 and 7.)

WHO ARE THE PEOPLE?

Information processing is done manually by everyone. Nowadays many people use computers in their jobs and also have a computer at home. Here, we will consider the people who work in an information processing department. (It may also be called a data processing department or computer department.) The people who work in this department may include:

- information processing manager
- project managers
- communications manager
- systems designers
- systems analysts
- programmers
- operations controllers and machine operators
- data input operators
- technical support staff
- management services staff.

INFORMATION PROCESSING MANAGER

The information processing manager has responsibility for ensuring that the department meets pre-determined objectives. The most important objective is to ensure that all the computer equipment in the organisation is working correctly, that everyone who needs access to a computer has it, that procedures are followed correctly, that when a problem arises, back-up facilities are available and the fault is dealt with speedily to avoid unnecessary disruption to the work of the organisation.

PROJECT MANAGERS

Project managers are responsible to the information processing manager for establishing, developing, controlling and implementing new projects. For example, installing a new computer system or upgrading hardware (i.e. installing equipment that can deal with a greater volume of work and/or additional types of work). An organisation may wish to install the equipment necessary to provide access to the Internet (see page 55), for example.

COMMUNICATIONS MANAGER

The communications manager has to ensure that the networks (see page 54) and telephone lines linking the computer with its peripherals (see page 50), the terminals and external telephone lines, are extended when necessary and maintained to a very high standard of reliability. The viability of integrating new technology into the communications system also has to be assessed as appropriate.

SYSTEMS DESIGNERS

Systems designers are the people who decide what is needed to meet the requirements of a system, and prepare a design to meet those requirements. For example, if the personnel manager in an organisation decided that he would like to have all the employee records on computer, a systems designer would prepare a design from the information obtained by the systems analyst (see below). The design would include how the program should be written, what information should be input, how the database (see page 53) should be set up, what forms would be needed for input/output, what security against unauthorised access would have to be included.

SYSTEMS ANALYSTS

Systems analysts review the existing system, if there is one, establish what is required by the users of the proposed computer system and determine the feasibility of meeting the requirements. A feasibility study is carried out to establish the costs and whether the benefits to be gained from a new system would be cost-effective.

If the feasibility study result is positive and the system is a fairly standard commercial activity, the systems analyst would then design the system. In a large organisation where more high-level, complex systems are required, the systems designer (see above) would take over the findings of the systems analyst and design the system.

PROGRAMMERS

Programmers write the **code** that makes up the programs or **software** (see page 52). It is possible to buy prepared software for many standard operations such as invoicing and payroll. Sometimes standard software, which can be bought from a software house, needs to be adapted to a particular organisation's systems. A programmer would do this.

OPERATIONS CONTROLLERS AND OPERATORS

These are the people who keep the computers working. They schedule the jobs to be done (e.g. payroll has to be done on a certain day of each month, invoicing may be done daily or weekly, but statements are prepared monthly). They have to ensure that the right program is loaded on to the computer for each job to be done. Disks have to be backed up (i.e. duplicated) and properly stored. The control console in the computer room has to be monitored constantly so that any hiccup in the system can be identified immediately and corrected. The operations manuals, stored in the computer room library, have to be kept up to date.

DATA INPUT OPERATORS

Data input operators are keyboard operators who key in the relevant data from forms, ready for processing.

TECHNICAL SUPPORT STAFF

Technical support staff deal with problems experienced by computer users in the various departments of the organisation. They may man one or more **helpdesks**, which users call when they have a problem. A careful record must be kept of all calls received.

Technical support staff need a wide knowledge of the organisation's computer systems. They need to be able to explain over the telephone what the user needs to do to extricate themselves from a problem. In some cases they may need to train the person at their workstation.

MANAGEMENT SERVICES STAFF

This group may form a separate department but sometimes forms a section within the information processing department. They undertake **work study** (see page 8), and **organisation and methods** (a process to find the easiest and most efficient ways of working in the office). They may also be involved in organisational and departmental restructuring and its impact on the information processing systems in place.

In addition to the staff in the information processing department there are the **users** who are in every part of the organisation. They have responsibility for ensuring that they know how to operate the system, what software to use for various types of job, and how to identify and correct simple faults. They should be able to use the operating manual and should use their computer for any task that can be done more effectively on it than manually.

ACTIVITY 3.1 The head of the research & development department in a large organisation wants to be able to devise project plans on his computer. The organisation does not have a program for this. The information processing manager agrees to see what can be done.

Make a list of the steps that have to be followed, in the correct sequence, and by whom, from the point when the request is made to the point when the head of the R&D department is able to plan projects on computer.

COMPUTER EQUIPMENT

There are many types of computer and many **peripheral** devices – machines linked to a computer – that make up a computer system. We shall explain the following types of equipment and how they work:

- mainframe computers
- personal computers (PCs)
- laptop computers
- peripheral equipment.

As we discuss various aspects of computers we will explain the jargon used in connection with them.

You may hear the terms 'hardware', 'firmware' and 'software'. Hardware is the equipment, i.e. the machines themselves. The hardware cannot do anything on its own. It has to be instructed and, for this purpose, software, or computer programs, are compiled. Some programs have to be in the computer all the time. These programs are the firmware, so called because they can never be removed from the computer. Software can be changed, depending on what kind of work you want the computer to do.

MAINFRAME COMPUTERS

The big computers that run systems for a whole organisation are known as 'mainframe' computers. They are installed in a computer room, which is air conditioned because the machine generates a great deal of heat.

All computers have a **central processing unit** (CPU), which consists of three sections.

- A control unit, which ensures that the required information is retrieved from storage, processed in the correct sequence and correctly stored again.
- An arithmetic unit where the calculations are carried out. All processing is done in the form of binary arithmetic code. This is a series of two digits, 1 and 0, arranged in different sequences to represent numbers, letters, symbols, etc. The digits are in groups called **bytes**.
- A memory where the programs that control the operation of the computer are stored and where the data being processed are held. The amount of processing that can be done at any one time depends on the capacity of the memory, which is measured in gigabytes (Gb) or megabytes (Mb). (Giga, billion; Mega, million.)

The users need **terminals** on their desks linked to the CPU. Terminals are peripheral equipment, see page 50.

Parallel processing

There is a limit to how much information can be processed in a given time, even on a very large mainframe. It would be very expensive to upgrade large mainframes regularly; a solution to this problem has been achieved by a method known as parallel processing. This term is interpreted in various ways but basically it means that two or more processors, linked together, process simultaneously. A device called a **server** directs the flow of data into the processors and back to the user's terminal.

PERSONAL COMPUTERS (PCs)

When they were first produced PCs were so called because they were used by individual members of staff who needed to do specific types of work, e.g. prepare and maintain personnel records. This enabled specialised work to be done by one, or just a few, people without using mainframe capacity. However, many staff needed to use both a PC and a terminal. The next development was a PC that could be used both as a stand-alone machine and as a terminal.

Modern PCs usually have a Winchester hard disk (see page 51) and/or a compact disc (CD), and on some machines, diskettes. Work can be recorded on diskettes, backed up (duplicated) on to the hard disk for security and also transmitted to the mainframe for storage, to keep centralised records up to date. In some cases the work is stored on the hard disk and backed up on diskette. It may not be necessary to keep information on the PC hard disk after it has been transmitted to the mainframe; the operator can access the mainframe when the information is needed. If work is to be done on the information it can be **downloaded** from the mainframe storage on to the PC disk. After processing, updating or amending, the data can then be **uploaded** to the mainframe again.

PCs are now very powerful, which means they can process very quickly and have large storage capacity. They can also be programmed to do a wide variety of tasks.

LAPTOP COMPUTERS

A laptop computer (see Fig. 3.1) is a miniature PC, which can be carried easily. It has a CPU capable of fast processing and a hard disk with large storage capacity. It is possible to do virtually all the various types of work that can be done on a PC provided appropriate software is installed on it. E-mail can be transmitted from a laptop and the Internet can be accessed. (Transmission of information is explained on page 54.) A printer can also be linked to a laptop.

Fig. 3.1 Laptop computer.

PERIPHERAL EQUIPMENT

Items of peripheral equipment allow information to be input into the CPU and output to be received from it. The main items of equipment are:

keyboards and mice	for input
tape drives disk drives	} for input and output
printers visual display units	} for output

Keyboards and mice

Keyboards are normally the standard QWERTY keyboard with an additional calculator-style keypad plus function keys. The QWERTY keyboard varies for different languages. There are also keyboards for languages that use different symbols, e.g. Russian, Chinese, Japanese, etc.

A mouse is used for giving instructions (e.g. to store a file).

Tape drives

Tape drives are machines on which tape reels or cassettes are loaded. A cable links the drive to the CPU. Data is transmitted from drive to CPU and vice versa. This kind of cable is usually **full duplex**, which means that data can be transmitted both ways simultaneously.

Tapes are magnetic and hold records in numerical sequence. To access a particular record, the tape is scanned until the record is identified. This is known as **serial access** and, because it is fairly slow, it is used for **batch**

processing. For instance, invoices can be accumulated and processed in batches. Batch processing can be carried out overnight when the system is not being used so much for **on-line processing**. 'On-line' means that the information can be accessed by an authorised user at any time; if the user is not authorised to access certain information the computer will refuse to accept the command.

Information is **written** (recorded) on to a tape and is **read** (retrieved) from it.

Disk drives

These drives work in a similar way to tape drives but are loaded with disks or diskettes. The drives can stand separately from the visual display unit (VDU) on a PC, or be incorporated into it as in the case of a laptop. Disk drives for mainframes are large 'boxes' arranged in rows, usually in a computer room.

Disks may be magnetic or optical, and information is 'written' on to and 'read' from disk as it is with tapes. Magnetic disks are read by a magnetic read/write head. Information is written to and read from optical disks by laser beams. Optical disks usually have a much greater storage capacity than magnetic disks.

A particular kind of disk, used mainly on PCs, is the **Winchester** disk. This disk is a sealed unit that excludes dust and humidity to avoid **corruption** (distortion) of the data. PCs are often in rooms that are not air conditioned and this makes disks vulnerable to corruption.

When a user wishes to access information held on a disk the firmware in the CPU 'orders' the scanning of the disk until it finds the information required. The particular item can be anywhere on the disk, not in any particular order; this is known as **random access**. When new information is written to the disk, a space is found for it and it is coded into a **sector** of the disk. Each disk has sectors that are unidentifiable to the user.

Printers

Those printers commonly used with PCs are explained in Chapter 6 (page 166). For the massive amount of printing carried out in a computer room, **line printers** or large laser printers are used. Line printers are so called as the program instruction is 'print a line'. They are relatively slow, producing about 2000 lines a minute. Laser printers are very fast, producing from 50 to 135 A4 pages per minute. Laser print quality is excellent.

Visual display units

VDUs are a standard part of PCs or laptop computers. In addition to receiving information accessed from the disk, VDUs also serve for checking input. In some cases VDUs stand on their own, for instance in airports and railway stations, to display information for the public. The information is updated regularly by a central operator.

SOFTWARE

The computer will not do anything until it has a program to tell it what to do. We have already seen that there are programs that 'live' in the computer; these programs make the CPU perform the functions that are common to all tasks, e.g. insert, delete, update, store, etc. The tasks we want to do on the computer must each have an individual program. There are many different programs, the most commonly used being 'commercial' programs such as accounting and stock records. There are also specialist programs for weather forecasting, traffic control and finger printing, for example. Word processing and spreadsheets for numerical data such as budgets and forecasts are commonplace.

Any PC user has to access the appropriate program either from their own disk or from the mainframe in order to do a particular kind of work. It is possible to integrate work from one program, e.g. graphics, into work on another, e.g. word processing.

A program is a series of detailed instructions written in a programming language. There are many languages used for different purposes, some of them highly complex.

A small company may not employ its own programmers. It will usually buy standard programs such as payroll, from a software house. If they need a program for a specialist application they will have a 'bespoke' program specially written for them to their specification by a software house.

Some companies 'outsource' their standard computer operations, such as running the payroll, to a computer bureau. This enables the company to make better use of its own computer for the more specialist tasks.

DATABASES

A database is a very large file of information – e.g. a mailing list, personnel record of employees in an organisation, customer account records. Databases need huge storage capacity and must be updated regularly. Some types of information can be updated monthly, other types weekly, some daily, and some must be updated as changes occur.

Because there is now so much information on databases it is often necessary to retrieve information from more than one. The information obtained from a database may be used in conjunction with graphics, e-mail and other software. A database is accessed from a terminal by means of special software, usually referred to as a database management system.

SECURITY

There are 'levels' of access to information held on computers. Some information can be accessed by anyone, some by certain people, and some by only one or two individuals.

Everyone who works on a PC/terminal linked to a mainframe has to **log on** to the system at the start of each day. Usually each individual has to key in a **password** that enables them to access the routine work they have to do. Thus, people such as personnel staff would be able to access employee records, and senior managers would be able to access the records of staff in their department, but not necessarily everything on them.

In order to protect highly sensitive information a second password may have to be input before it can be accessed. It is usual for secretaries to be able to access their managers' correspondence and managers to access their secretaries' work, but no one else would be able to do so.

Every employee has an obligation not to tell anyone their password. In some organisations to do so would result in disciplinary action being taken against them.

CONSUMABLES

Various supplies are needed for use with computers. These include:

- tapes, disks and diskettes (floppy disks)
- printout paper, which may be continuous stationery or single sheets

- felt-tip marker pens of different thicknesses for graphic printers
- printer ribbons for impact printers, ink cartridges for ink-jet printers and toner for laser printers.

TRANSMISSION OF DATA

Data is moved from one machine to another by using telephone lines. Ordinary telephone lines are analogue, which means that they were designed to carry voices by a series of signals. Computerised data are digital, i.e. binary arithmetic (see page 48), which cannot travel along telephone lines without first being converted into analogue signals. When the digital data reaches its destination it has to be converted back into analogue mode. To do this there is a modem (which stands for modulator/demodulator) at each end of the transmission line. In a computer room there are banks of modems, each one serving groups of machines. Individual PCs not linked to a mainframe system have their own modem, as do laptops.

In some countries **fibre optics** are used for transmitting telecommunications of all kinds including television channels. Fibre optics transmit by light signals, which can carry both voice and digital data.

NETWORKS

Private individuals transmit from their own computers via a normal telephone line direct to another individual or organisation. In business it would be very wasteful to have a separate telephone line for each computer. To maximise the use of telephone lines there are networks of three different kinds: intranet, local area network and wide area network.

An **intranet** is a network within a network. Individual departments may have their own networks, which are then linked to create a **local area network** (LAN). LANs are usually on one site or on sites within a few kilometres of the main building. People whose computers are linked to LANs can transmit messages, i.e. e-mail, to any other computer users similarly linked. Each user has an e-mail address. When the message has been keyed in and the address checked, pressing the 'send' key activates transmission to the addressee.

A **wide area network** (WAN) provides the same facility nationally. Some very large organisations have their own WAN, which creates a national network of the LANs in their branches. Banks, for example, rent 'private lines' from the national telecommunications company so that they have sole use of them.

It is not necessary to have a permanent telephone link to transmit data. Anyone with a laptop can plug it into a telephone point anywhere in any country that has appropriate telecommunications facilities, in order to send messages. This is known as a **dial-up** facility. It is particularly useful for people who travel.

WANs can be linked to international telephone lines, enabling organisations to have computers in many different countries linked to a mainframe in just one of the countries.

With the introduction and expansion of networks there has been a move towards having smaller mainframes. This is called **downsizing**. Instead, **file servers** are located at various points on the network for storage of data, in addition to the servers for routing the data from one station to another. However, because of the vast increase in data transmission and the file storage capacity needed, there is a trend towards reinstating large mainframes.

INTERNET

The Internet is an international network, which can be accessed by any computer that has appropriate software and is linked to a telephone line. The link does not have to be permanent.

The Internet consists of:

- millions of computers worldwide
- telephone lines
- routers
- information services providers (ISPs)
- servers
- software.

Computers and telephone lines have been explained already. **Routers** are machines that work as 'traffic policemen' finding the best route for the 'package' being sent. This equipment is located in various key places in every country that has the facilities for transmitting data.

Information service providers (ISPs) are companies that provide a service enabling business and private computer users to access e-mail, the web and download/upload capabilities, see page 223. There are other services that may be of use to the private individual, such as newsgroups. Some ISPs provide services free, others make a monthly charge.

The ISP enables computer users to access the Internet via a **server**. This is a system on a network that provides access to other services on the network, e.g. the World Wide Web (see page 57).

The computer user needs specific **software** to access the Internet. Most users would consider it essential to have an e-mail program, a World Wide Web browser and a file transfer protocol (FTP) program for downloading and uploading files. Some commonly used software incorporates these programs.

ACCESSING THE INTERNET

When you have an ISP service agreement and the appropriate software you can send e-mails, surf the net and download pages of information on to your own disk. The steps are:

- dial a local telephone number provided by the ISP
- log on – this automatically connects you to the Internet, enabling you to use any of the services included in your ISP service agreement.

Business organisations need to be on-line to the Internet, i.e. able to access it permanently. They have a permanent link via their own computer to the ISP and are referred to as a host. People who access the Internet only when required are known as 'clients'.

E-MAIL ADDRESSES

When you want to send a letter you need to know the address. The letter is placed in an envelope, which is addressed to the destination, and posted.

E-mail works in the same way. You have to know the e-mail address of the person or organisation to whom/which you are writing. By keying in both your own and the addressee's e-mail address you are creating an 'envelope' for the package, which is the message converted into binary digits.

Each user has an account name, which some ISPs designate and others allow the client to choose (e.g. annjones). This is followed by @ followed by the name of the server, e.g. freenet.com (referred to as 'dot com'). The complete e-mail address would be 'annjones@freenet.com'.

When someone sends you an e-mail its arrival may be indicated on your VDU or you may have to access your mailbox to check for messages, depending on your software. E-mail is thought to be received almost instantaneously after transmission. It can be, but depending on the traffic through the servers and routers, it can take longer.

USING THE INTERNET

The **World Wide Web** (WWW) is linked to the Internet, and enables organisations and individuals to rent a **website** on which to give information to other organisations and the general public. Many organisations spend a lot of money creating an attractive and informative website. It serves both for advertising and providing information.
For example, a professional institution posts details on its website of requirements for membership, the services it provides to members, its examination syllabi and calendar of events. The website has an address, which it quotes on all its printed documentation.

To access the web, you first access your WWW browser program and key in the address of the website you wish to visit, if you know it. If you do not know the address you will have to search. The most common facility used for searching is a **search engine**. Search engines vary in their usefulness. Each one seems to be particularly good in certain areas. Commonly used search engines include AltaVista, Excite, Google and Yahoo! but there are many more. You key in a key word, or words, which generates a list of related topics. In some cases you could have a list of thousands of topics, so you have to be more specific. Consider a subject such as 'law'. In what country? What kind of law – case, civil, criminal, history of, etc.? Being as specific as possible will reduce the list considerably. Within, say, criminal law, are we looking for cases, a specific case, penalties, defence lawyers or prosecution lawyers? You go on reducing the options until you find the precise topic you are looking for. An example of a website is shown in Fig. 3.2.

For everyday use the web is valuable for:

- advertising
- checking airline flight schedules and costs, arrival and departure times
- publishing what you write
- research on almost any subject
- shopping

Fig. 3.2 A website screen.

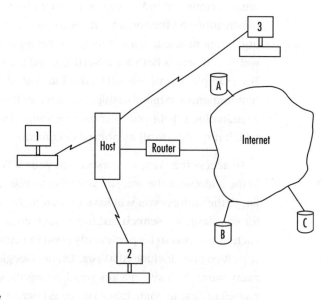

Key

1, 2 and 3	PCs in different locations around the world
Host	Server of the Information Service Provider (ISP) linking individual PC to the Internet website of a person or organisation
Router	Directs transmission from the individual PC to the website required
A, B and C	Servers of the individual websites

Fig. 3.3 Linking up with the Internet.

- starting a business
- taking training courses.

The web is growing all the time with new uses constantly emerging.

The diagram in Fig. 3.3 shows how the Internet works. The Internet cannot be seen: information is transmitted through the ether. A similar example is the way in which radio programmes are transmitted from broadcasting studios to transmitting masts and out into the ether to be picked up by individual radio receivers.

E-COMMERCE AND E-BUSINESS

These two words tend to be used synonymously. To make a distinction it is useful to say that e-commerce is for the individual who wishes to shop on the Internet, while e-business is for organisations that wish to do business with other organisations on the Internet.

If you know the web address of the shop or company from which you wish to make a purchase, you can key it in and access the shop's website. If you wish to see what is available you can work your way through the pages. If you want a specific item, e.g. a book, you would key in the title, author or ISBN (International Standard Book Number) and that would take you straight to it. If you are satisfied that what you see is what you want, you go through the process of giving your name, address and credit card details.

Some people are concerned about giving their credit card details on the web. A reputable supplier will have a security message on its web page. It is also worth making enquiries to other sources, e.g. a bank or your credit card company. Bear in mind that when you buy goods from abroad you will have to pay customs duty and any other taxes levied on imports.

Where organisations are moving into e-business it is essential that security procedures are established. What was 'safe' in a paper-based system may not be so safe when every part of the process is carried out on the Internet. Accuracy is of paramount importance and the slightest inaccuracy should be followed up. It may be computer or human error but it needs to be traced.

E-business raises many issues that are causing organisations to think hard about the future. The law relating to buying and selling is different in different countries, as is the law on copyright and financial dealings such as hire purchase. Taxes are different both in type and amount across the world. Some countries have problems with foreign exchange, which means that their nationals cannot buy from overseas.

HACKING AND CORRUPTION

Hacking is the term used to describe unauthorised entry into a system. It means that someone, either within or outside an organisation, has found a way to access information. It is a criminal offence to hack into another person's or organisation's computer system.

There are various ways of corrupting information on a computer system. There have been serious instances of 'bugs' and 'viruses' being transmitted over networks into the computer systems of major commercial and financial institutions throughout the world. 'Viruses' may be programmed to replicate themselves to every address held on a company's database, bringing the system to a halt by the sheer volume of transmission. It is, of course, a criminal offence to transmit anything that would interfere with anyone's computer.

COMPUTERISED PRESENTATION

There is now software that enables a presentation to be given using a laptop and a projector. Powerpoint is a commonly used program; the 'slides' are keyed in on a PC or laptop computer. Photographs, diagrams, sketches, etc. can be used either individually, or with text or statistical data. If a PC is used to design the slides, the file of prepared 'slides' is downloaded on to a laptop. This is then linked to a projector by a cable. The file is retrieved and each slide projected on to a screen at the press of a key. The images, in colour, are of excellent quality. Computerised projection of this type is not suitable for very large audiences because the distance at which projection is clear is limited. (Presentation of text, etc. on charts, projectors and video is explained in Chapter 5.)

PRACTICE QUESTIONS

1. What is the difference between a mainframe computer and a personal computer (PC)?

2. Give three examples of peripheral equipment.

3. Briefly explain each of the following:
    - *i.* log on
    - *ii.* binary arithmetic
    - *iii.* software
    - *iv.* memory
    - *v.* compact disc

   vi. download
   vii. consumables
   viii. disk drive
   ix. database
   x. password.

4. Briefly explain the role of the following people who work in an information processing department:
  i. project manager
  ii. programmer
  iii. systems analyst
  iv. operator
  v. data input operator.

5. State and briefly explain the four parts to a stand-alone personal computer.

6. What equipment is needed when digital data are transmitted over a normal voice telephone line? How does it work?

7. *a.* Explain the term 'network'.
  b. List and briefly explain three types of network.

8. *a.* Describe the Internet.
  b. Explain the terms e-business and e-commerce.

9. How does a user access and use the Internet?

10. What is an e-mail address? Give an example.

11. What is meant by the terms 'hacking' and 'corruption'?

12. How is a computerised presentation prepared?

SHORT ANSWER QUESTIONS

Complete the following sentences.

1. Programmers write the ...., which is a list of instructions called a ....

2. Management services staff undertake .... and ....

3. The machines linked to a central processing unit are called ....

4. CPU stands for ....

5. A very large file of information is called a ....

Choose the most appropriate ending for each of the following sentences.

6. A password is a code:
   a. needed to access a computer system
   b. allowing an individual access to certain files
   c. used for entering a building
   d. used only by managers.

7. A modem is used:
   a. to convert plain English into binary digits for transmission over telephone lines, and convert it back to plain English at the other end
   b. to transmit data from the computer to individual terminals
   c. to transmit data over external telephone lines
   d. to transmit and receive data.

8. E-mail is a means of:
   a. transmitting data over telephone lines very quickly
   b. directing mail from one computer to another
   c. corresponding with any person who has an e-mail address, within or outside an organisation
   d. transmitting data throughout the world.

9. Hacking is a term used:
   a. to indicate that a program is being changed
   b. to indicate a computer crime
   c. to describe unauthorised entry into a system
   d. to access information on another computer.

10. Computer presentation means:
    a. giving a talk about computers
    b. using a computer to produce overhead projector transparencies
    c. writing a program on computers
    d. using computer equipment to show visual aids while giving a talk.

EXAMINATION QUESTIONS

1. The term .... describes a two-way system that enables information stored in a central database to be displayed on a number of screens.
   (Pitman Office Procedures Level 1 1998 Pt 1A)

2. List THREE ways of reducing possible health hazards for computer operators.
   a. ....
   b. ....
   c. ....

3. Name THREE items of hardware found in a computer system.

a. ....

b. ....

c. ....

(Pitman Office Procedures Level 1 1998 Pt 1B)

4. Prepare a notice to be distributed to staff listing EIGHT rules to be followed in connection with the care and maintenance of floppy computer disks.

(Pitman Office Procedures Level 1 1998 Pt 2B)

5. Commands can be given to a computer using a/an .... or keyboard.

6. A spreadsheet is a computer .... often used for forecasting sales figures.

(Pitman Office Procedures Level 1 1999 Pt 1A)

CHAPTER 4

RECEIVING VISITORS AND USING TELEPHONE EQUIPMENT

OBJECTIVES When you have studied this chapter you should have acquired the knowledge and understanding to be able to:

1. explain the importance of the receptionist's role in an organisation
2. deal efficiently with visitors with or without appointments
3. make appointments, obtaining and giving all relevant information
4. deal with deliveries and collection of mail and goods
5. list and briefly explain the main types of switchboard and their facilities
6. receive and make telephone calls, including taking messages, courteously and efficiently
7. use the facilities of direct line and extension instruments effectively
8. explain the different ways in which mobile telephones can be used
9. list and explain the facilities of answer-recording machines
10. list and explain the types of call available on the national telecommunications network
11. create a professional image when receiving visitors and using the telephone.

Anyone who works in an office is likely to have to receive visitors and use telephone equipment. The way in which they do this creates the public 'face' of the organisation. This places a great responsibility on all staff to create and maintain a first-class image for their organisation.

RECEPTION

All organisations have visitors of one sort or another. They may range from couriers to Members of Parliament, from maintenance staff to business tycoons, from suppliers to overseas clients. These people need to be directed to the person or location (e.g. a meeting room) they are visiting. Some visitors come seeking information but have no idea whom they should see. Their needs must be established so that they see the person who can satisfy those needs.

Certain types of visitor are dealt with in reception without reference to anyone else. Couriers and delivery drivers may leave packages, which the receptionist signs for. In some types of organisation people make their appointments at reception (health centres, dentists and hospitals are examples of such organisations).

The function of reception can be defined as the clearing house for all visitors, every one of whom must leave the building with a high regard for the organisation.

MANNING THE RECEPTION DESK

In a large organisation there may be more than one person working at the reception desk. In a small organisation the receptionist may combine reception duties with operating the telephone switchboard, typing and various clerical/administrative tasks.

VISITORS WITH APPOINTMENTS

At the end of each working day the receptionist should receive from a secretary and/or other staff, lists of visitors expected the next day, at what times and where they should be directed. Alternatively, staff may tell the receptionist when they make an appointment so that the names of the visitor and the person to be visited can be entered under the appropriate date and time in the reception appointments diary.

Having the information beforehand enables the reception to prepare the necessary badges and/or passes before the visitor arrives. This creates an impression of efficiency.

The receptionist may find it helpful to compile a single list of appointments for the day made up from the individual lists provided. The lists of people who are to attend interviews and meetings should be kept separately. In organisations where visitors first report to a security checkpoint the list should be available at the security officer's desk. There may be a departmental reception area where a list of appointments for the department should also be held.

As each visitor arrives there should be an immediate smile and a greeting. The visitor should give their name, who they wish to see and state that they have an appointment. Some visitors present a business card (see Fig. 4.1). If this information is not volunteered the receptionist must ask for it. From this point on, various courses of action can be taken, depending on the organisation, the circumstances of the visit and the security arrangements.

Fig. 4.1 Business card.

VISITORS' REGISTER					
Date	Name of visitor	Name and address of organisation	Referred to	Time in	Time out

Fig. 4.2 Visitors' register.

Fig. 4.3 Visitors' badge.

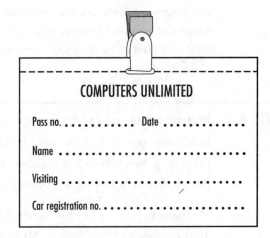

Fig. 4.4 Visitors' pass.

The following list of activities may not all be common practice in every organisation but some of them will be.

1. Check the visitor's name against the list of visitors expected.
2. Ask the visitor to sign the visitors' register (see Fig. 4.2). (This is for security and in case of fire.)
3. Telephone the person the visitor has come to see, or the person's secretary, and inform them that the visitor has arrived.
4. Give the visitor the prepared badge or pass (see Figs 4.3 and 4.4) or prepare one (always check that the name is spelt correctly).
5. Ask the visitor to take a seat until someone comes to collect them; or check whether the visitor knows where to go and, if not, give precise directions to the correct floor and room number and indicate the lift if appropriate; inform the visitor if they will be met at the lift if this is the practice.
6. If the visitor is early for the appointment, offer refreshment if it is possible to do so.

7. If the person being visited does not answer their telephone within a few minutes, the receptionist should try to contact them either by **paging** (see page 81) or by telephoning someone in the same department who might know where they are. The visitor must be kept informed.

VISITORS WITHOUT APPOINTMENTS

If the visitor does not have an appointment the receptionist should ask them to take a seat while they check whether the person they wish to see is available. It may be that the person's secretary or someone else could help. If someone is available, ask the visitor to sign the register while you prepare a badge and/or pass for them. They will then either be asked to take a seat until collected or be directed to the right place.

ACTIVITY 4.1 Prepare a page of a visitors' register as shown in Fig. 4.2. Then enter the appropriate details from the business cards (see below) presented by each of the visitors. The visitors arrived to see the people listed below at the times shown:

Mr Badsey	1115	Mrs Emily Peters	Personnel Dept
Miss Cassandra	0950	Mr James Casson	Purchasing Dept
Mrs Kinley	1055	Mr Paul Jones	Sales Dept
Mr Jameson	1110	Ms Victoria Payne	Marketing Dept
Ms de la Cour	1050	Standards Meeting	
Mr Passmore	1055	Standards Meeting	

George Badsey
Personnel Computers Limited
15 Beach Road
Port-of-Spain
Trinidad and Tobago

Tel. (868) 622 1357
Fax (868) 622 5683
E-mail georgebadsey@trinidad.net

Frederick R Jameson FIMgt
Overseas Promotions
63 Victoria Street
Chichester
East Sussex
England

Tel./Fax +44 1243 67678
E-mail jameson@overseas.co.uk

(continued)

ACTIVITY 4.1 *(continued)*

Kitty Cassandra Gentian Publishing Co. Ltd 18 Buckingham Road Oxford OX2 5PU England Tel. +44 1865 346814 Fax +44 1865 346819 E-mail kitty@gentian.com	Victoria de la Cour Department of Labour and Co-operatives PO Box 456 Port-of-Spain Trinidad and Tobago Tel. (868) 622 1234 Fax (868) 622 4321 E-mail delacour@labour.gov.tt
Margaret Kinley Ace Stationers Limited 48 Main Street Port-of-Spain Tel. (868) 622 6934 Fax (868) 622 6363 E-mail kinley@ace.com	Jamil Passmore 46 High Rise San Fernando Tel./Fax 622 8978

RECEIVING DELIVERIES

Letters, packages and parcels, even consignments of goods such as stationery, may be delivered to the reception area of an organisation. The receptionist may be asked to sign a delivery note or a goods received note (see Chapter 10, page 285). It is advisable to check the following points:

1. the item(s) are addressed to the organisation or a member of staff
2. the item(s) have been ordered by someone in the organisation
3. the item(s) are in good condition, i.e. the packaging is not torn or wet, or dented
4. the item has not been opened or damaged so that small items could have dropped out
5. there is no sign of any wire, which could indicate a letter bomb.

When satisfied that the package is as it should be, the receptionist should sign for it. However, if goods are being signed for it is best to write 'not examined' under the signature. If the goods are found to be damaged when the package is opened a claim can then be made for a replacement.

ORGANISING MAIL AND PARCEL COLLECTIONS

Often couriers call to collect items for delivery. It is common to have a collection tray in reception from which couriers collect items placed there by staff. The receptionist should keep an eye on the tray to ensure that no unauthorised person removes anything.

In some organisations the reception staff are responsible for contacting couriers and parcel carriers to arrange collection of items. Have a list of the companies used with their telephone numbers and names of contacts. Ensure you have a note of the following details:

- number and type of packages
- destinations
- what type of service is needed (see Chapter 8, page 243 and Chapter 9, page 263).

Also check that you have the documentation to be handed over with the item to be collected.

RELIEVING A RECEPTIONIST

When a receptionist is relieved for a break or change of shift it is essential that there is a handing over procedure; this may take a few seconds or a few minutes but must not be neglected. It is useful to have a checklist of points to ensure that all information is given. This list may include the items listed below.

- Visitors currently in the building who will be required to sign out/hand over identification passes.
- Visitors expected, including guests for lunch.
- Messages to be passed to staff when they are available.
- Items waiting for collection with any special instructions.
- Any equipment fault that has been reported.

UNMANNED RECEPTION

There are a few organisations where the visitor is asked to key in their personal details on a computer. In such cases the computer is always user friendly – instructions appear on the screen so that each step can easily be followed.

There are also unmanned reception areas where a notice instructs the visitor to use the telephone on the desk and call a particular number.

Such an arrangement may be regarded as unwelcoming; it is usually employed as a way of reducing costs.

INFORMATION NEEDED BY THE RECEPTIONIST

In order to do a professional job as a receptionist there is a need for essential information to be available and gradually assimilated. The things to know are listed below.

1. Names and functions of the departments and key people in the organisation. (It is useful to have an organisation chart.)
2. Names of executives' secretaries.
3. Names of related organisations, e.g. companies within the same group.
4. Names of people/organisations who call regularly and to whom they usually wish to speak, though never assume you know, always check.
5. References/codes used to identify departments, etc.
6. Staff movements, holidays, absences for sickness.
7. Appointments and meetings for the day.

There should be a procedure for passing information to reception so that the receptionist is always up to date on events and situations. The reception should always be on circulation and distribution lists for notification of changes. It may take time and effort to persuade people that this is necessary – for their benefit.

Every receptionist should have a guided tour of the building as part of the induction process (see Chapter 16, page 502) and whenever major changes are made.

MAKING APPOINTMENTS

Whatever your role, you may need to make appointments. When doing so you need to know:

- the person/people involved
- place
- the preferred time and date, and estimated duration
- the purpose of business to be discussed and any documents/files needed.

You should give the following information to anyone visiting your organisation for the first time:

- address and directions to the location – offer to send a map
- which entrance/gate to use

- car parking facilities – on premises/public (including location and distance from site)
- security and/or reception procedures as appropriate.

When making appointments check:

- time is free (refer to your own and/or manager's diary)
- travelling time (if appropriate) bearing in mind rush hours.

Immediately after you have made an appointment:

- enter the details in the appointments book, your own and/or your manager's diary as appropriate
- prepare a note of documents required to be filed in the bring-forward file (see Chapter 7, page 222)
- write a diary note of any arrangements to be made, e.g. booking an interview/meeting room, ordering refreshments and/or lunch.

If appropriate, confirm the details of the appointment in writing.

RECEIVING VISITORS IN THE OFFICE

If you are a secretary or assistant to a manager it may be one of your duties to receive visitors. When you are informed that a visitor who has an appointment is in reception, tell the receptionist what you will do – go to reception to collect the visitor, meet them at the lift on your floor, or wait for them in your office. Check with your manager that they are ready for the appointment.

When you meet the visitor the following sequence is appropriate.

1. Smile, greet by name ('Good morning/afternoon Mr Banks'), introduce yourself (your name and who you are) if you have not met before.
2. Tell the visitor where you are taking them and ask them to accompany you. Walk with them, not in front of them.
3. If the visitor has travelled some way, ask if they would like to freshen up.
4. Offer refreshment if it is available. Ask how they like their tea/coffee, etc. – with or without milk and sugar.
5. On arrival at the destination (meeting room, office) open the door for the visitor to pass through.
6. Introduce the visitor by saying the name of the person in the room first, followed by the name of the visitor: 'Mrs Shepphard, Mr Banks to see you.'

If your manager is not ready, ask the visitor to take a seat and offer them something to read. You can provide the refreshment while they wait. If they have not finished by the time your manager is available, offer to take the cup into the room for them if they have something to carry, e.g. a briefcase.

If you take the visitor straight to your manager, ask both of them if they would like refreshment. Prepare the refreshment on a tray, preferably with the milk and sugar separately. Serve the visitor first. Have a supply of coasters available so that the surface of the manager's desk is not spoiled.

The visitor may ask you to telephone their next appointment as they expect to be delayed, order a taxi, check on train times or confirm a flight booking. However busy you are, give no indication that the request is a nuisance: 'Of course I'll do that for you Mr Banks', with a smile, is not only courteous but also creates a very good image of your manager, the department and the organisation – an image which indicates that your visitors are important people, whoever they are.

There may be occasions when you have to arrange transport to meet a visitor arriving by air or by train. Always reconfirm on the day of the visit that the transport will be available as arranged. You may be asked to meet the visitor yourself. Allow plenty of time for the journey, especially during rush hour – far better to be 10 minutes early than 10 minutes late.

TELEPHONE EQUIPMENT

There is a vast array of telephone equipment available. New and more sophisticated items are being developed all the time. It is impossible to describe every type of equipment available so we shall consider the various categories – switchboards, direct-line instruments, extensions, intercommunications, mobile phones, pagers, answering machines and videophones.

SWITCHBOARDS

A switchboard is equipment at which incoming calls are received by an operator and directed to the appropriate extension user. Switchboards are of two basic types. Small systems are suitable for an organisation that needs

Fig. 4.5 Digital switchboard.

up to about 60 extensions. An extension is a telephone instrument located away from the switchboard but linked to it. Larger systems, known as PBXs (private branch exchanges), are made up of computerised programmable equipment, which can take hundreds of exchange lines and several thousand extensions, typically 10 extensions to each exchange line. Exchange lines, often referred to as 'outside lines', are provided by the telecommunications company from the business to the area telephone exchange.

In a large organisation, which has sophisticated equipment, there may be several small switchboards – key telephone systems – located in various sections or departments. Calls received at the main switchboard are directed to the appropriate 'mini' switchboard, which may be operated by a member of the staff – a secretary, for example.

Switchboards suitable for a small number of extensions and for a large number of extensions are illustrated in Fig. 4.5.

DIGITAL TELEPHONE SYSTEMS FACILITIES

The list in Table 4.1 explains the facilities commonly used in large computerised telephone systems. (The facilities listed may be known by different names depending on the equipment.) Not all facilities are provided on all extensions. The switchboard supervisor programs the extensions and updates them as necessary. For example, if a member of staff moves office, their extension number is transferred to the extension at the new location.

Table 4.1 *Digital telephone systems facilities*

Abbreviated dialling	An exchange controlled by computer can be programmed to automatically dial up to 100 telephone numbers when two or three digits only are dialled. This is particularly useful when overseas numbers, which can contain up to 15 digits, are dialled frequently.
Absent extension answering	When a computer-controlled exchange connects a caller to an extension that is not answered, the call is automatically transferred after 3, 4 or 5 rings, to another extension on a pre-arranged circuit. This process is repeated on all the extensions on the circuit (up to five) until the call reaches an extension that is answered.
Automatic callback	By lifting the receiver, dialling a code and replacing the receiver, the telephone instrument can be made to ring. Used by engineers for testing.
Automatic transfer	A call can be transferred from one extension to another by the extension user without referring back to the switchboard.
Barred extensions	Extensions on which external calls cannot be dialled directly; this can be applied selectively, e.g. to subscriber trunk dialling (STD) and/or international direct dialling (IDD). This facility is also referred to as 'route restriction', 'level 9 busying' or 'level 9 access barred'.
Call forward/follow me	When extension users leave their locations they may key in a code and extension number, which enables their calls to be forwarded to another extension.
Call logging	The origin, destination and duration of calls is recorded for cost control purposes.
Call waiting signal	A signal introduced into an existing call to inform the two people talking that another caller is waiting to speak to one of them.

(continued)

Table 4.1 *(continued)*

Camp-on busy/ring when free	An extension user, on finding any extension engaged can dial a code that will leave their call in the system. The caller can replace their receiver and the call will automatically be made when the extension called is free. This facility has now been developed so that the originator of the call is recalled first to ensure their availability.
Conference call	Several people are able to speak to each other in one call (see Chapter 13, page 422).
Direct dialling in (DDI)	Outside callers can dial directly to an extension, if they know the extension number, without first being answered by the switchboard.
Extension metering	A series of meters is installed, which records the number of units used by an extension on a PABX, usually installed in hotels so that guests can dial their own calls to be charged to their account.
Group calling/hunting	When incoming calls are connected by the operator to an extension the call is automatically rerouted to other extensions in turn on a programmed circuit. This facility is also available from internal extensions.
Hold for enquiry	The telephone operator can hold a call while enquiring of the extension user whether they wish to take the call.
Inter PABX connection – private wires	When a private wire is connected into the PABX system an extension user can use the private line, usually by dialling the digit 7 or 8 and the number of the private line.
Message waiting facility	Used mainly in hotels, a light on a panel is illuminated indicating that the operator should be contacted for a message.
Night busying	It is usual for night service (see page 77) to operate on selected extensions only. Where a switchboard has several lines on the

(continued)

Table 4.1 *(continued)*

	same number with automatic transfer of incoming calls to second and subsequent lines on that number, it is possible to have an engaged signal on the lines not connected to night extensions.
Night service	There are three types of night service. 1. A series of bells can be located throughout the premises. An incoming call will ring all the bells so that anyone who hears a bell goes to the nearest telephone, dials one digit and receives the call. This is known as unattended night service. 2. Exchange lines are plugged to specific extensions, e.g. senior managers. In some cases the night-service numbers are different from the day-time service numbers (known as 'changed identity') though the calls are routed on the same lines. 3. Night-service switchboard – calls are routed to a smaller switchboard, which may be manned by a security officer. There is limited facility for connection of incoming calls.
Transfer and enquiry	A subscriber may hold a call, dial another number within the exchange area and later revert to the original call, or transfer the caller to the new number. This is a similar facility to automatic transfer between extensions applied to direct lines.
Trunk offering	When an operator wishes to interrupt a call, e.g. for an overseas call, they can press a button that creates a pipping tone over the call indicating to the extension user that the operator wishes to speak. This facility is also available between extensions on some systems.
Voicemail	An answering facility integrated into a digital telephone system.

DIRECT-LINE INSTRUMENTS

A direct-line telephone is one that is connected to an 'outside' line. It may have exclusive use of a line, as a private telephone at home does. In a business organisation it is usually an extension telephone connected to an outside line through the switchboard. An external caller dials one or two digits in front of the extension number to be routed directly to the extension. The extension user dials a digit to access an outside line and then, on hearing the external dialling tone, can dial directly to an external number. Direct dialling bypasses the switchboard operator.

Telephone companies both sell and rent telephones and telephone systems. Many retailers sell telephone instruments; it is wise to buy equipment approved by the national telephone company to ensure that it is compatible with the national telephone system.

DIRECT-LINE AND EXTENSION TELEPHONE FACILITIES

There are many facilities available on extensions to electronic telephone systems. The most common facilities are listed in Table 4.2.

INTERCOMMUNICATION

Because most systems, even the simplest, allow communication between extension users it is not necessary to have a separate intercommunication system, which requires separate installation.

Table 4.2 *Direct-line and extension telephone facilities*

Amplifying handset	Increases the volume for hard-of-hearing users.
Base-to-phone intercom facility	On a cordless telephone the person carrying the handset can be called by someone at base.
Base-to-phone pager facility	On a cordless telephone the person carrying the instrument can be alerted to the fact that they are needed at the base.
Bell	An additional bell located at a distance from the telephone, e.g. in another room.
Call timer/clock	The duration and cost of the call is displayed after completion of the call.

(continued)

Table 4.2 *(continued)*

Caller identification	The caller's name and/or telephone number is displayed on a small display panel on the instrument (see Fig. 4.6).
Cordless	An instrument consisting of a base plugged into electric and telephone sockets, and a cordless handset that can be carried anywhere within range (which varies depending on the set and conditions).
Display	The display panel shows the number dialled or displays prompts to guide the user through each aspect of the telephone's use.
Hands-free	The user can speak and listen via a loudspeaker without lifting the handset.
Headset	Earphones that allow the telephone to be used without lifting the handset.
Inductive coupler	A device that provides greater clarity for a person wearing a hearing aid.
Lamp signalling	A light that flashes when the telephone rings.
Last number redial	By pressing one button the last number dialled will be redialled automatically.
Notepad memory	The next number required can be stored while a call is still in progress.
Number memory	Telephone numbers can be held in memory and dialled by pressing one or two buttons only.
On-hook dialling	The number wanted can be dialled with the handset on the hook. The handset is lifted when the call is answered.
'Phone in use' indicator light	A light on a cordless telephone base which indicates that a call is in progress.
Ringer volume selection	The ringer can be on or off, soft or loud.
Secrecy button	When pressed, the secrecy button enables the user to talk with someone who is in the room with them, without the person at the other end of the phone line being able to hear.
Touchtone capability	Modern telephone instruments have touchtone facilities, for which a rental is paid (see page 85).
Voice amplifier	A device to boost the voice so that the person at the other end can hear better.
Wall mount	A wall-mountable holder in which to insert the handset when not in use.

Fig. 4.6 Direct-line touchtone telephone.

MOBILE TELEPHONES

Sometimes called cellphones, mobile telephones are now used worldwide. There are many different makes of telephone but all have similar facilities. All new mobile phones are digital but there are some places in the world where the digital equipment on the telephone has to be replaced by analogue equipment. This is done by sliding the back off the phone and replacing it with a bigger, heavier item. This enables the user to access the network in difficult terrain such as mountainous areas.

All mobile phones operate on batteries. The number of hours for which the instrument can be switched on and for which calls can be made or received, depends on the particular model. On some models the standard battery can be replaced with a long-life battery. Battcries have to be charged; the frequency at which this is necessary depends on the length of time the phone is switched on and also for how long it is used. The phone is placed in a special stand, which is plugged into a standard electric socket, or connected direct to the socket via a jack-plug connection. Many cars now have telephone sockets, or the phone can be plugged into the car's cigarette lighter. The charging equipment is quite compact and light, so is easy to carry.

Mobile telephones can be hands-free, which is useful for car drivers as they can use the phone without removing their hands from the steering wheel. In some countries it is illegal to use a telephone while driving unless it is hands-free; however, speaking on the telephone is a distraction in any case, and is therefore dangerous when driving.

Various companies sell mobile telephones and provide 'cellnet' services. There are two ways of using a mobile phone. You can pay an installation charge for connection to a line and allocation of a number; you then pay a monthly rental fee and calls are charged at a standard rate per minute with cheaper calls at certain times. Alternatively, you can buy a card, which you insert into the telephone. You can then make calls until the value of the card has been used. A new card is then bought and used in place of the spent one or you can call a number and key in a code to 'top up' your card. Both incoming and outgoing calls are charged.

Mobile phones have virtually all the features of standard telephones. The mobile phone companies provide facilities such as a message service, both voice and written. This enables callers to leave a message when a mobile phone is switched off, not answered or engaged. The phone user receives a signal when the phone is switched on again, and keys in a number to access the messages. The messaging service can be charged on a monthly rental basis or, for people who do not receive many messages, a charge is made for each message accessed.

Mobile phones can now provide transmission facilities for fax and e-mail messages to be sent from laptop computers. This means that when travelling a business person can be in communication with colleagues, clients and others by three different methods.

PAGERS

There are many kinds of pager available. The simplest ones bleep and the user responds by calling the central paging point, which is usually the switchboard, from the nearest telephone. Some bleepers have more than one tone so that different groups of people, telephone numbers or locations can be identified. One of the tones can be linked to a message system.

Number pagers display telephone numbers to be called back. Message pagers display a message. This type of pager can be linked to a mobile phone so that, when the latter is switched off, calls are automatically switched to the pager. This is convenient for people who do not wish to have their mobile phones switched on when they are in public places. A pager is shown in Fig. 4.7.

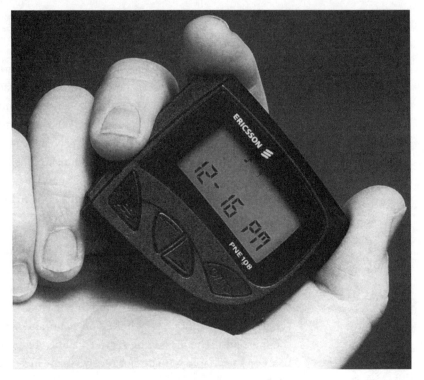

Fig. 4.7 An electronic pager on which both national and international messages can be received.

ANSWERING MACHINES

There are two types of answering machine:

- those that play a pre-recorded message to the caller, usually directing them to call another number, and
- answer-recording machines, which allow the caller to record a message.

Answer-recording machines provide access for callers 24 hours a day. They can be linked to a single instrument, a line on a switchboard or an extension. Advertisements frequently indicate a 24-hour service. This means that messages can be recorded to be replayed by staff during office hours. Answer-recording machines are often used by small businesses where it is not possible to have someone available to answer the telephone at all times, even during office hours. This means that callers do not waste a call. It is important that their use is not abused, though. It is not acceptable for an answer-recording machine to an extension to be switched on during office hours except in an emergency. It is very useful for anyone working late, either internally or externally, or for an overseas caller to be able to leave a message to be picked up the following day.

The latest answering machines are electronic. The user's message and callers' messages are recorded digitally. The machines have additional message capacity and better quality of voice reproduction.

Answering machines can be accessed from a remote location. The subscriber dials the home/office telephone number and when the answerphone clicks into operation, the subscriber keys in a personal code number. The messages are replayed and can either be left on the tape or deleted. The tape is then reset at the beginning. Table 4.3 lists details of answer machine recording facilities.

Table 4.3 *Answer machine recording facilities*

Answer delay	The number of times the telephone rings before the machine is activated
Digital announcement	User's message recorded electronically
Memo message recording	Enables the user to leave a message for an outside caller who has remote access
Message erase	Enables the user to delete the message after playback
Message indicator	May be either a flashing light or a counter
Message save	Enables the user to retain a message on the tape playback
Remote announcement	Enables the user to change the recorded announcement by remote control
Remote switch on/off	Facility for caller with remote control to access the machine to switch it on or off
Security code	The code a remote control user has to key in before messages can be played back
Tape full alert	Indicates when the message tape is full
Time/day announcement	Records the time and date of each message
Voice-activated remote control	Enables the user to play back messages by speaking instead of keying in a code

Many answering machines are combined with a telephone or a telephone/fax machine. These instruments incorporate many of the facilities of a direct-line telephone (see pages 78–9).

Machines that combine telephone, answer-recording and fax facilities (see Fig. 4.8) are appropriate for the small office or home where the volume of traffic in any one of the three is limited but all three are needed.

Fig. 4.8 Combined telephone, answer-recording and fax machine.

VIDEOPHONES

Videophones are not in common use yet but are available from various suppliers. A miniature screen is integrated into the telephone and shows the speaker's head and shoulders. Videophones may be used with digital telephone lines only.

TELEPHONE SERVICES

Telephone services are provided by the national telephone company.

TYPES OF CALL

There are four types of call that can be made from any territory.

- **Local call** – the subscriber wanted has the same area code as the caller so that you have to dial only the subscriber's number.
- **Toll call** – the subscriber has to dial the local area code before the number of the subscriber wanted; the local area code changes depending on where you are calling from.
- **Intra-island calls** made by direct distance dialling (DDD) – the subscriber has to dial '0' followed by the territory code and area code of the subscriber wanted, followed by the subscriber's number.
- **International calls** can be made by international direct dialling (IDD) to most countries in the world. The country codes and area codes of main cities/towns are given in the 'International Codes' section of the telephone directory. Refer to this when telephoning overseas to ensure that you are calling at a time when you can expect to be answered,

unless you know that the overseas subscriber has an answer-recording machine on which you can record a message.

Some calls have to be made via the operator.

- **Advice of duration and charge (ADC)** – tell the operator you want an ADC call before giving the number you require. When the call is completed you will be informed of the duration of and charge for the call.
- **Collect** – charged at a higher rate, you ask for a collect call when the person you are calling (or who answers) agrees to pay for the call.
- **Credit card** – a credit card can be obtained from the national telephone company to be used to make toll, intra-island and overseas calls. You tell the operator that it is a credit card call and give the credit card number. This is useful for people who have no mobile phone.
- **International** – there are a few countries you cannot access by direct dialling; calls have to be made via the international operator (the number to call is in the phone book).
- **Personal** – when you wish to speak to a particular person you ask the operator for the name, department or reference number of the person followed by the telephone number. A fee is charged but you are not charged for the call until the person wanted is 'on the line'. If they are not available the call is valid for 24 hours and attempts will be made by the operator to obtain the person wanted.
- **Ship's radio telephone** – when calling a person on board ship in port, ask the operator for the Ship's Telephone Service. When connected, give the name of the ship, and the name and designation of the person required.
- **Station** – if you are willing to speak to anyone who answers a toll call. The rate for this type of call is lower than standard toll call rates.
- **Time and charge** – ask the toll operator for a 'T and C' call and you will be advised of the charge on completion of the call.

TSTT CALL MASTER SERVICES

TSTT provides a range of services for which a rental is charged. For subscribers who have a 'touchtone' telephone, full details of the services and how to use them are given in the telephone directory. The list includes:

- **Caller ID** – know who is calling before you answer
- **Anonymous Caller Rejection** – when in active mode your telephone will automatically reject any caller who has blocked their 'Hold Number Delivery' (see below)
- **Hold Number Delivery** – You can prevent your telephone number from appearing on the Call Master display unit of a Call Master Telset if you wish to keep your number private.

CALLING PLUS SERVICES

Some additional services, fully explained in the telephone directory, include:

- **Call Forwarding** – allows you to transfer calls from your telephone to any other telephone, including mobile telephones
- **Call Waiting** – allows you to answer two calls on one line
- **My Call** – a standard ring plus up to 3 additional different rings allocated to individual people within the home or office
- **Speed dialling** – you can programme in up to 30 numbers that you call frequently enabling you to call the number by pressing one or two keys only
- **3-way Calling** – three parties can talk together from different telephones.

MISCELLANEOUS SERVICES

There is a range of useful services provided by TSTT. These include:

- duplicate bills
- interim bills
- integrated services digital network (ISDN) – very useful for people working from home or in a small office; up to three lines can be connected to one telephone number, e.g. telephone, fax and computer – when only one is in use, speed of transmission is faster
- Internet (see page 55)
- itemised bills
- leased lines – organisations can lease one or more telephone lines from one location to another for their exclusive use; the lines may be local or international for voice or data transmission
- phonecard and coinphone services (see page 87)
- radio/telephone (see page 85)
- telegram service (see Chapter 5, pages 131 and 132)
- traveller services
- 800 services – Call Free, International Inbound, Pay 800, etc.

There are slight differences in the services offered by the national telecommunications company in each territory. Some services may be called by a different name. For example, 'Hold Number Delivery' is called 'Blocking' in Barbados; the TSTT 'My Call' service is called 'Smartring' in Barbados. Some of the services are used differently depending on where they are used.

ACTIVITY 4.2 Look at the various types of telephone call listed on pages 84-6. Obtain a phone book and look in the section that explains the various calls and services available. Make a list of the names of these calls and services. Beside each call/service, write in the type of person who might find it useful.

Example
Duplicate bills – accounts department if bill for payment is lost.

PUBLIC PHONE BOXES

Coinphones and cardphones may be installed in private buildings or in public kiosks. The person using a coinphone inserts coins into the box either before dialling or when the subscriber called answers. Coinboxes take certain denominations of coin only (these depend on where you are based). Overseas calls can be made from a public coinphone only as collect or credit card calls (see page 85). Instructions on how to make a call are displayed in the kiosk.

Cardphones operate when a phonecard is inserted. Phonecards can be bought at post offices and various shops. When a call is made, the units used are cancelled from the card, which can be re-used until all the units have been cancelled. When the card is inserted into the slot the register on the telephone indicates the amount of money still unused.

Some cardphones operate when a credit card is inserted. Instructions on how to make a call with a phonecard or credit card are displayed in the kiosk.

TELEPHONE DIRECTORY

Every subscriber receives a copy of the telephone directory. In addition to listing subscribers' names and telephone numbers there are pages of information about the types of call and how to make them, services available and how to use them, and information services with the numbers to access them. Whenever a new telephone directory is received the information pages should be checked for updated information. New services are being introduced and it is important to be aware of them and think how they might be useful in your own office. Some services are free and can be used by any subscriber; others can be used for a rental charge (usually quite small).

USING TELEPHONE EQUIPMENT

Switchboards, direct-line and extension telephones, mobile telephones and other equipment must be used correctly if they are to help us achieve effective communication.

OPERATING A SWITCHBOARD

The main function of a switchboard operator is to receive incoming calls and direct them, quickly and accurately, to the extension of the person wanted. Various situations may arise, e.g. the caller not knowing the name of the person or extension number wanted, extension engaged or no answer from the extension. The following procedures provide guidelines for efficient operating. Individual organisations have their own procedures, designed to complement the telephone system and meet the needs of the system's users. Procedures must be followed by all operators as they reflect the corporate image.

Receiving incoming calls

Greet ('Good morning/afternoon') and give the name of the organisation. Listen to the caller's requirement(s). Repeat names and telephone numbers requested.

If the caller knows the name of the person wanted but not their extension number, look in your list of extensions to find the number (see page 91 for computerised telephone list).

If the caller asks to speak to someone who can help with a particular need, either:

- tell them the name of the person you will put them through to, or
- ask them to hold while you check who can deal with the problem; if this takes more than a minute go back to the caller to reassure them that you are dealing with their call.

If the extension is engaged, inform the caller and ask 'Do you wish to hold?' If the caller does hold, go back to them regularly, every 30 seconds or so, when the call is returned to the switchboard. The caller may then choose to ask for another person or extension.

If there is no answer from the extension, this situation is dealt with differently, depending on the system and the operator's circumstances.

The call may be transferred automatically to other telephones on a group circuit until the call is answered (known as group hunting), or it may be answered by another extension user. If this facility is not available the operator should inform the caller that there is no answer and, depending on circumstances, ask:

- 'May I put you through to A's secretary?'
- 'Would you like to speak to someone else?'
- 'May I ask A to ring back?'
- 'May I take a message?' (telephone operators are usually too busy to take full messages).

A 'ring back' message should include:

- the name of the caller and their organisation
- the telephone number, including STD, DDD or IDD code, the number and extension number; when passing on the message include the country code for overseas callers.

The details of the message should be repeated to the caller to ensure accuracy. It may be necessary to spell out names. To avoid any misunderstanding use one of the accepted 'telephone alphabets' when spelling. The British and international versions (the latter used when speaking to international exchange operators) are given in Tables 4.4 and 4.5.

Variations to the words are acceptable provided they are clear and usually understood by anyone who speaks English.

Telephone numbers are spoken in different ways in different countries. There are four basic ways.

1. Say each figure separately except for round hundreds up to 900 and round thousands up to 10 000.

Table 4.4 *Telephone alphabet (as used by British Telecom operators)*

A	Apple	J	Jack	S	Sugar
B	Benjamin	K	King	T	Tommy
C	Charlie	L	London	U	Uncle
D	David	M	Mother	V	Victory
E	Edward	N	Nellie	W	William
F	Frederick	O	Orange	X	X-ray
G	George	P	Peter	Y	Yellow
H	Harry	Q	Queenie	Z	Zebra
I	India	R	Robert		

Table 4.5 *Telephone alphabet (as used by international operators)*

A	Alpha	J	Juliet	S	Sierra
B	Bravo	K	Kilo	T	Tango
C	Charlie	L	Lima	U	Uniform
D	Delta	M	Mike	V	Victor
E	Echo	N	November	W	Whiskey
F	Foxtrot	O	Oscar	X	X-ray
G	Golf	P	Papa	Y	Yankee
H	Hotel	Q	Quebec	Z	Zulu
I	India	R	Romeo		

2. Pause between each pair of figures, working from the right:

   a. 3-figure numbers   346   3 46
   b. 4-figure numbers   1286   12 86
   c. 5-figure numbers   63218   6 32 18
   d. 6-figure numbers   781523   78 15 23.

   Use the word 'double' only when the figure is doubled on either side of a pause, and never at the beginning of a number, e.g.:

   a.   78812   7 double 8 12
   b. but   78112   7 81 12
   c. or   778456   77 84 56.

3. Say the figures in pairs as pairs, not as separate digits, e.g.:

   789123   seventy-eight or, in French,   *soixante-dix-huit*
                  ninety-one   *quatre-vingt-et-un*
                  twenty-three   *vingt-trois.*

4. Say the figures in groups of three, e.g.:

   789123   (written 789.123 in some countries)
          say – 789 123
   788499 say – 788 499 (not 7 double 8).

The switchboard operator has a very important role in creating an image of courtesy and reliability. Voice and speech are discussed on pages 101–2. The points raised are particularly important because voice is the medium of establishing a relationship with the caller. As systems become more sophisticated there is an ever greater need to create and maintain a personal rapport with the caller.

Quick reference lists

Telephone numbers are often needed quickly. If you have a computerised system you will be able to call up extension users' names and numbers, and other important numbers, speedily. If you do not have this facility keep written lists readily accessible and update them daily.

1. Extension users' names and numbers – internal directory preferably arranged alphabetically by individual name and by department. Staff of the same name with initials/first names, departments and titles.

2. Extension numbers of senior and key people – separate list on a single sheet.

3. Telephone numbers needed regularly or in emergency:
    a. company doctor (in case of illness)
    b. courier (for collection of mail)
    c. fire officer(s) (in case of smoke/fire alarms operating)
    d. first aiders (in case of accidents)
    e. health and safety officer (in case of accidents)
    f. maintenance staff (in case of emergency, e.g. water pipe burst)
    g. security officer (in case of theft or assault)
    h. taxis
    i. travel agents.

Handing over

There should be a procedure for one operator to hand over to another. The information to be given should include the following:

- faults reported but not yet corrected
- messages to be passed to staff when they are available
- promises to return calls with information
- changes notified during the day.

Bomb alerts

No matter how small the organisation or how unlikely a bomb alert may seem, it is important to have a procedure worked out and practised regularly. Keep the caller talking for as long as possible and ask questions regarding the location of the bomb and how long before it goes off. The form in Fig. 4.9 shows the information needed by the police when they have to follow up a bomb alert.

As soon as the caller ends the call, follow the procedures laid down.

BOMB THREAT

This form should be completed as far as possible by an operator receiving a bomb threat.

Part 1   Date .... Time of call ....

          Call received by ....

Part 2   Record the exact language of the threat:
....
....
....

When is it set for? ....
Where is it? ....
What kind of bomb? ....
Why are you doing this? ....
Who are you? ....

Part 3   VOICE ON THE PHONE (tick those applicable)

Man .... Woman .... Child .... Age ....
Intoxicated .... Speech impediment ....
Accent .... Other ....

Part 4   BACKGROUND NOISE (tick those applicable)

Music .... Children .... Aeroplane ....
Conversation .... Traffic .... Typing ....
Machines .... Other ....

OTHER INFORMATION

Fig. 4.9 Bomb threat form, to be completed by person receiving a call.

Making calls

It is rare for switchboard operators to be asked to make calls as staff can usually access a line from their own extensions and dial the number they require. The procedure for making a call from a switchboard is the same as from a direct line (see page 97) but the operator would then have to connect the person called to the extension of the caller.

Additional duties

There are other duties that the switchboard operator may be asked to carry out, including maintaining call records, reporting faults, updating a computerised internal directory and reprogramming extensions on a digital system.

An operator who is required to carry out one or more of these duties would be given appropriate training. Each organisation has its own procedures for such duties.

USING DIRECT-LINE AND EXTENSION TELEPHONES

Receiving calls

One sure way to impress callers is to receive calls correctly. The techniques involved are simple but they must be followed. Always remember that you are in a business situation and until you know who is calling it is essential to maintain a slight formality. This is not being unfriendly but ensures that you do not offend.

- When the telephone rings, identify the type of call – internal or external – and lift the receiver promptly.
- Do not continue a conversation with another person while holding the receiver off the cradle. Excuse yourself at the appropriate moment *before* lifting the receiver.
- Hold the receiver correctly so that you speak *into* the microphone, not across it.
- Greet the caller (external calls) – 'Good morning/afternoon' – and identify yourself, your office or department. Speak clearly – it is irritating and a waste of time if the caller has to ask you to repeat yourself.
- Listen carefully and make brief notes. Check that you have the name of the caller correctly – ask for it if the caller has not given a name.
- Make sure you know as exactly as possible what the caller wants, whether it is something you can do, whether you need to contact someone else for information or whether it is necessary to transfer the call.
- If the call is cut off replace the receiver and wait for the caller to telephone again.

Connecting calls

The calls you receive often have to be passed on to a colleague or to your superior. Fast, accurate connections are vital to keep the caller's costs to a minimum and avoid frustration and, consequently, ill-feeling.

- If the caller does not give a name ask 'May I know who is calling please?' It may also be important to know the caller's designation and organisation.

- If the caller wishes to speak to a colleague or your manager, say 'I will find out if Mr X is available. Will you hold the line please Mr Caller?' Never commit anyone to taking a call. (Note the use of the caller's name to establish a good working relationship.)
- Unless you know why the caller wishes to speak to the person requested ask the reason for the call: 'May I tell Mr X what you wish to speak to him about?' Most people respond positively.
- Put the caller on hold and inform the person wanted immediately, giving the name and other appropriate details of the caller, including the reason for the call.
- If the person wanted is willing and able to take the call, replace the receiver as soon as you hear that the connection has been made.

Handling calls when the person wanted is not available

It is essential to be positive. If the person wanted is not available there are several steps you can take to convey to the caller that you want to help.

1. Apologise that the person wanted is not available: 'I am sorry Mr Caller, Mr X is not available at present.'
2. Offer alternative help, which may include one or more of the following.
   a. 'Would you like to speak to someone else?'
   b. 'Can *I* help you?'
   c. 'Would you like to leave a message?'
   d. 'May I ask Mr X to telephone you when he is free?'
3. If the person wanted is engaged ask the caller 'Will you wait?' If the caller decides to wait keep in contact about every 30 seconds. (A minute seems a long time when you are waiting.)

Taking messages

Your telephone image is enhanced enormously by your reliability in taking messages accurately and delivering them promptly. Sound competent and people will have confidence in you. After experiencing your reliability they will have no hesitation in leaving messages in future.

1. Obtain the name, designation, organisation, address (in certain circumstances), telephone number (including STD, DDD or IDD codes) and extension number of the caller. Repeat the details as you write. To ensure that no detail is forgotten, use a message form such as the one illustrated in Fig. 4.10.
2. Use the telephone alphabet to check the spelling of names and difficult words (see Tables 4.4 and 4.5) and take special care with numbers.

```
                                                          URGENT: YES/NO

     Message for: ..................................................................................................
     Time: ........................... Date: .................................................


                              WHEN YOU WERE OUT

     M            .........................................................................................
     Of:          .........................................................................................
     Telephone:   .........................................................................................
     Address:     .........................................................................................
                  .........................................................................................


     Message:










     Taken by: .............................................................................................
```

Fig. 4.10 Telephone message form.

3. Check the main points of the message: say 'I'd like to check the details please', and read back the key points.
4. Close the call with a promise to deliver the message to the person concerned. Thank the caller.
5. Make a neat copy of the message and include the time and date at which it was taken, and your initials. Check that all the details you recorded are included in the neat copy.
6. Deliver the message immediately if urgent, otherwise in accordance with standard practice.

Follow-up action

When you have taken a message and/or promised that the person wanted will call back or take some other action at a certain time, make sure that your promise is fulfilled. If the promise cannot be kept, at least call the person from whom you took the message and explain the circumstances.

If you have responsibility for ensuring that messages are followed up it may be useful to use a duplicate book for recording them. You can then tick off the copy in the book when you have checked that the message has been dealt with.

In some offices staff are out a lot and regularly call in for messages. Anyone taking a message should record it in a book accessible to everyone.

ACTIVITY 4.3 Imagine that you are holding the following telephone conversation. Write the message that you will give to Miss Little, your manager.

You   Good morning. St Vincent Yacht Hire.

Caller   Good morning. May I speak to Jane Little please?

You   I am sorry, Miss Little is on leave today. Can I help you or would you like to leave a message?

Caller   I'll leave a message please. My telephone number is 620451. I'd like to know whether she would be willing and able to give a presentation to my staff on developments in sea navigation computers. If she could do this, the ideal time would be on the Tuesday or Wednesday of the second or third week of next month.

You   May I know your name please?

Caller   Sorry, I should have told you. I'm John Downs of Computers Incorporated. My telephone number is 620451.

You   Mr Downs, your telephone number is 620451. I will tell Miss Little that you would like her to give a presentation to your staff on developments in sea navigation computers if she is willing. The best time would be Tuesday or Wednesday of the second or third week of next month if that is possible.

Caller   Thank you very much. I will look forward to hearing from Miss Little tomorrow if possible.

Ideally, you should have a large book ruled in columns, each column headed with the name of a member of staff. The messages are then written in the appropriate column(s). This makes it easy to relay the messages (which are often simply call-back names and numbers) when a particular staff member calls in.

Making calls

Preparation is essential to making a successful telephone call. Here is a checklist that will help you.

1. Check the name, telephone number and extension number of the person you wish to speak to. (Details of people you contact should be kept in a personal telephone directory.)
2. List the points you wish to discuss and get the information/documents/files you think you may need *before making the call*. Decide what action you will take if the person you want is not available. You may wish to call again, leave a message, speak to someone else or be called back. Also be prepared to leave a message if your call is answered by a recorded message or an answer-recording machine.
3. Dial or key correctly.
4. When answered by an operator, greet them and ask for the person you wish to speak to, by name and extension number. If you do not know the person's name be ready to explain what help you are seeking. You may be dialling a direct line – always check that you are speaking to the person you want before starting the conversation.
5. When the person wanted answers, greet them, identify yourself and state the purpose of your call. Check that you are speaking to the person you want if no identification is given. If the person you want is not available act as you have decided (see 2 above).
6. If you leave a message ensure that the person who takes it checks the main points by reading it back to you.
7. If the call is cut off replace your receiver and redial the call.
8. Make a note for the file if decisions or actions have been agreed.
9. If answered by a message on an answerphone or voicemail, leave the following information.

    a. If a simple message can be left:
      - who the message is for
      - your name
      - company name
      - message
      - telephone number (in case the person wishes to return your call).

b. If you wish the person wanted to return your call, all the above points plus:
- when available to be called back if you are likely to be out at any time
- a brief word on what you wish to speak about.

10. If answered by a recorded voice from a call centre you will be asked to key in certain digits to access the department or person who will be able to help you. Some call centres ask callers to go through a series of access digits. For example, you may be answered as follows.

> 'This is ABC Bank Limited. To enable us to deal with your call as quickly as possible please listen carefully to the following instructions.
> - If you have a query on your account, please press 1.
> - If you wish to pay an outstanding account, please press 2.
> - If you wish to arrange to pay by direct debit, please press 3.

You may then get a second, third and even fourth set of instructions, after which you will be spoken to by a 'live' person.

USING THE TELEPHONE DIRECTORY

When preparing to make a telephone call you may need to find the telephone number of the person/organisation you want. Subscribers are listed in the telephone directory in alphabetical order of individuals' surnames and organisation names. The subscriber's address, area code and subscriber number are given. In the front pages of the phone book there are details of services available from TSTT and how to use them. As new services become available they are advertised on radio, TV and in brochures. There is also information on how to handle obscene calls. All Caribbean territories have telephone directories that give similar information.

It is always useful to keep to hand your own list of numbers that you call often or may need quickly. Such a record enables you to add other details that may be useful, such as addresses, contact names, and extension or direct-line telephone numbers, and other relevant information such as product names if the organisation is a supplier, for example.

USING A MOBILE TELEPHONE

The procedures for using a mobile telephone for business purposes are the same as those for using a direct-line or extension telephone. There are also some courtesy rules that should be followed. Your personal mobile telephone should always be switched off when you are working in your office. Callers can leave a message for you to access in your lunch break or after working hours. Except in an emergency, mobile telephones should not be used in public. It is very disturbing for other people to hear a conversation being carried on beside them when they wish to concentrate on what they are doing.

USING AN ANSWERPHONE OR VOICEMAIL

It is important to record a message for callers that reflects an image of courteous business efficiency. When recording a message, give the following information:

- your name
- your department, if appropriate
- an apology for not being able to answer the call
- a request to the person calling to leave their name, telephone number so that you can return their call, and details of what they wish to speak about
- an indication of when you will return the call (not 'as soon as possible').

When you have recorded the message, play it back to ensure that you have given all the details and that it sounds friendly but businesslike, that your voice is well modulated (see page 101) and speech is clear.

> **ACTIVITY 4.4** Write out the message you would record on an answerphone or voicemail to greet people calling you when you are not available to answer their call.

It is essential to check the answerphone/voicemail for messages when you have been away from your office. Answerphones have a flashing light, which indicates that there are incoming messages. Listen to each message carefully, making a note of the person's name, telephone number, the time they will be available and any other key points. Call them back as soon as you can or at the time stated. If the caller has indicated what they wish to talk about, obtain any relevant files/documents you may need.

USING SYSTEM FACILITIES

It is important to become familiar with all the system facilities you may need to use on an extension telephone, direct line, answerphone/voicemail. Some facilities are activated by using a series of digits. Keep a note on a card of the codes for the facilities you need to use. Place the card by the telephone.

CREATING A PROFESSIONAL IMAGE

The receptionist, telephone operator and all staff who use the telephone share a responsibility for creating a courteous and efficient image of the organisation. There are some key points to consider in relation to image. These are:

- attitude to people and the situations they sometimes create
- attitude to the telephone
- voice and speech
- what you say and how you say it.

We shall now look at each of these in turn.

ATTITUDE TO PEOPLE

Your attitude to people depends to some extent on the individual with whom you are in contact, what they expect of you, their attitude to you and how you feel when you meet them. Some people 'go on' about a problem or query, which is a waste of time; they are indecisive; they do not know what they want; they are abrupt and rude, dismissive of speaking with you, preferring always to speak to someone more senior. On the other hand there are so many people who give pleasure in one way or another: they are always cheerful; they say something nice; they have a very pleasing voice; they always say 'please' and 'thank you'; they apologise for troubling you. To get the best out of people, be one of those people who gives pleasure to others.

Try to understand why people are difficult. Perhaps they are not well, have had a disagreement with someone, or are worried. Few people set out to be unpleasant. By ignoring their attitude and being friendly, helpful, concerned and sensitive to their feelings, you may well help them to overcome their anger. Show respect for people by addressing them correctly. Never use a person's first name unless you know them personally or they ask you to do so.

Occasionally you may have a caller or visitor who is angry about a real or imagined wrong. Follow the three golden rules below and you should be able to deal with such situations in a dignified manner.

1. Do not take the comments personally. You happen to be the person being spoken to as a representative of the organisation, but it could just as well be someone else.
2. Never get angry in return. The unpleasantness is amplified and nothing is solved.
3. Ask the person to tell you exactly what is wrong and *make notes*. This reassures them that you are taking the matter seriously.

ATTITUDE TO THE TELEPHONE

'The phone rings all day.' 'I'm constantly interrupted by the phone.' 'I can't get any work done if I don't use the answering machine.' These are constant cries of despair. You are under pressure to meet tight deadlines, people come into your office wanting information or answers to queries, and each of your managers is wanting their work done 'now'. In spite of all this the telephone is a valuable tool that enables you to do your job efficiently.

When the telephone rings think of it not as an 'interruption' but as a possible opportunity for something positive – a decision you have been waiting for, an invitation to undertake some task that will be a challenge, a good business opportunity for your manager and your organisation, a request for help that it will give you pleasure to fulfil. Regard the telephone as an ally rather than an enemy and you will be well on the way to creating and maintaining a desirable image.

VOICE AND SPEECH

Voice and speech are not the same thing. Voice is the raw sound produced when the breath vibrates vocal chords in the throat. Speech results from the process of shaping into words the sound of the voice.

A voice of good 'quality' helps to achieve effective communication. A voice that is pleasant to listen to gains attention. A voice that is high pitched can be a distraction from what is being said.

Speech must be clear. Some people speak with very little movement of the lips so that they 'mumble'. It is worth making an effort to speak clearly; by doing so you gain confidence and are not interrupted by the listener.

What you say when you are speaking on the telephone is important. There are expressions that are inappropriate in business conversations. Some words and phrases are listed in Table 4.6 with suggested alternatives.

Table 4.6 *Guidelines on professional telephone conversations*

Unprofessional	Professional
Hello, Hi	Good morning/afternoon
Who?	I beg your pardon/I'm sorry I didn't hear your name
Who do you want?	Who do you wish to speak to?
What?	I beg your pardon
Hold on	Will you hold the line please Mr Smith?
He's out/not in	I'm sorry, Mr X is not in (deal with this situation as discussed on page 94)
He's engaged	I'm sorry, Mr X is engaged. Will you wait/hold?
He's busy/tied up	I'm sorry, Mr X is not available at present (deal with this situation as you would when Mr X is out)
I'll tell him	I'll tell Mr X you rang/I'll give Mr X your message as soon as he returns. Thank you for calling
OK/all right	An appropriate affirmative
OK?/all right?	Is that acceptable?
Thanks (a lot)	Thank you (very much)
'Bye	Goodbye (preceded by 'Thank you for calling' if appropriate)

These phrases, spoken in a friendly, but not over-familiar, manner generate confidence in your ability to deal with a caller's needs.

APPEARANCE

In addition to voice and speech, the appearance of staff working in an organisation plays an important part in creating its image. Good grooming and appropriate dress make anyone look professional. Ladies should not wear excessive jewellery or make-up for work. Save them for parties!

Look at the young lady in Fig. 4.11 and identify what gives her a professional appearance. Also look at the reception area and consider what is attractive to visitors.

> **ACTIVITY 4.5** A young person is starting her first job after leaving school. She is to be a trainee receptionist in a large organisation. She asks you for advice on what to wear and how she should present herself.
>
> Discuss the question with colleagues and others and make a list of the advice you would offer the young person.

Fig. 4.11 A reception area.

PRACTICE QUESTIONS

1. A gentleman comes into reception and asks to see Mr Liddell, the sales manager. He does not have an appointment. You know that Mr Liddell is not in the office today. How would you deal with the visitor?

2. A lady comes into reception looking very angry. She demands to see the chief executive. A product she bought recently was faulty. How would you deal with the situation?

3. Why is it important that each visitor should sign the visitors' register and should be given identification to wear?

4. As a junior secretary it is one of your duties to relieve the receptionist for an hour at lunchtime. When you take over reception duty what information do you need from the receptionist?

5. You apply for a job as a receptionist and are offered the post, which you accept. What information would you expect to be given about the practices used in your company:
   a. during your induction
   b. on a regular basis after your induction?

6.   *a.* If you are asked to make an appointment state four details you need to know.
      b. Mrs James, who has an appointment with the personnel manager of your organisation, rings to ask how to find your organisation. What question(s) would you ask Mrs James, and what information would you give her?

7. Give a brief explanation of each of the following:
   i. switchboard
   ii. direct-line instrument
   iii. extension
   iv. intercommunication
   v. pager
   vi. mobile phone
   vii. answering machine
   viii. videophone
   ix. PABX
   x. amplifying handset.

8. Digital telephone systems have many facilities. Briefly explain each of the facilities listed below:
   i. message waiting
   ii. group hunting
   iii. barred extension
   iv. call waiting signal
   v. DDI
   vi. ring when free
   vii. hold for enquiry
   viii. call logging
   ix. conference call
   x. night service.

9. There are various facilities available on direct-line and extension telephones. What are the following facilities:
   i. caller identification
   ii. hands-free
   iii. cordless
   iv. touchtone
   v. on-hook dialling?

10.   *a.* What is the difference between an answering machine and an answer-recording machine?
      b. List the details you should include in the message you record on an answer-recording machine or voicemail to be replayed to callers when you are not able to answer their call.

     c.   List the details you should give when answered by a recorded message.

11. Write the following abbreviations in full:
  i. DDD
  ii. IDD
  iii. DDI.

12. List and explain three types of call that have to be made via the exchange operator.

13. National telephone companies are now providing a range of services to subscribers. List and explain five such services.

14. Explain how you would deal with each of the following situations when operating a switchboard:
  i. receiving a call
  ii. the caller asks to speak to someone who is not available
  iii. the extension of the person wanted is engaged
  iv. you need to check the spelling of a name
  v. the caller wishes to leave a message for the person wanted to call back.

15. Prepare a list of instructions for a new junior member of staff on how to answer the telephone and deal with three situations that commonly occur.

16. What information should be given to a relief telephone switchboard operator?

17. *a.* As an extension user you may often have to take messages. List the details you must obtain from the caller.
  b. What is the procedure for taking a message?

18. How would you prepare to make a telephone call to a customer?

19. List five points to be followed when using a mobile telephone.

20. It is very important to create a good image of yourself, your department and your organisation when using the telephone. List and briefly explain four key points involved in creating the right image.

SHORT ANSWER QUESTIONS

Complete the following sentences.

1. When a visitor arrives at a reception desk the receptionist should immediately .... and ....

2. A large telephone system in a company is called a ....

3. A telephone call can be transferred from one extension to another without going through the switchboard operator by ....

4. The simplest type of pager .... to alert its owner to the fact that they are wanted.

5. Videophones can be used with .... telephone lines only.

Choose the most appropriate ending for each of the following sentences.

6. The **main** reason for asking people to sign a visitors' register is:
  a. to know how many visitors each member of staff receives
  b. so that someone can check whether they are with the person they have been directed to see
  c. for future reference, to find out the name of the person who came from a particular organisation or vice versa
  d. to be able to check that all visitors are accounted for in the event of fire.

7. Barred extensions are telephones that:
  a. are used as direct-line telephones
  b. restrict the facilities that can be used on them
  c. may be used by certain people only
  d. cannot receive incoming calls.

8. The message waiting facility is usually indicated by:
  a. a buzzer
  b. a message on a register
  c. a light
  d. a bleep.

9. A credit card obtained from a national telephone company cannot be used to make:
  a. a local call
  b. a toll call
  c. an intra-island call
  d. an overseas call.

10. When a relief operator takes over on a switchboard they should be told:
  a. how many calls have been received during the preceding period
  b. messages to be passed to staff when they are available
  c. how many calls have been made during the preceding period
  d. staff who are expecting visitors.

EXAMINATION QUESTIONS

1. The equipment that enables telephone calls to be recorded whilst the office is closed is called a/an ....

2. A receptionist keeps a/an .... diary.

   (Pitman Office Procedures Level 1 1998 Pt 1A)

3. State THREE disadvantages of using the telephone rather than writing a letter.

   a. ....
   b. ....
   c. ....

   (Pitman Office Procedures Level 1 1998 Pt 1B)

4. A receptionist is an essential member of staff.

   a. Why is it important for a receptionist to have knowledge of the company structure, product and personnel?
   b. Why does a receptionist maintain a register of callers?
   c. Apart from receiving and directing visitors, state SEVEN other duties a receptionist may perform.

   (Pitman Office Procedures Level 1 1998 Pt 2B)

5. To ensure telephone messages are given correctly, the caller should have all the relevant .... to hand.

   (Pitman Office Procedures Level 1 1999 Pt 1A)

6. List the actions a receptionist would take in the following circumstances.

   a. When a visitor with an appointment arrives
   b. When parcels are delivered to the reception desk

   (Pitman Office Procedures Level 1 1999 Pt 2A)

7. *a.* Identify THREE possible complaints about the way telephone calls are handled and suggest how these could be overcome.
   b. State the difference between mobile phones and portable phones, and explain situations where the use of each is advantageous.

   (Pitman Office Procedures Level 2 1998 Pt 2)

CHAPTER 5

WRITTEN COMMUNICATIONS

OBJECTIVES When you have studied this chapter you should have acquired the knowledge and understanding to be able to:

1. explain the advantages and disadvantages of written communication
2. compose clear, concise, well-written and correctly structured desk and file notes, memoranda, and letters
3. produce reports from handwritten drafts and/or dictation
4. complete a form, and design a simple form for a specific purpose
5. explain and produce the types of telegram that may be sent within and/or from your territory
6. compose and transmit a fax with cover sheet including a disclaimer
7. compose and transmit an e-mail document
8. list and explain the considerations involved in choosing the appropriate type of document in different circumstances
9. proofread to identify the main types of error that occur in typewritten and printed documents
10. mark a draft with appropriate manuscript correction signs
11. read documents to achieve clear understanding.

Some people find it easier to express their thoughts by speaking, others by writing. Everyone has to develop the skills necessary to express their thoughts clearly and fluently in both ways. Often a choice has to be made as to whether to contact a person by a spoken medium or by a written medium. The criteria for making this choice is discussed at the end of the chapter. First let us consider the advantages and disadvantages of communicating in writing.

ADVANTAGES OF WRITTEN COMMUNICATION

- The writer has time to think carefully about how to express their thoughts so as not to create misunderstanding or to give offence.
- There is a record for both writer and reader to refer to later.
- When figures are involved, the recipient of the information does not have to make notes, which may be inaccurate.
- The reader can read the document as many times as necessary to understand the message.
- Information can be presented in a systematic and logical sequence, e.g. by lists, tables, charts, etc.
- It provides a record for people who could not be present at a discussion.

DISADVANTAGES OF WRITTEN COMMUNICATION

- It can be difficult to express ideas clearly in writing.
- Not being able to see or hear the other person may lead to misunderstanding.
- Words need to be chosen carefully to avoid ambiguities.
- Formal language, sometimes used in business documents, gives an impression that the writer is pompous.
- The writer cannot be sure that the reader will concentrate sufficiently to understand the message.
- The reader cannot immediately question the writer on any point that is not clear.
- The writer may not have an adequate knowledge of grammar to convey exactly what he wants the reader to know.
- Written documents have to be filed.
- The writer cannot receive feedback immediately and may have to follow up to get it.

TYPES OF WRITTEN COMMUNICATION

TRANSMISSION BY MESSENGER, COURIER, POSTAL SERVICES, FACSIMILE (FAX) AND ELECTRONIC MAIL (E-MAIL)

These types of transmission might include:

- notes (desk and file)
- internal memoranda
- letters
- reports
- notes, minutes, reports of meetings (see Chapter 13)
- forms
- legal documents such as contracts.

TRANSMISSION BY TELEGRAPH OR RADIO

This might include:

- telegrams.

TRANSMISSION BY TELEPHONE LINES

This type of transmission covers:

- telex
- facsimile (fax)
- electronic mail (e-mail).

COMPOSING WRITTEN DOCUMENTS

Before we consider each type of document we will discuss the skill of writing clearly and concisely. This is fundamental to effective communication being achieved between writer and reader.

The best writing is precise and concise. To achieve this skill the writer needs a good knowledge of grammar, punctuation, spelling and vocabulary. If you know that you have difficulty with any of these key aspects of writing, it is essential that you take steps to improve. We will now consider the common difficulties that writers may have.

GRAMMAR

Obtain a good book on English grammar and check that you do not make the 'common errors' in your writing. These are listed, with examples, in Appendix 1.

PUNCTUATION

Tips on punctuation are given in Appendix 2.

SPELLING

When you are uncertain how to spell a word, do not guess, refer to a dictionary (see Chapter 15, page 476). Also keep an alphabetical index book and write in it every word you have to look up in the dictionary. This will help to fix the correct spelling in your mind and will provide a quicker source of reference if you forget the spelling in future. You can also include words that are new to you that you come across when you are reading.

VOCABULARY

Choosing the word that most clearly expresses what you mean is very important. The best, perhaps the only, way to improve your vocabulary is to read – newspapers, magazines, books and business documents. If you come to any word that you do not understand, look it up in a dictionary and write it in your index book. You will soon extend your vocabulary.

WRITING CONCISELY

There are four rules for writing concisely.

Short sentences

Long complex sentences obscure meaning. Often, a long sentence is two sentences joined by 'and'. Replace 'and' with a full stop, and the two sentences will be easier to read and understand. For example:

It is in the interests of the department that there should be staff on duty throughout the day *and* to achieve this it will be necessary to draw up a rota for staff to take their lunch breaks at different times.

Replace 'and' with a full stop and you have two good sentences.

Short words

Use short words in preference to long ones unless the long word expresses your meaning more precisely. There are many examples of short words that can replace long ones. Here are a few.

Commence – start, begin   Purchase – buy
Adjacent – next to   Innumerable – many

There is nothing wrong with long words but shorter words are usually more easily understood.

Word instead of a phrase

There are many phrases that can be replaced with a single word:

at this moment in time   now
take into consideration   consider
with immediate effect   immediately
owing to the fact that   since or because

Phrase instead of a clause

It is *sometimes* possible to replace a clause, which contains a finite verb, with a phrase or even a single word (although be aware that this can change the emphasis of the message you are trying to put across). For example:

The table, which is made of oak, needs polishing.

Replace 'which is made of oak' (adjectival clause) with 'oak' (an adjective).

The oak table needs polishing.

WRITING PRECISELY

There are many 'vague' words and phrases – vague because they are open to interpretation by the reader. For example, 'I should be grateful if you would let me have this information as soon as possible.'

The writer may think this will be within a day or two. The reader, who may be very busy, may think that a week will be 'soon' from their point of view. It would be much more precise to give a time limit, e.g. 'within a week'.

As well as using precise words and phrases, it is essential that facts and figures are given accurately. Information should always be checked to ensure

> **ACTIVITY 5.1** Think of more precise expressions that could be used in place of the following.
>
> 1. a short period
> 2. considerable progress
> 3. periodical tests
> 4. frequent meetings
> 5. a few days
> 6. about three months
> 7. a number of
> 8. substantial amount
> 9. up to 10 per cent
> 10. urgent

that it is accurate. Once in writing it can be legally binding. For example, if it is stated in a letter that the cost of a project will be $10 500 when it should be $20 500, the incorrect figure, which may be a typing error, has to be honoured.

SENTENCES AND PARAGRAPHS

Write in complete sentences and build up paragraphs.

A **sentence** is a group of words that have a subject and a verb. It makes sense when standing alone. The meaning of a sentence depends on the order in which the words are arranged. The parts of a sentence that 'go with each other' must be positioned as near as possible to each other.

A **paragraph** should be built on a topic sentence (usually the first). All other sentences should have a direct bearing on the subject matter in the topic sentence and will develop the point. Do not include irrelevant information. Keep the paragraph moving forward so as not to divert attention from the main point.

STYLE AND TONE

Style – the way you write – is created by the words you choose, the way you phrase your sentences, the concise explanation of information and the standard of presentation, i.e. display. You cannot write as you speak because speech is much less concise, and probably less precise, than writing should be.

There are a few rules to follow that will help to ensure that your writing creates the right impression.

Avoid:

- verbosity, writing more than is necessary
- ambiguity, leaving the reader asking 'does it mean this ... or that?'
- pompousness/affectation, using long words and complex sentences
- colloquial language, perfectly acceptable in speech but inappropriate in a business document (see examples below)
- slang – never
- clichés (see examples below)
- metaphors (see examples below)
- commercial jargon (see Table 5.1).

Colloquial phrases

bear with me	over the top (OTT)	be hung up
run it past them	it's cool to be untidy	at every turn

Clichés

far be it from me	at the end of the day	explore every avenue
let's face it	leave no stone unturned	grind to a halt

Metaphors

The plank of the financial investment ('plank', normally a piece of wood, is used here to mean 'mainstay')

The foundation on which to build a project ('build' normally refers to construction but is used here to mean 'develop')

Table 5.1 *Commercial jargon*

'Commercialese' expressions	Preferred expressions
Advise	Inform, tell
And oblige	(Omit)
As per	As in
As previously stated	(Omit – do not repeat the point)
At an early date	Soon

(continued)

Table 5.1 *(continued)*

'Commercialese' expressions	Preferred expressions
At the time of writing	Now
Attached hereto	I attach
Due to the fact that	Because
Duly	(Omit)
Enclosed herewith	I enclose
Enclosed please find	
I shall be obliged if you will	Will you please
I shall furnish you with	I shall send you
I shall keep you advised	I shall let you know / I shall inform you
I trust	I hope
In due course	(Give a deadline or omit)
In the amount of	For (amount)
It is anticipated that	I expect that
It was delivered to your good selves	It was delivered to you
Kindly	Please
On Friday next	Friday (date)
Re	About
Thank you in advance	(Omit)
Thank you in advance for your assistance	I shall appreciate your help
Thanking you in anticipation	(Unnecessary and ungrammatical)
The writer	I, me, my
This matter	(Omit)
Trust	Hope
Under separate cover	Separately
We are able to quote you	Our quotation is
We acknowledge receipt of	Thank you for
We are in receipt of	
We beg to	(Omit)
We look forward to hearing further from you	We look forward to receiving your reply *or* omit
We shall have pleasure in arranging	We shall arrange
We would ask you to	Will you please ... ?
With reference to	I refer to
With regard to	Regarding
Would ask/remind/say	Wish to ask/remind/say
Your esteemed/valued order	Your order

PLANNING AND PREPARING TO WRITE

If you follow the steps listed below you will find that the composition of your text will be easier and more fluent.

1. Decide the objective and bear it in mind all the time you are writing.
2. Jot down key words for each of the topics you wish to include.
3. Obtain all the information you need to meet your objective.
4. All writing needs to be structured. There should be a beginning, middle and end, even though each part may be one sentence only.
    i. The beginning usually 'sets the scene', i.e. tells the reader what to expect.
    ii. The middle is the 'meat' in which you deal with the topics needed to meet your objective.
    iii. The end is the summing up, which may draw conclusions, encapsulate the content of the middle and/or indicate what action will follow.
5. Present your facts in a logical sequence, connecting them with each other.

DESK NOTES

In Chapter 4 we discussed writing a telephone message, stressing the importance of including all the details necessary for the person receiving it to take action. When writing any kind of note, the same rules apply. It should not be so brief that it makes no sense to the reader. It should contain all relevant facts to enable the reader to react positively.

ACTIVITY 5.2 Read the following desk note. Comment on it and rewrite the note as you think it should be written.

Fred

I need some figures from you about the expenditure on fitting out the offices in the new building. Can you let me know what we have spent so far? Perhaps we had better have a meeting.

JT

FILE NOTES

It is common practice to write a file note after a telephone conversation or a meeting with someone, e.g. a client. This contains the key points of the conversation including any decisions taken or actions agreed.

In government ministries/departments, the same document is called a 'minute', not to be confused with minutes of a meeting (see Chapter 13).

A useful form for a file note is shown in Fig. 5.1. (This form would not be used in government.)

FILE NOTE

Conversation with: _____

Company/
department: _____

Telephone number/
fax number/e-mail: _____

Subject: _____

I telephoned/caller telephoned*
My/caller's* message was _____

_____

_____

_____

My/caller's* reply was _____

_____

_____

_____

Follow-up/action* _____

_____

_____

Signed: _____

Date: _____ Time: _____

*Delete as appropriate

Fig. 5.1 File note.

INTERNAL MEMORANDA*

Staff who wish to communicate in writing to other members of staff in the same organisation write a memorandum (generally referred to as a memo, plural memos). Memoranda may be typed/printed on pre-printed forms or on plain paper.

PARTS OF A MEMORANDUM

A memorandum has up to seven parts:

1. heading – 'Memorandum', 'Internal Memorandum' or 'Inter-office Memorandum'
2. to – the name of the addressee
3. from – the name of the writer
4. date
5. your and our references
6. subject heading
7. message.

Notice that there is no salutation and no complimentary close. Initials or a signature may be added but are not required.

MULTIPLE MEMORANDA

A memorandum is often of interest to more than one person. Each person may be sent a copy, in which case a **distribution list** is given. This is shown as either:

To: Mr A
       Miss B
       Mrs C

or:

To: See distribution list below

and at the bottom of the memorandum the list of people is given.

---

*The word 'memoranda' is the plural of 'memorandum'. The plural 'memorandums' is now acceptable.

Sometimes the memorandum is to one person but other people need copies for information. This would be shown:

Copies for information: Mr P
                            Mr Q
                            Mr R

An alternative to distributing copies to everyone is to send one copy with a circulation slip attached (see Chapter 8, page 234). As each person on the list receives the memo, they read it, sign the slip and pass it to the next person on the list.

The sequence of people's names on a list can be important. The list can be:

- in alphabetical order, which prevents individuals resenting their place in the list
- according to rank/seniority, which can cause resentment if people think they are being placed below someone less senior
- according to job priority, to ensure that action will be taken in order of urgency
- by location, so that the shortest route is followed for passing on the memo
- 'for information only' at the end.

An internal memorandum is illustrated in Fig. 5.2.

INTERNAL MEMORANDUM

FROM: JM Ramsay, Claims Department, Head Office

TO: Claims Department, Kingston

DATE: 5 May 2002

SUBJECT: MR J FOSTER – CAR ACCIDENT CLAIM No. 4568/02

The estimate for repairs to Mr Foster's car has been approved. Please inform him accordingly.

CPC/JMR

Fig. 5.2 Internal memorandum.

> **ACTIVITY 5.3** Write an internal memorandum to Mrs Mary James, the training manager of your organisation, asking for an appointment to discuss your career development. You would like advice on an appropriate course of study.

LETTERS

There are four main types of letter:

- personal
- semi-personal
- business
- official, i.e. government.

PERSONAL LETTERS

These are written among friends and relatives. They are normally informal and are written in language closer to speech than a business letter.

SEMI-PERSONAL LETTERS

These are written by business people to other business people whom they know very well and with whom they have a very good working relationship.

BUSINESS LETTERS

These are written by individuals to companies, etc., and by the staff of businesses to staff in other businesses and individuals.

OFFICIAL LETTERS

These are written by civil servants in government departments to staff in other government departments, companies and individuals.

PARTS OF A LETTER

A letter can have up to 13 parts:

1. printed heading, which includes
    - *i.* the name of the organisation
    - *ii.* the address

>> *iii.* the telephone and telex/fax numbers, e-mail address and website details, and, if relevant, the telegraphic address (an abbreviated name to be used on telegrams)
>> *iv.* the names of the directors if the organisation is a limited liability company
>> *v.* the address of the company's registered office, i.e. the address held on the register of companies' list
>> *vi.* sometimes a description of the organisation's business, e.g. solicitors, health food specialist
>> *vii.* sometimes there are headings for insertion of our reference (our ref.), your reference (your ref.), direct telephone no. (of the individual who writes the letter), date
>> *viii.* sometimes an instruction to address all correspondence to a certain person, e.g. the company secretary
> 2. our reference, which may be a file reference (e.g. 16.46/6) or the initials of the person who signs the letter and the person who produces the letter (e.g. JKP/RET, or JKP/ret, or jkp/ret)
> 3. your reference, taken from the letter under reply
> 4. date, in Canada and the USA the date is typed in the order of month, day and year (e.g. August 1 2002), in the UK the day precedes the month (e.g. 1 August 2002)
> 5. the inside address – the name and address of the addressee (it is very important that people's initials, first names and surnames are spelt correctly, and that they are correctly addressed); gentlemen are normally addressed as 'Mr', ladies as 'Mrs', 'Miss' or 'Ms' – the latter can be used when it is not known whether the lady is Mrs or Miss; people with titles, e.g. Sir, Lord, Rev, etc., must be addressed correctly (this information will be found in reference books); honours, degrees and professional qualifications are inserted after people's names – they must be in the correct sequence, which is
>> *i.* orders of chivalry, civil honours and decorations, e.g. Trinity Cross, Chaconia Medal (Trinidad), Order of the National Hero, Order of the Nation (Jamaica), KCMG, OBE, etc., conferred by the Queen on citizens of other Caribbean territories
>> *ii.* military decorations, e.g. VC, DSO
>> *iii.* academic qualifications, e.g. MA, BSc
>> *iv.* professional qualifications, e.g. MCIPD
> 6. salutation – 'Dear Sir/Madam' if the name of the addressee is not known
>> 'Dear Mr/Mrs/Ms/Miss Smith'
>> 'Dear Julie' (if the writer knows the reader)
> 7. subject heading, which indicates the topic of the letter

8. body of the letter in paragraphs, with any lists of points itemised and identified by numerals or letters
9. complimentary close which must 'match' the salutation

    'Dear Sir/Madam' - 'Yours faithfully'
    'Dear Mr Green'   - 'Yours sincerely'
    'Dear John'   - 'Yours sincerely' sometimes preceded by 'Kind regards' or 'Best wishes'

10. signature of the person who has authority to sign, or another member of staff may sign on behalf of the authorised signatory by prefixing the authorised signatory's typed name with 'pp', which stands for 'per pro' and means 'for and behalf of'.
11. the name of the person who signs the letter – this can be in brackets and can have the title of a woman, e.g. Mrs Paula Clarke, Miss Jane Shepherd (this is useful when someone who does not know the writer wishes to telephone them)
12. 'ENC.' or 'Enc.' or 'enc.' to indicate that there is an enclosure; this may also be indicated in the left-hand margin by a row of stops beside the line in which the enclosure is mentioned
13. copies to – name(s) of the person/people to whom copies are to be sent; note that 'blind copies' are not shown on the original document – this is because the writer does not want the addressee to know that other people have received a copy.

ADDRESSING COMPANIES

In Chapter 1 we discussed the various kinds of organisation. They are addressed as follows:

- Partnership — Messrs (plural of Mr)
- Private and public limited liability companies – ABC Company Limited

It is usual to address a letter to an individual in an organisation either by name or, if the name is not known, by job title, e.g. Sales Manager.

Sometimes letters are addressed 'for the attention of', for example:

- For the attention of the Marketing Manager
  Three Trees Honey Limited *or*

- For the attention of Mr Mark Elson
  The Acre Hotel Limited

LAYOUT (DISPLAY) OF A LETTER

There are two typical styles of display:

- full block
- modified full block.

These two styles are illustrated diagramatically in Fig. 5.3.

The date shown on the right in modified block is useful when searching for a particular letter in a file. It is usual to look for letters by date. With full block the file has to be fully opened at each page in order to see the date. It is much easier to flick through looking at the date on the right-hand side of each page.

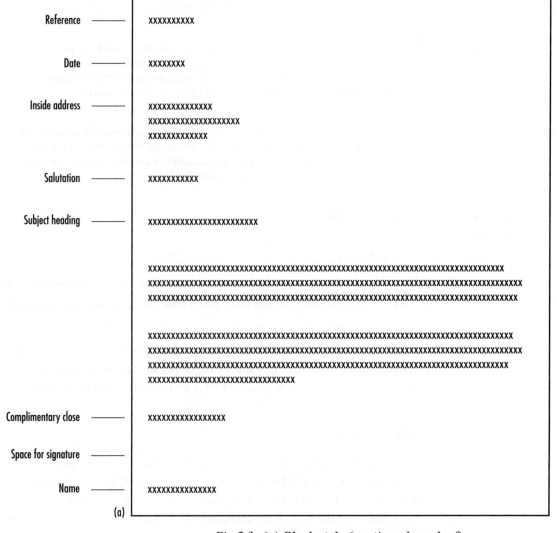

Fig. 5.3 (a) Block style (continued overleaf).

```
Reference ——— xxxxxxxxx                          Date ——— xxxxxxxxx

Inside address ——— xxxxxxxxxxxx
                   xxxxxxxxxxxxxxxxx
                   xxxxxxxxxxxx

Salutation ——— xxxxxxxxxxx

Subject heading ——— xxxxxxxxxxxxxxxxxxxxx

                    xxxxxxxxxxxxxxxxxxxxxxxxxxxxxxxxxxxxxxxxxxxxxxxxx
                    xxxxxxxxxxxxxxxxxxxxxxxxxxxxxxxxxxxxxxxxxxxxxxxxx
                    xxxxxxxxxxxxxxxxxxxxxxxxxxxxxxxxxxxxxxxxxxxxxxx

                    xxxxxxxxxxxxxxxxxxxxxxxxxxxxxxxxxxxxxxxxxxxxxxxxx
                    xxxxxxxxxxxxxxxxxxxxxxxxxxxxxxxxxxxxxxxxxxxxxxxxx
                    xxxxxxxxxxxxxxxxxxxxxxxxxxxxxxxxxxxxxxxxxxxxxxxxx
                    xxxxxxxxxxxxxxxxxxxxxxxxxxxxxxxxxxxxxxxxxxxx

                    xxxxxxxxxxxxxxxxxxxxxxxxxxxxxxxxxxxxxxxxxxxxxxxxx
                    xxxxxxxxxxxxxxxxxxxxxxxxxxxxxxxxxxxxxxxxxxxxxxxxx
                    xxxxxxxxxxxxxxxxxxxxxxxxxxxxxxxxxxxxxxxxxxxxxxxxx
                    xxxxxxxxxxxxxxxxxxxxxxxxxxxxxxxxxxxxxxxxxxx

Complimentary close ——— xxxxxxxxxxxxxx
Space for signature ———
Name ——— xxxxxxxxxxxx
                                                                     (b)
```

Fig. 5.3 (continued) (b) modified block style – note the date on the right.

Many companies have a house style, which may be one of the two styles illustrated or an adaptation of one of them. House style is an important factor in creating an organisation's image and must be used by all staff.

CONTINUATION SHEETS

Occasionally a letter will be too long for one page. The second page, or continuation sheet, will be headed with the page number, the name of the addressee and the date. This information is in case the second sheet becomes detached from the first. Some companies have printed continuation sheets. Two continuation sheet layouts are shown in Figs 5.4a and 5.4b.

```
        Page 2
        24 May 2002
        Mr Peter Diaz




        have reached a stage where we feel able to assure you of production dates in the future.
(a)
```

```
                                                                        Page 2
                                                                        24 May 2002
                                                                        Mr Peter Diaz




        have reached a stage where we feel able to assure you of production dates in the future.
(b)
```

Fig. 5.4 (a) Left-axis block continuation sheet; (b) right-axis block continuation sheet.

ACTIVITY 5.4 Write a letter to the Head of Business Studies at your local college asking for details of evening-class courses in secretarial subjects. Include details of any qualifications you have already gained.

INVITATIONS

There are occasions when customers, clients and others are invited to attend a company event such as a product launch or a special anniversary. Formal invitations are issued in these cases.

A formal invitation is written in the third person (see Fig. 5.5). The names of the guests may be handwritten.

Guests may be asked to telephone their reply (see the example in Fig. 5.5).

> The President and Board of Directors of the
> Caribbean Arts Centre
> request the pleasure of the company of
> Mr and Mrs John Smith at the
> 50th Anniversary Celebrations
> at 6 pm on Thursday 22 August 2002
> at the Centre
> for a tour of the Golden Exhibition
> followed by a buffet supper
>
> RSVP Cynthia Ifill
> Tel. 622 4976

Fig. 5.5 Example of a formal invitation.

The reply is written in the same way:

Mr and Mrs John Smith are very pleased (*or* regret that they are unable) to accept the kind invitation of the President and Board of Directors of the Caribbean Arts Centre to attend the Centre's 50th Anniversary Celebration at 6 pm on Thursday 22 August 2002.

REPORTS

There are two kinds of report: informal and formal. Informal reports may be written as a memorandum, a letter or a short attachment to a letter or compliments slip.

A formal report usually has the following sections:

- introduction – explaining the objective of the report and how the information was obtained
- findings – setting out the facts
- conclusions – summarising the findings
- recommendations – suggesting what action should be taken
- appendices – usually lists, visual presentation such as charts and graphs, and/or documents referred to in the findings.

It is unlikely that you would be expected to write reports but you may have to produce them. If the organisation has a house style for reports, this must be followed. Otherwise, set out the report so that it is easy to read and understand. Fig. 5.6 shows a specimen report displayed with a main heading, section headings and sub-headings within a section heading. Section and sub-headings are numbered.

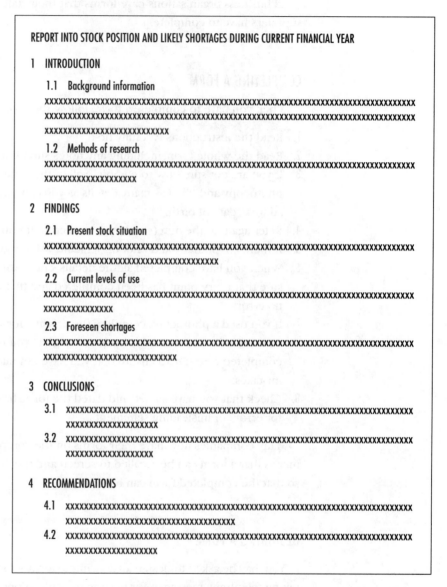

Fig. 5.6 Specimen report layout.

NOTES, MINUTES AND REPORTS OF MEETINGS

Note-taking at meetings, and drafting of notes and minutes are covered in detail in Chapter 13. Examples of display are also shown.

FORMS

All business organisations have forms that their staff, customers and suppliers have to complete.

COMPLETING A FORM

When you have to complete a form, follow these rules.

1. Read the instructions carefully first.
2. Read the whole form, including any notes supplied with it.
3. If you are not sure how to complete all of the form, make a photocopy and fill in as many details as you can, e.g. your name, address, date of birth.
4. Refer again to the note(s) relevant to each point on the form.
5. If there are points you do not understand, ask for guidance.
6. When you have completed all the details, check them to make sure that every point has been completed and that there are no errors.
7. If you used a photocopy, complete the original form and keep your draft for your record. Check the original you have completed carefully to ensure that you have not made any mistakes.
8. Check that you have signed and dated the form, having read the penalty for errors or misleading statements.

Many companies now have their forms on the computer system. This means that a form can be recalled to screen and the details can be inserted so that the completed form can be printed.

DESIGNING A FORM

You may be asked to design a very simple form – for example, for taking telephone messages, for logging in applications for a vacancy or to obtain a signature when money is handed over to the cashier.

The basic rules of form design are:

1. have a heading so that it is immediately evident what the form is to be used for
2. leave enough space for each of the details required

3. if instructions are needed on how to complete the form, put them immediately after the heading
4. consider the sequence of the details so that they are logical to the person completing the form.

An example of a simple form is shown in Fig. 5.7.

CAR MILEAGE LOG

Week beginning 2002

Day	From	Destination	Miles
Monday			
Tuesday			
Wednesday			
Thursday			
Friday			
Saturday			
Sunday			
		TOTAL	

Signature .... Date ....

Authorised .... Date ....

Fig. 5.7 Simple form.

ACTIVITY 5.5 Registered mail is received in the mail room of your company and is then delivered to the appropriate member of staff. Design a form for the member of staff to sign when a registered letter is delivered to them.

COLOUR CODING

It can be useful to use colour coding to differentiate one form from another. Each form is printed on different coloured paper or can be printed in different colours on white paper. If there is a large number of forms, colour coding could be by group, e.g. a particular colour for all forms related to one subject or to one department.

LEGAL DOCUMENTS

You will not be asked to write legal documents but you may have to type them. Contracts, agreements, etc. are normally typed in a specific format. Very often you would copy a document, just changing details such as names, dates and amounts of money.

A legal document must be 100 per cent accurate. If a document is produced on a typewriter an error may not be erased, so you have to be a very accurate typist! On a word processor or computer, it is much easier to produce a perfect document.

In either case, a legal document should be 'read over' with a colleague. This means that you read the original draft and a colleague reads the document you have produced. It is always easier for someone else to pick up your mistakes than it is for you to pick up your own errors.

TRANSMISSION

All of the documents we have discussed can be transmitted internally by messenger, facsimile and electronic mail.

In addition they can be transmitted externally by courier and postal services.

TELEGRAMS

Telegrams are transmitted by telegraph or radio and are dealt with by a special office. They may be sent overseas but not to an inland addressee in some Caribbean territories.

An overseas telegram, also called a cable, is a written message sent from a sender in one country to an addressee (individual or business) in another country. Completed telegram forms (see below) may be handed in at any telegraph office, telephoned or telexed. Telegrams to private addressees are delivered by hand or are sorted into a private post office (PO) box. Government departments and businesses are usually informed by telephone or telex of the contents of a telegram, a confirmatory copy being delivered or sorted into the private post box later.

SENDING A TELEGRAM

A form provided by the Telegraph Office must be completed with the class indicator (see pages 132-3), the name and address of the addressee, the message, and the name and address of the sender.

Organisations that send and receive telegrams usually have a telegraphic address. This is an abbreviated address consisting of a name, usually made up from the name of the organisation and the town. Here are examples of telegraphic addresses.

- Trinidad and Tobago External Telecommunications Company Limited
  1 Edward Street PORT-OF-SPAIN TRINIDAD
  Telegraphic address: TEXTEL PORT-OF-SPAIN

- Ransom and Jones Ltd 432 Holborn LONDON WC1R 4SR GT BRITAIN
  Telegraphic address: RANJON LONDON

The telegram form can be typed with three or four spaces between each word, or written in block capitals. A copy should be made for the relevant file. The date and time of handing in, telephoning or telexing the telegram, and the cost should be noted on the copy. It is advisable to write a letter to the addressee confirming the details contained in the telegram.

CHARGES

The cost of sending a telegram overseas is rated according to the number of words and the destination, with a minimum number of words charged.

A table of rates for the various facilities can be obtained from T & T External Telecommunications Company Limited (TEXTEL) or Jamaica International Telecommunications (JAMINTEL).

CLASSES (OR RATES)

Some types of telegram have an **indicator**, which must be the first word of the telegram before the name of the addressee. The classes most commonly used are explained in Table 5.2.

Table 5.2 *Telegram classes*

Type of telegram	Indicator	Explanation	Minimum charge
Ordinary	none	a full rate telegram, may be written in plain or secret (code or cipher) language or any combination of these	7 words
Notification of delivery *or* reply to paid service advice	ST	sender of telegram is notified of date and time of delivery to addressee; extra charge equivalent to 7 words at ordinary rate to the same destination	
Telephone delivery	TF	sender can request delivery by telephone; telephone number and name of the exchange with indicator are counted in the address as 1 word; when the telegram is received at the telegraph office, the addressee is telephoned and the contents are read; a printed copy is then sent by post	
Telex delivery	TLX	sender can request delivery by telex; telex number with indicator in the address as 1 word	
Phototelegraph service		pictures, photographs, drawings, typed or written documents and plans may be telegraphed in facsimile (exact copy) from JAMINTEL and TEXTEL to many places in the world; printing must be on one side of paper only; charges calculated on size of item	

(continued)

Table 5.2 *(continued)*

Type of telegram	Indicator	Explanation	Minimum charge
Official free in Jamaica OJGS (On Jamaica Government Service)	none	accepted free of charge if handed in by an authorised person or department; must contain official business only; must be written on blue OJGS form, franked with an official stamp, and signed by or for an authorised person or department; can be sent priority rate without charge; can be sent reply paid but the minimum flat rate charge for first 12 words at ordinary rate must be paid by sender (a list of people authorised to send OJGS telegrams is obtainable from any Post Office in Jamaica)	

WRITING A TELEGRAM

Because each word costs money, telegrams are written in an abbreviated form. For example, in a letter you might write:

I am sending you a set of samples. When you have decided which of the samples you prefer, will you please let me know so that I can order it as quickly as possible. (34 words)

As a telegram, the message could be written:

SENDING SAMPLES STOP INFORM CHOICE SO ORDER PLACED QUICKLY (9 words)

A specimen full rate telegram is shown in Fig. 5.8.

BARTHOLOMEW GRANDHOTEL HAVANA
PLEASE SEND FULL INFORMATION RE CONFERENCE FACILITIES BY RETURN
JAMES HIGHTEC PORT-OF-SPAIN

Fig. 5.8 Specimen full rate telegram.

ACTIVITY 5.6 Write a telegram to a friend telling him/her that you will be arriving at London Heathrow Airport next Thursday (give date). You will arrive from Heathrow and stay with your friend for three days.

TELEX

Telexes are transmitted via a telephone line. Businesses that wish to use the telex service must have a telex machine and be subscribers in the same way as anyone who uses a telephone.

Each subscriber has a telex number (which is shown in the letter heading) and is provided with a telex directory, in which all subscribers are listed alphabetically.

A telex machine has a telephone dial and a keyboard very similar to a typewriter. The operator dials the number of the addressee subscriber and, when an 'answer back' signal is received, types in the message. The text is transmitted as the message is typed and is reproduced on the receiving machine.

The telex machine enables the subscriber to send a written message to any other telex subscriber anywhere in the world. Providing the telex machine is switched on, it can receive messages 24 hours a day even when unattended.

PUNCHED TAPE MACHINES

An attachment can be fitted to a telex to enable the letters and figures typed to be translated into a series of holes punched in tape. Difficult text, such as tabulations, can be typed in and checked before the message is transmitted.

ELECTRONIC TELEX MACHINE

A machine similar to a word processor (see Chapter 6, page 164) is now commonly used. The typist keys in the message, checks it on screen, amends any errors and stores it on diskette before dialling the telex number of the addressee. When contact with the receiving machine is made the message is transmitted from the diskette. If the receiving machine is engaged, the sending machine will automatically redial at intervals until contact is made. The same message can be sent to many different addressees by keying in the message and a list of names with their telex codes and numbers.

The rental for the line to the telex exchange is controlled by the telephone company. International switching, the technical term for dialling telex calls in the exchange for onward transmission to the addressee, is carried out by TEXTEL or JAMINTEL. Charges are made in time units with a minimum charge of three minutes.

WRITING A TELEX

Because transmission by telex is quite slow, the message is written as briefly and concisely as possible. This reduces transmission time and therefore cost. A telex is not usually as abbreviated as a telegram but is shorter than a letter.

FACSIMILE TRANSMISSION

The great advantage of fax over telex transmission is that any type of material – typed/printed/handwritten text, drawings, sketches, etc. – can be sent. Only text can be sent by telex.

As we showed on page 110, most types of document can be sent by fax. An internal memorandum or letter can be typed in the usual format. Many companies use a fax form, which is sent on its own with the necessary details and a brief message. For a long message, the fax form is used as a cover sheet to the document. A report to be faxed would have a cover sheet that would merely indicate what the attachment is.

The details required on a fax are:

- the name, address, telephone/fax/telex numbers and e-mail address of the organisation sending the fax
- the name, organisation and fax number of the addressee
- the name of the individual sending the fax
- reference (if any)
- date
- number of pages, usually expressed as
  – 'Page 1 of (the total number of pages)' *or*
  – 'Pages: 16 including this page'
- message
- no signature is required but it is usual to 'sign off'.

A fax cover sheet is shown in Fig. 5.9.

A disclaimer is often printed at the bottom of a fax. This is to cover the sender against confidential information being seen by someone other than the addressee. A typical disclaimer states:

This fax and the information it contains may be confidential being intended solely for the use of the named addressee. If you are not the named addressee and/or have received this fax in error, please contact

```
Letter heading


FAX MESSAGE

To              Jean Ifill

Company         Confectionery Company Limited

Fax No.         624 1357

From            Andrew Chang

Fax No.         623 2468

Tel. No.        623 1245

Ref.            AC/458

Date            28 May 2002

No. of pages    3 including this page


This fax and the information it contains may be confidential being solely for the use of the named
addressee. If you are not the named addressee and/or have received this fax in error, please contact us
immediately by telephone or fax. We will accept a reverse charge call. You should neither disclose the
contents of this fax to any other person nor make copies of it.
```

Fig. 5.9 Fax cover sheet.

us immediately by telephone or fax. We will accept a reverse charge call. You should neither disclose the contents of this fax to any other person nor make copies of it.

When the fax has been prepared it is printed and put on a fax machine. Most fax machines work on a similar basis. They have a feed tray, a paper tray (or fax roll), a keypad similar to that of a telephone, a keypad of function keys and a register. Some fax machines have a telephone handset so that the machine can be used for making telephone calls as well.

The process of sending a fax consists of the following steps.

1. Place the document face down on the feed tray.
2. Press the appropriate keys to allow you to key in the addressee's fax number.
3. Press the START key to have the document read into the fax memory.

4. The addressee's fax may ring as a telephone for a few seconds and then change to a fax signal (like a whistle).
5. The register on the fax will then indicate that the document is being transmitted.
6. When all the pages have been transmitted the register indicates TRANSMITTED OK.

A fax machine is illustrated in Fig. 5.10.

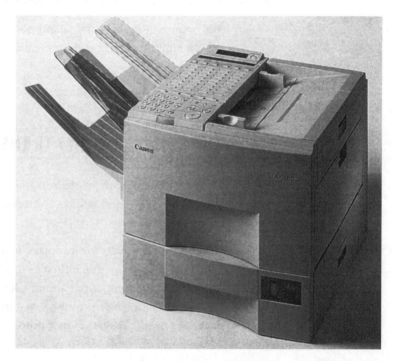

Fig. 5.10 The Canon Fax L-800 high-volume plain paper laser fax machine has a 20-page memory and facility to record 172 telephone numbers for abbreviated dialling.

Sometimes the addressee's fax will be engaged. The register will show this by indicating REDIAL. This means that the machine will automatically redial after a few minutes, usually twice more. If it still cannot transmit, a 'report' is printed showing that the fax could not be sent.

Most modern telefax machines recognise a fax signal and automatically switch to fax mode. Some older machines are not automatic and the telephone may be answered by the subscriber who has to switch to fax mode manually.

To receive a fax the only thing that has to be done is check the paper tray or fax roll regularly to ensure that there is a sufficient supply of paper. Most fax machines (called 'plain paper fax machines') use plain copier paper.

There are also faxes that use sensitised paper which is supplied on a roll (fax roll). As faxed documents are received the printed paper has to be torn or sliced off the roll. (The procedure for distributing faxes is explained in Chapter 8 on page 235.)

As with electronic telex machines, it is possible to send a fax to multiple addressees. Their fax numbers are keyed in one after another, up to a maximum number, depending on the machine; the document is fed into the fax memory and the machine automatically works through the list of fax numbers.

Many large organisations have the facility for sending faxes direct from computers. This eliminates the need for printing the faxes. (For more details see Chapter 3.)

ELECTRONIC MAIL (E-MAIL) TRANSMISSION

As with faxes, any document, printed/diagrams/charts, etc., can be sent by e-mail. The word 'e-mail' is used both as a verb, i.e. to transmit by e-mail, or as a noun, i.e. to send an e-mail.

E-mail is used very informally for internal communication. As with a fax, e-mails can be in desk note, memorandum or letter format. They can be very informal. Typically a minimum of preliminary details are given. The sender's and addressee's e-mail addresses must be keyed in and are usually followed by the message. A friendly salutation may precede the message. A typical e-mail is shown in Fig. 5.11.

From: Gloria James gloriaj@printshop.net
To: michaelali@hotmail.com
Date: 27 May 2002 15.50
Subject: Invitation cards

I am pleased to tell you that we have been able to meet the deadline you gave for the proof of your invitation card. This is being sent to you this morning by courier.

If you can let me know by 1700 today what amendments, if any, are needed I will 'pull out all the stops' to get 200 printed and delivered to you by midday on Wednesday 29 May.

Regards

Gloria

Fig. 5.11 Typical e-mail.

The e-mail address is made up of three parts:

1. the name by which the sender wishes to be known, e.g. patjohnson@ (at)
2. followed by the name chosen for the computer and a dot, e.g. magic.
3. followed by the type of organisation that the service provider's computer belongs to, e.g. com

The complete address then looks like this: patjohnson@magic.com

The Internet is explained in detail in Chapter 3, page 55.

E-mail is a wonderful invention but, as with so many other very useful innovations, it can be abused. Follow the guidelines below to ensure that the e-mails you send are businesslike and effective.

1. Give all the information needed by the addressee to achieve your objective: to, from, reference, subject; a date for reply is useful too.
2. Never comment on other people in an e-mail. There can never be total confidentiality and there are legal implications relating to libel.
3. Do not use words such as 'Urgent' unless the matter is genuinely urgent.
4. Do not send documents with a huge number of pages or e-mail attachments unless absolutely necessary – the system slows down when there is too much traffic.
5. Send to the people who need the information or who can answer your query; copy only to other people who need to know or would benefit by knowing.
6. If you cannot reply to an e-mail quickly, send a standard reply that says when you will reply.
7. Use normal initial capital and small letters – text in capital letters is difficult to read and is regarded as the equivalent of shouting.
8. If you are not advised automatically on your PC of receipt of mail, access your mailbox regularly (ideally at least hourly).

CHOOSING THE TYPE OF COMMUNICATION TO USE

With so many different ways of communicating in writing, how do you decide which method to use in each case?

The considerations are:

- urgency – determines the speed of delivery required
- distance to destination – relates to urgency
- content – the complexity of the information may require a certain type of document

- confidentiality – may preclude the use of certain types of transmission, e.g. fax
- the relationship between the writer and the addressee – what degree of formality/informality is appropriate
- cost – depending on the preceding points
- the need for discussion – the telephone would be better *but* send a fax or e-mail beforehand to brief the person on what topic(s) you wish to discuss so that they can prepare.

PROOFREADING

Proofreading is checking a document to ensure that there are no errors. It needs skills of concentration and sharp observation. The most common errors are:

- grammatical
- spelling
- redundancies
- lack of consistency.

GRAMMATICAL ERRORS

Common grammatical errors are explained in Appendix 1.

SPELLING ERRORS

Most computers have a 'spellcheck' facility. This is valuable for unusual words or words relating to particular fields such as medicine. The use of the spellcheck does not eliminate the need for proofreading. It does not differentiate between homophones such as 'were', 'where' and 'wear'. It does not recognise typing errors, so if 'hot' has been typed instead of 'got' it will not be highlighted as it is not a spelling error. If in any doubt as to whether a word is incorrectly spelt, check in a dictionary.

REDUNDANCIES/TAUTOLOGY

There are many examples of words used unnecessarily because they are a duplication of the meaning of the word they follow. Here are some examples with the redundant word highlighted.

- reverse **backwards** – 'reverse' means to go backwards
- meet **up with** – you cannot meet 'up', and 'meet' means to get together with
- return **back** – 'return' means to go back

- very **unique** – 'unique' means 'completely different from anything else' so cannot be 'very'; examples of similar words that should not have 'very' before them are relevant, definitely, perfect, perceptible.

LACK OF CONSISTENCY

There must be consistency of spelling, layout and tone.

- Spelling – when there is a choice of spelling, e.g. organise or organize, either one or the other must be used consistently throughout the document. Other examples of such words include other words ending in ise or ize, judgment or judgement, acknowledgment or acknowledgement, etc.
- Layout – there are many aspects of layout that need to be observed carefully, including:
  - line spacing
  - spaces after punctuation
  - emboldening
  - headings in upper-case characters (capital letters) and/or lower-case characters (small letters)
  - use of side headings
  - numbering of paragraphs and sub-paragraphs
  - use of small roman numerals and letters for itemising
  - open punctuation, i.e. no punctuation above or below the body of the letter
  - date in full.
- Tone – depending on who will read the document, the same degree of formality (or informality) must be retained throughout. If a report is started in the third person, the third person must be used consistently.

ACTIVITY 5.7 There are various types of error in the following memorandum. Rewrite the memo, correcting the errors and underlining the corrections.

> Walking throuhg the office, last night, I was apalled to see the large amount of spoint letter headings in the wastepaper baskets. In these times of inancial difficulty you, will I am sure realise the necesity for the greatest economy to be exercises in the use of all materials. With word procesing there are no excuse for spoilt work. It is simply a matter of proofreading carefully before printing. To say that you have used spell check is not a valid excuse because you know that spellcheck does not pick up all errors.
>
> I hope that I shall not have cause to write in this vien again.

READING OVER

If legal documents or documents containing a lot of figures are to be checked they should be 'read over'. This means one person reads from the original and a second person, preferably not the person who typed it, checks the typed document.

MANUSCRIPT CORRECTION SIGNS

When proofreading text that has been typed, each error should be marked with an appropriate manuscript correction sign. A list of the most commonly used signs, with examples of how they are used, is shown in Fig. 5.12.

Margin indication	Meaning	Amended text	Corrected text
Caps	capital letters	Examination Tips	EXAMINATION TIPS
uc	upper case (capital letters)	The wind in the willows	The Wind in the Willows
lc	lower case (small letters)	The Next Day	The next day
⌀	delete	Take the new books away	Take the books away
		I will send it ac/ross to you.	I will send it across to you.
ʌ	insert	The cast will be here shortly.	The cast will be here shortly.
		It is good acommodation.	It is good accommodation.
trs	transpose	on Friday I shall go	I shall go on Friday.
		You will redieve it next week.	You will receive it next week.
NP	new paragraph	... in a month. Meantime it ...	... in a month. Meantime it ...
run on	not a new paragraph	I visit Paris every month. While there I always see my aunt.	I visit Paris every month. While there I always see my aunt.
stet	let it stand	I hope to go there soon.	I hope to go there soon.
stet	let the underdotted stand	I expect to go there soon.	I expect to go there soon.
#	leave a space	The fax is#expected tomorrow.	The fax is expected tomorrow.
⌒	join	It will be done at the week end.	It will be done at the weekend.

Fig. 5.12 Manuscript correction signs.

READING

It takes two to communicate. The writer must make the effort to write concisely and precisely. It is equally important that the reader makes the effort to read with concentration in order to achieve understanding. In some cases this may mean reading a document more than once. Pick out the key points in order to identify the important facts.

ACTIVITY 5.8 Read the following letter and make a list of the key points.

The publishers of *Training Today* have identified a need for a regionally targeted series of training journals that would provide in-depth feature reports on subjects that are of common interest to training officers and instructors.

We are inviting companies that specialise in training to contribute regularly to the editorial content of the particular regional edition of *Training Today*.

In September we shall cover the subject of 'Training for Efficient Use of Information Technology'. Any company, based in each territory, is invited to submit comments, case studies or articles that are relevant to this subject.

Regional editions of *Training Today* are circulated on a controlled basis to named directors, owners, partners and senior executives of up to 6000 companies. During the next two years this number will increase to 10 000.

We hope that your company will be a regular contributor to *Training Today* and that you will also consider it as a promotion medium for your training services. We would welcome an opportunity to discuss both our needs and your needs.

PRACTICE QUESTIONS

1. What are the advantages of written communication over spoken communication?

2. What is:
    i. a desk note
    ii. an internal memorandum

      iii. a telegram
      iv. an e-mail
      v. a telex?

3. Explain the difference between an internal memorandum and a letter.

4. State four key points you would look for if you were asked to say whether a letter is good or bad.

5. What is meant by 'precise and concise'? Give an example of each.

6. Give one word in place of each of the following phrases:
    i. as of now
    ii. in connection with
    iii. with regard to
    iv. acknowledge receipt of
    v. furnish you with.

7. Write a letter ordering a book from The Mail Order Bookshop, 16 High Street, ANYTOWN. Use fictitious details.

8. List and explain the four main types of letter.

9. List six points that are normally included in a printed letterhead.

10. Write the complimentary close that goes with each of the following salutations:
    Dear Sir or Dear Madam
    Dear Mr Green or Dear Mrs Green
    Dear Frederick.

11. How do you indicate that there is an enclosure to a letter?

12. You have typed a letter for your manager who has said 'Sign it for me please'. How would you sign it?

13. Read the following letter and then rewrite it without the 'commercial jargon'.

    Dear Mr Bloggs

    I am in receipt of your letter of yesterday's date. The information contained therein is useful but I am in need of more detail than you have included.

    I should be most grateful if you would be kind enough to let me have the additional information I requested in my letter of the 15th ultimo.

If you think that a face-to-face discussion would be of benefit I shall have pleasure in arranging a convenient time and place for a meeting.

I would greatly appreciate hearing from you within a few days.

Thanking you in anticipation
Yours sincerely

[Signature]
JF Findlay

14. What is meant by:
   i. full block letter layout
   ii. house style
   iii. continuation sheet
   iv. block paragraph
   v. blind copy?

15. *a.* A video recorder that you bought recently is not working properly. Write a letter of complaint to the manager of the shop where you made the purchase.
   b. As manager of the shop, write a reply to the customer.

16. Write a letter to the firm responsible for cleaning your office windows, complaining about the poor and irregular service, and high charges.

17. Your manager has been invited to present the prizes on speech day at a local school. Write a letter of acceptance for his/her signature.

18. Design a letterhead for The Smart Fashion House, which does a lot of business overseas. The address is:
The Design Studio
41–51 New Street
SAN FERNANDO
Include telephone and fax numbers, telegraphic and e-mail addresses.

19. List all the details that may be included in a letter in addition to the main body of information.

20. Gerald Fletcher of 24 High Road, Bridgetown, Barbados, is to be offered an appointment as stores supervisor at The Caribbean Building Materials Co. Ltd PO Box 257, Bridgetown, starting on 1 July 2002. As personnel officer at The Caribbean Building Materials Co. Ltd, write a letter to Mr Fletcher and include the following details.
   i. Salary scale G1 – $14 000 pa with increments of $300 up to a maximum of $18 000.

ii. The offer must be accepted by 31 May 2002, otherwise it will be withdrawn.

iii. There will be a six-month probationary period during which either the company or Mr Fletcher may give two weeks' notice to terminate the appointment. The appointment will be confirmed on satisfactory completion of the probationary period.

21. What sections would you expect to find in a formal report?

22. List eight rules you should follow when you have to complete a form.

23. Design a simple form to be completed by staff who wish to order a few items of stationery.

24. Write a telegram to be sent to The Peacock Trading Company Limited asking why you have not received your order No. 4581 of [date two weeks ago]. The china you ordered is needed urgently. The company's telegraphic address is Peacock New York. Your telegraphic address is Island Traders Kingston.

25. What details should be given on a fax cover sheet?

26. What is an e-mail address? Explain how it is made up.

27. What has to be considered when you have to decide the best method of communicating with other people?

28. All documents should be proofread. What types of error do you look for when proofreading?

29. Lack of consistency is a common error found when proofreading. List eight examples of this kind of error.

30. What is meant by 'reading over'? When is it done?

31. In the paragraph below there are 10 errors. Type, write out or photocopy the paragraph as it is shown below. Mark each error and insert the appropriate manuscript sign in the margin with the correction.

> Faster motoring means longer breaking distances are needed. At 80 miles an hour on a dry road with tyres, car and driver in tip-tup condition, it takes 300 feet to stop completely. This is eqivelent to 23 car lengths. If the road is weh the tyres worn or the drivers' reactions are slow this distance can increase to more than 600 ft. It cannot be stressed to stronglythat adequate spacing between veickles on motorways is essential.

SHORT ANSWER QUESTIONS

Complete the following sentences.

1. If you write more than is necessary you are being ....

2. Three types of phrase should not be used in business documents. They are ...., ..., and ....

3. Honours, degrees and professional qualifications after a person's name must be shown in the correct order: orders of chivalry, e.g. OBE, precede ...., e.g. ....

4. When completing a form the first step is to ....

5. Many companies include on the cover sheet of a fax a .... that covers the company against confidential information being seen by someone other than the addressee.

Choose the most appropriate ending for each of the following sentences.

6. Sometimes an addressee's fax machine is engaged. After trying to transmit once the sender's machine:
   a. indicates number engaged and aborts the transmission
   b. automatically tries twice more with an interval between each attempt
   c. instructs the sender to redial
   d. prints out a report indicating that the fax cannot be sent.

7. Proofreading requires certain skills, including:
   a. quick reading
   b. a good knowledge of language
   c. concentration
   d. ability to use a dictionary.

8. 'Reading over' means:
   a. glancing at a document very quickly
   b. proofreading
   c. checking the content of a document
   d. one person reading from the original with another person checking the typed document.

9. A file note is:
   a. a record of key points of a conversation to be kept on file
   b. minutes of a meeting
   c. a record of a telephone conversation
   d. a handwritten note slipped on to a file.

10. The name of the person who signs a letter is often typed below the space for the signature. This is to:
   a. make the letter official
   b. enable the addressee to refer to the person's name when the signature is illegible
   c. show that the person works in the organisation
   d. indicate their position.

EXAMINATION QUESTIONS

1. If a letter or memo has an enclosure, ... is written at the end.
   (Pitman Office Procedures Level 1 1998 Pt 1A)

2. The address on a letter should match the address on the ....
   (Pitman Office Procedures Level 1 1999 Pt 1A)

3. Name THREE types of external written communication.
   a. ....
   b. ....
   c. ....

4. State THREE advantages of using electronic mail.
   a. ....
   b. ....
   c. ....
   (Pitman Office Procedures Level 1 1999 Pt 1B)

CHAPTER 6

DOCUMENT PRODUCTION AND REPRODUCTION

OBJECTIVES When you have studied this chapter you should have acquired the knowledge and understanding to be able to:

1. explain the methods of producing hard copy
2. explain the use of recording and transcribing equipment
3. select the correct size and weight of paper and envelopes for specific types of document
4. list and briefly explain the facilities of electronic typewriters and word processors
5. explain the use of software, and the facilities it provides on computers
6. explain the different types of printer, their advantages and disadvantages
7. explain and use the range of facilities available on copiers
8. explain the use of copy printers
9. explain the machines used in the professional presentation of documents.

DOCUMENTS

What are documents? They are correspondence (see Chapter 5), forms, commercial documents (see Chapter 10) and records of all kinds (see Chapter 12).

They contain information consisting of one or more of the following: text, statistics (numeric and graphics), drawings, sketches, photographs. The information can be presented on white, black or coloured paper or screen background, in black, white or coloured print.

Information printed on paper is referred to as **hard copy**. Information held on magnetic or optical media (see Chapter 3, page 51) is referred to as **digital information**.

Before a document can be produced it has to be **composed**. This can be done by drafting in handwriting, dictating to a shorthand writer or stenotypist, by audio, or by keying in directly on to a means of production (see below). This is the process needed to transfer thoughts from the mind of the writer to a medium that can be used by the reader.

Production of hard copy means printing the first, or original, document.

Reproduction means making more copies from the original document, either from the hard copy or from a magnetic/optical medium.

METHODS OF PRODUCING HARD COPY

These include:

- typewriting
- keying in on a word processor and printing
- keying in on a personal computer/computer terminal (see Chapter 3)
- printing from personal computer/computer terminal.

METHODS OF REPRODUCING DOCUMENTS

These include:

- copying
- copy/printing
- offset printing.

PRESENTATION OF DOCUMENTS

Depending on the type of document, its purpose and uses, and its reader(s), a document has to be presented appropriately. This may involve:

- collating and 'jogging'
- trimming, punching and fastening
- binding.

We shall consider the processes of production and reproduction in sequence, as follows:

1. Recording equipment
2. Supplies for typewriters and printers
3. Typewriters
4. Word processors
5. Word-processing software
6. Printers
7. Copiers
8. Copy printers
9. Offset-litho printers
10. Collators and joggers
11. Guillotines, punches and fastenings
12. Binding.

RECORDING EQUIPMENT

There are two types of recording equipment:
- stenotyping machines
- audio-dictation equipment.

STENOTYPING MACHINES

Some people prefer to dictate 'live' to a shorthand writer. This is time consuming and constrains both dictator and transcriber to working at times when the other is available. Another disadvantage is that few people can read anyone else's shorthand. The use of a **stenotyping machine**, most frequently seen in courts and at public enquiries, overcomes this problem.

Stenotyping is a system of note-taking using a machine that produces, on a paper roll, a phonetic record of words keyed in by the stenotypist. The operator presses a combination of keys, using both hands, to represent each sound in the same way that a shorthand writer records a letter or a sign for each sound. The great advantage of the stenotype record is that anyone can be taught to read and transcribe it in a very short time.

AUDIO-DICTATION EQUIPMENT

This consists of:
- desktop recording machine with handset for dictation *or* hand-held dictation machine
- transcription machine with headset and foot control for transcriber.

Recording machines

The desktop recording machine has control buttons for recording, rewinding, listening and forward winding. The dictater speaks into a handset, which also has a set of control buttons. The hand-held machine does not have a separate handset but has the same facilities as the desktop machine. It has the advantage of being compact and easily portable. Dictation of up to an hour (30 minutes on most machines) is recorded on a cassette.

Examples of audio equipment are shown in Fig. 6.1.

In large organisations there may be a **remote dictation system**. The dictator accesses the system by dialling a code on a telephone extension. The dictation is recorded on machines located in the office where the transcription is done, usually in a secretariat (or pool).

Modern machines have a magnetic facility, which enables the dictator to indicate the end of each document by pressing a button. Another button allows the dictator to give 'special instructions' out of sequence. For example, the dictator might wish the transcriber to produce a particular letter first or change something dictated in a previous letter.

Transcription machines

Some desktop machines are dual-purpose, i.e. they can be used for both recording and transcribing. The disadvantage is that only dictation *or* transcription can be done at any one time.

The transcriber uses a headset so that the dictation remains private, and a foot control to start and stop the dictation as necessary. Before starting to type or key in, the transcriber should first check the tape for any special instructions. It is also important before starting each document to identify what it is, e.g. letter/memo/minutes, the approximate length and any instructions, e.g. double line spacing, extra wide margins.

Advantages of audio-dictation are:

- the writer can dictate whenever and wherever it is convenient
- the transcriber can plan transcription into their work schedule
- the dictator can send cassettes by post for transcription when away from the office.

Disadvantages of audio-dictation are:

- it takes time for the transcriber to raise queries with the dictator

(a)

(b)

Fig. 6.1 (a) Audio dictation machine with handset; (b) audio transcription machine with headset and foot control.

- if there is background noise on the tape it may be difficult to hear the dictation
- if the dictation is poor it will take time to correct grammar, etc.

SUPPLIES FOR TYPEWRITERS AND PRINTERS

Supplies are also called 'consumables', the most commonly used being paper. When producing a document, the size of the paper (see Table 6.1) and its grammage (see page 156) are important.

PAPER SIZES

Most countries now use paper made to sizes based on International Standards Organisation (ISO) standards, known as International Paper Sizes (IPS).

The IPS system is based on three series of sizes. These are:

- Series A, most widely used for letters, reports, forms, etc.
- Series B, used for larger items such as posters and wallcharts
- Series C, used for envelopes.

Look at the table of sizes (Table 6.1); you can see that the largest Series A size is A0, which is approximately 1 square metre. A0 is divided in half to get A1, which is divided in half to get A2, and so on. The Series B sizes are divided in the same way. The width of the paper is always given first. You will see that the long side of a size becomes the width of the next smaller size.

When the paper is used with the short side at the top it is in **portrait** format. When the long side is at the top it is in **landscape** format. Any size of paper can be used either way depending on how the text needs to be presented. The maximum width of paper a printer can take must also be taken into account.

The standard size for letters is A4. A3 is generally used for statistical tables. In Fig. 6.2 you can see how it is divided for various types of document:

- A5 – short letters, memoranda, commercial documents
- A6 – compliment slips, invitation cards
- A7 – message slips, desk notes
- A8 – business cards.

The two additional sizes, ⅓ A4 and ⅔ A4, are used:

- ⅓ A4 – compliment slips, paying-in slips and other forms
- ⅔ A4 – short letters, commercial documents.

Table 6.1 *Paper sizes*

Designation	Size in inches	Size in millimetres
Series A		
A0	33.1 × 46.8	841 × 1189
A1	23.3 × 33.1	594 × 841
A2	16.5 × 23.3	420 × 594
A3	11.7 × 16.5	297 × 420
A4	8.3 × 11.7	210 × 297
⅓ A4	8.3 × 3.9	210 × 99
⅔ A4	8.3 × 7.8	210 × 198
A5	5.8 × 8.3	148 × 210
A6	4.1 × 5.8	105 × 148
A7	2.9 × 4.1	74 × 105
A8	2.1 × 2.9	52 × 74
A9	1.5 × 2.1	37 × 52
A10	1.0 × 1.5	26 × 37
Series B		
B0	39.3 × 55.7	1000 × 1414
B1	27.8 × 39.3	707 × 1000
B2	19.7 × 27.8	500 × 707
B3	13.9 × 19.7	353 × 500
B4	9.8 × 13.9	250 × 353
B5	6.9 × 9.8	176 × 250
B6	4.9 × 6.9	125 × 176
B7	3.5 × 4.9	88 × 125
B8	2.4 × 3.5	62 × 88
B9	1.7 × 2.4	44 × 62
B10	1.2 × 1.7	31 × 44

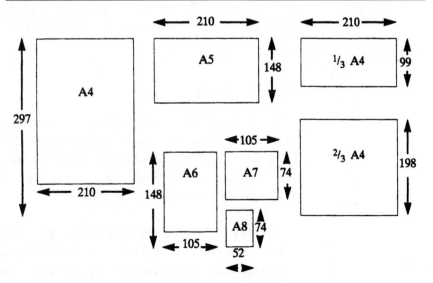

Fig. 6.2 A4 paper divisions.

In addition there is **American quarto**, called 'letter size', which is slightly longer than A4. This is commonly used in the Caribbean, in American organisations outside the USA and international agencies such as the World Health Organization (WHO).

CONTINUOUS STATIONERY

Continuous stationery is used for computer printout. A very long length is composed of large sheets of paper, joined with perforations, which are folded concertina-style. There is a strip of holes on either side of the paper, a hole for each line space. The tractor (or traction feed) moves as each line is printed and the next hole is caught by the ratchet.

A stack of printout paper is loaded on a large printer (generally in the computer room) and feeds through automatically as lines are printed. As each sheet is printed it drops behind the printer and is folded concertina-style again, ready for the sheets to be separated by 'bursting', i.e. tearing the perforations so that the stack is separated into single sheets.

Continuous stationery is shown in Fig. 6.3a used for printing a list; Fig. 6.3b shows it used for printing labels.

Continuous stationery has been adopted internationally on a non-metric basis. It is based on six lines to the inch down the page and ten characters per inch across. The line and letter spaces for typewriters and printers that use single sheets of paper are explained on page 161.

PAPER GRAMMAGE

This refers to the weight of paper. It is measured per square metre and ranges from 45 gsm (grams per square metre) to 120 gsm for special-quality paper used for prestige letterheads. Heavier grammages become thin card and then card of varying thicknesses. Commonly used grammages are 45, 70, 80, 90 and 100 gsm (see Table 6.2).

Carbon paper is used with lightweight paper to make copies of a document at one printing. Carbon copies can be made only on typewriters and 'impact' printers (see page 166), so are now rarely made.

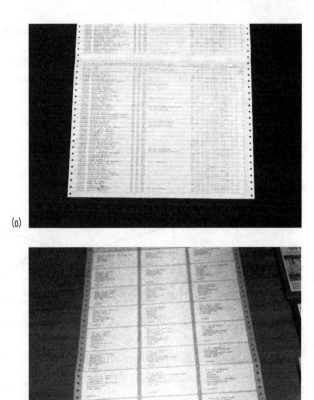

Fig. 6.3 (a) Continuous stationery printout of a list; (b) continuous stationery printout of labels.

Table 6.2 *Paper grammage*

Types of paper	Grammage
Airmail and carbon copies	45 gsm
Copy paper for copiers and fax machines	70 and 80 gsm
Commercial documents, e.g. advice notes	70 gsm
General business documents, e.g. reports	80 gsm 'bond'
Letterheads	90 and 100 gsm

ENVELOPES

Envelopes are manufactured in a variety of styles, shapes and sizes. There is also a wide range of quality (weight), cutting and sealing.

There are two main styles (illustrated in Fig. 6.4):

- banker – the opening is on the longer side
- pocket – the opening is on the shorter side.

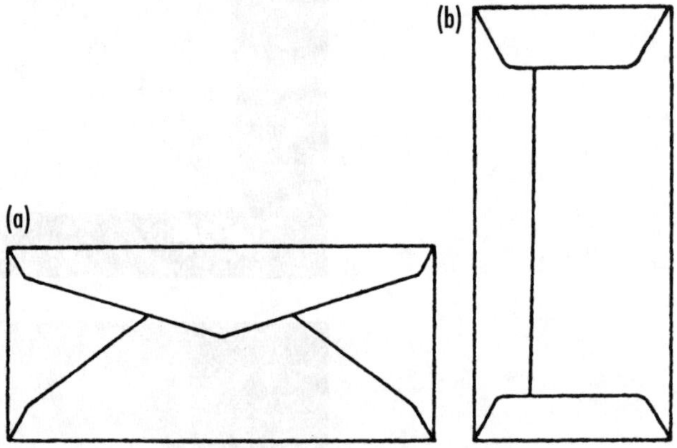

Fig. 6.4 (a) Banker envelope; (b) pocket envelope.

Envelope sizes are shown in Table 6.3. The second measurement of each envelope indicates the open side.

Table 6.3 *Envelope sizes*

Designation	Size in inches	Size in millimetres
C3	12¾ × 18	324 × 458
B4	9⅞ × 13⅞	250 × 353
C4	9 × 13⅝	229 × 324
B5	7 × 9⅞	176 × 250
C5	6⅜ × 9	162 × 229
B6/C4	4⅞ × 12	125 × 324
B6	4⅞ × 7	125 × 176
C5	4½ × 6⅜	114 × 162
C5/6 or DL	4¼ × 8⅝	111 × 120
C7/6	3¼ × 6⅜	81 × 162
C7	3¼ × 4½	81 × 114

The most commonly used sizes are C4, C5 and DL (C5/6). The folding of paper to fit different sizes of envelopes is shown in Chapter 8, Fig. 8.8.

The **quality** of envelope used is generally chosen to match the paper. A letter will be in an envelope of the same weight and colour as the letterhead. Manilla (buff-coloured) or thinner white envelopes (70 or 80 gsm) are used for commercial documents such as invoices.

Many organisations have their name and/or logo printed on the top left-hand corner of the envelope, or they may have their name and address printed on the flap.

Envelopes may be gummed or self-sealing. The latter cost a little more but are much quicker to seal.

Window envelopes are commonly used for commercial documents and also for letters. An oblong 'window' is cut out of the front of the envelope and is covered by a transparent sheet gummed inside. The document is folded so that the inside address is in the right position to show through the transparent 'window'. A window envelope is shown in Fig. 6.5.

Fig. 6.5 Window envelope.

Airmail envelopes may be printed with a blue and red border on both sides and/or the 'airmail' flash in the top left-hand corner. They are commonly produced in DL and C6 sizes.

RIBBONS

Ribbons for electronic typewriters and printers are supplied in cartridges, which are fitted into the machine very easily. The ribbon may be made of nylon or carbon. The latter gives sharper outlines and so is preferred.

CARTRIDGES

Non-impact printers (see page 166) are fitted with ink cartridges. The ink is in powder form. The cartridges must be kept in their boxes until needed and, when opened, they must be handled with care.

CORRECTION PAPERS AND FLUID

These are for use with typewriters and are used to correct mistakes without using an eraser. One side of the correction paper is coated with a white substance. The strip of correction paper is placed between the ribbon and the paper, over the error, with the coated side against the paper. The error is then typed again: this covers the mistake with the white substance, thus blanking it out. The paper is removed and the correct letter/word is then typed. This correction paper is also supplied in a cassette for certain makes of typewriter.

Alternatively, a white liquid can be painted over the error. When dry, it should be invisible if just one stroke of the brush has been applied. The correct letters/word can then be typed over the correction. Other shades of liquid are produced for use with coloured paper.

COPYHOLDERS

A copyholder helps the typist to read accurately line by line, especially when complicated schedules are being copied. Copyholders range from simple devices for keeping a shorthand notebook upright and making it easier to see, to the more complicated machines with a cursor or line guide, which moves automatically down the page, guiding the typist's eye to the line of text to be typed. These appliances are sometimes operated by foot control. A copyholder is illustrated in Fig. 6.6.

Fig. 6.6 Copyholder with line guide.

> **ACTIVITY 6.1** Gather together sheets of paper and envelopes of different sizes. Measure them, referring to Tables 6.1 and 6.3. Check the designation of each sheet of paper and each envelope so that you become familiar with the common sizes of paper and envelope. This will be useful when you have to look in catalogues for stationery supplies.

TYPEWRITERS

There are various kinds of typewriter, including manual, electric and electronic, both desk and portable models. Manual and electric typewriters are no longer manufactured but there are some still in use in people's homes and very small offices.

Electronic typewriters have a variety of facilities, which differ slightly depending on the manufacturer. Facilities may include:

- auto demonstration – when a code is typed in, the machine shows the typeface, pitch, margins, etc. that are set on the machine
- paper width up to 381 mm – A4 landscape (see Table 6.1)
- print speed up to 16 characters per second (a character is one letter or figure)
- pitch (type size) – 10, 12 and 15 characters to the inch
- proportional spacing – allowing the exact amount of space required for each letter/figure instead of a standard width for all letters/figures
- line spacing – 1, 1½ and 2 between the lines of type
- tabulation stops for specific parts of a document such as the date on a letter or for typing columns of words and/or figures
- automatic carriage return – when the end of the carriage is reached, any letters starting a new word that will not fit on the line are carried over to the next line
- interchangeable daisywheels, enabling different type styles, known as fonts (or founts), to be used
- automatic centring, enabling words, phrases, lines or paragraphs to be centred either on the page or between the margins
- right flush – see 'justification'
- bold type – heavier type achieved by a double impression for the words or phrases to be highlighted

- automatic underline – underlines each letter as it is typed
- line indent – starting the line a set number of spaces in from the left margin, used for either indented or hanging paragraphs (see page 163)
- paragraph indent – automatic indent when starting a new paragraph
- justification – even right-hand margin achieved by leaving extra spaces between words when a standard pitch is used or by proportional spacing (see page 161)
- memory holding up to two lines in which errors can be corrected
- word/character delete – delete key to erase a letter/figure or a word
- super-/sub-script – letters/figures above or below the line of type, e.g. for fractions or footnotes (a note at the bottom of the page explaining some word or phrase used in the text)
- end of page warning – indication that the last line on the page has been reached
- memory for storing documents so that they can be used again – for example, standard letters to customers; the number of pages that can be stored and the duration of storage varies depending on the machine
- user dictionary up to 80 000 words – for holding the typist's own words relating to specialist fields, such as medicine
- spelling verifier (or spellcheck) up to 90 000 words – enables the typist to check the spelling of the text; errors are highlighted but see Chapter 5, page 140 for the dangers of not proofreading
- small display screen, up to two lines.

An electronic typewriter is illustrated in Fig. 6.7.

Fig. 6.7 Electronic typewriter.

The format required for each particular document has to be set up. The format consists of:

- text margins – top, bottom, left-hand and right-hand, see Fig. 6.8
- line spacing – the number of spaces (1, 1½ or 2) between each line of type
- page length – the number of lines of type between the top and bottom margins
- pitch (type size)
- font (type style)
- tabulation stops
- indents.

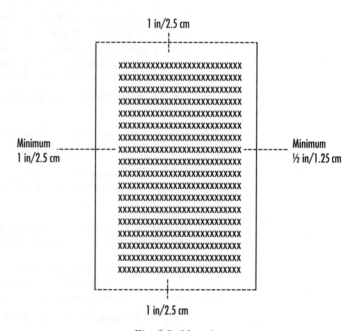

Fig. 6.8 Margins.

The usual **margins** for most documents are 1 in (2.5 cm) at the top and bottom of the page, at least 1 in (2.5 cm) for the left-hand margin to allow for the paper to be punched for filing, and at least ½ in (1.25 cm) for the right-hand margin.

Standard pitch is 10, 12 and 15 letters/figures to the inch. These three sizes are illustrated in three different font styles in Fig. 6.9.

Paragraphs may be block or hanging. Examples are shown in Fig. 6.10.

Headings are main (blocked on the left or centered), subside or shoulder. Examples of each of these types of heading are shown in Fig. 6.11.

```
Elite
The quick brown fox jumped over the lazy dog.

Courier 10
The quick brown fox jumped over the lazy dog.
```
Gothic
The quick brown fox jumped over the lazy dog.

Fig. 6.9 Standard type pitches in specimen font styles.

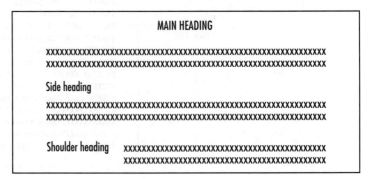

Fig. 6.10 Block and hanging paragraphs.

Fig. 6.11 Main, subside and shoulder headings.

WORD PROCESSORS

The step between an electronic typewriter and a personal computer is the word processor. It looks very similar to a typewriter but has a screen (visual display unit), which may be very small, showing just two lines of type, or as big as a computer screen, showing about thirty lines of type.

The main difference between a typewriter and a word processor is that the typewriter's memory has very limited capacity, usually only a few pages. When typing on a word processor, the documents are stored on a diskette so they are normally safe for as long as they are needed.

Word processors have all the facilities of an electronic typewriter plus at least some of those listed below:

- faster print speed
- built-in fonts – up to five
- built-in print sizes – up to 45 type sizes from 4 point to 792 point (see page 167)
- shading – shaded areas can be printed, usually with words over-printed
- working memory up to 100 Kb (100,000 bytes) (see Chapter 3, page 48), enabling a document to be typed and checked before being saved on diskette and printed
- storage memory on 3½ in diskette up to 1.4 Mb (see page 48)
- multilingual characters for various languages
- scientific and graphic symbols for mathematics and science formulae
- non-impact printing (see 'Printers', page 166)
- delete and insert, removing or adding text (from a single letter/figure to a whole paragraph); this can be done while a document is being typed or with documents saved on diskette; by recalling a document from the diskette to screen, alterations can be made and the revised document can either replace, or be filed in addition to, the original version
- save (or store) text on diskette after it has been keyed in; the document must be given a reference so that it can be retrieved when required; saved documents are listed in an index or directory, which can be recalled in order to identify the particular document to be recalled
- label print mail merge, enabling a list of names and addresses to be 'merged' with labels so that a number of labels can be printed without keying in the name and address between each one.

A word processor is illustrated in Fig. 6.12.

Fig. 6.12 Word processor.

COMPUTER WORD-PROCESSING SOFTWARE

In Chapter 3 we discussed the types of software used on computers. Word-processing software provides instructions for the computer when the operator is keying in text such as letters and reports.

All the facilities available on electronic typewriters and word processors are contained in word-processing software. Generally, the speed of operation is faster and the working memory capacity greater. Most PCs have hard disks, often as well as diskettes, providing a great deal more storage capacity.

Additional facilities of word-processing software are explained below.

- **Moving text** – allowing text to be moved within a page or from one page to another within a document. For example, this facility would be used when a report is edited and the writer wishes text to be reorganised.
- **Search and replace** – when a particular word or phrase needs to be replaced with a different word or phrase throughout the document, a command can be given to find the word/phrase and replace it with the new word every time it occurs.
- **Keystroke memory** – storing of words or phrases to be repeated frequently within a document.
- **Pagination** – automatic numbering of pages.
- **Reformatting** – changing the format of a document by changing one or more of the settings, for example, margins, pitch, line spacing, offset/header (depth of top margin), footer (depth of bottom margin), page length, page width (left/right margins), e.g. from portrait to landscape (see page 163).
- **Merging** – used to produce personalised letters and other documents with variable items of information, e.g. date, name and address, amounts of money.

PRINTERS

The two main types of printer are 'impact', by which the paper is imprinted directly through a ribbon with a character on a daisywheel, and 'non-impact' by which the print is created on the paper by a special ink. Non-impact printers are dot matrix, ink-jet and laser.

DAISYWHEEL PRINTERS

These are used with word processors and are relatively slow, taking approximately 30 seconds to print an A4 page. The daisywheel has to be changed if a different pitch or style is required.

DOT-MATRIX PRINTERS

These are produced in varying qualities, including letter quality (LQ). Each letter/figure/sign is made up of very small dots. The dots are packed closely together to create a clear impression.

INK-JET PRINTERS

These print by spraying ink on to the paper to create the character required.

LASER PRINTERS

These produce very high-quality print in a wide variety of styles. Individual pages can be coded to print in different styles within a page.

Daisywheel and dot matrix printers are fairly noisy when in operation, whereas ink-jet and laser printers are virtually silent.

GRAPHICS PRINTERS

These are used for producing documents containing diagrams such as line graphs, pie charts, bar graphs (see Chapter 12). By using various thicknesses of felt-tip pens to 'print', many different shapes can be filled with colour as, for example, on a pie chart. A common application of the graphics printer is the production of transparencies for overhead projectors (see Chapter 13, page 420).

PRINT SIZES

There is a tremendous range of sizes in which text and figures can be printed.

The average size of print used is 12 point. Larger sizes may be used for headings or for notices to be placed on noticeboards. Varying larger sizes are used for visually impaired (VI) people. Many banks produce bank statements in large print for their VI customers.

> **ACTIVITY 6.2** Consider the following facilities that are found on electronic typewriters, word processors, word-processing software and printers. Decide how you might use each facility. An example is given.
>
> Example: automatic centring
>
> Uses:
> - headings for any type of document, e.g. minutes, reports
> - menus with each line centred
> - advertisements
>
> Now think about the rest.
> - right-hand margin justification
> - interchangeable daisywheels
> - bold type
> - multilingual characters
> - standard letters
> - shading
> - very large print
> - pagination
> - shoulder headings
> - right flush

COPIERS

Copiers, copy printers (see page 172) and offset-litho machines (see page 173) are machines used for the process of **reprography**. Some organisations have a reprographics department where all large amounts of copying and printing are done. It is usual now for copiers to be found in most departments or on each floor of a building.

Copiers are sometimes called by their original name of 'photocopiers', but modern machines do not work on a photographic principle. Copies are now produced on plain paper instead of on the sensitised paper used with photographic machines.

Modern copiers encompass most, if not all, of the facilities listed below.

- Single or multi-feed, which means that a single page can be inserted for immediate copying, or a stack of pages can be placed on the feedtray to be copied in sequence from the bottom of the pile upwards.
- Copies can be made on different weights of paper and card, from 65 gsm to 130 gsm (see Table 6.2).
- Paper trays take different sizes of paper, usually A4 portrait and A4 landscape (see page 155), A3 and 'universal' for almost any size.

There may be two A4 trays (as these are used most often) to save constant refilling. Larger machines take a stack of 5 reams of paper.
- Up to 999 copies can be made at one run, though small paper trays will need to be refilled during the run.
- The density, or 'darkness', of the print can be adjusted so that it is not too faint or too dark.
- Copies smaller or larger than the original can be produced. Copies can also be enlarged or reduced vertically or horizontally.
- Copies can be made from books, with a facility for making a copy of first one page and then the facing page of a book opened flat.
- The coloured background of an original printed on coloured paper can be faded so that there is no shading on the copy and the print is clear.
- Most coloured printing can be copied in black but print in some colours (such as red) may not reproduce clearly.
- Originals printed on both sides of the paper can be copied on both sides of the copy paper without turning over the master. This is known as reverse, back-to-back, or 'recto verso' printing.
- Originals that include photographs can be lightened so that the photographs do not come out too 'solidly' black.
- A run can be interrupted so that another original can be copied.
- Overhead projector transparencies can be made by using an acetate sheet instead of paper for the copy. The transparencies can be interleaved with sheets of paper.
- Collating bins can be attached to the machine. Most bins stack 10 or 20 sets of copies. More than one bin can be attached to the machine.
- Collated copies can be stapled as the copying of each document is completed.
- Front and back covers can be inserted in front of and behind each document before stapling, or in readiness for binding (see page 181).

A standard black and white copier with collating bins is illustrated in Fig. 6.13.

A wide range of copiers is available and it is important to choose a model that is appropriate for the organisation's needs. In addition to the facilities listed above, other factors that have to be considered when buying or leasing a new copier include:

- the volume of copying to be done regularly, in order to determine the speed of operation needed
- whether colour copying is needed regularly
- whether colour copies of 35 mm film slides are required on either paper and/or acetate sheets

Fig. 6.13 Canon NP 6050 high-volume black and white copier with collating bins.

- whether a key-code system is needed whereby each user keys in their allocated code before the machine will operate; the copy cost for each code is recorded so that the appropriate department can be charged.

Modern colour copiers reproduce either by laser or by bubble-jet printing. The depth and tone of the colours is 'measured' electronically and reproduced exactly. The operator can make adjustments to enhance particular colours. Some machines can enlarge a standard A4 sheet to A1 in full colour on matt- or gloss-finish paper.

It is possible to make colour copies of 35 mm film slides either on to paper or on to transparencies. A film slide projector is attached to the copier and the projected image is copied (see Fig. 6.14).

The speed of colour copying depends on the size of copy to be produced. An A4 copy may be produced in about 1 minute; an A1 copy might take up to 6 minutes.

A copier should be used efficiently in order that the process is carried out cost-effectively. When using a copier, follow the simple rules listed below.

1. If you are unfamiliar with the machine, read the manual before using it.
2. Check the register to ensure that the previous user has not left it set for more than the number of copies you need.

Fig. 6.14 The Canon CLC 800 colour copier, which produces copies of 35 mm film transparencies; the projector at the right-hand end of the copier projects the image of the film slide in the carousel at the left-hand end of the machine; the film reproduced on the visual display unit is then copied in colour on paper.

3. Check the paper size indicator to ensure that it will copy on to the size of paper you want.
4. Check the paper tray to ensure that there is an adequate supply of paper for a run. Check it after you have made a lot of copies to ensure that you do not leave it empty for the next user.
5. Run off one copy to check that:
    a. the print density is correct
    b. the print is not faded in places
    c. there are no ink 'streaks'
    d. the copy is 'straight' on the paper.
6. Make the exact number of copies required. Extra copies are a waste of money (cost of paper, copy cost and cost of time). If 100 staff members each make five extra copies a day, that adds up to a ream of paper and 500 copy charges, an annual wastage of 260 reams of paper and 130 000 copy charges!
7. If the register indicates that a new ink cartridge or a new copy cartridge is needed, read the instructions in the manual carefully before attempting to change it. Both types of cartridge need to be handled with great care. The copy cartridge will be irreparably damaged if it is in the light for more than a minute or so.

8. If the machine ceases to function the register will show a code. Look up the code in the manual to identify the fault. Then follow the instructions precisely.
9. If you cannot rectify the problem, write an 'OUT OF ACTION' notice and place it on the machine, securing it with tape. Report the fault to the person responsible for the machine. If you go to a machine and find an 'OUT OF ACTION' notice on it, do not attempt to use it. You could make the fault a lot worse.
10. Never leave originals on the machine; they may not be confidential but it may not be desirable that other people see them.
11. Destroy spoilt copies by tearing them into small pieces or, if they are confidential, taking them to your own office for shredding.

COMPUTERISED IMAGE COPIER/PRINTER

This sophisticated digital machine is linked into a network so that PC users can prepare their copy on disk and transmit the finished document to the copier. The document may consist of text, spreadsheets and/or graphics produced by merging different types of software. For example, text produced in Word (a word-processing application) may be merged with a spreadsheet produced in Excel. Documents can also be merged with material sent to a mailbox (see Chapter 3, page 57).

A proof copy can be run for checking and, if necessary, amending before the print run is done. Each document, of any number of pages, is produced individually. As it is completed it can be punched for insertion into a ring binder, e.g. a technical manual, or stapled centrally and folded into a booklet.

This system can also be used with an external printer. The document is transmitted to the printer's computer system where it is reproduced on disk. The disk drive linked to the computer then enables the document to be reproduced as many times as needed.

COPY PRINTERS

You may occasionally find an ink duplicating machine in an office. Originally this was the only machine on which to produce a large number of copies. In this method, a wax stencil is 'cut' on a typewriter; the ribbon is removed so that the typeface impacts directly on to the wax sheet, indenting the shape of the character into it. The stencil is then placed on the machine round a drum. Ink, inside the drum, is squeezed through the impression to reproduce the characters on the paper.

A copy printer reproduces copies very cheaply by a combination of the basic method of duplication with fax and programming technology. Although the quality of reproduction is not quite as good as copies produced on a copier, it is very good and the machine is easy to operate.

The stencils are located inside the machine, a roll of 255 on a drum. The document to be reproduced is placed on a glass platen and is then scanned by a fax head, which 'cuts' the stencil. When completed, the stencil moves into position on the ink drum and the number of copies required (up to 9999 in one run) is run off. On completion of the run the stencil is automatically removed from the drum and dropped in a bin. Up to 20 masters can be placed in the feed mechanism, so that multi-page documents can be reproduced without constant attention to the machine.

Some of the useful facilities available on the copy printer include:

- reduction and enlargement
- blanking out of different parts of the document on separate runs in order to produce multi-coloured copies
- separation of stacks of different documents with a coloured sheet between each stack
- printing of photographs.

It is possible to link a specially designed copy printer to a PC. The text is keyed in and recorded on disk. The disk is then transferred to the copy printer for cutting the stencil from digital data. The process of reproduction then continues as on the less sophisticated machines.

Because copy printers are cheap to operate they are used a great deal in schools, colleges and in organisations such as churches. Administrative documentation, lesson material, notices, etc. can all be produced at minimum cost.

OFFSET LITHOGRAPHY AND OFFSET-LITHO MACHINES

Offset lithography, or offset-litho as it is more commonly called, is a high-quality method of reproducing many copies from one master.

'Lithography' is based on the principle that water does not adhere to a greasy surface, while ink does. The 'image' (typing, writing, drawing or photograph) is made in a greasy medium on a 'plate' affixed to a drum.

The remainder of the surface of the plate is covered with a film of water. The printing ink from the inking roller will adhere only to the image.

Plates are made of paper, parchment, plastic or metal. Metal plates are made by photographing a master copy of the text, drawing or photograph to be printed. The master photograph is then imprinted on to an aluminium plate from which up to 25 000 copies can be made, or a copper plate, from which an unlimited number of copies can be made. The other types of plate can be prepared directly by hand, by typewriter or on a printer linked to a computer, or by a special machine called a platemaker. These cheaper plates can be used to make between 1000 and 10 000 copies, depending on the quality.

When the prepared plate has been fixed to the cylinder of the machine, it is first wetted with a solution, generally known as the 'fountain solution'. Then the inking rollers are brought into contact with the cylinder, inking the image but not the wetted background. The inked image is then brought into contact with a second roller on the machine, around which is wrapped a soft rubber sheet, known as a 'blanket'. In this way the image from the inked plate is 'set off', i.e. it appears in reverse, on the blanket roller.

Fig. 6.15 Automatic offset-litho printing machine.

When the blanket roller is brought into contact with the paper, the reverse image is transferred the right way round. This process is known as 'offset', hence the term offset lithography.

Modern offset machines are automatic so do not require a trained operator. Offset printing is a cheaper process than reproducing on a copier, so it is used for large-quantity reproduction such as books and letterheads. However, in commercial organisations most printing is done by copier because the choice of facilities enables the most suitable machine to be obtained for the type of work to be done.

An automatic offset-litho printer is illustrated in Fig. 6.15.

COLLATORS AND JOGGERS

MANUAL OPERATION

Many documents consist of several pages. If the copier does not have collating bins it will be necessary to collate the pages by hand. The most efficient way to do this is to set the stacks of pages as shown in Fig. 6.16.

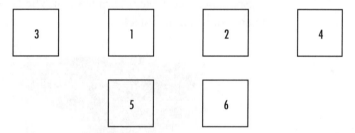

Fig. 6.16 Arrangement of piles of pages for manual collating.

The stacks are arranged by page number in a way that makes it easy to lift a page from two stacks at a time in sequence from the last page. Before the pages can be fastened (see page 177) they must be aligned so that the edges are even. The loose pages of the document are held at each side and the pack is 'knocked' on the work surface until all the pages are in alignment at the top and sides. This is known by printers as 'knocking up'.

MANUAL MACHINES

To speed up the process, a collating frame can be used. The frame consists of a number of trays (corresponding to the piles of paper) into which the piles of each numbered sheet are placed. A foot lever lifts the top sheet of each pile and allows the operator to use both hands for gathering the papers in their right order. Each document has to be 'knocked up' as explained above.

AUTOMATIC MACHINES

Modern collating machines run for several hours, automatically delivering five or six sheets of paper in their correct order at a speed of several sets per minute. **Joggers** are used in connection with collators to shake the pages into alignment.

GUILLOTINES

Sometimes it is necessary to trim paper, or to cut sheets to a smaller size. A guillotine, also called a paper cutter, consists of a metal surface on which is printed a guide for various sizes of paper, a weight with rollers to hold the paper firmly in position, a knife blade with handle, and a perspex screen to ensure that the user's fingers or hand cannot be placed under the knife blade, see Fig. 6.17. Depending on the machine, from 5 to 400 sheets of 70 gsm paper (see Table 6.2) can be cut. The heavier the paper, the fewer sheets can be cut in a stack.

Fig. 6.17 Guillotine (or paper cutter) with safety guard.

PUNCHES

Papers have to be punched for insertion into files, ring binders, presentation folders, etc. There are various kinds of punch, including:

- miniature – useful for carrying in a briefcase
- standard desk, some with a guide to ensure that the holes are central down the side of the page
- heavy duty – for punching thick documents.

If a punch does not have a guide it is necessary to put a slight fold at the left-hand side edge of the paper to indicate the halfway mark. The sheet is then inserted into the punch with the fold level with the centre mark on the punch.

When very large piles of paper have to be punched, a **drill** is used. This is an electrically operated machine that bores down into the paper, the distance between the holes being pre-set.

FASTENINGS

There are many methods of fastening papers together, including:

- paper clips
- fasteners
- treasury tags
- staples.

PAPER CLIPS

Paper clips are obtainable in metal and plastic, in a wide range of shapes, sizes and designs. Sizes range from just under 1 in (20 cm) to 3 in (76 mm) with square or round ends. Bulldog clips are used for holding together large packs of paper. A selection of paper and bulldog clips is shown in Fig. 6.18.

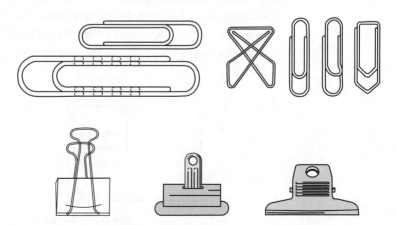

Fig. 6.18 Paper and bulldog clips.

FASTENERS

Fasteners are produced in various types. There are plastic fastener strips that hold up to 10 sheets of paper, steel paper fasteners, some with washers, and metal clips for use with punched paper. Examples of these types of fastener are shown in Fig. 6.19.

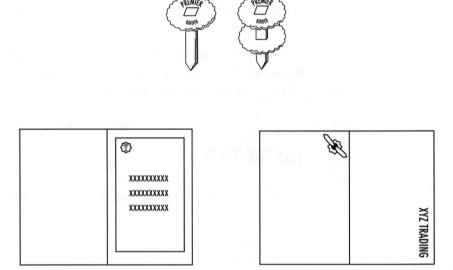

Fig. 6.19 Paper fasteners.

TREASURY TAGS

Treasury tags are used mostly in government offices. The tag consists of a piece of coloured cord, from 1 to 6 in long, with metal or plastic end tags. The tag is passed through the hole in the left-hand top corner of the document and the hole in the manilla folder (see Fig. 6.20), or through two central holes in the paper and folder. It is difficult to remove or insert documents from a file of papers secured in this way.

Fig. 6.20 Treasury tag.

STAPLERS

Staplers are commonly used for fastening the pages of documents from 2 pages up to 100 pages or more. If the document is for internal use, stapling is perfectly adequate. If it is for external use it may be punched and placed in a plastic or ring binder, or be bound (see page 181).

There is a variety of stapling machines, including:

- miniature (or pocket), useful for people who travel
- standard desk – permanent fastening, the prongs close inwards (see Fig. 6.21a)

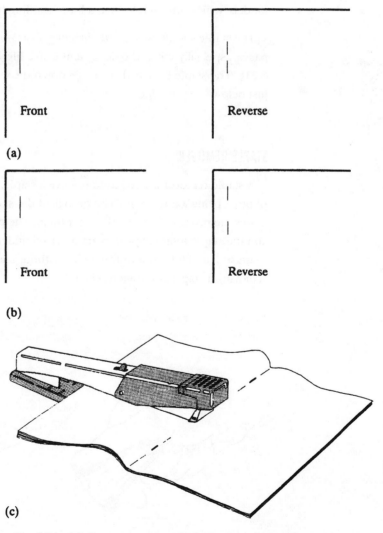

Fig. 6.21 (a) Permanent staple fastening; (b) temporary staple fastening; (c) long-arm stapler.

- standard desk – permanent and temporary fastening; the open prongs of a temporary fastening enable the staple to be removed easily (see Fig. 6.21b)
- long arm, also called 'long reach' – has a long base, which allows papers to be inserted for stapling several inches in from the edge, e.g. in the centre of a landscape A4 sheet to form a booklet (see Fig. 6.21c)
- heavy duty – takes staples of various sizes to allow for larger packs of paper up to 175 sheets; available in both standard and long-arm styles.

All types of stapling machine are available in electric and electronic models, which are useful when a lot of stapling has to be done.

The staple should be placed correctly so as not to impede turning the pages, especially when the document is in a file. Look at Figs 6.21a and 6.21b. The staple is placed vertically down the left-hand side of the page just below the top edge.

STAPLE REMOVER

A staple remover is needed to remove a staple, for example when photocopying a document. The prongs of the staple remover are inserted under the prongs of the staple to lift them. The paper is then turned over and the staple remover prongs are inserted under the flat front of the staple to grasp it and lift it out of the paper without tearing it. The process of removing a staple is shown in Fig. 6.22.

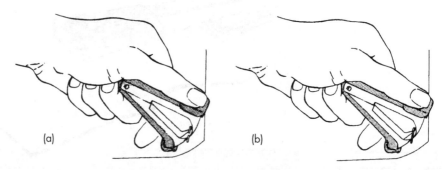

Fig. 6.22 (a) Staple remover under staple prongs; (b) staple remover under flat front of staple.

BINDING

Documents that are to be sent to clients are usually presented bound in some way. There are various types of binding, including:

- spine covers
- comb
- wire
- thermal.

The choice of binding depends on the type and size of the documents to be bound. Most bound documents have a card cover, usually with the company name and logo printed on it, and a card back.

SPINE COVERS

These covers are attached manually. The left-hand side of the collated document is pushed into the open side of a plastic strip, as shown in Fig. 6.23. The strips are available in different widths to accommodate from 4 or 5 pages to about 50, depending on the thickness of the paper. The disadvantage is that, when bound, it is difficult to keep the document open at a particular page.

Fig. 6.23 Spine binding.

COMB BINDING

This requires a machine that consists of a punch to make a line of holes in the margin where the binding is required. A plastic strip with 'prongs' is then placed on the machine, which is operated so that the prongs slip into the punched holes. This type of binding overcomes the problem of keeping the document open, making it easier to handle and read.

WIRE BINDING

Wire binding is similar to comb binding, using a metal wire instead of a plastic strip. The processes of punching and wiring are shown in Fig. 6.24.

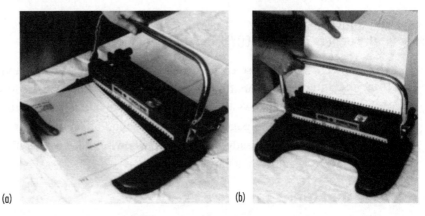

Fig. 6.24 (a) Wire binding – punching the pages; (b) pressing the wire into the holes.

THERMAL BINDING

Thermal binding is achieved by placing a strip of linen or plastic over the spine of the document and inserting it in a heat machine, which seals the cover on to the paper. Alternatively, an adhesive is melted on to the spine. It is difficult to hold the document open with this kind of binding.

All the types of binding described are available in a variety of colours.

THE IMPORTANCE OF PRESENTATION

The presentation of a document creates a major impression on the people who receive it. This in turn becomes a major factor in the image of the

> **ACTIVITY 6.3** Go to a good office equipment and stationery store and ask for an old catalogue. (Most larger stores issue new catalogues at least once a year.) Look for the items of equipment and supplies described in this chapter and see the wide variety available. Read the specifications that explain the facilities of the machines illustrated. Make a note of any that you think might be particularly useful in a general office. This could be helpful if you are involved in ordering stationery and/or equipment.

organisation. Attention to detail is the key to achieving the best possible presentation of documents. Consistency and accuracy are paramount.

Consistency means ensuring that:

- the right type of paper is used for each document
- an appropriate style of typing/printing is used for the particular document
- the document is correctly collated with all the pages in the right order, the right way up and facing the right way
- punch holes are central on the page and not too near the left-hand side
- the correct type of fastening is used, depending on the volume of the document and its destination
- staples are in the correct position
- a bound document can be opened and read easily.

Accuracy means ensuring that:

- the document is proofread, as well as spellchecked, and figures are read over with a colleague
- anything that does not *seem* right is checked.

PRACTICE QUESTIONS

1. Your manager has decided to start using an audio-dictating machine instead of drafting his letters, etc. He asks you to explain to him how the machine works.

2. Explain the following terms:
    i. paper grammage
    ii. portrait format

   iii. pocket envelope
   iv. correction fluid
   v. ink cartridge
   vi. A2
   vii. hard copy
   viii. DL
   ix. digital information
   x. reprography.

3. What size paper would you use to print:
   i. a letter
   ii. an invoice
   iii. an invitation card
   iv. a business card
   v. a compliment slip?

4. Describe the main differences between an electronic typewriter and a word processor.

5. What is the difference between memory storage and diskette/disk storage?

6. Name 10 facilities you would expect to have on a word processor. Give examples of the use of each.

7. Explain the following terms:
   i. pitch
   ii. embolden
   iii. window envelope
   iv. ISO
   v. C6
   vi. gsm
   vii. American quarto
   viii. banker envelope
   ix. justified margin
   x. A3.

8. List and explain two types of paragraph.

9. When would you use the following:
   i. copyholder
   ii. continuous stationery
   iii. heavy duty punch
   iv. long-arm stapler
   v. guillotine?

10. Describe three types of printer that you might use with a word processor or PC.

11. You are secretary to the principal of the Stenotype College. The principal tells you that she is considering replacing the existing office copier. You are asked to suggest what facilities the new copier should have. Prepare a list with reasons for including each facility.

12. The office copier in the department where you work is not being used cost-effectively. You are asked to write a memorandum to all staff giving instructions on what they should do to ensure that the machine is being used efficiently.

13. What is a computerised image copier/printer?

14. Explain how a copy printer works and what facilities it has.

15. What method of reproduction would you choose to produce the following:
    i. 5000 copies of a book
    ii. 50 copies of a 10-page report
    iii. 500 copies of a coloured sketch
    iv. 100 000 copies of a circular letter for direct mailing
    v. 10 copies of a 500-page scientific paper?

16. List and briefly explain four ways of fastening papers.

17. There are five types of stapling machine. What are they?

18. Explain the following terms:
    i. cutting a stencil
    ii. staple remover
    iii. drill
    iv. alignment.

19. Write a step-by-step guide for a school-leaver on how to use a stapling machine.

20. List and briefly explain four ways of binding a document.

SHORT ANSWER QUESTIONS

1. In some organisations staff can dictate letters, etc. for typing by using the telephone. This is known as a ....

2. The size of paper most commonly used in Caribbean territories is ....

3. The weight of paper is known as ....

4. An envelope with the opening on the short side is known as .... style.

5. Daisywheel and dot-matrix printers are known as .... printers.

Choose the most appropriate ending for each of the following sentences.

6. A block paragraph is one:
   a. with a justified right-hand margin
   b. with every line indented from the margins
   c. with every line starting at the left-hand margin
   d. printed in a different type style from the rest of the text.

7. Reformatting a document means:
   a. printing it in a smaller or larger print size
   b. changing the margins
   c. placing the first line lower down the page
   d. changing one or more of the settings.

8. Copy printers differ from office copiers in that:
   a. they produce better copies
   b. they copy from a stencil master
   c. they operate faster
   d. they can enlarge and reduce the size of the original.

9. There are different types of plate for offset printing. The greatest number of copies can be obtained from:
   a. a plastic plate
   b. an aluminium plate
   c. a copper plate
   d. a parchment plate.

10. Collating documents means:
    a. placing all the pages together in a pile
    b. placing all the pages with the same number in separate piles
    c. sorting the pages into numerical order
    d. sorting the pages into sets, each set in page number sequence.

EXAMINATION QUESTIONS

1. An example of a letter-quality printer would be a/an .... printer.

2. A/an .... can be used to align the pages of a document before stapling or binding.

(Pitmans Office Procedures Level 1 1998 Pt 1A)

3. Apart from making copies, state THREE facilities that may be offered by a modern photocopier.
   a. ....
   b. ....
   c. ....

4. List THREE main actions you should take if a photocopier stops working during use.
   a. ....
   b. ....
   c. ....
   (Pitmans Office Procedures Level 1 1998 Pt 1B)

5. Explain briefly the purpose of the following equipment.
   a. jogger
   b. collator
   c. binder
   (Pitman Office Procedures Level 1 1998 Pt 2B)

6. A photocopier can enlarge and .... the size of documents.

7. Accurate transcription of pre-recorded dictation is one of the main duties of a/an ....
   (Pitman Office Procedures Level 1 1999 Pt 1A)

8. State THREE ways to help ensure a photocopier produces good-quality copies.
   a. ....
   b. ....
   c. ....
   (Pitman Office Procedures Level 1 1999 Pt 1B)

CHAPTER 7

DOCUMENT STORAGE AND RETRIEVAL

OBJECTIVES   When you have studied this chapter you should have acquired the knowledge and understanding to be able to:

1. explain what a filing system comprises
2. explain the advantages and disadvantages of central, departmental and individual filing
3. explain the various types of equipment used for filing
4. explain the three main filing classifications, their advantages and disadvantages
5. list and follow the rules for alphabetical filing
6. explain the importance and methods of indexing
7. explain the uses of guide cards and colour coding
8. explain the procedures for filing, and control of access to files and file movements
9. explain retention policy and archiving, and their importance
10. explain the different types of microcopy and the purposes for which microcopying is used
11. explain and use a bring-forward system
12. briefly describe electronic storage, its advantages and disadvantages.

All organisations, from the sole trader to the international corporation, must keep records of various kinds. Letters, commercial documents, etc. are fundamental to administration. All government ministries and departments have records of everything that is said to and done for everyone within and outside the organisation.

Information can be held on a variety of media, both visual and electronic. The principles are always the same but there are many different ways of storing and retrieving information. We shall consider information held on visual media and, later in the chapter, electronic storage and retrieval.

'Storage and retrieval' may be referred to as 'records management' or 'filing'. For simplicity we will use the latter term, bearing in mind that what is stored must be retrievable. There is no point in storing information and then not being able to find it when needed.

WHAT FILING IS

Filing is the storing of various types of media, which hold information contained in correspondence, records, reports, etc.

WHAT A FILING SYSTEM COMPRISES

As we saw in Chapter 2, a system involves much more than just the end result. A storage system starts with the receipt of information on some kind of medium, e.g. paper or on screen (e-mail). It progresses through action if appropriate – this may be a lengthy process – and then reaches the storage stage.

The storage system involves:

- types of media to be filed – what is filed
- people involved in the action and storage – who files
- the location of information – where information is stored
- equipment appropriate for the media – what equipment is used
- content/topics of information ⎫ – how files are
- the ease with which information can be retrieved ⎭ arranged
- regular and accurate filing – when and how filing is done
- the attitude of people involved in filing – why filing is a vital task
- the control of access to information ⎫ – procedures for dealing
- the security of the information ⎭ with classified documents.

We will now look at each of these areas in turn.

WHAT IS FILED

Visual media include:

- paper, often referred to as 'hard copy', as single sheets or documents, leaflets, booklets, magazines and journals, reports, books
- overhead projector transparencies (or overhead slides or acetates).

Miniature visual media include:

- microcopy
- film slides
- video cassettes.

Electronic media include:

- magnetic tapes, disks and diskettes
- optical disks.

Information held on paper can be read directly. Information held on microfilm, film slides, video cassettes and computer tapes/disks can be read only by using a machine, which means that access is indirect.

WHO FILES

Almost everybody files, however informally. At home, people keep letters, invoices, etc. in drawers, either loose, in envelopes or in folders. In business the people who file include:

- filing clerks in a **file registry** (see below)
- secretarial and administrative support staff
- managers who hold their own confidential and 'work in progress' files
- librarians
- computer operations staff.

WHERE INFORMATION IS STORED

There are three locations for filing – centrally for the whole organisation, departmentally for a whole department or group of sections, and personally by individuals in their offices.

CENTRAL FILING

This means that there is a **file registry** in the organisation. This may be combined with the mail room (see Chapter 8). The file registry is staffed by filing clerks, usually with a supervisor. Hard-copy items for filing are sent to the registry for storage and are retrieved by staff for individuals when required.

Advantages of central filing

1. Filing is done by staff trained for the job, who become familiar with the types of information stored, so there is less likelihood of documents being filed incorrectly.
2. Duplication of filing in various offices can be avoided.
3. Files can be arranged in the most appropriate way for the types of information and types of media.
4. File movements can be documented and controlled.
5. Classified information can be kept securely.
6. Appropriate equipment for the different types of media can be provided most cost-effectively.
7. Files can be kept in good order with documents in chronological (date) order and are not allowed to get too thick.
8. Closed and non-active files can be archived systematically (see page 214).
9. Individuals do not have to spend time filing.

Disadvantages of central filing

1. Some managers and others like to keep their own files; they do not send all documents to central registry for filing so they are not available for anyone else who may need them, and neither the individual nor registry have a complete file.
2. Some organisations cover a very wide range of topics and it may be difficult to design one system that is suitable for all topics.
3. When an individual needs a file it may take a long time for it to be delivered, and fetching it could be time-consuming.
4. If a file is needed by someone talking on the telephone it could be embarrassing to have to delay giving information.
5. Anyone working late or at a weekend would be unable to obtain a file.
6. A file may be out on loan to a person who has locked it away in a drawer and is away from the office.

Some uses of central filing

1. Large numbers of files on individual topics, e.g. insurance company clients' policies, mail-order customers or college students.
2. Technical files.
3. Standing orders, reports and public documents that are needed by a variety of people in the organisation.

DEPARTMENTAL FILING

This is done centrally within a department, usually by support staff.

Advantages and disadvantages of departmental filing

These are similar to those for central filing. There are some additional disadvantages, including the following.

1. The person or people responsible for filing may be too busy with their other work to keep the files up to date.
2. Departmental staff may 'help themselves' to files without leaving a record of the loan, and may replace files in the wrong places.
3. It is usually more difficult to keep classified files confidential.

Some uses of departmental filing

1. Confidential files, such as personnel records where personnel staff have their own office with security access.
2. Technical files relating to one department or group of sections only.
3. Files needed regularly by members of staff within a department.

INDIVIDUAL FILING

This means that files are kept in individual offices or in a section of an open-plan office (see Chapter 2, page 23) and is done by managers and/or their support staff.

Advantages of individual filing

1. The cost of space and staff for a central registry is eliminated.
2. Temporary staff are not needed to cover for sickness and holidays.

3. The individual can have a system that is exactly right for them and their type of work.
4. Files can be obtained immediately at any time, including outside working hours.
5. The individual is completely familiar with the system.

Disadvantages of individual filing

1. Several people may file the same documents in their systems, e.g. circulars, resulting in a lot of paper and space being used unnecessarily.
2. If an individual keeps all files locked away, access is not possible when the individual is away.
3. Systems may be designed in such a way that only the individual understands how they work, or they may be haphazard, i.e. not systematic at all.
4. Time has to be allocated for filing to avoid a backlog as filing is not regarded as a priority.

Some uses of individual filing

1. When the information is highly specialised and unique to the individual.
2. When only the individual needs access to the information.
3. When the information is generally needed immediately because of the nature of the work.

WHAT EQUIPMENT IS USED

Equipment includes the means of keeping documents, etc. together, e.g. file folders, and the storage space for the files, e.g. cupboards.

Means of keeping documents together include:

- slip files (plastic and card)
- plastic pockets
- manilla folders
- envelope/wallet/flat-pocket folders
- file covers with various kinds of devices for securing the papers
- ring binders (commonly two-ring, but these can be made with four or more rings)
- lever arch files in various widths of spine, from 2.5 cm to 7 cm
- box files

- very large binders to hold computer printouts
- magazine files for leaflets, journals, maps, etc.

A variety of file covers, binders, etc. is illustrated in Fig. 7.1

The files are stored on open shelves or in cabinets. Cabinets may have two, three, four or five drawers. The files are stored from front to back of each drawer. If the drawers have suspension cradles, the files are placed in suspension pockets that remain in the cabinet when files are removed. Both the file cover and the suspension pockets must be marked clearly with the title of the file. If there are no suspension cradles, the files are placed on their spines. Storage in drawers is known as **vertical** filing.

In cabinets with shelves, files are placed side by side, i.e. **laterally**, on their spines. Cabinets may have racks from which suspension pockets can be hung instead of shelves. Some cabinets are arranged so that they have a combination of suspension files and shelves for ring binders, box files, etc., and/or drawers for microfilm (see page 216). Lateral filing takes much less space than vertical filing.

Vertical and lateral shelf and suspension files, and combination cabinets are illustrated in Fig. 7.2. You will see in Fig. 7.9, **guide cards** (or dividers) are used to separate groups of files. Those shown are for alphabetical filing but there are other types of file arrangement (see Table 7.1).

Cabinets with drawers have locks and a safety device, to ensure that only one drawer can be opened at a time. Cabinets are also available with varying degrees of fireproofing.

Cabinets with shelves may have doors or a metal 'blind', which can be locked. If non-confidential files only are kept in a cupboard it may have a linen blind, used at night to keep the files free from dust and insects.

There are cabinets designed especially for storing plans. These can be cabinets with very shallow drawers in which the plans are laid flat in the drawer, one on top of another (this is known as **horizontal** filing). This term also applies to documents/files stored in pigeon-holes. Alternatively, plans are filed in a deep cabinet with 'wavy' dividers, which hold the plans upright. The two types of plan filing are shown in Fig. 7.3.

Not all files need to be kept in cabinets. Ring binders and lever arch files, in particular, are bulky, and are often kept on **rotary** files (see Fig. 7.4).

Some information is kept on cards, e.g. an index of addresses and stock records. The cards must be kept in sequence, just the same as files. This can be done in card index boxes, horizontal and vertical rotary 'wheels' and 'visible' card indexes. In box and rotary wheels, the cards are placed one

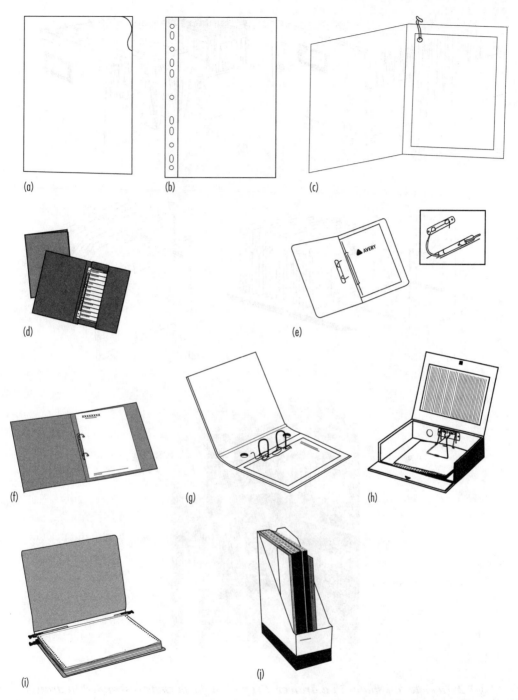

Fig. 7.1 (a) Plastic slip file open at top and right-hand side (note the thumb-cut slot for easy opening); (b) plastic pocket open at the top; (c) manilla folder with treasury tag; (d) flat-pocket folder; (e) file cover with prongs and coil springs; (f) two-ring binder; (g) lever arch file; (h) box file; (i) computer printout binder; (j) magazine file.

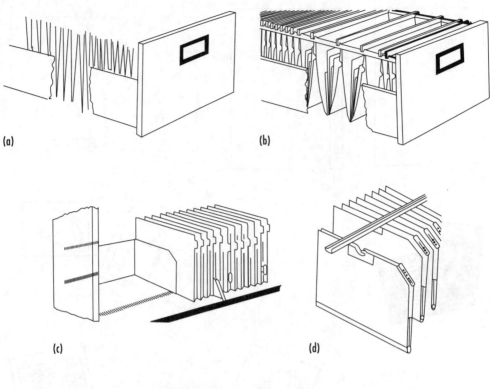

Fig. 7.2 (a) Files on spines in a drawer; (b) files in file pockets suspended in drawer; (c) files on spines on shelf; (d) files suspended laterally (in cabinet); (e) cabinet arranged for suspension and shelf filing.

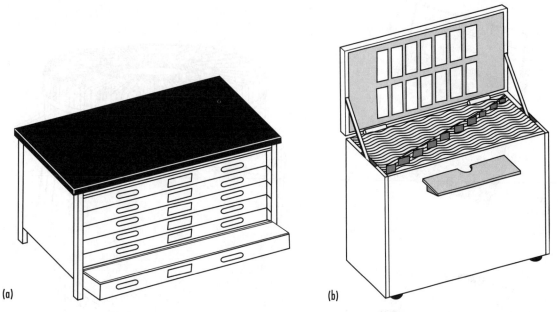

Fig. 7.3 (a) Plan drawer filing cabinet; (b) vertical plan filing cabinet (note the 'wavy' dividers to hold the plans firmly).

Fig. 7.4 Rotary stand file for ring binders or lever arch files.

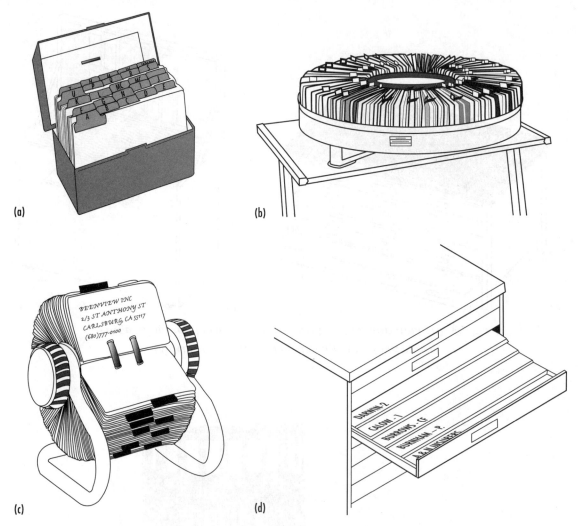

Fig. 7.5 (a) Card index box; (b) horizontal rotary card index; (c) vertical rotary index; (d) visible card index.

behind the other. The visible card index has the cards overlapping in a shallow drawer, with the bottom of each card visible showing the identification, e.g. name or stock part number. These various methods of storing cards are shown in Fig. 7.5.

HOW FILES ARE ARRANGED

Files must be arranged so that they can be found quickly. There are three main methods of arranging files in sequence: alphabetical, numerical and chronological (in date order). The alphabetical sequence may be used for **classification** by name, subject and geographical area; numerical can be used for most types of classification; chronological sequence is generally used in conjunction with other classifications (i.e. the documents are placed in the files in date order); it is also used for numbered commercial documents such as invoices.

Alphabetical filing is an example of **direct filing** because the files can be identified without reference to an index. Numerical filing requires an index to cross-reference the number with the name or subject.

When filing alphabetically **by name** there are certain rules to be followed.

1. File according to the initial letter of the surname and each subsequent letter, e.g.:

    - Dean PM
    - Deekin LR
    - Dexter MB
    - Dobbs TS.

2. If the surnames are the same, file according to initials, e.g.:

    - Peters AN
    - Peters DA
    - Peters DL
    - Peters ST.

3. Ignore titles unless the surname and initials are the same, e.g.:

    - Lara Dr A
    - Monroe Dr D
    - Monroe Miss D
    - Sillitoe Mrs R.

    Note that the title should be included in the identification on the file and suspension pocket.

4. A surname alone comes before a surname with an initial, which comes before a surname with a first name – that is, 'nothing' comes before 'something', e.g.:

    - Jensen
    - Jensen SR
    - Jensen Peter
    - Jensen Peter A.

5. Names with a prefix are filed by the first and subsequent letters of the prefix and then the surname, e.g.:

    - De Groot NP
    - De la Bastide PW
    - Le Breton DI
    - Legrande WC.

6. Names with the prefix M', Mc and Mac are treated as if they are all spelt 'Mac', whether separate from or joined to the surname, e.g.:

   - McAdam OF
   - MacBride Prof LM
   - Macdonald KR
   - McElvie Mrs DI.

7. Names beginning with 'St' or 'Saint' are treated as if they are all spelt in full, e.g.:

   - Saint Peter's Church
   - St Theresa's Convent
   - Saint Thomas' Hospital
   - St Vincent College.

8. Names consisting of initials are placed before full names, e.g.:

   - AA Road Services
   - A-Z Office Services
   - Anglican Church Bookshop
   - Apartments Limited.

9. Numbers in names are treated as words, e.g.:

   - 5 Arts Exhibition Centre (Five)
   - 4 Oak Restaurant (Four)
   - 7-Day Club (Seven).

10. File government ministries and departments under the key word, e.g.:

    - Consumer Affairs and Social Security, Department of
    - Sport and Youth Affairs, Ministry of
    - Works and Transport, Ministry of.

11. Sub-divide files for local councils into departments, e.g.:
    XYZ Council

    - Housing Department
    - Personnel Services Department
    - Treasury Department.

12. Ignore 'The', '& Co.' or '& Company', Limited, plc, e.g.:

    - Caribbean Shipping Company Limited, The
    - John Doull & Co. Ltd
    - Same Day Couriers, The.

13. File under the name of the organisation, not the individual who signed the document.

> **ACTIVITY 7.1** Rewrite the following list of names in the correct order for filing.
>
> Dr A Dalton
> Tree Felling Company
> Peter Le Motte
> Lady Margaret Forde
> Georgina Dress Shop
> Caribbean Jewellery Co. Ltd
> Port-of-Spain Trading Co. Ltd
> Ministry of Health
> Instant Copying Company
> 8-hour Cleaning Service
> St Mary's Episcopal Church
> Dr Adrian Phelps
> Mrs LM Lebrun
> Miss Jane Wilkins
> Sahara Gift Shop
> Castries City Council Traffic Dept
> Jamaican Rum Company Limited
> Department of Social Security
> The Computer Shop
> TEC Computer Software

Using the name classification, files can be identified by letters and/or numbers. Using the initial letter plus a number is known as alpha-numeric. Look at the list of files below and see how they can be identified alpha-numerically.

Argentine Football Association	A1
Ayling Import/Export Co. Ltd	A2
Adriatic Shipping Company	A3
Amsterdam Airport Services	A4
Beach Hut Manufacturers	B1
Brazil Nut Company	B2
Bank of Nova Scotia	B3

You will notice that the names are not in alphabetical order. It would be impossible to remember the numbers of hundred of files so it is necessary to create a cross reference index, either on cards or on computer.

The index gives the names in alphabetical order with the file number. The examples given would be indexed as follows:

Adriatic Shipping Company	A3
Amsterdam Airport Services	A4
Argentine Football Club	A1
Ayling Import/Export Co. Ltd	A2
Bank of Nova Scotia	B3
Beach Hut Manufacturers	B1
Brazil Nut Company	B2

Names can be added to the list under each letter and can go on indefinitely. This system is not recommended, as preparing and using an index takes time. The direct filing method is easy to use, each new file being slotted into its right place in the alphabetical sequence.

> **ACTIVITY 7.2** Write an index list for the files listed below.
>
> | | | | | |
> |---|---|---|---|---|
> | Driscoll, Peter | D1 | Hendrie, Michael | H1 |
> | Dark, Leo | D2 | Hamilton, Lady M | H2 |
> | De la Tour, Victor | D3 | Hadley, Hamish | H3 |
> | Drax, James | D4 | Healey, David | H4 |
> | Dando, Deirdre | D5 | Hawkes, Marilyn | H5 |
> | Deveril, Jeffrey | D6 | Hope, Denise | H6 |

Alternatively, names can be numbered without a letter, each new file being added to the end of the list. This is known as sequential numerical filing. It is commonly used for personnel files. As a file is opened for each new employee, say, the next number is allocated. The file number is then used on all documentation relating to that employee.

> **ACTIVITY 7.3** The following files need to be put in order ready for insertion into the numerical filing system. Write the list in numerical sequence.
>
> | | | | | | |
> |---|---|---|---|---|---|
> | 10923 | 12151 | 16343 | 11800 | 17447 | 13414 |
> | 16828 | 19000 | 10806 | 18622 | 18991 | 15347 |
> | 14116 | 11009 | 10994 | 12943 | 11100 | 11010 |

Filing **by subject** means that the content of the document, not the name of the sender or addressee, determines where it is filed. Because some subjects are complex it is often necessary to sub-divide the main subject and have a file for each sub-division. Take BUDGET and TRAINING as examples. Each topic might be sub-divided as follows.

```
BUDGET    - Capital
            Revenue
            Expenditure
TRAINING  - Support staff
            Supervisory
            Health and Safety
            Management development
            Apprentice
            Graduate
```

Numerical sequence can also be applied to subject classifications. The main subject and each sub-division is given a number. For example

BUDGET is 1, Capital Budget would be 1.1, Revenue Budget 1.2 and Expenditure Budget 1.3. An index card for this subject is shown in Fig. 7.6.

BUDEGET	1
Capital	1.1
Expenditure	1.3
Revenue	1.2

Fig. 7.6 Index card.

ACTIVITY 7.4 Look at the list of Training files on page 202. Training is 16. The sub-divisions are numbered from 1. Support staff training is 16.1, Supervisory training 16.2, etc. Draw index cards for the six files and complete them to provide cross-references.

Filing by **geographical area** can be arranged alphabetically or numerically, though the former is more usual. Files may be identified by country, region, city/town and even street. Study the following example.

Caribbean	- Antigua	- Caxton, Joseph & Co
		Mainwaring China Company
	Barbados	- Barbados Wine Company Limited
		Bridgetown Book Suppliers
		Pharmaceuticals Limited
	Jamaica	- Johnson, Abel & Company
		Kingston Sailing Supplies
		Montego Bay Hotel
	St Lucia	- Castries Grocery Co. Ltd
		Pearls Unlimited
	St Vincent	- Kingstown Warehouse
	Trinidad and Tobago	- Gina Dress Fabrics
		Gina Hairdresser
		San Fernando Estate Agents

With a large number of customers it would be difficult to remember the location of each one. A cross-reference index would again be needed, showing the name of the client and the location (see Fig. 7.7).

> ROBERT JOHNSON DESIGNS
> see
> JAMAICA, Kingston

Fig. 7.7 Cross-reference index card.

Earlier, we said that **chronological** filing is used in conjunction with alphabetical, numerical and geographical filing. Documents are inserted into the appropriate individual file with the latest-dated document on top. It is important that when documents are removed and re-inserted in a file, they are replaced in date order.

Documents such as requisitions and expense claims may be filed in date order. Since the originator of the documents keeps a copy of them they can refer to the date if they have need to follow up.

The uses, advantages and disadvantages of the various ways in which the classifications are used are listed in Table 7.1.

IDENTIFICATION OF FILES

Depending on its classification, each file should have the:

- name of the person or organisation, or
- subject (main) and sub-division, or
- geographical area (country or region) with sub-division.

If the files are numbered or alpha-numbered, this must also appear on the file. Similarly, the suspension pocket must be identified in the same way.

A suspension pocket with a file, both identified, are shown in Fig. 7.8.

GUIDE CARDS (OR DIVIDERS)

These are used to separate files into groups when they are placed on their spines in drawers or on shelves. Alphabetical files have guide cards labelled A, B, etc. Some letters have more names under them than others, for example the letter B. This section can be sub-divided into Ba, Be, Bi, Bo, Bu.

Subject guide cards would have the main subject indicated.

Table 7.1 *Classification types (uses, advantages and disadvantages)*

Classification	Examples of use	Advantages	Disadvantages
Alphabetical by name	Clients/customers Students Personnel/staff Index cards for numerical files and cross-reference	Direct filing Simple to operate Maximum flexibility for inserting and extracting files	Sub-division possibilities limited Danger of misfiling if files are grouped, e.g. customers in one group and staff in another group, unless some form of coding, e.g. colour, is used Cross-reference may be necessary
Alpha-numeric sequential, i.e. in numerical sequence	Names, e.g. clients, trainees Single topics not sub-divided	Provides a file reference	Index and file list essential Time-consuming if number of files is large
Alphabetical by subject	Products Services Projects Contracts Index cards for cross-reference	Direct filing Subjects can be numbered	Not suitable for a large number of files Cross-references may be necessary
Numerical – sequential	Customers, etc. Subjects if no sub-division	Provides a file reference A block of numbers can be allocated	No sub-division possible Files cannot be grouped in any way Index and file list is essential if many files are held
Numerical – subject	Products Supplies Services Functions of an organisation	Flexibility – easy to sub-divide and add topics Can be combined with alphabetical or numerical coding for departments/sections of the organisation	Index and file list essential Danger of misfiling when contents of a document are not understood by person filing
Alphabetical by geographical area	Sales regions Import/export Survey areas Provision of services Mail order Insurance	The names of organisations do not have to be remembered Cross-reference not usually needed	Index and file list is necessary for a large number of files

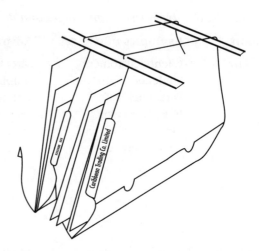

Fig. 7.8 Suspension pocket with file identification.

Numerical guide cards are usually placed after every 10th file, so are labelled 1, 11, 21, 31, etc. Alpha-numeric files have a combination of letters and numbers, e.g. A1, A11, etc., B1, B11, etc.

Guide cards are illustrated in Fig. 7.9.

COLOUR CODING

This is a useful way of differentiating groups of files. For example, if files are classified by subject, each group of files within a subject area could be in a different colour. Similarly, if there are a number of projects in progress, each project would have a group of files. Each project group could be in a different colour. The files for each project can then readily be recognised, e.g. when they are on a desk.

WHEN FILING IS DONE

Records must always be up to date. This means that files, whether visual or electronic, must be updated daily. Storing of papers and other visual media should ideally have a time of day allocated, e.g. first thing in the morning or immediately after lunch. When a member of staff needs information from a file they must be able to rely on that information being the most up to date. Decisions are made on the basis of information, including that held in files. A bad decision could be made if it is based on out-of-date facts.

Filing is a priority task. It is unfortunate that many managers do not understand this and ask their staff to do other tasks rather than the filing. Try to avoid being 'put off' from doing it; it is much easier to allocate 10 minutes a day to filing than an hour at one session once a week.

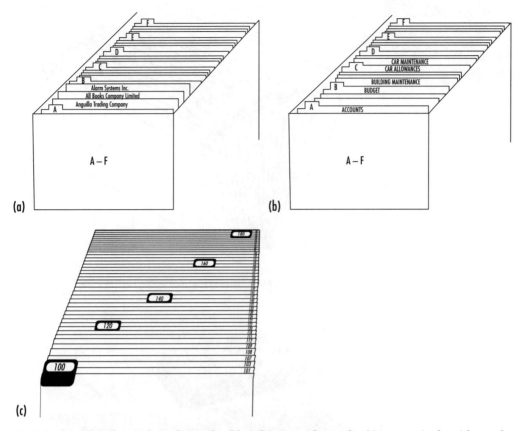

Fig. 7.9 (a) Alphabetical guide cards; (b) subject guide cards; (c) numerical guide cards after every twentieth file.

HOW FILING IS DONE

Documents for filing should have been 'marked off', i.e. the initials of the person authorising filing have been written in the top right-hand corner.

Documents awaiting filing should be kept in a tray marked 'FILING' or in an expanding wallet or concertina file (see Fig. 7.10). This is useful because documents can be placed in the appropriate pocket, either alphabetically or numerically. A document awaiting filing in a concertina file can be found more quickly if needed than a document in a tray.

PRE-SORTING

Pre-sorting is the first stage in the process of preparing documents for filing. If a concertina file has not been used it may be helpful to pre-sort the documents using a letter sorter (see Fig. 7.11).

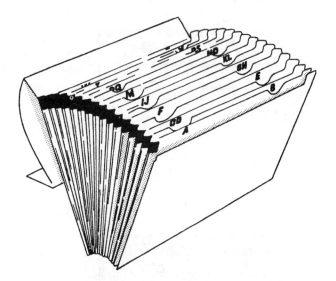

Fig. 7.10 Concertina (or expanding) file.

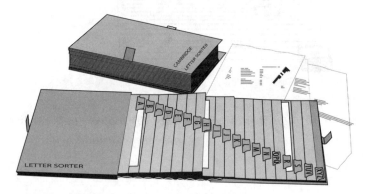

Fig. 7.11 Letter sorter.

If sorting alphabetically, all documents being filed by letter A would be placed under the first flap, documents being filed by letter B would be placed under the second flap, and so on.

Each group of letters is then taken and sorted in accordance with the filing rules (see pages 199-200) or number sequence.

PREPARING THE DOCUMENT FOR FILING

This involves ensuring that:

- attachments are attached
- the pages of documents are stapled together
- pins (which are dangerous) are removed

- paper clips are removed, unless it is absolutely necessary to keep them
- documents are punched centrally for insertion into the file.

OPENING A NEW FILE

This is necessary when a new filing system is set up, an existing filing system is re-organised, or as new names, subjects and geographical areas are added to the organisation's business. It is essential to follow a set sequence of steps.

- Check that a new file is necessary. It must not duplicate an existing file, nor should a new file be opened for a single document when it is unlikely that there will be more documents. In this situation it is permissible to have a 'Miscellaneous' file with the single documents filed alphabetically.
- Obtain the appropriate type, size and colour of folder to match the others in the system and suspension pocket if used.
- Check the title of the new file, and label the folder/binder and suspension pocket.
- If the file identification is numerical, prepare an index card with the alphabetical cross-reference and add to the file list.
- Insert the document in the file.
- Insert the suspension pocket and file in the appropriate place, in alphabetical or numerical sequence, in the drawer or on the shelf.
- It is only in such a circumstance as that stated above that a Miscellaneous file should be opened. It can so easily become a dumping ground for documents that are not immediately identified as relating to a file in the system.

OPENING A CONTINUATION FILE

When a file becomes thick (say about 150 to 200 pages), a continuation file should be opened. The first file is marked 'Volume 1' with the dates of the first and last documents on the front cover. The continuation file is marked 'Volume 2'. For a while, Volume 1 will be needed for reference but can eventually become semi-active (see page 213).

WHY FILING IS A VITAL TASK

Filing systems exist so that:
- the media on which information is held is kept clean and safe
- the office is kept tidy

- information is arranged systematically and can be found quickly when needed
- movement of files/documents can be controlled
- classified information is kept secure.

It is essential that everyone who files recognises the responsibility involved. Filing is often regarded as a time-consuming chore, but if it is integrated into the daily work schedule it need not be.

Accuracy is vital. A misplaced file can be lost for weeks or even for ever, with serious consequences. Looking for 'lost' files can be extremely time-consuming so it is well worth the little extra time needed to ensure that a file is replaced in the correct place.

SECURITY

There are two aspects to security:

1. controlling access to information
2. controlling the movement of documents and files.

CONTROLLING ACCESS TO FILES

There are various levels of confidentiality that must be maintained for certain files. 'Classified information' (i.e. files) is accessible to certain named people or categories of people, e.g. senior managers or chief officers. Classified files can be:

- top secret
- secret
- staff in confidence
- confidential.

Two other classifications – 'for your eyes only' and 'private and confidential' – are used on envelopes when documents or files are sent to individuals.

Access to classified files may vary in different organisations. Generally one can say that:

- the chairman, managing director, directors and chief executive would have access to all levels

- selected senior managers would have access to secret files relevant to their roles, staff files relating to their own departmental staff and confidential files
- personnel staff would have access to all staff files
- any staff could have access to confidential files if they were relevant to their roles.

Classified files should always be kept in a locked drawer or cabinet. They should never be taken out of the building by anyone, however senior. Certain files may not be taken from the registry, personnel department or the office/department in which they are kept.

It is essential that the people responsible for filing have a list of the staff who may have access to classified files.

- Top secret and secret files are generally kept by the personal assistant to the chairman/managing director/chief executive or by the company secretary.
- Staff in confidence files are kept in the personnel department.
- Confidential files are kept in the central registry or by the secretary to the departmental manager.

CONTROLLING THE MOVEMENT OF DOCUMENTS AND FILES

Documents should *never* be removed from a file. If a document is needed, e.g. to take to a meeting, it should be copied. Should it be absolutely essential to remove a document or documents, a **substitution note** should be put in their place.

The substitution note must state:

- details of the document – sender's name and organisation, date of the document(s), subject
- details of the borrower – name, department, date the document(s) borrowed.

The substitution note should be secured in the file and 'flagged' so that it can be seen immediately that a document has been removed (see Fig. 7.12).

When files are borrowed there must be a procedure to ensure that they can be traced at any time. If only a few people have access to files, e.g. in a section or small department, there is an easy way of indicating who has borrowed the file: coloured cards are made available near or in the filing cabinet(s); each person is allocated a colour (Fred is blue, Mary is green, etc.); when Fred borrows a file he slips a blue card in the place of

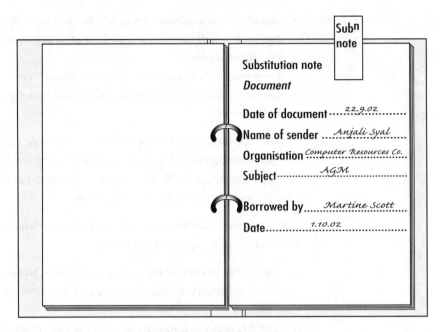

Fig. 7.12 Flagged substitution note.

the file he has taken; should anyone else need that file they will know that Fred has it.

When more than a few people have access to files, '**Absent**' or '**Out**' **cards** are used. The borrower has to complete the details as shown in Fig. 7.13. The borrower is responsible for their security and should be sure to lock them away, especially at night, even if they are not confidential.

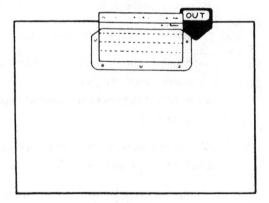

Fig. 7.13 Out or Absent card.

There should be a policy as to how long staff may keep files. On returning a file, the borrower must write in their initials and the date. The person in charge of filing should check the filing cabinets on a weekly basis to see if any of the files borrowed have been out for more than the permitted time. If so, the borrower must be contacted to find out whether the file is still needed.

ACTIVITY 7.5 Mildred Yates, who works in the engineering department, borrows a report from a file on 31 May 2002. The title of the report is *Design of New Water Pump*, and it is dated February 2002. It was produced by the Water Engineering Company in Port-of-Spain, Trinidad and Tobago.

Draw up a substitution note and complete it with the information above.

ACTIVITY 7.6 The following people have borrowed files. Draw four 'Out' cards and enter the details of each loan on a card. Sort the completed cards into date order.

- Doris Arkwright borrowed file no. 16.4 on Monday 8 July 2002. She works in the accounts department.
- Gerald Graham, who works in the engineering department, borrowed file no. 4.11 on Tuesday 16 July 2002.
- Arthur Jansen from the sales department borrowed file no. 38.2 on Thursday 11 July 2002.
- Jacqueline Day borrowed file no. 8.3A on Friday 5 July 2002. She works in the advertising department.

There is a policy that files must be returned within five working days. Write a list of names and file numbers, showing the dates, in chronological order of when the files were due to be returned.

RETENTION POLICY

Files may be active, semi-active, non-active or closed (dead).

- Active files are up to date and in regular use.
- Semi-active files are up to date and occasionally in use.

- Non-active files are often the early volumes of ongoing subjects; they are not used but may be needed for reference at some time.
- Closed or dead files are files on matters that have been finalised, e.g. a project, an investigation or a case.

It is essential to have a policy that sets out how long different types of document should be active, semi-active and non-active/closed before they can be destroyed. There are legal requirements for some types of file, e.g. financial documents and employee records must be kept for a minimum number of years. There are recommended minimum periods for other documents but it is up to individual organisations to set their own limits. An example of suggested time limits is given in Table 7.2

Table 7.2 *Suggested time limits for documents*

Type of document	Active	Semi-active	Non-active	Closed
General correspondence	1 year	1 year	3 years	Nil
Technical correspondence	3 years	3 years	7 years	Nil
Employee records*	During the period of employee's service	1 year after termination of service	12 years after termination of service	Nil
Invoices*	1 year	1 year	1 year	3 years
Projects	Duration of project	1–3 years	1–3 years	Indefinite

*Statutory requirements in Great Britain.

ARCHIVING

Files should be reviewed annually in order to remove non-active and closed files at the end of their period. Semi-active files should be changed to non-active status when their semi-active period ends. Active files should become semi-active at the end of their active period.

Non-active and closed files should be **archived**. This means that they can be taken out of the cabinets and cupboards, and placed in storage boxes, which are taken to the archive room. Sometimes archives are stored off site.

The storage boxes should be marked clearly with the identification of the files and the dates of the documentation (see Fig. 7.14). A record of

Fig. 7.14 Archive storage box.

the files sent for archiving must be kept so that, if any file is needed, a reference can be given to extract it from the archives.

When the time comes to destroy non-active and closed files, the person who sent them for archiving should be contacted to check that the files can be destroyed. Methods of destruction are explained on page 220.

Instead of keeping the documentation in archives, it can be microcopied and the original hard copy destroyed (see page 220).

ACTIVITY 7.7 It is the end of the year: time to review the files in the personnel department. Your filing system contains the following active and semi-active files:

- correspondence
- employee records – during the year five employees left the company
- projects – during the year two projects were completed.

When files become non-active they are sent to archives.

Using the suggested time limits shown in Table 7.2, decide:

a. which files will you send to archives
b. which files will you move from active to semi-active.

THE ESSENTIAL ELEMENTS OF A GOOD FILING SYSTEM

To summarise, a good filing system must be:

- simple to operate, using direct filing if practicable
- arranged in a classification appropriate to the content of the documents, with an alphabetical index for numerical and geographical classifications
- in an appropriate location for the users of the system
- stored in the right type of equipment
- possible to expand and reduce without disrupting the system
- operated in accordance with a retention policy.

MICROCOPY

The dictionary definition of 'microcopy' is 'a greatly reduced photographic copy of a printed page, drawing, etc., on microfilm or microfiche' (often called 'fiche'). The reduction in size is achieved by photographing the original hard copy with a special microfilm camera.

PREPARATION OF DOCUMENTS FOR FILMING

Before the records can be filmed they must be prepared. This involves checking to ensure that:

1. the print of each page is of good enough quality for filming
2. the pages of each document are in sequence
3. the documents are in date order
4. all fastenings are removed
5. each batch of documents is clearly identified with the file name/number.

FILMING THE RECORDS

The documents are fed on to a platform under an electronic camera. As each page is in position the camera 'snaps'; a 'plan camera' is used for large documents such as plans, drawings and maps. Computerised cameras can film up to 4000 A4 sheets, i.e. 8000 pages an hour. The film can then be processed into a microfilm roll in about 10 minutes.

The output can be in any one of the five types of microcopy: roll, cassette, jacket, microfiche and aperture card.

Roll

The film is first processed as a roll and can be stored on a reel. The major disadvantage of this form of storage is that finding the particular image required is time-consuming.

Cassette

The roll of film is inserted into a plastic box, which keeps the film free from dust and is quicker than the roll to insert into the machine.

Jacket

Small strips of film are placed in slots of varying widths on a transparent folder. Different film sizes can be filed in the same folder.

Microfiche

This is a sheet of A6 plastic (105 × 148 mm) on to which the images are printed. The number of images varies from 60 to 240 for most documents but can be up to 3000 for such information as stock lists in stores and motor parts held at garages.

Aperture card

This is an individual microfilm, usually 35 or 70 mm, mounted in an aperture in a card. For example, the image of a drawing can be inserted in the aperture and information about the drawing can be printed or written on the card.

The five types of microcopy are shown in Fig. 7.15.

MICRO-IMAGES ON DISK

Large volumes of documents can be micro-copied onto magnetic or optical disk (see Chapter 3, page 51). A 5¼ inch optical disk can store up to 30,000 page images.

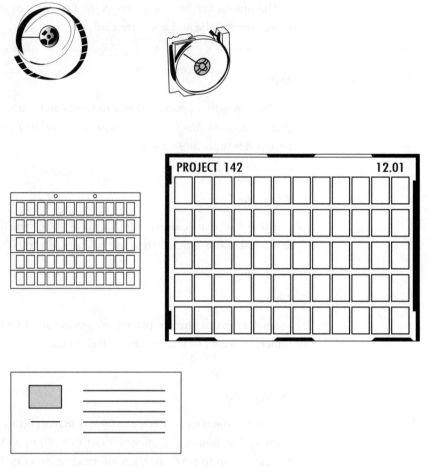

Fig. 7.15 Five types of microfilm storage: roll (or spool), cassette, jacket, fiche and aperture card.

READING THE IMAGES

Each film roll, cassette, jacket, fiche and card must be clearly identified and filed in an appropriate sequence. A microfilm reader is used to enlarge the image on a screen. A reader/printer is used if hard copies of images are required. A microreader/printer is shown in Fig. 7.16.

Images stored on disk are indexed or coded so that a group of images or an individual image can be recalled on screen. Documents can be printed out if needed.

A micro-image enlarged on screen, to which a printer is linked, is shown in Fig. 7.16.

Fig. 7.16 Computer micro-image reader linked to a printer.

WHY MICROCOPY?

There are many benefits to be gained from microcopying.

- Vast space saving – microcopy needs only 2 per cent of the space needed for hard copy.
- Copying is six or seven times faster than any other method of copying.
- Difficult to destroy by tearing or crumpling, and lasts longer than paper in a fire, so gives greater security than is possible with hard copy.
- Greater durability than paper so lasts much longer in good condition.
- Where constant reference to records is required, a vast amount of information can be held in a small box on a desk or in a drawer. It is also very easily transportable so is ideal for service engineers to carry details and drawings of various kinds of equipment. There are now some hand-held microreaders.
- Cheap to post so large amounts of material can be distributed widely very cheaply, e.g. reports consisting of several hundred pages, magazines and large documents such as plans.
- Microcopy can be held on electronic media, so can be viewed at any time, incorporated into new documents and transmitted by e-mail.

There are some disadvantages to microcopy.

- The preparation of the records for filming can be time-consuming.

- If the documents are reduced in size too much, they may be difficult to read on a reader.
- The equipment is costly.

USES OF MICROCOPY

Microcopy is used for many reasons. Here are a few examples:

- to distribute technical and professional articles worldwide
- maintenance manuals for equipment of all kinds
- commercial documents – for example, all documents relating to one transaction or one financial period.

MICROFICHE STORAGE

Microfiche can be stored in index boxes, separated by cards. Alternatively, they can be stored in pockets on panels, with a strip visible at the top of each fiche to show its identification. The panels can be stored in ring binders, which bend to form an easel (see Fig. 7.17).

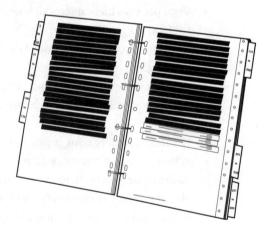

Fig. 7.17 Microfiche ring binder/easel.

DOCUMENT DESTRUCTION

Unwanted documents need to be destroyed. When they have been microcopied, the original hard copies can be disposed of. When the non-active and closed file periods end, the documents can be destroyed.

Non-confidential documents should be torn up and placed in a wastepaper bin. Confidential records, classified documents, financial information and commercial documents should always be shredded or burned in an incinerator.

Various sizes of shredder are available, from a small portable machine that will shred two or three pages at a time to heavy-duty automatic machines. Paper can be shredded into strips, cross-cut into small chippings for classified documents or micro-cut into tiny pieces for highly sensitive documents and microfilm. A heavy-duty shredder is shown in Fig. 7.18.

Fig. 7.18 Large-volume shredder.

A company that has large volumes of scrap paper, e.g. computer printout, may shred all unwanted documents and sell the shredded paper to packers.

Before shredding, documents must be checked to ensure that all staples, pins and paper clips have been removed, as these would damage the cutting blades. It is also extremely important to ensure that the operator is not wearing anything 'dangling' that could be caught in the cutters, e.g. a tie or scarf, hair or jewellery.

WORKING FILES

There are various files that relate to the day-to-day work of many people employed in offices.

WORK-IN-PROGRESS FILES

These files are those that contain working documents used by engineers, accountants, copywriters, etc. The papers in these files may be destroyed when the work is completed or may be placed in the main file.

PENDING FILE

A pending file is one in which to keep documents awaiting action. For example, an invoice needs authorisation but there is a query; when the query has been answered, the invoice can be authorised and sent to the accounts department for action.

DAY FILE

A day file is used in some offices to circulate copies of all outgoing mail to senior managers, partners in accountants' and solicitors' offices, or staff within a department. Staff are kept up to date with correspondence from clients and others. A day file may also be called a 'chron' (chronological) file.

BRING-FORWARD SYSTEMS

Action has to be taken on many matters at a later date. To ensure that nothing is overlooked, a system of 'bring forward' must be maintained. This can be done in a file, or set of files, on cards, in a diary or on computer.

File documents should never be put in the bring-forward system. If necessary, a copy can be made or a written note placed in the file. The bring-forward date should be written in the top right-hand corner of the paper and the papers should be placed in date sequence, the nearest date on top.

If there is a lot of bring-forward matter, it can be kept in 12 monthly files. At the end of each month, the documents/notes in next month's file are placed in daily files, 1 to 31 (see Fig. 7.19). First thing each morning, the documents are removed from the day's bring-forward file, which is then placed at the back of the daily files.

Alternative methods are to write notes on dated cards, which are kept in chronological sequence, or in a diary. Entries can be made in a computer diary if you have appropriate software (see page 52).

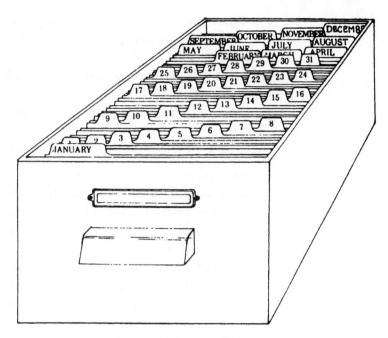

Fig. 7.19 'Bring-forward' file system.

ELECTRONIC STORAGE AND RETRIEVAL OF COMPUTER FILES

The storage of documents on disk, whether it be a hard disk on a mainframe or a PC, or a diskette, follows the same basic principles as manual storage. The single most important fundamental principle is that each document must be stored and identified in a way that will enable it to be retrieved immediately it is wanted.

In a manual system we have a cabinet or cupboard containing files, which contain documents. In an electronic system you create your document and file, or save it on disk. Your document is held in a file, or folder, which must be identified with a name, number, date or code. Each document, or record, in the folder should also be identified so that it can easily be located. The identification should be as short as possible, consistent with being recognisable.

It is common to store records on the hard disk and, ideally at the end of the day, download and duplicate the records created that day on to a floppy disk. In this way, **back-up** of folders is assured. Should any records be lost on the hard disk, they can be uploaded from the floppy disk to replace them. Each floppy disk must be labelled clearly to show what folders are stored on it.

Although hard disks have a large storage capacity they do eventually become full. It is just as important to have a retention policy for electronically stored records as for a manual system. For example, correspondence should be retained on both floppy and hard disks for a certain time. Eventually certain types of record can be erased from the hard disk but retained on the floppy disk, or vice versa.

The advantages of storing documents and records electronically are:

- space saving
- paper saving, if users do not print out unnecessarily
- a vast amount of information can be stored
- access to information can be controlled by passwords
- updating is a simple operation
- documents from various files can be integrated
- a database (large number of records) can be accessed in various ways in order to extract precisely the information required.

The disadvantages are:

- the system can become overloaded if users do not erase documents that do not need to be kept
- a database is time-consuming and expensive to establish
- if the system breaks down, documents cannot be accessed and may be lost
- all documents should be backed up, i.e. duplicated, on to another medium
- 'hacking into' or 'bugging' the system could create major problems (see Chapter 3).

PRACTICE QUESTIONS

1. A filing system is more than just a cabinet containing documents. List 10 points that a storage system involves.

2. List 10 types of media that may be filed.

3.
   a. Explain central, departmental and individual filing.
   b. State five advantages and five disadvantages of central filing.
   c. The disadvantages of departmental filing are similar to those of central filing. List three additional disadvantages.
   d. State four disadvantages of individual filing.

4. Explain the following and give one example for the use of each:
  i. manilla folder
  ii. ring binder
  iii. plastic slip file
  iv. wallet folder
  v. box file
  vi. lever arch file
  vii. plastic pocket
  viii. magazine file.

5. Explain:
  i. vertical filing
  ii. lateral filing
  iii. horizontal filing
  iv. rotary filing.

6. Explain alphabetical filing giving three examples of how it may be used.

7. State 10 alphabetical filing rules and give an example for each.

8. Explain the difference between direct and indirect filing. Give an example of each.

9. Type or write each of the names listed below in order on a 125 mm × 75 mm card. Sort into alphabetical order.

101 Galleries Ltd
The British Council
7-Up Bottling Co. Ltd
The T & T Electricity Company
Jamaican Distilleries Ltd
Dr JB Smythe
The General Building Society Ltd
National Council of Labour
Hotel Victoria
T & T Shipping Corporation Ltd
The Premier Engineering Co. Ltd
BWEE
Mrs Janet Smith
Saint Luke's Community Centre
Smiths Motor Accessories Ltd
Barbados Association of Chemists
The Reliance Telephone Co. Ltd
St Lucia Business Women's Association
Puerto Rico Chemicals Ltd
National Association of Secretaries

10. Give one example of the use of each of the following classifications:
   - *i.* alphabetical by name
   - *ii.* alpha-numeric
   - *iii.* numerical – sequential
   - *iv.* alphabetical by subject
   - *v.* numerical – subject
   - *vi.* alphabetical by geographical area.

11. Explain the following terms:
   - *i.* semi-active files
   - *ii.* colour coding
   - *iii.* a cross-reference
   - *iv.* suspension filing
   - *v.* an 'Out' card
   - *vi.* guide cards
   - *vii.* archive files
   - *viii.* chronological order
   - *ix.* a continuation file
   - *x.* pre-sorting of documents for filing.

12. Draft some 'hints on filing' for the guidance of junior staff in your department.

13. If you were setting up a filing system, what procedures would you establish to control file movement, i.e. ensure that the location of a particular file could always be traced?

14. Some organisations operate a centralised filing system, others operate a fully decentralised system, yet others operate a combination of the two. What are the main factors you would take into account in deciding which of these three possibilities was right for an organisation in which you worked?

15. Consider how you might file each type of document listed below (include type of equipment, classification and other relevant details in your answer):
   - *i.* stock record cards
   - *ii.* confidential staff records
   - *iii.* petty cash vouchers
   - *iv.* plans on microfiche
   - *v.* invoices from suppliers
   - *vi.* catalogues from wholesalers
   - *vii.* minutes of meetings
   - *viii.* staff training records
   - *ix.* sales ledger cards
   - *x.* invoices to clients awaiting payment.

16. **a.** Describe two types of 'bring-forward' system.
    b. Why is it essential to have a 'bring-forward' system?

17. Why is it essential that references and dates should be quoted on all documents?

18. **a.** What is microcopying? State three purposes for which it is used.
    b. Explain the five types of microcopy.

19. **a.** State the benefits and disadvantages of microcopy.
    b. Explain what has to be done to prepare documents for microcopying.

20. When documents are no longer required they should be destroyed. Confidential paper and microcopy documents are usually shredded.
    a. Explain what checking has to be done before documents are shredded. Explain what types of shredding there are.
    b. Explain the safety procedures that should be followed.

SHORT ANSWER QUESTIONS

Complete the following sentences.

1. To hang files in a cupboard you need .... in a .... cabinet.

2. Plans can be filed either in .... or .... with ....

3. Files may be colour coded to .... groups of files.

4. Filing must be done .... to ensure that files are always up to date.

5. Before opening a new file check that ....

Choose the most appropriate ending for each of the following sentences.

6. Guide cards are used:
    a. to indicate the files behind them
    b. list the files in a drawer or on a shelf
    c. list the files that have been borrowed
    d. separate files into groups, e.g. A, B, etc.

7. Microcopying is done:
    a. for historic purposes
    b. to provide back-up to computer printout
    c. to store a massive amount of information in a very small space
    d. to keep the original confidential.

8. A concertina file is used:
   a. to file papers when a drawer is too full to take more
   b. for pre-sorting documents awaiting filing
   c. to keep documents for archiving
   d. to keep miscellaneous papers.

9. A substitution note:
   a. is put in place of a file that has been borrowed
   b. is put in a file in place of a document that has been borrowed
   c. is kept in a file where notes of all files borrowed are kept
   d. is located in a drawer for safe keeping.

10. A retention policy means that:
    a. it provides a timescale for keeping different types of document
    b. you can destroy documents whenever you wish
    c. you destroy all documents after a certain number of years
    d. you archive documents and files as soon as they are no longer needed.

EXAMINATION QUESTIONS

1. An aperture card is used in connection with ....

2. .... filing is the method whereby correspondence is classified according to the country, town, etc.

3. An office processes .... for future reference.

4. For security and fire protection purposes, files are usually stored in a/an ....

   (Pitman Office Procedures Level 1 1998 Pt 1A)

5. State THREE ways in which microfilm documents can be stored.
   a. ....
   b. ....
   c. ....

   (Pitman Office Procedures Level 1 1998 Pt 1B)

6. a. Describe briefly a vertical filing cabinet. State one advantage and one disadvantage of a vertical filing cabinet.
   b. Describe briefly a lateral filing cabinet. State one advantage and one disadvantage of a lateral filing cabinet.

c. Write a memo to your office manager stating why you need a special storage method for very large drawings, maps, etc., and state one method that is available.

(Pitman Office Procedures Level 1 1998 Pt 2B)

7. The .... method of filing is capable of indefinite expansion.

8. The filing system that reminds you to pass a file to your manager on the right date is called ....

9. Paperless office filing systems include electronic, computerised and ....

(Pitman Office Procedures Level 1 1999 Pt 1A)

10. Re-arrange the following names in the correct order for alphabetical indexing: The Smith Hotel, J Smith, St Smith's Hospital.
    a. ....
    b. ....
    c. ....

11. Give THREE advantages of numerical filing.
    a. ....
    b. ....
    c. ....

(Pitman Office Procedures Level 1 1999 Pt 1B)

12. State the problems that can arise if a firm's filing system does not have a retention policy.

(Pitman Office Procedures Level 1 1999 Pt 2A)

13. a. State how the geographical and subject filing classification systems work, giving an example for each, and name the type of organisation/department that might use each system.
    b. i. Explain a file retention policy.
       ii. What should be taken into account when deciding on such a policy?
    c. In connection with filing, when would you use:
       i. a cross-reference card
       ii. an 'Absent' card?

(Pitman Office Procedures Level 2 1998 Pt 2)

14. Prepare a list of rules that should be followed to ensure that files in a centralised filing section are kept safe and tidy, and that the process of filing is efficient and not time-consuming. Give a reason for each rule. (This question does *not* relate to classification systems.)

(Pitman Office Procedures Level 2 1998 Pt 2)

CHAPTER 8

MAILING

> **OBJECTIVES** When you have studied this chapter you should have acquired the knowledge and understanding to be able to:
>
> 1. explain and carry out the procedures for dealing with incoming and outgoing mail
> 2. maintain relevant records for incoming and outgoing mail
> 3. deal with special types of mail to ensure confidentiality and security of contents
> 4. carry out the procedure for dealing with classified documents
> 5. briefly explain the machines that can be used in the mail-handling processes
> 6. wrap parcels neatly and securely
> 7. explain the principles on which a mail room is arranged.

The process of mailing is carried out in various ways in different organisations. Larger organisations have a mail room (see Chapter 1, page 14). In smaller organisations mail may be opened in and despatched from a general office. In other organisations the mail addressed to a particular person or department is sent to the appropriate office unopened.

In this chapter we shall discuss the procedures for dealing with incoming and outgoing mail, regardless of whether this is done in an individual office, a department or a mail room.

INCOMING MAIL

Incoming mail may be delivered to the organisation or it may be collected from a Post Office box. Special delivery, registered and recorded mail has to be signed for and should be dealt with separately from normal mail. The stages of opening the mail are explained below.

1. **Face the envelopes**, i.e. turn them so that the address can be read, and check that each envelope is addressed to the organisation. At the same time sort into piles according to size and place envelopes marked 'personal', 'private' and 'confidential', and envelopes not addressed to the organisation in separate piles.
2. **'Tap' the envelopes** at their bottom edge so that the contents drop out of the way of the paper opener (knife or machine).
3. **Opening envelopes manually** – turn the stacks upside down, take a paper knife (see Fig. 8.1) and slit each envelope, placing them in fresh piles.

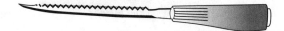

Fig. 8.1 Letter opener (paper knife) with straight edge for letter and saw edge for parcels.

4. **Opening envelopes mechanically** – place a stack of envelopes on a letter-opening machine (see Fig. 8.2). Each envelope passes through the machine, the cutter taking a fractional slice off the top of the envelope.

Fig. 8.2 Electric letter opener.

5. Take each envelope and **remove the contents**. Check that the inside address on the document is your organisation's and that enclosures are with the document if they should be. If they are not, write a note to that effect on the letter. Attach the enclosures if not already attached. Put aside the empty envelopes.
6. **Date stamp** each main document, e.g. letter, preferably under the date of the document. Date stamps are available in various sizes and are either

self-inking or inked by placing the face on an ink pad. Self-inking stamps, which use an ink cartridge, are quicker and cleaner to use. The day, month and year are changed by rotating wheels on the machine. Fig. 8.3a shows a standard self-inking date stamp; the date can be incorporated with some other information (see Fig. 8.3b).

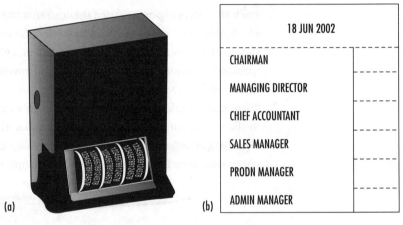

Fig. 8.3 (a) Self-inking date stamp; (b) Combined date stamp and distribution list.

7. If an **incoming mail register** is kept (either as a book or on computer) enter details of each document received. A register is useful to check to whom a document was sent if it cannot be found later. If the register is rarely used for reference it is probably not worth maintaining it as this is a time-consuming task. Fig. 8.4 shows a page of a typical incoming mail register.

Date received	Date of letter	Sender	Subject	Sent to	File no.	Remarks
21.5.02	17.5.02	JUKES Builders Ltd	Extension	Co. Secretary	BLDG/101	
	16.5.02	Ministry of Labour	Job creation	Personnel	TRG/6	
	17.5.02	Joan Idell	Application	Personnel	REC/17	

Fig. 8.4 Incoming mail register.

8. Some or all items of incoming mail may have to be **attached to the appropriate file.** The file identification should appear on the document but, often, the writer omits to include it. The subject of the document should indicate the appropriate file. Attach the document to the outside of the front cover.
9. **Identify who should deal with the document.** This will be the person to whom the document is addressed or the department that deals with the subject of the document, e.g. the sales department would deal with an enquiry for goods, the accounts department with a query on an account.
10. If staff collect their mail from the mail room, **place each document in the appropriate tray or pigeon-hole.** Personal, private and confidential mail should not be opened. If an unmarked envelope is opened and the document is marked, e.g. 'confidential', insert it and the envelope into another envelope, seal it, mark it 'confidential' and write the addressee's name on the envelope. If mail is delivered by a messenger, sort it into piles for each destination. The messenger will then put it in the delivery trolley in the sequence of the mail round.
11. In larger organisations the **mail may be delivered** to an assistant in each department. The mail will be sorted there for distribution to staff.
12. **Check the empty envelopes** to ensure that no piece of paper has been left inside. They can then be recycled or destroyed.
13. **Mail incorrectly delivered** should be reposted. If the envelope is correctly addressed but the inside address on the document is that of another organisation, telephone the sender and ask what they would like done, i.e. sent on to the addressee or returned to the sender.
14. **Circulation slips** (see Fig. 8.5) are attached to documents that should be seen by several people. As the item is passed from one person to another the list is initialled and eventually the document is directed to the person who will file it. Magazines may be sent to the library where the librarian will attach an appropriate circulation slip. The last person on the list will send the magazine back to the library. Circulation lists can be obtained as rubber stamps.
15. An **action slip** (see Fig. 8.6a) or **routing slip** (see Fig. 8.6b) is used to indicate what the person receiving the document has to do. It is usually used by a manager sending the document to a member of staff.
16. **Special delivery, registered and recorded mail** should not be opened if it is marked 'personal', 'private' or 'confidential'. It should, however, be entered in the incoming mail register kept specially for documents that are signed for on receipt from the Post Office. Details to be recorded include:

- the number of the special delivery/registered/recorded sticker on the envelope

CIRCULATION	
FROM Registry	DATE 10.5.02
SUBJECT Production Report	
	INITIALS
Personnel Officer	mm
Company Secretary	JP
Chief Accountant	....
Sales Manager	....
Chief R & D	....
PLEASE RETURN TO	FILE

Fig. 8.5 Circulation slip.

ACTION SLIP	
TO CTO	FROM Cashier
SUBJECT Travel Claim	DATE 10.6.02
Please let me have a cheque for this claim a.s.a.p. *D.A.*	

ROUTING SLIP			
TO John Gains			
FOR APPROVAL		NOTE AND RETURN	✓
FOR INFORMATION		NOTE AND RETAIN	
FOR SIGNATURE		FOR TYPING	
FOR COMMENT		FOR RUNNING OFF	
FOR REVISION			
DATE 27.6.02		FROM Gina Marks	

(a) (b)

Fig. 8.6 (a) Action slip; (b) Routing slip.

- the name of the addressee
- if the envelope is opened in the mail room, details as in a normal incoming mail register.

The envelopes should be retained with the documents. When the documents are delivered to the appropriate person or people, a signature should be obtained.

17. All **financial documents** are normally sent to the accounts department.
18. **Cash and cheques** received must be recorded in a remittance book and checked by the mail room supervisor or a colleague, before being sent to the cash office. Details of each cheque – date, cheque number, amount and name of drawer (see page 318) – must be entered in the register.
19. **Faxes and telexes** (see Chapter 5, pages 134–5) may be received by individual staff in their offices. In some organisations there may be a central fax and/or telex machine, sometimes located with the telephone switchboard. Each fax message may be photocopied and a copy kept in a chronological file (see Chapter 7), or details of the fax may be handwritten in a register, or entered on computer. The person to whom the fax/telex is addressed would be telephoned or e-mailed to inform them that a fax is awaiting collection. This would be done only for urgent items if there is a messenger who collects and delivers faxes on the mail round.
20. **Mail delivered by courier** may have to be signed for. Couriers often deliver to reception or a 'front desk'. This mail should be sent to the mail room, department or individual as quickly as possible.

ACTIVITY 8.1 Rule up a page of an incoming mail register, as shown in Fig. 8.4. Then enter the following letters received today. (You will need a calendar to identify the dates given on the letters.) In the fifth column write the name of the department to which you would send the document.

- Letter from John Abraham, dated Friday last week, complaining about the poor quality of a product.
- Invoice from Frederick Lara & Company for consultancy services.
- Letter from Miss Candida Thompson, dated Thursday last week, asking if there are any vacancies.
- Letter from Mrs Celeste Franks, dated Friday last week, asking for details of a product.
- A catalogue from Caribbean Manufacturing Limited.

(continued)

> **ACTIVITY 8.1**
> *(continued)*
>
> - Statement of account, dated Wednesday last week, from Gerald Barker, Accountant.
> - Letter dated last Thursday, with brochure from Ms Tina Forde, offering training services.
> - Letter dated last Tuesday from J Tippett & Son, enclosing samples.

OUTGOING MAIL

When a document has been checked and signed, it can be prepared for mailing.

MANUAL PROCESSING

In small offices mail is usually processed manually as explained below.

1. If an outgoing mail register (see Fig. 8.7) is maintained, each document to be sent out must be entered.

Date	Document no./ref.	Addressee	Subject	Date reply requested
13.5	027	Peter Jenkins ABC	Copier – infn.	16.5
	028	Computer Networks	Service charges	Immediate
	029	Computer Services Ltd	Photographs	17.5

Fig. 8.7 Outgoing mail register.

2. Select an appropriate size of envelope for the document. This is likely to be a C4, C5 and DL (or C6) envelope (see Table 6.3). Fig. 8.8 shows the folding of documents to fit the various sizes. The envelope must be big enough to take the document and enclosures without too much folding.
3. Address the envelope, or a label for a larger envelope.
4. Secure the enclosures to the document if appropriate, fold and insert in the envelope, checking that the addressee on the letter and the envelope are the same and that any special marks, e.g. 'Personal', have been shown above the address on the envelope.
5. Before sealing the envelope check that everything is enclosed.
6. Check the method by which documents are to be sent. The various services are explained on page 243.

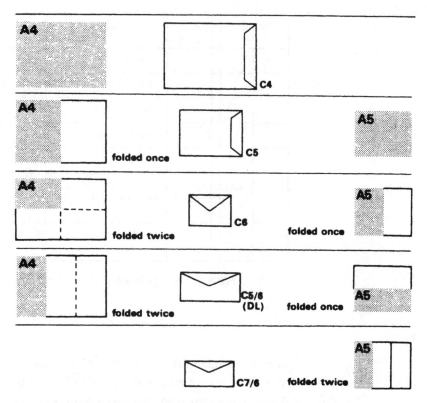

Fig. 8.8 Folding paper to fit international envelope sizes.

7. If the Post Office postal service is to be used, weigh the envelope and note the weight in grams.
8. Refer to the appropriate Post Office leaflet/booklet to find out the cost of sending within the country, or overseas (airmail or surface mail).
9. Attach the appropriate stamps, which may be gummed or self-adhesive. In a small office that does not have a large volume of mail, postage stamps are used. Various denominations of stamps are kept in a book containing dividers for the different values of stamps.
10. Enter the item in the outgoing postage book. A specimen page of a postage book is shown in Fig. 8.9. You will see that things such as invoices are shown as one item.

CLASSIFIED DOCUMENTS

Documents marked 'top secret', 'secret', 'private and confidential', 'confidential', 'for your eyes only', 'staff in confidence', etc. are known as **classified.** This means that the documents may be opened and seen by

Received $		Date 2002	Name	Address	Postage $	
50	00	10.6	Villiers	Liverpool, UK	5	80
			Schmidt	Bonn, Germany	6	40
		11.6	Circulars (20)		6	00
			Invoices (10)		3	00

Fig. 8.9 Postage book with individual and block entries.

certain named individuals or categories of staff, e.g. senior managers only. Top secret and secret documents are treated differently from ordinary mail. They are inserted in an envelope marked 'top secret' or 'secret', and sealed. This envelope is then placed in another envelope, identically addressed but not marked in any special way. The envelope may be opened in the mail room of the addressee but the inside envelope is not opened. It is delivered to the appropriate individual and a signature should be obtained for its receipt.

Envelopes marked with other classifications are treated as confidential and are delivered unopened to the individual addressee.

MACHINE PROCESSING

Where a large volume of magazines, circulars and standard letters is mailed regularly there are machines to deal with this efficiently. Most of the procedures explained for manual handling can be carried out by machine. These include:

- label printing
- collating
- folding
- inserting into envelopes

- envelope sealing
- franking of envelopes with the required value of postage.

Individual machines for each procedure can be combined to enable the whole process, from collating to sealing, to be done in one operation. Such a machine is shown in Fig. 8.10. The processes are explained below.

Fig. 8.10 Mailing machine with integrated modules, which collate, fold, add inserts such as coupons, insert into envelopes and seal them.

Label printing

Labels are now commonly produced electronically, but in offices where this facility is not available an addressing machine is used. 'Plates' are prepared with the name, address and possibly customer code number of the addressees. 'Stencil' type plates must be prepared on a typewriter or printer that works on the 'impact' principle (see page 166). The plates are stacked in the machine and the envelopes, cards or labels to be printed are placed in the feedtray. When the 'print' lever is depressed, the address from the first stencil is printed on the first envelope, which is passed to its own receiving tray, and the second plate and second envelope move into position. A 'skip' lever enables some plates to pass through without printing if this is required.

The frame of the stencil may be used for recording additional information. The plates can then form a card index, which can be notched, punched or flagged for reference.

Collating

When a document consists of several pages, they have to be collated. Collating is the process of placing the pages in the correct sequence with each page the right way up. It is common for a document of more than one page to be photocopied and collated by the copier (see Chapter 6, page 169). However, there may be several collated documents to be enclosed. These also have to be collated, usually manually, so that a complete set is sent to each individual.

Folding

In Fig. 8.8 we saw how paper can be folded to fit different sizes of envelope. This folding can be done on a machine, which is set to the size and number of folds required. The machines are adjustable for different sizes of paper and various folds. Machines can process up to 20 000 items an hour.

Inserting

The documents and envelopes of the correct size are fed into the machine, the documents being inserted into the envelopes as they are folded. In addition to inserting the same documents in all envelopes, some machines can be programmed to select additional inserts to specific addressees.

Sealing

The filled envelopes are passed between rollers, which moisten the gummed flap, fold it over and squeeze it to ensure that it sticks. Self-adhesive envelopes are now more commonly used in place of gummed envelopes.

Franking

All mail can be franked. Letters are passed through a machine that prints an impression denoting the amount of postage pre-paid. The impression also indicates the place and date (but not the time) of posting (see Fig. 8.11). Some users include a logo or an advertisement in the impression. This must be printed on the left-hand side of the cover, quite separate from the postage frank and postmark.

As it is not possible to frank a packet or parcel, an adhesive label is franked with the correct amount of postage and affixed to the package.

Postage meter franking machines (see Fig. 8.12) can be hired or purchased from the manufacturers or their agents by private people or

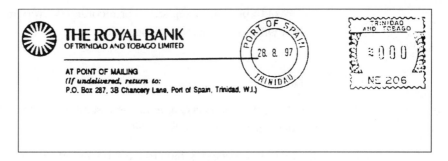

Fig. 8.11 Franked envelope showing logo, postage and postmark.

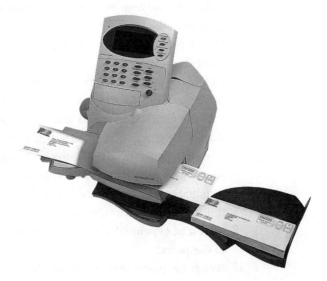

Fig. 8.12 Franking machine with sealing and stacking facilities.

business firms. A licence has to be obtained from the Postmaster-General. The licensee makes an advance payment, which is registered on the franking machine meter by the Post Office; the machine is then sealed. As letters are franked the machine indicates how much of the advance payment of 'credit' has been used (the ascending register). Some machines also show how much credit remains unused (the descending register).

The correspondence franked by the machine must be faced, securely tied in bundles (certain separations are required) and handed in at a specified Post Office. Letters may not be posted at any other Post Office.

When the credit is exhausted or reaches a certain minimum level a further advance payment must be made. This may be done at a Post Office, by credit card or electronically by telephone.

Mail to be sent by registered or recorded delivery must be taken to the Post Office (see Chapter 9, page 260).

PARCELS

Wrapping parcels can be time-consuming but if you follow a few basic rules, a lot of time can be saved.

1. Make a space in which to work on a work surface.
2. Get together wrapping paper, string and/or parcel tape, ready-addressed labels for addressee and sender, scissors.
3. Make sure the item to be wrapped is clearly identified with the name and address of the sender *before* it is wrapped.
4. Ensure you use a large enough piece of wrapping paper. If it is too big, cut it down to size.
5. Ensure the edges of the paper overlap and hold them together with a small piece of adhesive tape.
6. Fold the paper at each end in an envelope-flap shape, pull the flap up the side of the parcel firmly and seal at the top.
7. If using parcel tape, strip across from one of the flap sides across the top and down the other flap side. It is advisable to strip the tape down the diagonals of the flap on each side.
8. If using string make sure that it is pulled tightly and knotted firmly.
9. Stick a label printed with the addressee's name and address on the front of the parcel.
10. Weigh the parcel and determine the necessary postage, including the cost of any special service such as recorded delivery.
11. Take the required value of stamps from the stamp book or print a franked mail label.
12. Stick the stamps or a franked mail label at the top right-hand corner of the front of the parcel.
13. Stick a sender's address label on the back of the parcel.
14. Complete any special forms, e.g. customs declaration.

INTERNAL MAIL

Mail from one office or department to another within the building is usually sent without an envelope unless it is classified. Some organisations have more than one building, with deliveries of mail between them at regular times. The mail room usually has a large envelope for each building and places mail as it arrives in the appropriate envelope for each building.

Mail that needs to be in an envelope, e.g. because there are several documents together, should be placed in an envelope. There are specially printed internal envelopes that can be passed from one person to another. An example of an internal envelope is shown in Fig. 8.13.

```
FOR INTERNAL USE ONLY
Please deliver to:
```

~~Cynthia Williams~~	~~Personnel Dept~~
~~Jean Bartholomew~~	~~Marketing Dept~~
~~Robert James~~	~~Accounts Dept~~
~~John Chang~~	~~Sales Dept~~
James Courtney	Purchase Office

Fig. 8.13 Internal envelope.

METHODS OF MAILING

There are various methods of sending mail. Post Office postal services have been mentioned. Full details of these services are explained in Chapter 9. Other methods include fax, electronic mail and couriers. (Fax and e-mail are explained in Chapter 5.)

There are local, national and international couriers. The normal procedure is for the organisation to arrange for an envelope, package or parcel to be collected and delivered to an addressee. Many companies have regular collections at a certain time or times each day. A form has to be completed and the packages are signed for by the collector, usually either a motorcyclist or van driver.

National couriers have a variety of services, e.g. same-day, overnight, next-day and 48-hour delivery. Shorter delivery times are the most expensive. International couriers work in the same way as national couriers. They will guarantee next-day delivery to some countries to which there are several flights daily. Arrangements can be made for highly secret or extremely valuable goods to be taken by a courier personally to their destination.

THE MAIL ROOM

In an organisation where a large volume of incoming/outgoing mail is dealt with, it is usual to have a mail room where the processing is done.

The Post Office and couriers deliver and collect mail to and from the mail room entrance. Huge volumes of mail, such as are normal in, for example, mail-order companies, are delivered in large canvas sacks.

The layout of the mail room is important to ensure that there is no interruption to the flow of the procedures. It is designed as a production line with mail coming in at the entrance and moving smoothly to where the mail is either collected by staff or taken by messenger for delivery to the

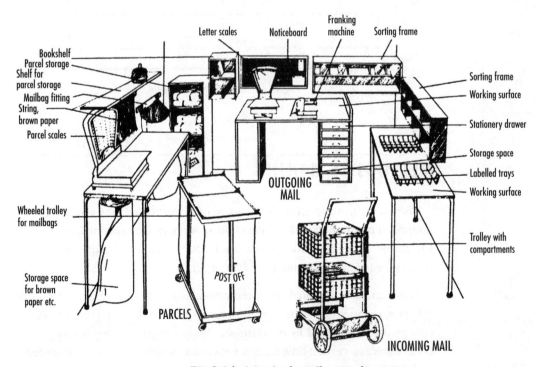

Fig. 8.14 A typical mail room layout.

offices. Similarly, outgoing mail must flow smoothly from the point where it is received from the offices to the mail room exit where it will be collected. A specimen layout of a mail room is shown in Fig. 8.14. It will be seen that special furniture and fittings are required in order to deal with mail quickly and efficiently.

The procedures that have been explained are carried out by different people in various organisations. There is no one right system of processing mail. It is important, however, that whoever deals with mail at any stage follows correct procedures.

PRACTICE QUESTIONS

1. A newly recruited junior clerk is to start work in your office in a week's time. One of her duties will be to open and distribute the mail. You will explain to her what she has to do and how she will do it as part of her induction. You decide to provide her with an *aide-mémoire* so that she does not have to make a lot of notes.

    Prepare a list of the steps to take in opening and distributing the mail. There is a letter-opening machine and a messenger distributes the mail.

2. How would you deal with a letter which indicates an enclosure although there is no enclosure in the envelope?

3. How would you deal with a letter addressed to your organisation but on opening the envelope you find the letter is addressed to another organisation?

4. What is the procedure for dealing with cash and cheques received in the mail?

5. *a.* What headings are usually found in an incoming mail register?
   b. What is the purpose of keeping an incoming mail register?

6. Write a procedure for dealing with outgoing mail.

7. How do you deal with outgoing mail marked 'top secret' or 'secret'?

8. Describe the steps you would take in wrapping and despatching a parcel from the office.

9. *a.* In an organisation where large amounts of mail are received and despatched daily, what machines could be installed?
   b. What would be the benefits of installing machines?

10. What sources of reference would you need in a mail room for finding out services available for sending mail?

SHORT ANSWER QUESTIONS

1. Before opening letters they should be .... and ....

2. Cash and cheques received must be entered in a ....

3. The most common sizes of envelope used for sending mail are ...., ... and ....

4. Internal mail is normally sent .... unless it is confidential.

5. Documents marked 'secret' 'private and confidential', etc. are known as ....

Choose the most appropriate ending for each of the following sentences.

6. An incoming mail register is kept:
   a. to know how many letters are received each day
   b. to ensure that all letters are acknowledged
   c. to check in the future that a missing letter has been received
   d. to identify the frequency of letters from particular people.

7. Parcels cannot be put through a franking machine. Instead:
   a. they should be taken to the post office
   b. they should be sent by courier
   c. postage stamps are used
   d. a label is put through the franking machine and stuck on to them.

8. The first thing to do when wrapping a parcel is to:
   a. gather the items needed
   b. prepare labels
   c. make space on a work surface
   d. check the size of paper needed.

EXAMINATION QUESTIONS

1. A franking machine can be used to print envelopes with the name and address of the .... as well as the postage paid.

   (Pitman Office Procedures Level 1 1998 Pt 1A)

2. Give THREE rules for efficient handling of outgoing mail.

a. ....

b. ....

c. ....

(Pitman Office Procedures Level 1 1998 Pt 1B)

3. A .... machine will ensure that documents fit neatly into an envelope.

4. A paper knife is used in the mail room to ....

(Pitman Office Procedures Level 1 1999 Pt 1A)

5. State THREE checks made daily or weekly on a franking machine.

a. ....

b. ....

c. ....

(Pitman Office Procedures Level 1 1999 Pt 1B)

CHAPTER 9

POST OFFICE SERVICES

> **OBJECTIVES** When you have studied this chapter you should have acquired the knowledge and understanding to be able to:
>
> 1. explain the importance of addressing mail correctly
> 2. identify the sizes of envelopes recommended by the postal authorities
> 3. find the correct rates of postage for the various types of mail and special services
> 4. explain the services available for receiving mail
> 5. explain the services available for speed, security and tracking of mail
> 6. identify appropriate services available specifically for businesses
> 7. briefly explain the non-postal services available at Post Offices
> 8. recognise when service standards are not achieved, and contact the appropriate section/department to complain or ask for advice.

In Chapter 8 we discussed the procedures for dealing with incoming and outgoing mail. The possible methods of transmitting mail were explained. In this chapter we shall explain the postal services available. We shall also explain additional services offered by the Post Office.

Staff who are responsible for despatching mail should have a good knowledge of postal regulations and know where to find information on the services available. Post Offices* in the Caribbean are undergoing reform and improvements are being introduced; it is essential to check frequently to find out what new services there are that might be useful to your organisation.

THE SEVEN STAGES OF THE POSTAL COLLECTION AND DELIVERY SERVICE

It is helpful to know how the postal service is operated because it indicates the need for following regulations carefully. There are seven stages in the processing of mail, from the point where it is posted to the point of delivery.

1. **Collection** – Letters and small packets are collected by Post Office staff from posting boxes placed at roadsides, on Post Office compounds and at other strategic locations, and from individual companies.
2. **Segregation** – After collection, mail is taken to a Post Office sorting office where the items are separated according to size and destination, e.g. local and foreign addresses.
3. **Cancellation** – The next stage is the cancellation of the postage stamp. This is done either manually with a date stamp or by passing the letter through a stamp-cancelling machine.
4. **Sorting** – Mail is then sorted according to destination, tied into bundles and containerised ready for despatch.
5. **Despatch** – Containers of mail labelled with their destinations are despatched to their respective destinations. Letters addressed to local destinations are forwarded to the Post Office nearest to their addresses. Overseas letters are despatched either to the airport or sea port, depending on whether they are to be sent by air or sea.
6. **Sorting for delivery** – Upon arrival at the office of delivery, mail is sorted into delivery districts. Each district may be a specific area for one postman. Next the mail is sub-sorted into streets and order of houses/buildings in each street. The mail is then in the correct sequence for the postman or woman to deliver to each address as they follow the round.

---

*The term Post Office is used to represent the national organisation in each territory that provides postal services and, in some cases, other services. A list of postal authorities is given in Table 9.1.

7. **Delivery** – Each item of mail is delivered to its address. It may be handed to the addressee or anyone residing at the address, put into a post box on the premises of the addressee or placed in a private letter box or bag. In the case of a registered letter, proof of identity may be required, as well as a signed acquittance (or receipt).

ADDRESSING FORMAT

The Post Office requires mail to be addressed in a specific format. The key points are listed below.

1. Start the first line about one-third of the way down from the top of the envelope, depending on the length of the address.
2. Show the name of the town, with an initial capital for an inland address, in block capitals for overseas, and the postcode in block capitals.
3. Do not use words such as 'Local', 'By', or 'Near' in the address.
4. Write the names of the town or parish in full, unless there is a recognised abbreviation (e.g. 'POS', for Port-of-Spain). Abbreviations are discouraged in Jamaica.
5. Leave a space between each line of type.
6. Put the correct postage stamp in the top right-hand corner of the envelope.

The address should contain:

- the name of the addressee
- the name of the house or block of offices, if any
- the number of the house/office and name of the avenue/road/street, etc.
- the name of the village, suburb or district, if any
- the name of the town (see 2 above) followed by the correct postal district number, if any
- the name of the parish, where appropriate
- the postcode/zipcode, if any, in BLOCK CAPITALS.

A correctly addressed envelope is shown in Fig. 9.1.

The address may include a Post Office box or private bag number, which takes the place of the name or number of the house/office, and the name of the road. For example:

Mrs Jane Fisher
PO Box 168
KINGSTON 5
JAMAICA

Mr Peter Le Maitre
Private Bag 243
FORT DE FRANCE
GUADELOUPE

```
┌─────────────────────────────────────────┐
│                                         │
│                                         │
│          Miss K White                   │
│          100 Keate Street               │
│          PORT-OF-SPAIN                  │
│                                         │
│                                         │
└─────────────────────────────────────────┘
```

Fig. 9.1 Correctly addressed envelope.

POSTCODES/ZIPCODES

Postcodes and zipcodes are not used in the Caribbean except in Kingston, Jamaica. They are used in many countries including the USA and most European countries. In countries where mail is sorted electronically it is very important to include the postcode/zipcode in the address. If there is no code the letter/package is put aside and sorted manually, causing delays in delivery.

- On an overseas letter the postcode precedes the name of the country, which should be in BLOCK CAPITALs.
- The postcode should appear on a line by itself but, if it is necessary to restrict the number of lines, the town or county/state/region/parish/district name may be on the same line. In this case leave a space of at least two characters (and preferably six), between the postcode and preceding name.
- Never underline the postcode or join the characters.
- Do not use full stops or any other punctuation marks within or at the end of the postcode. For example:

Miss K White	Mr James T Robson
100 South Street	158 Twenty-second Street
PURLEY	CHICAGO
Surrey CR2 4TJ	Illinois 60602
ENGLAND	UNITED STATES OF AMERICA

When letters are sorted electronically the code is keyed in on the envelope in magnetic ink. The letter is then passed to a machine called a magnetic ink reader. The code is 'read' and the letter moves by conveyor belt to the correct pigeon-hole, from which it is collected for delivery.

RECOMMENDED ENVELOPES AND CARDS

The Post Office asks all its customers to post their mail, whenever possible, in envelopes within a preferred range of sizes. The sizes have been recommended by postal administrations worldwide. Their use enables electronic sorting machines to deal with more mail, more quickly, so providing a better service to customers and keeping costs down.

Postcards are treated as letters, which means they should be of the same standard sizes as envelopes. The materials for postcards should not:

- be more than 250 and not less than 25 micrometres (0.01 in) thick
- exceed 13.97 cm (5½ in) in length by 10.48 cm (4⅛ in) in width
- be less than 13.02 cm (5⅛ in) long by 8.89 cm (3½ in) wide.

The mail-recommended sizes of envelope are:

- maximum 240 mm (9½ in) in length and 165 mm (6½ in) in width
- minimum 140 mm (5½ in) in length and 90 mm (3½ in) in width.

The longer side of the envelope should be at least 1.4 times the length of the short side. Envelope sizes C5, C6 and DL (see Table 6.3) fall within these dimensions.

Sometimes it is necessary to use bigger/smaller envelopes. The Post Office can handle mail of other sizes provided it is:

- minimum 150 × 90 mm (6 × 3½ in)
- maximum 610 × 460 mm (24 × 18 in).

Roll-shaped packets should be a maximum of 900 mm (35½ in) in length. The total length of the roll plus twice the diameter should not exceed 1040 mm (41 in).

Black printing on white background is ideal. Envelopes in other colours are acceptable provided that the printing is darker than the background. Red should not be used, except with a light-coloured panel or label. Machines read red as black so cannot differentiate between the background and the printed or written address.

Window envelopes should have a transparent oblong area with the longer side parallel to the longer side of the envelope, and this should be:

- a minimum of 38 mm (1½ in) from the top of the envelope
- a minimum of 15 mm (⅝ in) from the left- and right-hand edges
- a maximum of 60 mm (2⅜ in) from the bottom edge of the envelope if the window is within 115 mm (4½ in) of the right-hand edge of the envelope.

POSTAGE RATES

Postage rates change from time to time so you must find out from a Post Office the rates in force for various types of mail when a change takes place. There are two main categories of mail: **inland** and **overseas.** Within these categories there are letters, postcards, small packets, printed papers, literature for the blind, newspapers and parcels.

Caribbean territories are members of the Universal Postal Union, which sets the regulations and classifications for international mail.

INLAND MAIL

There can be multiple classes of mail for items sent to a destination within a territory. In Jamaica, first class is reserved for letters and postcards while other types of mail are sent second class. In Trinidad and Tobago, there is only one class of mail, which has a next-day delivery standard. TTPost now charges by **size** rather than by weight. Letters may be transmitted by surface or air depending on the local transport networks. Parcels are sent by surface mail.

OVERSEAS MAIL

Letters and parcels may be sent surface mail, the postage rate depending on weight and destination. Trinidad and Tobago currently has only one category of airmail with no second class option. A slower surface Air Lift service was introduced in 2000.

Items being sent by airmail should have an airmail label affixed in the top left-hand corner of the envelope. Alternatively, specially printed airmail envelopes with a printed edging can be bought (see Fig. 9.2). Details of

Fig. 9.2 Airmail envelope.

postage rates, weight and size restrictions, and other facilities available can be obtained at any Post Office.

Aerogrammes/airletters and air parcels

Airletters can be bought at any Post Office and may be sent to any address in the world. The cost includes postage. **Air parcels** may be sent to many parts of the world. The maximum weight is 20 kg (44 lbs).

Customs declaration forms

A **customs declaration form** (see Fig. 9.3) has to be completed for any article to be sent overseas. In some cases a despatch note is also needed. The customs declaration form is used for parcels being sent to Great Britain, the USA, Canada and Commonwealth countries (see Appendix 3 Part 2). A slightly different form is used for parcels to be sent to other destinations. The duty payable in the country of destination is paid by the addressee.

The Post Office competes for postal delivery with local and international couriers (see Chapter 8), and for international mail with services such as Skybox.

PROHIBITED GOODS

There are certain articles that may not be sent by post. These include dangerous items such as chemicals and explosive materials, and illegal articles such as guns and drugs.

(a)

BEFORE COMPLETING THIS DECLARATION, READ INSTRUCTIONS ON BACK CAREFULLY

(Postal administration)

CUSTOMS DECLARATION

CN 23
(old C 2/CP 3)

From — Name and address of sender

Sender's reference (if any)

No of item/parcel (bar code, if any)

To — Name and address of addressee, including country of destination

The item/parcel may be opened officially

List of contents (and number of articles)	Country of origin of goods	Tariff No (if known)	Net weight	Value (Customs)

☐ Commercial sample ☐ Documents ☐ Gift.

Observations

Number of certificates and invoices

Office of origin/Date of posting

Total gross weight

I certify that the particulars given in this customs declaration are correct and that this item does not contain any dangerous article prohibited by postal regulations

Date and sender's signature

(b)

CN 23 (Back)

Instructions

The customs declaration should be completed in French or in a language which is accepted in the country of destination

To clear your item the Customs in the country of destination need to know what the contents are. You must therefore complete your declaration fully, accurately and legibly, otherwise delay and inconvenience may be caused for the addressee. Moreover, a false, misleading or incomplete declaration may lead, for instance, to the seizure of the package

It is also your responsibility to inquire into import and export regulations (prohibitions, make-up, etc) and to find out what documents, if any (certificate of origin, health certificate, invoices, etc) are required in the country of destination and to attach them to this form

Box "From (Name and address of sender)"	Indicate the sender's name and address
Box "To (Name and address of addressee, including country of destination)"	Indicate the addressee's full name and address, including the country of destination
Boxes "Commercial sample", "Documents", "Gift"	Make an "x" in the appropriate box. The insertion of a cross in this space does not relieve you of the obligation of completing the declaration in detail; nor does it necessarily imply that the goods will be admitted free of duty in the country of destination: – "commercial sample" means: articles considered by Customs as being of negligible value, which are merely used in pursuit of orders for merchandise of the kind they represent; – "documents" means: any medium intended to contain and actually containing information which, by virtue of its quantity or nature, is considered by Customs as being of negligible value
Box "List of contents (and number of articles)"	Indicate separately different kinds of goods and their number. General terms, such as "foodstuffs", "samples", "spare parts", etc, are not permitted
Box "Country of origin of goods"	Indicate the name of the country of origin for each kind of goods
Box "Tariff No (if known)"	If known, state customs tariff number in the country of destination
Box "Net weight"	State net weight of each kind of goods
Box "Value (Customs)"	State the value of each kind of goods separately, indicating the monetary unit used
Box "Date and sender's signature"	Your signature on the front is your pledge that the item does not contain any dangerous article prohibited by postal regulations
Box "Observations"	Insert here any other relevant information (eg "returned goods", "temporary admission")

G.P., TR./TO.—M 2675—25,000— /96

Fig. 9.3 Customs declaration form CN 23; (a) front (b) reverse.

ACTIVITY 9.1 Obtain the appropriate Post Office leaflets to determine the cost of postage of the following items of mail.

- Postcard to be sent airmail to an Eastern Caribbean island
- Letter weighing 35 grams to be sent recorded delivery and airmail to London
- Letter weighing 142 grams to be sent to an inland address
- Letter weighing 74 grams to be sent by the cheapest service to Puerto Rico
- Letter weighing 256 grams to be sent recorded delivery and airmail to an inland address
- Small packet weighing 268 grams to be sent airmail to Paris
- Small packet weighing 125 grams to be sent by registered airmail to Grenada
- Parcel weighing 2.3 kg to be sent to an inland address
- Parcel weighing 6.5 kg to be sent surface mail to Cape Town
- Parcel weighing 8.7 kg to be sent airmail to Bermuda

COLLECTION SERVICES

The Post Office collects mail from public post boxes, which are located outside Post Offices and at various other locations. Collection times are shown on the post boxes.

Some very large companies arrange to have their mail collected daily by TTPost between 0800 and 1200. Other organisations can pay a courier to collect their mail.

RECEIVING MAIL

There are four services available relating to receiving mail. These are:

- delivery to the addressee
- sorting into Post Office box or private bag for collection by addressee

- post restante
- redirection.

DELIVERY TO ADDRESSEE

Delivery of letters and packets is made by postal staff to residential areas and businesses that are reasonably accessible by road. Deliveries are once daily Monday to Friday. A card is delivered to an addressee to collect recorded delivery or registered letters/packages.

POST BOXES AND PRIVATE BAGS

Individuals and organisations may pay a fee to have a **box number** allocated for use as their address. All correspondence, except recorded and registered mail, is placed in a locked box, for which the renter holds a key, at selected Post Offices.

Private bags can be rented for an annual charge. The Post Office sorts mail into the bag ready for collection. The Post Office provides two bags and the renter provides the locks and keys, one of which is kept by the Post Office. Arrangements can be made for the private bag to be collected at a Post Office convenient for the addressee.

On payment of the annual fee applicable to the service required, the user may have his letters conveyed to and from the Post Office in a private bag either by an employee of the bag holder, or by a mail contractor or courier. With this service the advice list (see below) and the registered letters enumerated are enclosed.

Post box renters may call regularly at their Post Office for recorded and registered packages during office opening hours. Notification of a registered item for collection is sent to the addressee. In Jamaica the renter of a Post Office (PO) box or private bag can pay an additional annual fee to receive a serially numbered registered **advice list**. This gives particulars of the number and place of origin of each registered article received for them.

POSTE RESTANTE

Letters and packets may be addressed to any Post Office (except a town sub-office) to await collection by the addressee. The words 'Poste restante' or 'To be called for' must be written clearly in the address (see Fig. 9.4).

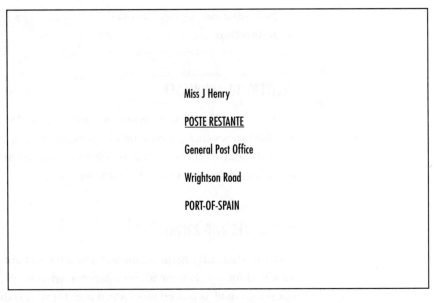

Fig. 9.4 Envelope addressed for poste restante.

The addressee will be asked to prove their identity when collecting the letters/packets. The service is used by travellers, but it must not be used in the same town for more than three months, after which time an application must be made to the General Post Office. No one with a permanent postal address can take advantage of this service.

Correspondence is held for collection at all offices from which there are no house-to-house deliveries. Postal items must be collected within certain time limits, which are:

- one calendar month if they originate in the island
- two calendar months if they originate from abroad
- three calendar months if addressed to ships.

REDIRECTION

When people move house, they may have their mail, addressed to them at their original private or office address, delivered to their new private address. They must have removed completely from the original address. The Post Office does not undertake to redirect mail from hotels, boarding houses, institutions, offices or private boxes.

The conditions under which redirection is allowed in Jamaica and Trinidad and Tobago are set out below.

Unless the sender has forbidden redirection by a note to that effect on the address side of the postal article, any member of the public may redirect any postal article from its original address to the same addressee at any other address in the island without payment of additional postage, provided that:

- the postal article is reposted not later than the day after delivery (Sundays and holidays excepted)
- prior to reposting it has not been tampered with in any way
- the name of the original addressee is not obscured if an adhesive label is used to indicate the new address.

Inland parcels can be redirected free of charge only if the addressee's new address is served by the same Post Office as the original address. Fresh postage is required if a parcel is redirected to an address in another town. Additional postage, representing the difference between the inland and the foreign rate of postage, must also be paid on all redirected postal articles involving an overseas address. Redirected overseas parcels and registered articles should be handed in at a Post Office counter and a **certificate of posting** obtained.

To avoid inconvenience to residents at a person's old address it is preferred that a printed notice of redirection, obtainable at any Post Office, should be completed and sent to the local delivery office serving the old address, or handed to the postman. This redirection service is free for three months. Thereafter a fee is charged for every three-month period.

GENERAL POSTAL SERVICES

There are various services, for which fees are charged, to enable the sender to have a quicker and/or more secure service.

EXPRESS DELIVERY

Both inland and overseas post may be sent by express delivery, for which a fee is paid in addition to the postage. The inland service can be used only to send to persons residing in certain delivery areas. The item will be delivered by special messenger immediately after it is received at the office of destination.

Overseas post can be accepted for express service at most branches of the Post Office for delivery to a number of selected foreign countries. The postage rate is charged according to the weight and destination of the item.

Incoming express mail comes to the General Post Office from all over the world for delivery throughout Trinidad and Tobago.

Express mail is a top-priority service provided by Post Offices worldwide. The fee paid includes money-back guarantee for non-delivery within the time stated, and a certain amount of compensation for damage or loss. It is necessary to check with the Post Office for precise details.

It should be borne in mind that the express mail service competes with international couriers such as DHL, Fedex, TNT, UPS, etc. (see page 263).

RECORDED DELIVERY (NOT AVAILABLE IN JAMAICA)

Any inland postal packet, except a parcel, can be sent by this service, which provides proof of posting and delivery.

Letters and packets for recorded delivery must be taken to a Post Office. A fee in addition to the postage is paid and includes an amount of TT$75 compensation in the event of damage or loss. The name of the addressee must be written on the recorded delivery receipt, and the gummed label at the bottom of the receipt must be detached and affixed to the left-hand corner of the envelope. The Post Office clerk date-stamps and initials the receipt, which should be kept by the person who posted the item. Recorded delivery packets must not contain bank notes, coins or jewellery. The addressee of a recorded delivery packet must sign a receipt.

REGISTRATION

All inland letters and parcels may be registered on payment of a registration fee in addition to the postage. Details of registration fees and compensation for loss or damage can be obtained from a Post Office.

Items to be registered must be clearly marked 'REGISTERED' and have blue lines drawn horizontally and vertically on both sides (see Fig. 9.5a).

All letters and parcels intended for registration must be handed to a Post Office clerk. A **certificate of registration** (see Fig. 9.5b), called a certificate of posting in Jamaica, must be obtained to prove that the registration fee has been paid.

A **notice of arrival** is delivered to the addressee, who can then collect the item from a named Post Office for registered articles during normal working hours. A receipt is obtained when the item is collected.

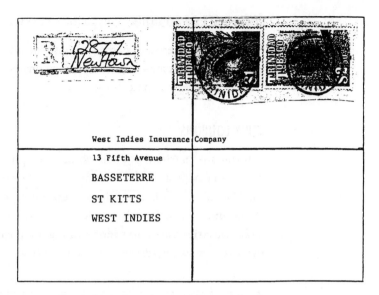

Fig. 9.5(a) Envelope addressed for registration.

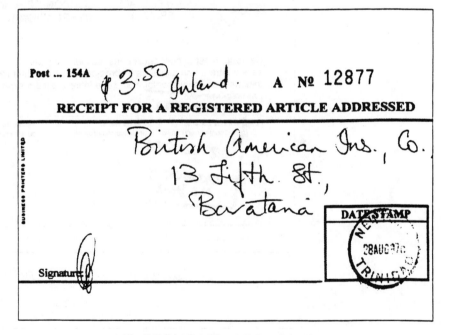

Fig. 9.5(b) Certificate of registration.

ADVICE OF DELIVERY

The sender of a recorded or registered article addressed to either an inland or overseas destination may at the time of posting obtain an 'advice of delivery' slip. The sender pre-pays stamps in addition to the normal postage and recorded delivery/registration fee.

CERTIFICATE OF POSTING

Senders of letters and parcels to both inland and overseas destinations can obtain certificates of posting free of charge. This service is available in Jamaica for overseas parcels only.

REPLY COUPONS

If you wish a friend or client abroad to reply to your letter without their having to pay postage you cannot send a stamped addressed envelope. You can instead buy an **international reply coupon** (see Fig. 9.6) from a Post Office and enclose it with your letter. These coupons may be exchanged in most countries for stamps representing the postage payable for a letter from that country to any territory in the Caribbean.

Fig. 9.6 International reply coupon.

BUSINESS POSTAL SERVICES

There is a number of services provided by the Post Office, primarily for use by businesses. These include:

- business reply
- bulk postage
- free post

- courier
- franked mail
- unaddressed mail.

BUSINESS REPLY SERVICE

Under this service business organisations may enclose in their letters, etc. an unstamped reply card, letter card or envelope enabling their customers to reply free of charge. The service is not available for overseas post.

Before using this service a licence must be obtained from the Post Office. The fee charged is less than the normal postage on each card or envelope returned by post to the licensee. The design of the card or envelope must conform to certain standards and a proof of the design must be approved by the Post Office before the cards or envelopes are printed.

FREEPOST

This service allows people to write or reply free of charge. The receiving organisation must apply for a freepost address. The address must include:

- the word 'freepost' and
- the name of the organisation, or
- the name of the competition, or
- any string of words referring to the promotion and
- the name of the city or town.

Organisations using this service pay the normal rate of postage depending on the size of each envelope or card received.

The TTPost 'Business Reply Paid and Freepost' leaflet gives full details of these services.

COURIER SERVICE

TTPost can provide a courier service to business and private addresses. Almost anything can be sent by courier, from letters to machine parts. The most important points about the service from the sender's point of view are:

- door-to-door collection and delivery
- nationwide delivery
- delivery up to three times a day

- traceability
- money-back guarantee
- signed acceptance of items
- convenience for both sender and addressee
- inter-branch satchels.

Articles can be sent in TrackPak red plastic envelopes with barcode stickers for quick, reliable tracking. Parcel tickets are used for items too big for a TrackPak envelope. Parcels must not be more than 1.5 m long, 25 kg weight and 0.125 m^3, i.e. the length $\times$ width $\times$ depth. TTPost's 'Couriers' leaflet gives full details of this service.

BULK POSTAGE

Many business organisations take advantage of the facility by which the postage on any postal packet may be pre-paid. This is particularly useful when a large number of packets must be despatched in one day. To use this service the sender must fulfil certain conditions. Postal packets should be tied in bundles before being handed in at the counter of the General Post Office. Letters and circulars must be faced (i.e. have the addresses facing up the same way round, and be tied up in bundles of 50). Bulky articles and newspapers must be tied in bundles of 10 and be handed in with a statement certifying that the articles all consist of the same category of correspondence, subject to the same postal charge.

FRANKED MAIL

Many businesses prefer to use a franking machine to print the postage on their outgoing mail. This avoids the need to buy stamps and the time to stick them on to envelopes, etc. (The operation of franking machines is explained in detail in Chapter 8, page 240.)

UNADDRESSED MAIL

The Post Office now has an 'unaddressed' service for advertising material such as flyers, leaflets, samples and catalogues. The items need not be enveloped and can be delivered to specific geographic areas and/or within specific timeframes. This service is a lot cheaper than normal mailing, but there are requirements for booking and a larger delivery window. Organisations using this service are offered price incentives for the use of mail as a response option. Discounts are also given for sending larger volumes of unaddressed mail, using courier services for delivery and choosing certain times of the year.

CHOICE OF SERVICE

There are various factors to be taken into consideration when choosing the most appropriate service(s) to be used for any particular item or type of mail. You need to think about:

- weight of the item
- speed of delivery required
- certainty of delivery achieved by tracking, and evidence of delivery
- value of the item and the relative importance of security
- cost of postage plus particular service.

For business organisations, choice of service is considered from the customer's point of view, i.e. how the customer wishes to do business. For example, a company might buy pre-paid courier envelopes to have to hand when needed.

OTHER SERVICES

There are services available at Post Offices other than those relating to the mail. These include:

- postal orders and money orders (see Chapter 11, page 325)
- savings
- pensions
- agency (Jamaica).

SAVINGS

The Post Office Savings Bank enables anyone to have a savings account. You may open a Savings Bank Ordinary Account with $1.00 at Savings Bank Post Offices throughout the Caribbean. You will be given a bank book in which deposits and withdrawals are recorded. Interest is paid on deposits, the rate being fixed by the government.

In order to withdraw cash from your savings account you must complete a Notice of Withdrawal form, obtainable from any Post Office. Complete the form, stating the Post Office at which you wish to collect the money, and send it to the Savings Bank Headquarters. The form will be returned to you within three days, authorised for payment. Take the form and your bank book to the specified Post Office and the money will be paid to you.

The Post Office Savings Bank in Trinidad and Tobago has been discontinued.

PENSIONS

Retirement pensions may be drawn at Post Offices throughout the territory. Retired people who are entitled to draw a government retirement pension are issued with a cheque that may be cashed at any convenient Post Office or commercial bank branch. Alternatively they may have their pension paid by direct credit into their bank account.

AGENCY SERVICES (JAMAICA)

In Jamaica, the Post and Telegraphs Department provides the following agency services:

- Workers Savings and Loan Bank
- Pensions – old age, invalidity, sugar workers, National Insurance Scheme
- fishing licences
- registration of births and deaths
- judicial stamps for resident magistrates' courts
- Crown witness expenses
- Family Court payments.

SERVICE STANDARDS

The Post Office has specified standards of service for many of the services it provides. For example, the one-class inland post aims to achieve next-day delivery throughout the territory. Courier delivery guarantees next-day delivery with a full fee refund if this is not achieved. Customers should ask what standard applies to a particular service when using it.

> **ACTIVITY 9.2** Obtain from your postal authority as many leaflets and booklets as you can that will give you information on postage rates and postal services.
>
> Check this information against the information given in this chapter. Make a note of anything that is different in your territory from the information given here.

ADVICE, INFORMATION AND COMPLAINTS

Customers in need of advice, seeking information or wishing to make a complaint can obtain help from several sources.

Advice can be obtained by calling at, or telephoning, Post Offices during working hours (usually 0900 to 1700 Monday to Friday and 0900 to 1300 Saturday).

Information can be obtained direct from Post Offices (as above), by fax, e-mail or on websites.

Complaints can be made in writing by letter, fax or e-mail, or by telephone during working hours. When making a complaint it is important to provide all relevant information. If a document is available, e.g. a receipt for a registered letter that has not been delivered, this should also be produced.

POSTAL AUTHORITIES

Table 9.1 lists Caribbean territories and contact details for their postal authorities.

Table 9.1 *Postal authorities in the Caribbean*

Territory	Name of postal authority
Bahamas	Postmaster General PO Box N-8302 NASSAU NP BAHAMAS

(continued)

Table 9.1 *(continued)*

Territory	Name of postal authority
Barbados	Postmaster General General Post Office Cheapside BRIDGETOWN BARBADOS
Grenada	The Director of Post Grenada Postal Corporation St George's GRENADA ANTILLES
Jamaica	Postmaster General Postal Corporation of Jamaica Limited Central Sorting office 610 South Camp Road KINGSTON 4 JAMAICA
St Lucia	Postmaster General General Post Office Bridge Street CASTRIES SAINT LUCIA
St Vincent and the Grenadines	Postmaster General General Post Office KINGSTOWN SAINT VINCENT AND THE GRENADINES
Trinidad and Tobago	Trinidad and Tobago Postal Corporation National Mail Centre PO Box 1 Golden Grove Road PIARCO TRINIDAD AND TOBAGO

PRACTICE QUESTIONS

1. Explain how you would address a letter to be sent overseas.
2. Draw an oblong 160 mm × 115 mm (6½ in × 4½ in) and write or type your own name and address in the correct place and format for posting.

3. Which commonly used sizes of envelope fall within the minimum and maximum dimensions set by the postal authorities?

4. Explain Post Office box numbers and private bag numbers.

5. In what circumstances might you wish to use the poste restante service?

6. Explain the following services:
   i. redirection
   ii. express delivery
   iii. certificate of posting
   iv. recorded delivery
   v. business reply service
   vi. courier service
   vii. registration
   viii. advice of delivery
   ix. reply coupons
   x. bulk postage.

7. Describe the postal services that can be used to ensure that written communications are received:
   i. speedily
   ii. safely.

8. *a.* How would you prepare a packet to be sent by registered mail?
   b. How would you arrange to pre-pay a reply to a letter sent overseas?

9. How would you prepare a parcel to be sent to an inland address by registered express post?

10. If you were asked by your employer to send a parcel needed urgently by the consignee to an address in your country, what service(s) could you use? What would you have to do to make sure the parcel was sent and then delivered to the consignee as soon as possible?

11. Explain:
    i. unaddressed mail
    ii. franked mail.

12. What factors do you need to take into consideration when deciding the most appropriate service for a particular letter, packet or parcel?

13. What is meant by 'service standards' in relation to postal services?

SHORT ANSWER QUESTIONS

1. The Post Office sets out guidelines for addressing mail. When addressing inland post, the .... should be printed with an initial capital letter.

2. .... envelopes may be used provided the address is printed on a label.
3. The cost of an aerogramme (airletter) includes ....
4. When an article is to be sent overseas a .... must first be completed.
5. A person travelling can collect mail from Post Offices on their route addressed to them ....

Choose the most appropriate ending for each of the following sentences.

6. Redirection is a Post Office service to someone:
   a. who travels a lot
   b. moving house
   c. on holiday for more than a month
   d. who wants to collect letters from a Post Office box.

7. A certificate of posting is given for:
   a. letters sent to overseas addresses
   b. parcels sent to overseas addresses
   c. letters and parcels sent to inland and overseas addresses
   d. parcels only sent to inland and overseas addresses.

8. When a company has a lot of mail is to be sent, the service to be used is:
   a. courier
   b. parcel
   c. recorded delivery
   d. bulk postage.

9. There are certain services available to businesses only. These include:
   a. bulk postage
   b. insurance
   c. freepost
   d. franking.

EXAMINATION QUESTION

1. Items of monetary value sent through the post should be ....

(Pitman Office Procedures Level 1 1998 Pt 1A)

CHAPTER 10

COMMERCIAL DOCUMENTS FOR BUYING AND SELLING

> **OBJECTIVES** When you have studied this chapter you should have acquired the knowledge and understanding to be able to:
>
> 1. list the documents used in a business transaction in their correct sequence for home trade
> 2. identify the information on each of the documents in the sequence
> 3. explain the key documents used in overseas trading with reasons for their importance
> 4. explain terms used in trading and give the meaning of abbreviations
> 5. recognise metric units of measurement.

Terms in the text followed by an asterisk are listed alphabetically and explained in Table 10.1.

The purpose of all businesses is to make a profit. The profit results from the difference between the cost price (of buying in or manufacturing products) and the selling price of the products sold. If the 'product' is a service such as repairs, training or hairdressing, the cost will include materials used, the time of the person/people who do the work and administrative costs. The profit will be the difference between the total cost and the amount charged to the client.

The complete process of buying and selling is known as a **transaction**. Each step of a transaction involves the transmission of information between buyer and seller in a specific sequence. With the exception of an enquiry, a form is used for each step. Forms may be sent by post, fax or telex, or be electronically transmitted by e-mail (see Chapter 5, page 138).

DOCUMENTS USED IN A BUSINESS TRANSACTION

Study the flowchart shown in Fig. 10.1. This shows the documents involved in a transaction, the sequence in which each document is produced and who is responsible for generating it. We shall look at each of the documents as it occurs in the sequence.

Refer to the list of terms in Table 10.1 before studying the various documents explained in this chapter. Terms explained in the table are shown with an asterisk the first time they appear in the text. Units of measurement used for goods are given on pages 300–1.

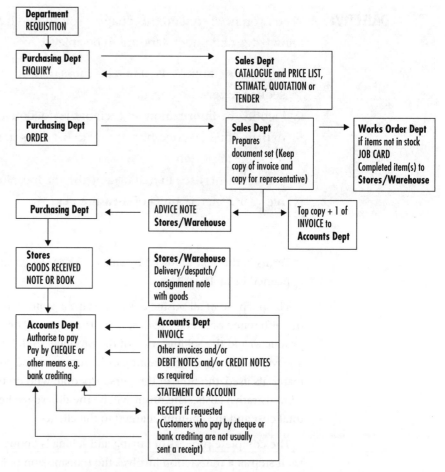

Fig. 10.1 Flowchart of business documents used in buying and selling.

HOME TRADE

There is **home trade** and **overseas trade**. Documents relating to home trade, i.e. trade within the home country, are dealt with first. Additional documents needed for overseas trade, i.e. trade with foreign countries, are dealt with later in the chapter.

REQUISITION

In a large organisation the department requiring the product or service completes a requisition, which is sent to the central purchasing department. The requisition states as many details of the product or service as are known.

```
REQUISITION                                                    34556
Name         Fred Jarvis                        Date    6.6.02
Department   Drinks
To Purchasing Department
Will you please order the following items:

Quantity    Code No.         Description              Supplier (if known)
            (if known)

10 cases                     Tinned grapefruit
                             juice concentrate        East Caribbean
5 cases                      Orange juice in          Export Co. Ltd –
                             cartons (1 litre)        trial order
                                                      as agreed
5 cases                      Lemon drink
                             in cartons (1 litre)

Authorised by ..... FJ .................................................
Job title ..... Supervisor .............................................
Date supplied to department ..........................................
Date received in department ..........................................
```

Fig. 10.2 Requisition.

These may include:

- name of product/service
- catalogue (or code) number*
- size/dimensions/weight
- colour
- quantity in units, e.g. boxes, reams, packs of 10
- preferred/essential delivery date*
- unit price*
- supplier (name, address, telephone/fax numbers, e-mail address).

The requisition must be signed, usually by the person requiring the goods, and authorised by the departmental manager. One copy is sent to the central purchasing department and one copy is retained in the department for reference, in date order, in a 'Requisitions pending' file. A specimen requisition is shown in Fig. 10.2.

ENQUIRY

In a large organisation the central purchasing department receives the requisition and then either orders the goods or sends out an enquiry. In a small organisation it is not usual to complete a requisition.

A buyer may use one supplier regularly for a particular product or type of product, e.g. stationery. There are times when a buyer requires an item not previously purchased. Sometimes a buyer becomes dissatisfied with a supplier and decides to use a different one. In these cases some research may be needed to find the names of potential suppliers. Sources include an index of suppliers (see below), files of catalogues*, the *Yellow Pages* directory (see Chapter 15, page 470), advertisements in appropriate newspapers or specialist magazines, e.g. computer magazines, or the Internet (see Chapter 3, page 55).

Most suppliers mail catalogues to companies they think may need their goods/services. It may not be practicable to keep all catalogues received but it may be useful to set up and maintain an index (on cards or computer) of their names, addresses, telephone and fax/telex numbers, e-mail addresses and types of product/service they supply. A specimen index card is shown in Fig. 10.3.

It is often desirable to enquire of two or three suppliers in order to obtain more than one quotation for comparison. When names of suppliers have been found, the first step in the transaction process can begin.

```
EAST CARIBBEAN EXPORT Co. Ltd
PO Box 456
KINGSTON
JAMAICA

Tel.:        264 7856
Fax:         264 7899
E-mail:      ecexport@jamaican.net

Contact:     John Trasco

Products:    Citrus juices
             Concentrated fruit drinks
             Fresh citrus fruit
```

Fig. 10.3 Index card.

```
Tel   784 8142                                THE FRUIT SHOP
Fax   784 1234                                City Street
                                              MONTEGO BAY
                                              JAMAICA

                                              7 June 2002

Mr John Trasco
East Caribbean Export Co. Ltd
PO Box 456
KINGSTON
JAMAICA

Dear Mr Trasco

ENQUIRY

Thank you for your visit last week. I was pleased to know the products you can offer.

Will you please send me a quotation for the following:

10 cases tinned grapefruit juice concentrate
 5 cases orange juice in 1 litre cartons
 5 cases lemon drink in 1 litre cartons.

This will be a trial order and if products and delivery are satisfactory I anticipate doing regular business
with you.

Yours sincerely
Mohammed Bashta
Mohammed Bashta
```

Fig. 10.4 Enquiry letter.

The buyer sends an enquiry to one or more suppliers, giving and requesting information. A supplier will need to know:

- the item(s) required – size/dimensions/weight, colour, etc.
- quantities required, in what units
- maximum delivery time*.

The buyer needs to know from the supplier:

- whether the item(s) required can be supplied
- cost including taxes* and delivery charges*
- whether trade discount* is allowed
- terms of payment*
- delivery method*.

The enquiry may be sent as a letter, fax, telex or e-mail, or the information can be requested on the telephone. The enquiry is sent to the supplier(s) and a copy is sent to the department that submitted the requisition. A copy of the document is placed in the purchasing department 'Enquiries pending' file, usually in date order, either as hard copy or on disk. A note should be made to check with the supplier if a reply has not been received by a certain date. An enquiry letter is shown in Fig. 10.4.

ACTIVITY 10.1 You have checked your stationery cupboard and found that you need to stock up on several items. You make a list of what you need: 50 wallet folders, 10 reams 80 gsm copy paper, 100 plastic slip files and a four-hole punch.

Find the name and address of a stationery supplier. Write a letter enquiring whether they can supply the items you need.
Use fictitious details (for colours and sizes, etc.).

QUOTATION, ESTIMATE, TENDER

The enquiry is received by the sales department of the supplier. A quotation is either given on the telephone, or sent by hard copy or e-mail. The quotation should include the following details:

- quotation identification, usually a number
- catalogue (or code) number, name and description of product (type, model number, size, colour, etc.)

- quantity with unit price
- cost with tax and delivery charges shown separately or inclusively
- delivery date and method
- trade discount agreed
- terms of payment, e.g. monthly, with cash discount*.

A catalogue and/or price list* is often sent with a quotation.

Prices may be quoted in various ways, including:

- fully inclusive – no extra charges for packing, delivery, installation
- ex works* – up to the point of leaving the factory, i.e. transport and installation are extra charges
- ex warehouse* – as ex works but from a store
- carriage forward* – to be paid by the buyer when taking delivery of the goods
- carriage paid* – amount paid includes delivery but if installation is required an extra charge would be made
- cash on delivery* – the full cost is paid by the buyer on receipt of the goods
- trade cost/price* – the price after deduction of trade discount
- gross cost/price* – before deduction of discounts
- net cost/price* – after deduction of discounts.

If the request is for services it is not always possible for the supplier to quote the cost precisely. In this case an **estimate** is given.

When major work is required, e.g. a specially built machine for a factory, or building construction, it is usual for the buyer to advertise for **tenders**. This means that suppliers are invited to submit a specification for the job with detailed costs of materials, labour and other services.

It is usual in government departments and in local government for at least two quotations/estimates/tenders to be obtained for all orders over a certain amount. The cheapest is not necessarily chosen, because the aim is to obtain best value.

A specimen quotation is shown in Fig. 10.5. The document is sent to the buyer and a copy is retained in a 'Quotations' file in the supplier's sales department. This may be kept in date order or alphabetically by customer name. Alternatively it may be filed in a customer's file. If no reply has been received to the quotation within a certain time it is followed up with either a letter or telephone call, offering further information.

```
EAST CARIBBEAN EXPORT Co. Ltd        Telephone    264 7856
PO Box 456                           Facsimile    264 7899
KINGSTON                             Email  ecexport@jamaican.net
JAMAICA
                                                  11 June 2002

Mr Mohammed Bashta
The Fruit Shop
City Street
MONTEGO BAY
JAMAICA

Your ref.   Letter of 7 June 2002
Our ref.    QUOT 2459

We are pleased to quote as follows:

Code        Quantity    Description         Unit price    Cost
G21         10 cases    Grapefruit juice
                        concentrate (tins)  J$30.00       J$300.00
O14         5 cases     Orange juice
                        (1-litre cartons)   45.00         225.00
L18         5 cases     Lemon drink
                        (1-litre cartons)   38.00         190.00
                                                          -------
                                                          715.00
Delivery                                                  10.00
                                                          -------
TOTAL                                                     J$725.00
                                                          =======

Terms: Payment against pro-forma invoice.
Delivery: Maximum five days after confirmation of order.
```

Fig. 10.5 Quotation.

ORDER

The buyer receives the quotation/estimate/tender and decides whether to accept it. It may be that certain points, e.g. delivery times, need to be negotiated. If the quotation is acceptable, or when the unacceptable points have been successfully negotiated, an order is placed.

If more than one quotation/estimate/tender has been received, each one must be compared against the others. Points for comparison include:

- discounts – trade, cash
- terms of payment

- after-sales service
- period of guarantee.

The details on the order form must include:

- purchase order number
- name and address of buyer
- name and address of supplier
- supplier's quotation number
- full details of the goods/services as stated in the quotation
- delivery date(s)
- delivery address* (if different from the mailing address given)
- whether 'one-off'* or 'part'* deliveries required
- cost with taxes and delivery charges
- trade discount (if any)
- terms of payment
- signature of person authorising the purchase, either the departmental head or a member of the purchasing department staff.

The document is sent to the supplier and a copy is kept in an 'Orders pending' file in date order with the requisition from the department and the copy quotation. A copy is sent to the department that has requisitioned the goods/services where it will be attached to the copy of the requisition.

It is important that the department requiring the goods is kept informed of the progress of the order. Any delay or variation in the order must be approved by the buying department. If the delay is not acceptable the purchasing department should try to find an alternative supplier.

Copies are also sent to the accounts department for checking the invoice, and to stores notifying the goods to be received and updating stock records (see Chapter 12, page 378). In some organisations 'goods received' and 'stores' are separate sections, and each would need a copy of the order.

A specimen order is shown in Fig. 10.6.

ACTIVITY 10.2 Obtain a catalogue for office furniture. Draw up an order form as shown in Fig. 10.6.

Choose three items from the catalogue and complete the order form using the details given in the catalogue. Any details not given in the catalogue can be fictitious.

```
Tel.  784 8142                                          THE FRUIT SHOP
Fax   784 1234                                          City Street
                                                        MONTEGO BAY
                                                        JAMAICA

ORDER No. 246/02                                        7 June 2002

East Caribbean Export Co. Ltd
PO Box 456
KINGSTON
JAMAICA

Your ref.   QUOT 2459

Code        Quantity      Description           Unit price      Cost
G21         10 cases      Grapefruit juice
                          concentrate (tins)    J$30.00         J$300.00
014         5 cases       Orange juice (1 litre)   45.00         225.00
L18         5 cases       Lemon drink (1 litre)    38.00         190.00
                                                                -------
                                                                 715.00
Delivery                                                          10.00
Mohammed Bashta                                                 -------
TOTAL                                                           J$725.00

Delivery: Maximum five days after confirmation of order.
```

Fig. 10.6 Order.

ACKNOWLEDGEMENT OF ORDER

The supplier may acknowledge the order with a printed postcard or a standard letter. The delivery date may be stated or an indication given, e.g. the goods will be delivered within seven days.

PROCESSING THE ORDER

Orders are processed in different ways depending on the organisation's systems and procedures. If the buyer is unknown to the supplier it is likely that the supplier will want **references**. This means that the buyer must give the names of organisations, usually a bank and another supplier, certifying that the buyer is a reputable and reliable customer. The supplier will take up these references before supplying the goods.

If the buyer is known to the supplier, the order may be sent to **credit control** to ensure that the credit allowed to the buyer will not be exceeded by the new order. When the order has been passed by credit control it is sent to stores where the items will be 'picked' (i.e. taken out of stock), and passed to despatch for packing and delivery.

Alternatively the supplier may send a pro-forma invoice to be paid before the goods are delivered. This may also be sent if the item(s) required have to be made specially.

PRO-FORMA INVOICE

If the buyer is required to pay in advance, the seller sends a pro-forma invoice, which is raised (produced) in the accounts department. The details on the pro-forma will include:

- date
- date and number of the buyer's order
- seller's order number
- details of goods as set out in the quotation
- delivery time (may be stated)
- period of validity of the pro-forma (may be included), i.e. the amount must be paid within a certain time – this is because prices may vary, or one or more of the items may be discontinued.

The pro-forma invoice is sent to the buyer and a copy is retained on the accounts department file. The buyer then pays the pro-forma so that the goods can be supplied. A specimen pro-forma invoice is shown in Fig. 10.7.

ADVICE NOTE

If the supplier does not require payment in advance an advice note may be sent to the buyer. This may be a brief note stating the order number and the date of delivery. More usually it will give:

- date
- buyer's order number
- seller's order number

```
EAST CARIBBEAN EXPORT Co. Ltd          Telephone    264 7856
PO Box 456                             Facsimile    264 7899
KINGSTON                               Email  ecexport@jamaican.net
JAMAICA

PRO-FORMA INVOICE No. 1578                    Date: 11 June 2002

Mr Mohammed Bashta
The Fruit Shop
City Street
MONTEGO BAY
JAMAICA

Your order no.   246/02                       Account No. B/4578
Our ref.         QUOT 2459

Code       Quantity     Description              Unit price      Cost
G21        10 cases     Grapefruit juice
                        concentrate (tins)       J$30.00         J$300.00

014        5 cases      Orange juice (1 litre)   45.00           225.00

L18        5 cases      Lemon drink (1 litre)    38.00           190.00
                                                                 -------
                                                                 715.00
Delivery                                                         10.00
                                                                 -------
TOTAL                                                            J$725.00
                                                                 =======

Delivery: Maximum five days after confirmation of order.
```

Fig. 10.7 Pro-forma invoice (payment is required before the goods are delivered as this is the first transaction between buyer and seller).

- name and address of buyer
- delivery address if different
- whether one-off or part delivery is to be made – part delivery may be required because the supplier does not have all the items in stock and will send outstanding items later or because the buyer wishes to 'call off'* from a bulk order as required
- date and method of despatch, e.g. parcel post, courier, carrier, delivery van
- request for the buyer to inform the supplier if the goods are not received within a certain time.

The document is sent to the buyer with one copy being sent to stores and another placed on the 'Order' file.

PACKING, DESPATCH, DELIVERY, CONSIGNMENT NOTES

Depending on the method by which the goods are delivered, one of these notes is sent with the goods. A packing or despatch note is included with the goods when they are sent by post. Goods sent by carrier may also include a despatch note, the goods being handed in at the buyer's address without a signature being obtained.

A delivery note is used when the goods are delivered by certain couriers or by the seller's own transport. Two copies of the delivery note are presented by the driver to the buyer, who signs one of the copies and returns it to the driver. The buyer retains the second copy.

A consignment note is used when goods are transported by road haulier. Again the buyer signs one copy of the consignment note and retains the second copy.

The details included on a packing/despatch/delivery/consignment note are usually:

- date
- address for delivery of goods, if different from the buyer's mailing address
- seller's and buyer's order numbers
- number of packages
- one-off or part delivery details
- space for signature of the person receiving the goods, the date and, in some cases, the time
- a statement informing the buyer that the seller must be notified within a specified time if all or some of the goods are damaged or incorrect.

A specimen delivery note is shown in Fig. 10.8.

The last point on the list above is very important. It is often not possible to open the package(s) immediately. It is important that they are opened and that all the goods are inspected carefully within the specified time. If there are any faulty goods, any that are not what was ordered (e.g. the wrong colour or size) or any that were not ordered, the seller must be notified. The seller will then tell the buyer what to do.

- The seller might send a 'return package kit', which provides the buyer with the documents required, including address labels, to return

---

EAST CARIBBEAN EXPORT Co. Ltd
PO Box 456
KINGSTON
JAMAICA

Telephone 264 7856
Facsimile 264 7899
Email ecexport@jamaican.net

DELIVERY NOTE No. 1578　　　　　　　　　　　　　　Date:　11 June 2002

Mr Mohammed Bashta
The Fruit Shop
City Street
MONTEGO BAY
JAMAICA

Your order no. 246/02
Our order no. T 1578

Code	Quantity	Description
G21	10 cases	Grapefruit juice concentrate (tins)
O14	5 cases	Orange juice (1 litre)
L18	5 cases	Lemon drink (1 litre)

Notification of incomplete or damaged items must be given within five working days.

Customer's signature .... Date ....

Customer's name ....
PRINTED please

Fig. 10.8 Delivery note.

the goods and details of how to contact the carrier so that the faulty goods can be collected from the buyer.
- The seller might ask the buyer to keep the faulty/incorrect goods until replacements are supplied, when the unwanted items can be handed to the carrier for return to the supplier.

ACTIVITY 10.3　Draw a delivery note as shown in Fig. 10.8. You are now the supplier who has received the order you prepared for Activity 10.2. Complete your delivery note for the items ordered.

GOODS RECEIVED NOTE

When the goods are received in the buyer's store, a goods received note is prepared. This states:

- the number of packages received
- the goods received (itemised)
- details of any items that are broken, damaged, faulty, missing, incorrect, i.e. not as ordered, or not ordered at all.

A copy of the goods received note is sent to the accounts department, where it will be placed with the copy of the order. In some organisations a copy is also sent to the stores section for updating stock records. A copy may also be sent to the department that ordered the goods.

A specimen goods received note is shown in Fig. 10.9.

```
GOODS RECEIVED NOTE                                        No. 1578

Supplier ...........................................................................

Order no. ................................

Date goods received ...............................................................

Our order no. ..............................

Quantity            Description




Order complete Yes/No*

Specify any damage .................................................................
......................................................................................
......................................................................................

Signed: ...................................................................  Storeman

Date: ...........................................

*Delete as appropriate
```

Fig. 10.9 Goods received note.

INVOICE

An invoice is sent to the buyer if they have not already paid on a pro-forma invoice. The invoice may be enclosed with the goods or may be sent immediately afterwards.

The details on an invoice include:

- invoice number
- date
- name and address of buyer
- buyer's order number
- seller's order number
- details of goods – catalogue/code number, brief description, unit price, net cost of each type of item, tax on each item, gross cost of each

---

EAST CARIBBEAN EXPORT Co. Ltd
PO Box 456
KINGSTON
JAMAICA

Telephone 264 7856
Facsimile 264 7899
Email ecexport@jamaican.net

INVOICE No. 1578

Date: 11 June 2002

Mr Mohammed Bashta
The Fruit Shop
City Street
MONTEGO BAY
JAMAICA

Your order no. 246/02
Our order no. T 1578

Account No. B/4578

Code	Quantity	Description	Unit price	Cost
G21	10 cases	Grapefruit juice concentrate (tins)	J$30.00	J$300.00
014	5 cases	Orange juice (1 litre)	45.00	225.00
L18	5 cases	Lemon drink (1 litre)	38.00	190.00
				715.00
Delivery				10.00
TOTAL				**J$725.00**

Terms: Strictly net cash within 14 days.

Fig. 10.10 Invoice (sent with or after delivery if the customer and supplier had already traded).

type of item, delivery charge, totals of net, tax and gross costs, trade discount (if any), terms of payment with cash discount (if any) allowed, total amount due
- due date* for payment and whether part payment can be made
- Errors and omissions excepted (E & OE)*, which enables the seller to submit a further debit note (see below) or credit note (see below).

Although the accounts department has a copy of the order it is usual for an invoice to be sent to the department that placed the order. There, the invoice is checked, signed by the person authorised to pass invoices for payment and returned to the accounts department.

A specimen invoice is shown in Fig. 10.10.

DEBIT NOTE

A debit note contains details of any under-charge or omission from the invoice. The details are the same as on the invoice. The amount involved would be debited to the buyer's account, i.e. added to the total amount owed by the buyer to the supplier.

CREDIT NOTE

A credit note is sent to the buyer when an over-charge has been made in an invoice, e.g. an item listed but not delivered. Some goods are delivered in returnable packaging, e.g. crates or on pallets that can be returned to the supplier. The buyer is then credited with the value of the returned items, known as 'returnable empties'*, which were included in the cost of the goods. The details are the same as on the invoice. The amount involved is credited to the buyer's account, i.e. deducted from the total amount owed by the buyer to the supplier.

STATEMENT OF ACCOUNT

When a buyer has an account with a supplier it is usual for the supplier to send a statement at the end of each month. The statement shows the details of the transactions during that month. Details include:

- date
- buyer's account number
- name and address of buyer
- listing of invoices, debit notes and credit notes by number, date and total amount payable, i.e. after deduction of trade discount
- terms of payment including the date by which payment has to be made.

A statement of account may include a **remittance slip** and/or a **paying-in slip**. The remittance slip contains details of the buyer's account number, the amount due and the address to which a cheque should be sent. The buyer then sends a cheque with the remittance slip to the seller.

```
EAST CARIBBEAN EXPORT Co. Ltd           Telephone    264 7856
PO Box 456                              Facsimile    264 7899
KINGSTON                                Email  ecexport@jamaican.net
JAMAICA

STATEMENT OF ACCOUNT                    Date: 30 June 2002

Mr Mohammed Bashta                      Account No. B/4578
The Fruit Shop
City Street
MONTEGO BAY
JAMAICA
```

Date		Debit J$	Credit J$	Balance J$
11.06.02	Invoice no. 1578	725.00		725.00

TOTAL now due   J$725.00

Terms: Strictly net cash within 14 days.

- -

Remittance slip   Please detach this slip and send it with your cheque to:

EAST CARIBBEAN EXPORT Co. Ltd   Account No. B/4578
PO Box 456
KINGSTON JAMAICA   **Amount due J$725.00**

Please make cheque payable to East Caribbean Export Co. Ltd and write the account reference on the back of the cheque.

Fig. 10.11 Statement of account with remittance slip.

A paying-in slip enables the buyer to pay the amount owing into a bank. The slip shows the name and account number of the seller, and the amount owing. There is space for the buyer to write the amount being paid in cash/by cheque, the date and their signature.

A specimen statement of account with remittance slip is shown in Fig. 10.11. (For details of how payments are made see Chapter 11.)

RECEIPT

It is rare for suppliers to issue receipts if payment has been made by cheque or through a bank. The buyer's bank statement will show the payment, which is adequate proof for accounting purposes.

OVERSEAS TRADE

The documents discussed so far in this chapter relate to home trade. A lot of trade, however, is done between different countries. This is known as **importing** when buying goods from overseas and **exporting** when selling goods to overseas buyers.

Trading overseas means that goods often have to be sent by sea or by air. There are various international trading laws that have to be obeyed, as well as paying customs and excise duties. The regulations of dock and harbour authorities, airport authorities and airline conditions have to be followed. All this involves additional documentation, and it is vitally important that documents are completed accurately with all relevant details.

BILL OF LADING

The bill of lading is a very important document because it provides proof that the goods have been shipped. Without this document the buyer is not able to collect the goods at their destination. A number of original copies must be produced. They are distributed to:

- the master of the ship on which the goods are shipped
- the buyer, to obtain customs clearance for the goods on arrival
- possibly the buyer's bank to enable payment to be made.

(Methods of payment for international trading are explained in Chapter 11.)

The information given on a bill of lading includes:

- document number
- name of supplier
- name of buyer
- name of vessel on which the goods are shipped
- number and kind of packages, e.g. chests, containers
- gross weight, i.e. the weight of the goods in their packaging
- conditions, such as temperature, would be included for particular types of goods, such as foodstuffs
- whether the goods are shipped cost, insurance and freight (cif)* or free on board (fob)*
- total number of packages received by the carrier – not all may be shipped at the same time
- number of original documents
- signature of a representative of the shipping company.

A specimen bill of lading is shown in Fig. 10.12.

AIR WAYBILL

When goods are sent by air the bill of lading is replaced by an air waybill but the information required is quite similar. A specimen air waybill is shown in Fig. 10.13.

CERTIFICATE OF INSURANCE

Goods sent by sea or air are normally insured. An insurance company agrees to insure the goods sent against damage or loss in return for a premium*. The buyer receives a copy of the insurance certificate so that a claim can be made if the consignment does not arrive intact. A certificate of insurance is shown in Fig. 10.14. (See also the entries for owner's risk* and company's risk* in Table 10.1.)

CERTIFICATE OF ORIGIN

Many countries require a certificate of origin for imported goods. This is an invoice on which a statement has been added declaring the country of

BILL OF LADING FOR COMBINED TRANSPORT SHIPMENT OR PORT TO PORT SHIPMENT

Shipper

B.P. DE LANGE B.V.
P.O. BOX 230
1800 AE ALKMAAR
HOLLAND

B/L No NLBURTMR4842

Reference

Nedlloyd

Incorporated in The Netherlands as
Nedlloyd Lijnen B.V. Rotterdam

Consignee or Order

TO ORDER

Notify Party Address (It is agreed that no responsibility shall attach to the Carrier or his Agents for failure to notify (see clause 20 on the reverse))

DORMAN ENTERPRISES
COR CENTENARY & RAMDATH STREET
PASEA, TUNAPUNA
TRINIDAD W.I.

Place of Receipt (Applicable only when this document is used as a Combined Transport Bill of Lading)

AMSTERDAM C.Y.

Ocean Vessel

CARIBIA EXPRESS/3435

Port of Loading

AMSTERDAM

Place of Delivery (Applicable only when this document is used as a Combined Transport Bill of Lading)

PORT OF SPAIN C.Y.

Port of Discharge

PORT OF SPAIN

Marks and Nos; Container Nos:	Number and kind of Packages; description of Goods	Gross Weight (kg)	Measurement (cbm)
ROYU 472596-9 RYAN: 1009768	1 40FT CONAIR CONTAINER STC.: 1150/50 LBS BAGS CONSUMPTION POTATOES. TEMP. +8/+14 CENTIGRADE	26105	

FREIGHT PREPAID/FLETE PAGADO
CLEAN ON BOARD
SHIPPED ON BOARD; 22/10/98
NEDLLOYD LINES NEDERLAND BV

ABOVE PARTICULARS AS DECLARED BY SHIPPER

• Total No. of Containers/Packages received by the Carrier

1/ONE CONTAINER(S)

Movement

FCL/FCL

Freight and Charges (indicate whether prepaid or collect):

Origin Inland Haulage Charge

Origin Terminal Handling/LCL Service Charge

Ocean Freight PAID

Destination Terminal Handling/LCL Service Charge

Destination Inland Haulage Charge

RECEIVED by the Carrier from the Shipper in apparent good order and condition (unless otherwise noted herein) the total number or quantity of Containers or other packages or units indicated in the box opposite entitled "• Total No. of Containers/Packages received by the Carrier" for Carriage subject to all the terms hereof (INCLUDING THE TERMS ON THE REVERSE HEREOF AND THE TERMS OF THE CARRIER'S APPLICABLE TARIFF) from the Place of Receipt or the Port of Loading, whichever is applicable, to the Port of Discharge or the Place of Delivery, whichever is applicable. One original Bill of Lading must be surrendered, duly endorsed, in exchange for the Goods. In accepting this Bill of Lading the Merchant expressly accepts and agrees to all its terms and conditions whether printed, stamped or written, or otherwise incorporated, notwithstanding the non-signing of this Bill of Lading by the Merchant.

Freight payable at

ROTTERDAM

Place and Date of Issue

Rotterdam 22/10/98

Number of Original Bills of Lading

3/THREE

IN WITNESS of the contract herein contained the number of originals stated opposite have been issued, one of which being accomplished the other(s) to be void.

For the Carrier Nedlloyd Lines Nederland B.V.

As Agent(s) only

ICS
CT B/L
April '78

ORIGINAL

R 302 (Original) 20000-3-'93

Fig. 10.12 Bill of lading.

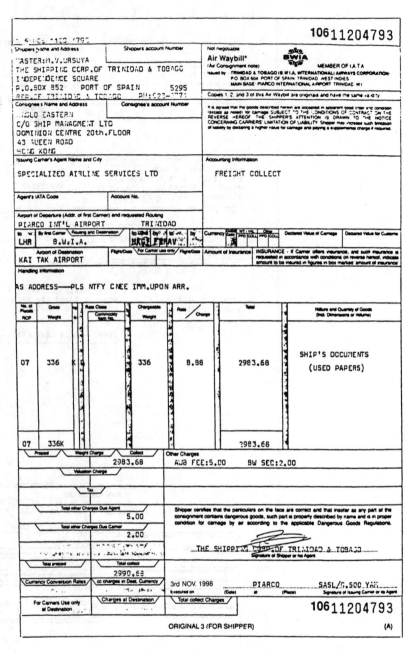

Fig. 10.13 Air waybill.

Hudig-Langeveldt insurance brokers

Amsterdam office

P.O. box 357, 1000 AJ Amsterdam 74 Grote Bickersstraat, Amsterdam
Telephone (31)-20-5572911

T 905 Certificate of Insurance no.   TC 851-LA/2   to be mentioned in all cases

Reference :

We, the Undersigned, in our capacity of sworn Insurance Brokers and therefore not as Insurers, certify herewith that insurance has been effected with Insurance Companies and/or with Underwriters on behalf of   B.P. DE LANGE B.V.

amounting to : US$. 7.850,--
say   : SEVENTHOUSANDEIGHTHUNDREDFIFTY US DOLLARS

                                                                                so valued
on   : 224/50 lbs bags CONSUMPTION ONIONS.
                 928/50 lbs bags CONSUMPTION POTATOES

                 Container nr. EWLU 461035-0

per   : mv "EWL VENEZUELA" on or about 9th March 1998
                 and/or other vessel (subject to Dutch Classification Clause) /conveyance and including transhipment, if any

from   : ROTTERDAM/HOLLAND   (from warehouse to warehouse)
to   : GEORGETOWN/GUYANA

Conditions   : All risks as per Institute Cargo Clauses (A).
                 Including the risks of war and/or strikes, riots civil
                 commotions and malicious damage as per Institute War
                 Clauses and Institute Strikes Riots and Civil Commotions
                 Clauses relevant to the particular form of transit
                 covered by the insurance.
                 Institute Radioactive Contamination Exclusion Clause
                 (1/10/90).
                 - 24 hours breakdown clause.
                 - 3 days' delay clause.

This certificate does not require endorsement and if issued in duplicate, triplicate etc., then one copy having been accomplished, the other(s) to stand void.
This certificate represents and takes the place of the original policy and if required can be exchanged for that policy (apply to Hudig-Langeveldt, Amsterdam Office).
Loss or damage recoverable under the insurance is payable on surrender of this certificate.

Amsterdam, 9th March 1998

Hudig-Langeveldt

In case of loss or damage the Assured and their Agents are to observe all stipulations printed at the back hereof. Claims to be presented to Hudig-Langeveldt, Amsterdam office, P.O. Box 357, 1000 AJ Amsterdam for adjustment and collection. Commercial registry Rotterdam 61634   p.t.o.

Commercial registry Rotterdam 61634

Fig. 10.14 Certificate of insurance.

© SITPRO 1976 Example 1

INVOICE FACTURE FACTURA RECHNUNG FACTUUR

Seller (Name, Address, VAT Reg. No.)
SITPRO EXPORT LIMITED
HIGH STREET
BURTON ON TRENT
STAFFS., DE15 1YZ, ENGLAND

Brussels Tariff No.

Invoice No. and Date (Tax Point): 16418 1 Nov 19—
Seller's Reference: 364/B205/190
Buyer's Reference: ED1814-97-10-3

Consignee
SITPRO TRINIDAD & TOBAGO LTD
P O BOX 412
SAN FERNANDO
TRINIDAD

Buyer (if not Consignee)

Country of Origin of Goods: United Kingdom

Terms of Delivery and Payment: CIF Bushire. Payment against sight draft accompanied by documents through British International Bank, Tehran

Vessel/Aircraft etc.: Bebington
Port of Loading: Liverpool
Port of Discharge

Marks and Numbers	Number and Kind of Packages; Description of Goods	Quantity	@	Amount (State Currency)
SITPRO ED1814A SAN FERNANDO VIA PORT-OF-SPAIN Nos. 1-3	3 Cases: Refills for ballpoint pens (Cat. no. 43-746)	18000	0.04	720.00
SITPRO ED1814B SAN FERNANDO VIA PORT-OF-SPAIN No. 4	1 Case: Electronic duplicator stencils (Cat. no. 42-648)	5000	0.193	965.00
SITPRO ED1814C SAN FERNANDO VIA PORT-OF-SPAIN No. 5	1 Carton: Self-adhesive labels size 70mm x 50mm boxed in packs of 1000 (Cat. no. 40-070)	24 pks	8.82	211.68
SITPRO ED1814D SAN FERNANDO VIA PORT-OF-SPAIN No. 6	1 Case: Self-inking hand operated rubber date stamps (Cat. no. 44-101)	1000	0.52	520.00
			TOTAL £	2416.68

Gross Weight (Kg): 492
Cube (M3): 0.712

We certify this invoice to be true and correct and in accordance with our books, also that the goods are of United Kingdom origin. We hereby certify that the prices stated in this invoice are the current export market prices for the merchandise described therein and we accept full responsibility for any inaccuracies or errors therein

Cost of freight £62.40
Cost of insurance £17.55

Name of Signatory: H J Helliar, Chief Clerk
Place and Date of Issue: Burton, 1 November 19—
Signature: H J Helliar.

It is hereby certified that this invoice shows the actual price of the goods described, that no other invoice has been or will be issued, and that all particulars are true and correct.

380

Fig. 10.15 An invoice certifying the origin of goods.

origin of the goods, which is not necessarily the country from which they are transported. A certificate of origin is shown in Fig. 10.15.

APPLICATION FOR LICENCE TO IMPORT GOODS

When goods are imported it is often necessary to obtain an **import licence**. There are also certain types of goods that cannot be exported

MINISTRY OF TRADE, INDUSTRY AND TOURISM

Application for Licence to import goods into Trinidad and Tobago
(under the Imports and Exports Control Regulation, 1941)

Applicant's B.I.R. No. 51324 Applicant's Name THE STENOTYPE COLLEGE
Address 17 TAYLOR STREET, WOODBROOK, TRINIDAD
Other I.D. No. 19330603008 Supplier's Name PLATIGNUM plc
Date of Application 31 August 1998 Address 20 GREENFIELD, ROYSTON, HERTS SG8 5XX
Customs Entry to be Processed at Date of Delivery 13 OCTOBER, 1998

Baggage ☐   Cargo ☒

Terms of Payment
thru a Local Bank S/D thru: ROYAL BANK T&T LTD

Customs Item No. CCCN	Ministry Negative List Code No.	Unit of Qty.	Qty. in Figures	Description of Article	Unit Price c.i.f. TT	Total Value $TT	Foreign Curr. Equiv.
960839	145		30	GRADUATE FOUNTAIN PENS code 100	$1.17 £9.36	280.80	£35.10
960891	144		30	NIB UNITS FINE code 801 (STD)	0.32 £2.56	76.80	9.60
				Country of Origin U.K. Country of Shipment U.K.	Total Value c.i.f.	357.60	£44.70

Stamp: MINISTRY OF INDUSTRY, ENTERPRISE VALID ONLY TO 31 DEC 1998 AND TO THE VALUE OF GOODS STATED AND TOURISM

THIS COPY TO BE PRODUCED TO CUSTOMS

This Licence is issued upon the condition that the goods described herein may be deemed products of the Comptroller of Customs and that where their importation does not satisfy the criteria laid down for such goods under the Rules of Caribbean Common Market Origin.

Note: (i) B.I.R. No. Necessary for Trade Transactions and Personal Use.
(ii) Other I.D. No. may be used for goods required for Personal use.
*Evidence of (i) and (ii) to be produced.

I/We hereby declare that the goods comprising this application are to be imported for

....Writing shorthand....

and that the statements, computations, additions and other contents of same or of any documents submitted in support of same are to the best of my/our belief and knowledge true and correct in all its particulars.

....
Signature of Applicant and Business Stamp

G.P. Tn/To.—J 2806—7,000— /98

Fig. 10.16 *Application for a licence to import goods into Trinidad and Tobago.*

without an **export licence**. Importers and exporters can obtain guidance from the appropriate government ministry or department, the local chamber of commerce and the appropriate embassy/high commission. The right documents must be completed accurately, and copies must be sent to the right people at the right time. If the goods are perishable, a delay of just a few hours can mean that the consignment is ruined.

An application for a licence to import goods is shown in Fig. 10.16.

ENTRY EX SHIP FOR GOODS LIABLE TO DUTY

Form C-20 (see Fig. 10.17) has to be completed, signed and witnessed when importing goods on which duty has to be paid.

CUSTOMS BILL OF SIGHT

There are occasions when the documents needed to import goods are not available for some reason. In such cases, a bill of sight has to be completed, giving details of the consignment and method of transportation. The document includes a declaration, which is signed by the importer or his agent and is then witnessed. Form C-21 – customs bill of sight – is shown in Fig. 10.18.

Standard documents agreed by member states of the International Standards Organisation (ISO) are now used by most countries for international trade. It is usual to prepare a master document, which contains all the details of the transaction. All other documents are reproduced from the master with appropriate details for each individual document.

TERMS USED IN TRADING

Table 10.1 lists the terms most commonly used in trading. (These are marked with an asterisk on their first appearance in the text of this chapter.)

TRINIDAD AND TOBAGO

ENTRY EX SHIP FOR GOODS LIABLE TO DUTY

Form C-20 Re-revised

PORT OF PIARCO/2

*PREFERENTIAL 010
GENERAL 000

MODE 3
PORT 1

ENTRY No. and DATE

See Note (B) IMPORTER'S NAME HI LO FOOD STORES LTD

CUSTOMS BROKER

See Note (B) CONSIGNOR CATROP SA

No. of Bill of Lading .... Dated 19.1. 19 98

1014956

19. 1. 98

Date of Importation			Rate of Exchange	Value Slip No.	Port or Place of Loading of Goods on Importing Ship/Aircraft
Day	Month	Year			
16	11	1997	B/S	NEW YORK	

Name of Aircraft or Ship	Rotation Number	Date of Report: Day	Month	Year	Country of Registry	Port or Place Whence Arrived
PARCEL POST	39165	16	11	1992	United States	NEW YORK

Invoice Examined by RJS.
Date 12/1/98

Amount Received $ 125.50
Cashier

Packages: Marks and Number	Packages: Number and Description	Tariff Heading Number	Statistical Classification Number	DESCRIPTION (See Note (C) Overleaf)	Quantity in Figures See Note (H)	Unit of Q'ty	Unit No.	Country of Origin and Consignment	No. of Country	VALUE C.I.F. See Note (D) $	c.	DUTY See Note (E) Rate	Amount $	c.
				SEE BILL OF SIGHT ATTACHED										
ADDE	EECL	33.06.50		COSMETICS	1	KG	41	USA	1 16	250	00	50%	125	00
IMP LIC NO 10297														
	VIDE D/E NO 1012700/9-1-81													
Total Number of Packages in Words: – ENCLOSURE					TOTAL					250	00		125	00

Total duty payable (in words) ONE HUNDRED AND TWENTY FIVE Dollars .... cents

I/We declare the above particulars to be true and complete

See Note (F) Signature of Importer or his Authorised Agent (1)* Peters Lic # 144X Grill
CUSTOM BROKER L. JOSEPH

Dated this 9th day of JANUARY 19 98

Status LIC. #0099

Signature of Witness (1)

for Comptroller of Customs and Excise

For Notes (A) to (H) See Overleaf.
*Delete whichever is not applicable

(1) The signature of the Importer or his Authorised Agent must be attested by the Comptroller or a witness whose signature is known to, and is approved by the Comptroller.

Fig. 10.17 Form C-20 Entry ex ship for goods liable to duty.

TRINIDAD AND TOBAGO.	**BILL OF SIGHT** Declaration under Section 79 of the Customs Ordinance, Ch. 32 No. 2		Form C 21—Customs

No. of Bill of Lading _#1_
Port of Importation _POINT LISAS, P.L.I.P.D.E.C.O._
Importer's Name _MRS. V. GOMEZ_

Name of Aircraft or Ship	Master's Name	Date of Report	Port or Place whence arrived
M.V. "TRINIDAD & TOBAGO"	HAROLD THOMPSON	10/1/98	HOUSTON, TEXAS

Marks and Numbers	Number and Description of Packages with such information as the Importer is able to give as to Quantity and Value of Goods.
NM/NN	ONE (1) BARREL STC PERSONAL EFFECTS C/O MRS. V. GOMEZ

I, _MRS. V. GOMEZ_ the Importer, or
_____ Agent of the Importer,
of the Goods above-mentioned, do hereby declare that I have not, and that to the best of my knowledge he has not received sufficient Invoice, Bill of Lading, or other advice from which the Quantity, Quality or Value of the Goods above-mentioned, can be ascertained.

Dated this _10TH_ day of _JANUARY_ 19_98_

Frances Abbott
FRANCES ABBOTT   Witness.   Importer or Agent (I)

Declared before me this _10TH_ day of _JANUARY_ 19_98_.

Trujillo Valentine
for Comptroller of Customs and Excise.

Note.—(1) The Importer or his Agent may examine the above-mentioned goods for the purpose of making entry according to law.
(2) The declaration and signature of the Importer or his Agent must be attested by the proper Officer, or by a witness whose signature is known to and who is approved by the Comptroller.

Fig. 10.18 Form C-21 Customs bill of sight.

Table 10.1 *Terms used in trading*

Term	Definition
Call off	the buyer purchases in bulk and then at intervals calls for some of the order to be delivered
Carriage forward	the price quoted does not include the cost of carriage, which must be paid by the buyer
Carriage paid	the price quoted includes the cost of carriage to the buyer's address
Cash discount	an allowance of a certain percentage, often 2.5 or 5 per cent of the amount due from the buyer to the seller, provided the buyer pays within a stated time
Cash on delivery	the cost of the goods and any delivery charges will be collected when the goods are delivered to the buyer
Catalogue	a book illustrating and describing the products available from a supplier; the units, unit prices (see below), sizes and colours are given; some suppliers print prices in their catalogues, others provide a separate price list (see below), which can be updated more regularly
Catalogue (or code) number	identifies a specific product, e.g. a red two-ring binder may be 5679, a green ring two-ring binder 5683
Company's risk	a carrier is responsible for loss or damage of goods while they are in transit
Cost, insurance and freight (cif)	the total amount paid for imported goods; includes the cost of the goods plus insurance and freight charges
Delivery address	the location to which the goods are to be sent; may be different from the mailing address
Delivery charge	a charge made for delivery within the home country in addition to the cost of the goods
Delivery date	a specific date given by the supplier for the goods to be delivered to the buyer
Delivery method	the means of delivering the goods, e.g. by post, courier, carrier, road haulier, train, delivery van
Delivery time	the number of days/weeks/months from the date the supplier receives the order to the date of sending the goods
Due date	the date by which an amount owed by the buyer must be paid to the seller
Errors and omissions excepted (E & OE)	printed on an invoice, indicating that any amount under-charged, over-charged or incorrectly charged to the account can be corrected by a debit or credit note
Ex works or ex warehouse	the price of the goods does not include delivery to the buyer from the works or warehouse to the buyer's address
Free on board (fob)	the supplier pays carriage, dock dues and handling charges for stowing the goods on a ship; the buyer pays the freight and importing

(continued)

Table 10.1 *(continued)*

	charges (dock dues, customs duty, carriage from the dock where the goods are landed to their final destination)
Gross cost price	the full cost of goods before deduction of any discounts
Net cost/price	the price of goods after trade discount and/or cash discount has been deducted
One-off delivery	a complete order is delivered to the buyer
Owner's risk	a carrier is not responsible for goods in transit being lost or damaged unless caused by his employees' deliberate neglect or dishonesty
Part delivery	the term used when part of an order only is delivered, either because the supplier does not have all the goods available or because the buyer does not wish to take delivery of the full order
Premium	amount paid to an insurance company to insure goods against loss
Price list	list of products with unit prices (see below), which may be sent to buyers on its own or with a catalogue (see above)
Returnable empties	empty containers, e.g. crates, special bottles, pallets on which large items are stored, can be returned, for which credit will be given by the supplier
Tax	amount added to the price of an item; amount of tax varies from one country to another; the name of the tax also varies – for example, in some countries it is called 'sales tax', in others 'value added tax'
Terms of payment	stated on an invoice and/or statement indicating that the amount due must be paid within a certain time; in some cases the terms of payment may include a cash discount if paid in a short time, e.g. within seven days
Trade discount	amount deducted from the full price, known as 'gross price', of goods; a percentage (often 20, 25 or 30 per cent), which is allowed by firms in a trade to other firms in the same trade; by a manufacturer to a wholesaler, or a wholesaler to a retailer; may also be allowed to other buyers who order in bulk
Trade cost/price	amount payable after deduction of trade discount
Unit price	cost of a unit, which might be a single item, or a box, e.g. a carton containing 5 reams of copy paper, or a pack, e.g. 100 slip files

UNITS OF MEASUREMENT

When buying or selling goods, precise details of size, dimensions, weights and quantities must be stated. The most common units are listed below in metric and imperial systems. (The name of the measurement is given with its standard abbreviation and an explanation where appropriate.)

Metric (based on units of 10, 100, 1000)

Linear measure (measurement of length, width and depth)

millimetre	mm	thousandth of a metre
centimetre	cm	hundredth of a metre
metre	m	

These linear measurements can be **squared**, e.g. a piece of metal of 3 cm length and 2 cm width would be 6 sq cm (6 cm^2).

square centimetre	cm^2	square metre	m^2

Liquid

millilitre	ml	
litre	l	1000 millilitres

Cubic measurement is volume. An item measuring 10 cm length, 2 cm width and 1 cm depth would be 20 cubic centimetres (10 × 2 × 1).

cubic centimetre	cm^3	cubic metre	m^3

Weights

gram	g	
kilogram	kg	1000 grams
ton	tn	1000 kilograms

Imperial

Linear measure

inch	in	
foot	ft	12 inches (ins)
yard	yd	3 feet (ft)

These linear measurements can be squared and cubed (see above).

Weights

ounce	oz	
pound	lb	16 ounces (oz)
stone	st	14 pounds (lbs)
hundredweight	cwt	8 stones (st)
ton	tn	20 hundredweight or 2240 lbs – long ton
		2000 lbs – short ton

PRACTICE QUESTIONS

1. Explain the following terms:
    i. transaction
    ii. tender

iii. trade discount
iv. consignment note
v. pro-forma invoice
vi. credit note
vii. home trade
viii. overseas trade
ix. cash discount
x. quotation.

2. Prepare sets of documents (on the typewriter if possible) to cover the following transactions.
   a. The purchase of office stationery supplies by the Standard Insurance Co. Ltd from Office Supplies Ltd
   b. The purchase of setting lotions, shampoos, pins, etc. by a hairdressing salon, Anna, from the Excellent Trading Co. Ltd
   c. The purchase of stock by The Cycle Stores Ltd from International Bicycle Accessories Ltd.

3. Study the document shown in Fig. 10.19, then answer the questions below.
   a. What is the name of the customer?
   b. What is the name of the supplier?
   c. What is the reference number of the account?

```
                          STATEMENT

                    EXCELLENT TRADING CO. LTD
                       Water Street, Grenada
                           Tel.: 2771

Mr PK Kyer                                              1 August 2002
31 Market Street
GRENADA
A/c4/F/91
```

Date	Balance from previous month	Dept	Purchases	Amount due
	$		$	$
1.7.02	250.00			250.00
8.7.02		H'ware	125.00	
22.7.02		F'ture	355.00	480.00
				$730.00

Terms: Strictly net

Fig. 10.19 Example of a statement.

d. What is the date of the statement?
   e. How much did the customer owe at the beginning of the month?
   f. How much did the customer spend during the month?
   g. How much did the customer spend in each department?
   h. What was the total amount due at the end of the month?
   i. What is the meaning of 'Terms: strictly net'?

4. Explain the following terms and abbreviations:
   i. carriage paid
   ii. ex works
   iii. trade price
   iv. net cash price
   v. carriage forward
   vi. fob
   vii. cif
   viii. E & OE
   ix. company's risk
   x. owner's risk.

5. a. i. What is the difference between trade discount and cash discount?
      ii. Why are they important when a buyer is considering a supplier's quoted prices?
   b. Prepare a receipt to give to a man who has just bought a secondhand filing cabinet from your organisation for $80.00.

6. The purchasing department of a firm wishes to order a large quantity of an item that it has not obtained previously. Outline the office procedures that will be followed and the documents that will be involved, with a brief explanation of the purpose of each, up to the stage when the organisation pays for the item purchased.

7. a. When might a credit note be used?
   b. Prepare a credit note form and enter the following details.

      On the 10th of last month, Alanson & Co., 13 Long Street, St Vincent, returned to YKK Co. Ltd, 14 Nook Avenue, Kingston, Jamaica, by T & L Steamship Co. Vessel *Enterprise* the following items:

      3 Ace word processors (damaged) $20 100 each
      12 Contact typists chairs (wrong model supplied) $1080 each
      2 Excel plain paper copiers $5865 each.

8. a. You are in charge of ordering stationery supplies for your department. Copy the order form shown in Fig. 10.20, which is used by your company A-ONE Equipment Ltd, and complete it for signature by the head of your department. The order is to go to Ideal Stationers Ltd, Barton Road, Kingston, Jamaica, with whom your company has an

```
                              ORDER
┌─────────────────┬──────────────┬──────────────┐
│ Tel. Townlea 4579│ Date         │ Order No.    │
├─────────────────┴──────────────┴──────────────┤
│        A-ONE Equipment, 2nd Avenue, Kingston, Jamaica │
├─────────────────────────────┬─────────────────┤
│ CUSTOMER ACCOUNT No.        │ Our Stock Ref.  │
├─────────────────────────────┴─────────────────┤
│ To                                            │
│                                               │
│                                               │
├───────────────────────────────────────────────┤
│ Please Supply and Deliver                     │
├───────┬─────────────────────────┬─────────────┤
│ Qty   │ Description             │ Price       │
│       │                         │             │
│       │                         │             │
│       │                         │             │
│       │                         │             │
├───────┴──────────────┬──────────┴─────────────┤
│ NO DELIVERIES ACCEPTED UNLESS AGAINST│ Signed │
│ OUR OFFICIAL ORDER                   │        │
│ PLEASE QUOTE ORDER NO. AND DATE      │ Purchasing Officer │
└──────────────────────┴─────────────────────────┘
```

Fig. 10.20 Example of an order form.

account, no. A1069. The stock reference is E818. The items required are:
50 shorthand notebooks, hard cover J$70.00 each (less 10 per cent)
100 Special ballpens J$7.00 for 10 (net)
24 Pencil erasers J$280.00 per dozen (less 10 per cent)
10 boxes medium-sized paper clips J$50.00 for 10 boxes
(less 15 per cent).

b. When your head of department sees the order he thinks the prices quoted are rather high. He asks you to obtain prices from other suppliers. In what ways might you do this?

c. What factors, in addition to price, would you check when making these enquiries?

9. The following transactions took place between Mr John Thomson of 16 Acre Street, Kingston, Jamaica, and The New Style Supply Co. Ltd of

Georgetown, Guyana. All the goods supplied to Mr Thomson are subject to 20 per cent trade discount off the catalogue prices quoted below.

2002

1 April	Balance owing by John Thomson $249.75
7 April	Goods supplied $271.41 (Invoice no. A3405)
12 April	Some goods supplied on 7 April returned damaged; credit note S.514 sent for $42.99
14 April	30 items supplied at $32.10 each (Invoice no. A4271)
23 April	40 items supplied at $16.00 each (Invoice no. A5413)
26 April	John Thomson returned packing cases and was allowed $60.00 (credit note S.689)
28 April	John Thomson paid by cheque the balance owing on 1 April 2002

a. Prepare a statement form for The New Style Supply Co. Ltd. Enter the transactions set out above and show the balance owing at 30 April 2002.

b. Prepare a cheque and complete it for the amount due at 30 April 2002. Mr John Thomson is allowed 2.5 per cent cash discount as he makes the payment on 4 May, i.e. within seven days of the date of the statement, which is 30 April 2002.

10. If you are sending goods by air on behalf of your company in San Fernando to a customer in Jamaica, on what factors do you think the freight charges, i.e. the amount to be paid for carrying the goods, would be based?

11. *a.* What are the principal means of transporting goods within the Caribbean territory in which you live?

b. State the factors you would consider for using each one.

12. *a.* What is a certificate of origin?

b. What is an air waybill?

c. What is a bill of lading?

13. As an invoice clerk for GAB Jewellery Supply Co. Ltd you have supplied J Goldsmith & Sons, 123 Broad Street, Bridgetown, Barbados, with the following items against their Order no. 312/JG.

Quantity	Item	Price ($)
3 only	Gents' watches	1275.00 each
10 only	Ladies' watches	950.00 each
1 only	Lady's gold brooch	1800.00 each
6 pairs	Gold cufflinks	3800.00 pair
4 only	Gold and diamond rings	4008.00 each
2 only	Gold filigree necklaces	3500.00 each
3 only	Silver filigree necklaces	800.00 each

Prepare an invoice form and complete it with the details above. A trade discount of 33.3 per cent is allowed, plus 2.5 per cent cash discount for payment within 30 days. Postage is included in the costs.

14.
   a. If you are sending goods by sea:
      i. what two documents are essential
      ii. what information does each document contain?
   b. If you could not produce the necessary documents when importing goods, what form would you have to complete?

15. Rewrite the following list of documents in the order in which they are used during the buying and selling process and state whether each one is produced by the buyer or the seller.

invoice	packing/despatch/delivery/consignment note
enquiry	quotation/estimate/tender
statement	credit note
pro-forma invoice	requisition
advice note	order
debit note	cheque

16. Explain the following:
   i. delivery address
   ii. delivery note
   iii. acknowledgement of order
   iv. reference for a new customer
   v. goods received note
   vi. debit note
   vii. remittance slip
   viii. certificate of insurance
   ix. customs bill of sight
   x. export licence.

17. What does the term 'part delivery' mean? When might a customer ask for goods to be supplied on this basis?

SHORT ANSWER QUESTIONS

1. The gross price of an article is the price before .... is deducted.

2. When a supplier has made a mistake on an invoice and charged less than the proper price, a/an .... is sent to the buyer.

3. When sending goods by air the equivalent of a bill of lading is a/an ....

4.
   a. A thousandth of a metre is a/an ....

b. A kilogram is .... grams.
 c. Eight stones is a/an ....
 d. Written in full, 6 m is 6 ....
 e. A/an .... is 2000 lbs.

5. Suppliers often offer customers an incentive to pay invoices within a prescribed time. The incentive is a/an ....

Choose the most appropriate ending for each of the following sentences.

6. When a customer asks for information on a particular product a supplier sends a/an:
 a. advice note
 b. pro-forma invoice
 c. catalogue
 d. acknowledgement of order.

7. A supplier receiving an order from a new customer will want:
 a. a letter of recommendation
 b. a bank draft
 c. authority from the chief executive of the company
 d. a reference from another organisation.

8. If a buyer is known to the supplier, checks are made when a new order is placed to ensure that the buyer:
 a. is within the agreed credit limit
 b. has paid the last account
 c. has ordered goods within the last three months
 d. has sufficient funds to pay for the new order.

9. A packing note is sent to the customer:
 a. before the goods are despatched
 b. with the goods
 c. after the goods have been despatched
 d. with the invoice.

10. When the buyer receives an order from the supplier the delivery is recorded:
 a. with an acknowledgement to the supplier
 b. on stock record cards
 c. on a copy of the original order
 d. on a goods received note.

EXAMINATION QUESTIONS

1. A/an .... note is sent if a customer is over-charged.

(Pitman Office Procedures Level 1 1998 Pt 1A)

2. List THREE documents that are connected with accounting for the sale of goods.

   a. ....
   b. ....
   c. ....

   (Pitman Office Procedures Level 1 1998 Pt 1B)

3. You are employed by Woodcraft Sheds Ltd. Complete the invoice in Fig. 10.21a using Invoice no. S4789 and today's date for the goods ordered by the fax in Fig. 10.21b. Use the prices listed on the 'Price list' in Fig. 10.21c.

   (Pitman Office Procedures Level 1 1998 Pt 2A)

WOODCRAFT SHEDS LTD
WINDSOR SAWMILLS
LONDON ROAD
WINDSOR WF4 6KP

Tel.: 01942 440045
Fax: 01942 446753

Invoice No.:

Order No.:
Order Date:

Date:

Terms: 3% for monthly settlement

Quantity	Description	Item price £	Erection each £	Total price £

TOTAL goods
LESS: 10% trade discount
NEW TOTAL
ADD: sales tax 15%
TOTAL BALANCE DUE

(a)

Fig. 10.21

FACSIMILE

No. of pages: 1

To: Woodcraft Sheds Ltd
Windsor Sawmills
London Road
WINDSOR WF4 6KP

From: Ford's Portable Buildings
22–42 New Street
MANCHESTER MA6 7LD

Date: 3 days ago

Please reply to:
Fax No.: 01274 65984

Copy to:

Please supply as soon as possible:

1 Feather Edge Shed – Apex style size 8' x 6'
2 Heavy Duty Sheds – Pent style size 6' x 4'
1 Super Range Shed – Pent style size 8' x 6'

Each shed will be erected by you on our site.
We assume 10% trade discount.
Order No. 5419

Signature *T. Sinclair*
Chief Buyer

(b)

WOODCRAFT SHEDS LTD
PRICE LIST

Approx SIZE	FEATHER EDGE		SUPER RANGE		LOG-LAP APEX	HEAVY DUTY		HOBBY APEX	OPTIONAL ERECTION
	APEX	PENT	APEX	PENT		APEX	PENT		
6' x 4'	£199	219	£249	256	£270	£297	305	£264	£39
7' x 5'	£226	246	£281	285	£302	£339	357	£305	£41
8' x 6'	£259	270	£305	333	£353	£402	407	£352	£45
10' x 6'	---	---	£386	397	£395	£512	490	£393	£54
10' x 8'	---	---	---	---	£526	£631	591	£463	£78
12' x 6'	---	---	£461	509	£464	---	562	£443	£70
12' x 8'	---	---	---	---	£588	£699	683	£525	£86

PRICES INCLUDE DELIVERY: ERECTION IS OPTIONAL AS PRICED

(c)

Fig. 10.21 (continued).

4. The price of items and the total cost of an order is not given on a/an .... note.

5. The first document in a selling transaction is a/an ....
(Pitman Office Procedures Level 1 1999 Pt 1A)

6. Put the following in correct sequence:
order
invoice
requisition
(Pitman Office Procedures Level 1 1999 Pt 1B)

7. Your company has received quotations from the four firms listed in Fig. 10.22a for the supply of a document safe. Using this information (see Fig. 10.22a), carry out the following tasks.
   a. Calculate the actual price to your company for a safe from each supplier. Then, using the blank sheet in Fig. 10.22b, rearrange the table in price order beginning with the cheapest.
   b. Write a memo to your manager, enclosing your new table. Let him know that all the suppliers can deliver within one week, except for S & N Safes who have quoted one-month delivery.
(Pitman Office Procedures Level 1 1999 Pt 2B)

8. Quotations have been received for the supply of two fire extinguishers for the office. Details are summarised below.

   QUOTATION 1 – £60 each, plus sales tax at 10 per cent payable on monthly statement or 2.5 per cent cash discount for payment within seven days. Delivery generally within two working days of signed order. Quotation price held for one month. Maintenance can be provided on demand. Minimum call-out charge £25 plus hourly rate and materials.

   QUOTATION 2 – £64 each, inclusive of all taxes and other charges. Cash required with order. Delivery usually within two working days. Price includes automatic reminder for annual maintenance available at £10 inclusive. Remedial work not usually required during first 10 years, but if needed separate quotation provided. Extinguishers guaranteed for 1 year. Explanatory literature enclosed.

   Draw up a table comparing the two quotations, including the total cost of each.
(Pitman Office Procedures Level 2 1998 Pt 2)

(a)

Firm	Price £	Trade discount	Sales tax 15%	Carriage £	ACTUAL PRICE
ANALYSIS OF PRICES AND TERMS OF QUOTATIONS FOR PURCHASE OF A DOCUMENT SAFE					
Link Security	120	Nil	Not included	Paid	
S & N Safes	100	10%	Included	£25	
Reed & Co.	150	15%	Included	Paid	
Lock & Safe Co.	90	Nil	Not included	£15	

(b)

ANALYSIS OF PRICES AND TERMS OF QUOTATIONS FOR PURCHASE OF A DOCUMENT SAFE

Firm	Price £	Trade discount	Sales tax 15%	Carriage £	ACTUAL PRICE

Fig. 10.22

9. You need to purchase a pedestal desk and a typist's chair for a new employee. Draft a standard letter of enquiry that could be sent to several office furniture suppliers. Include all the information you will require.

(Pitman Office Procedures Level 2 1998 Pt 1)

CHAPTER 11

METHODS OF PAYMENT

OBJECTIVES When you have studied this chapter you should have acquired the knowledge and understanding to be able to:

1. explain the three main types of bank account
2. explain the process and forms used to open a bank account
3. list and explain the various ways of making payments
4. complete a cheque and recognise different types of cheque crossings
5. explain when and why a cheque may not be valid
6. explain methods of payment when trading overseas
7. explain methods of withdrawing money from a bank account
8. give details of how to use other bank facilities, including borrowing money
9. reconcile a bank statement with accounting records
10. briefly explain the banks' clearing system
11. be aware of developments in banking as they occur.

In business, as in private life, goods and services have to be paid for, which means that we need funds on which to draw. It is usual to have a bank account, so we will discuss the types of bank account there are, how to open an account and what facilities are available to account holders, before we discuss the various methods of paying bills.

TYPES OF BANK ACCOUNT

Commercial banks offer three types of bank account: **savings** accounts, **term deposit** accounts and **demand deposit** accounts.

SAVINGS ACCOUNTS

Savings accounts enable people to put money that they do not need immediately into a bank so that it will earn **interest**. This means that the bank pays a percentage of the amount of money in the account and adds it to the original amount, usually on a specified date each year. If, for example, you were to deposit $100 in a savings account, and the annual rate of interest is 5 per cent, the bank would add $5 to your account. If you withdraw money during the year, the amount of interest will be less; if you deposit more money during the year, the amount of interest will increase.

TERM DEPOSIT ACCOUNTS (OR 'FIXED DEPOSIT' ACCOUNTS)

These accounts enable people to place their money **on deposit** for a longer fixed period, usually a year or more. The longer the term, the higher the interest. Interest is calculated annually and is added to the account on specific dates. If the account holder withdraws money during the fixed term they lose a certain amount of interest.

DEMAND DEPOSIT ACCOUNTS

Demand deposit accounts enable people to deposit money into an account and pay out of it as necessary. Generally banks do not pay interest on these accounts but some demand deposit accounts, such as bonus checking accounts, do earn a small amount of interest on money held in the account. This interest is calculated on the balance, i.e. the amount of money, held in the account at the end of each day.

A demand deposit account could be called a 'working account'. Money is paid in as creditors (people who owe you money) pay their bills and you pay money out to your debtors (people to whom you owe money).

CHOOSING A BANK

When an individual or a company wishes to open a demand deposit account at a bank, they have first to decide which bank they would like to use. Most companies choose a bank near their business premises so that it is easy to pay in cheques received and withdraw money when it is needed. Most business organisations encourage their employees to open bank accounts so it may be useful for an employee to use the same bank as the business. Working for the business serves as an introduction for the employees of the business. The later closing time on Fridays for banks is convenient when you wish to withdraw cash or have other business with the bank.

OPENING AN ACCOUNT

When a business wishes to open an account at a bank, a representative of the company, usually the chief accountant, arranges an appointment. An individual can go into the bank and tell one of the cashiers that they wish to open an account. They will then be seen by the bank manager (possibly in a small branch) or one of the bank manager's assistants.

The business or individual wishing to open an account must provide the names of referees. However, if a business owner already has a personal account at the bank, a reference will probably not be needed. An individual is asked for two forms of identification – their last utility bill and a letter of employment. The latter requirement applies to the opening of a chequing account only, not to a savings account.

FORMS

Various forms have to be completed. This is usually done by the bank assistant who asks the person to sign them, one of these being a **signature card**. This is a very important document because the signature on it will be used to compare the signature on cheques that you write and other instructions that you give.

Most businesses have two, sometimes three, signatories (i.e. people who have authority to sign cheques). A company's cheques are usually signed by two senior staff, e.g. the chief accountant and company secretary. This is to prevent fraud. The third signatory would sign if either of the other two were absent.

Another form to be completed is the **paying-in slip**, also called a **deposit slip** or **credit slip**. A minimum amount of money, cash or cheques, is needed to open an account.

As a paying-in slip (see Fig. 11.1) will have to be completed every time money is paid into the account, a **paying-in book** containing pre-printed

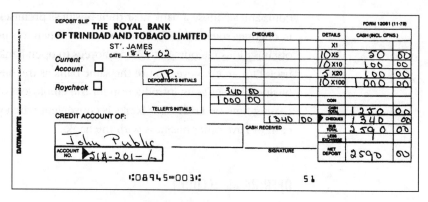

Fig. 11.1 Paying-in (or deposit) slip completed when paying money into a bank account.

slips will be ordered. The slips will be printed with the account holder's bank branch code, name and account number. This will enable them to pay money in at any branch of the bank (a method known as **crediting**).

CHEQUE FORMS

Legally, cheques can be written on anything but banks would certainly query a cheque written on anything other than a pre-printed cheque bearing the name of the drawee (i.e. the name of the bank on which the cheque is drawn). This is for security reasons and is in the account holder's interests.

Several banks print 'personalised' cheques at the request of an account holder. These are printed with a background scene and the account holder's name, address, telephone number and account number.

A **cheque book** will be needed in order to withdraw cash and make payments to suppliers, etc. A form is completed requesting cheques to be pre-printed with the same details as the paying-in slips. The cheques are also numbered. The bank branch code and account number on the paying-in slips and cheques, and the cheque number on the cheque are printed in MICR (magnetic ink character recognition) ink. This is to enable the slips and cheques to be processed electronically. These MICR characters are usually printed along the bottom of the cheque. Cheques are discussed in detail on pages 318–22.

The books of paying-in slips and cheques will be sent to the new account holder within a few days. When all but a few paying-in slips and cheques have been used, there is in each book a request form for a new book.

This must be completed and handed in or sent to the account holder's bank branch.

TAKING CARE OF A CHEQUE BOOK

The possession of a cheque book, whether business or personal, is a responsibility. As cheques represent money there must be safeguards to protect the bank, the drawer (the person who signs the cheque) and the payee (the individual/organisation to whom the cheque is payable). Anyone using a cheque book should adhere to the precautions listed below.

1. Keep the cheque book with you or in a safe place, ideally a locked drawer.
2. Never write a signature on the cover.
3. Never sign a blank cheque for it to be completed at a later date.
4. If the cheque book is lost, inform the bank immediately by telephone and then in writing so that the cheques can be 'stopped' (see page 321).
5. Write cheques in ink (preferably with a ballpoint pen). Begin writing as far to the left of each line as possible and do not leave spaces in which unauthorised words or figures could be written.
6. Initial or sign any alterations.
7. Use the same signature as the one written on the specimen signature card (see page 315).
8. Complete the counterfoil or copy slip (see page 319) so that you can give details in the event of losing the cheque and to check your record against your bank statement (see page 330).

MAKING PAYMENTS

There is a variety of ways in which to pay for goods and services:

- cheque
- bank draft
- crediting
- standing order
- direct debit
- credit card
- Switch card
- money order
- postal order
- documentary credit

- electronic transfer
- travellers' cheques.

PAYMENT BY CHEQUE

A cheque represents the amount of money written on it and is considered in law in many countries to be the same as cash. The cheque is a form of instruction to the bank to take money out of the demand deposit account of the drawer (the account holder who signs the cheque), and credit that amount to the account of the payee. The processes involved in this transaction are explained under 'Clearing a cheque' on pages 333-4.

Cheques can be used in several ways. A cheque can be given or sent to a creditor to settle an account; the drawer can withdraw money from their own account by **cashing a cheque**; or the drawer can give the payee a cheque that they can cash. Many organisations pay their employees by cheque to avoid keeping large sums of money on site.

A **crossed cheque** (see Fig. 11.2) must be deposited into the payee's account and cannot be cashed or transferred by the payee to another person (see pages 320-1).

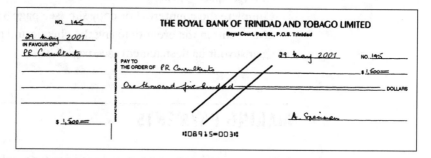

Fig. 11.2 Crossed cheque with counterfoil.

DRAWING A CHEQUE

There are five details to be completed on a cheque:

1. the date
2. the name of the payee
3. the amount to be paid in words
4. the amount to be paid in figures
5. the signature of the drawer.

On the left-hand side of the line on which the payee's name is written may be printed 'Pay to the order of' or, on the right-hand side, 'Or order'. This means that the cheque must be paid into the payee's account unless it has been endorsed, i.e. signed on the reverse, by the payee.

The drawer should also complete the cheque counterfoil with the date, name of the payee and the amount. Some counterfoils provide space to write the balance (amount of money) in the account before the cheque is paid, and the balance that will be left after the cheque is paid. A completed cheque and counterfoil is shown in Fig. 11.2. (The crossing on the cheque will be explained later.) Alternatively, the cheque book may have a copy slip (see Fig. 11.3) instead of counterfoils to individual cheques.

DATE	CHEQUE NO.	PARTICULARS	AMOUNT OF CHEQUE	√	AMOUNT OF DEPOSIT	BALANCE
		BALANCE FORWARD				

Fig. 11.3 Copy slip.

It is very important that each detail is written correctly. When the cheque is paid into the bank it will be checked to ensure that:

- the date is neither more than six months before the date of paying in nor that it is a future date; a cheque dated more than six months previously is known as a **stale-dated cheque** and a cheque dated ahead of time is a **post-dated cheque**
- the name of the payee is the same as the name on the paying-in slip if the cheque is to be deposited into the payee's account
- the amount written in words is the same as the amount written in figures
- the signature is correct.

POST-DATED CHEQUES

A person may wish to give a cheque to be paid at a future date (post-dated). The payee cannot pay the cheque into their account until the date written on the cheque. Banks do not approve of the practice of post-dating cheques.

AMENDING A CHEQUE

Only the drawer can amend a cheque. The amendment is written next to the detail(s) to be changed, initialled or, in some countries, signed. The date on stale-dated cheques (see page 319) can be amended in this way, although it is always safer to write another cheque and destroy the original. Never erase a detail to be changed as this invalidates the cheque.

CROSSING A CHEQUE

The purpose of crossing a cheque is to ensure that it is paid into a bank account or Post Office savings account. If a crossed cheque is lost (see page 321) it cannot be cashed by anyone. A cheque sent by post should always be crossed.

The crossing is two parallel vertical or diagonal lines drawn across the middle of the cheque (see Fig. 11.2). This is known as a **general crossing**. Many banks issue their cheques with the crossing printed on.

There are also **special crossings**, which provide additional safeguards. These include:

- 'Account payee only' and 'Not negotiable'
- the name of the account, e.g. 'Repairs a/c' (a/c = abbreviation for 'account')
- the name and branch of the bank, e.g. 'Barclays Bank, Bridgetown'
- the maximum amount payable, e.g. 'Under 10 dollars' would prevent a cheque for $8 being altered to $80 or $800.

Examples of cheque book crossings are shown in Fig. 11.4.

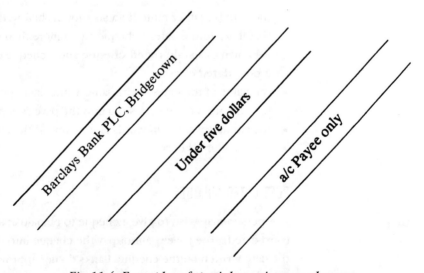

Fig. 11.4 Examples of special crossings on cheques.

'Account payee only' and 'Not negotiable' do not mean what they appear to mean. Cheques with these crossings can be endorsed (signed on the reverse) by the payee and passed on to another person for payment into their account. However, a cheque being paid into an account other than that of the named payee would certainly be checked by a bank cashier.

LOST CHEQUE

If a cheque is lost, whether it is an open or crossed cheque, the branch of the bank should be informed immediately by telephone. The account name and number, cheque number, the date on which the cheque was drawn and the amount should be given. Even if these details are not available when the loss is discovered, ring the bank anyway; the bank will then **stop payment**.

STOPPING PAYMENT OF A CHEQUE

Having informed the bank by telephone of the loss of a cheque, the details must be confirmed in writing. This validates the need to complete the cheque counterfoil or copy slip when drawing a cheque. The instruction to stop payment (see above) will result in the bank refusing to cash an open cheque. If a crossed cheque that has been stopped arrives at the drawer's branch it is returned unpaid to the payee's branch. The drawer's account is not debited (i.e. the money is not taken out of the drawer's account).

A lost or stolen cheque book should be reported to the bank immediately, giving the name and number of the account.

ACTIVITY 11.1 Make a drawing of a cheque with a counterfoil (see Fig. 11.2). Complete the cheque you have drawn with the following details:

- today's date
- cheque payable to Jacob Abraham
- an amount of $149.87
- signed by you
- crossed 'Account payee only'.

DISHONOURED CHEQUE

When a drawer writes a cheque for more than the balance in their account, their branch will refuse to pay the cheque unless an overdraft has been arranged (see page 325). The cheque will be returned to the payee's branch marked 'R/D' (refer to drawer). The payee then has to contact the drawer to get the money owed. Cheques marked 'R/D' are known as **dishonoured cheques** and are said to 'bounce'. It is illegal to draw cheques on an account in which there are insufficient funds, and legal proceedings may be taken against the drawer.

PAYMENT BY BANK DRAFT

People are not always happy to receive a cheque for a very large amount of money, e.g. when selling a car. A bank draft is a cheque from the bank, i.e. the bank is the drawer as well as the drawee, to the payee. The customer authorises the bank to debit the amount from their account to issue the draft in favour of the payee, to whom the draft is then given. The payee can then hand over the car to the customer, knowing that the payment is guaranteed absolutely and the money will be paid on presentation of the draft to the bank. A company or personal cheque takes time to process and in the meantime a company can go bankrupt or an individual can die, creating problems for the payee.

PAYMENT BY CREDITING

In the section about forms, we explained that money paid into an account with a paying-in slip via a different branch from that where the account is held is known as crediting (see page 316).

Many businesses pay their staff by crediting their accounts. A list is prepared of the employees' names, bank, branch codes and account numbers, and the amount to be paid to each. Individual credit slips are prepared. One cheque for the total amount, made payable to the bank, is taken with the slips to the organisation's bank branch. Alternatively the business may supply the list on diskette. The bank transfers payments to the individual bank branches.

Anyone without a bank account can use the service but pays the total of the payments in cash plus a service charge.

PAYMENT BY STANDING ORDER

When an account holder wishes to make a payment of a specific amount on a regular basis, this can be arranged by standing order. Standing orders are a useful way of making regular payments, e.g. annual subscriptions and monthly rent or leases. The account holder completes and signs a standing order form (see Fig. 11.5) giving details of the payee's account number, and bank branch name and code, the amount to be transferred and the dates on which payments are to be made, e.g. the last day of each month. The bank makes the credit transfers to the payee on the specified dates without further instruction. An account holder can cancel the standing order at any time. There is a charge for standing order payments but it is waived for customers who enjoy certain facilities, e.g. Plan 55 customers at the Royal Bank of Trinidad and Tobago.

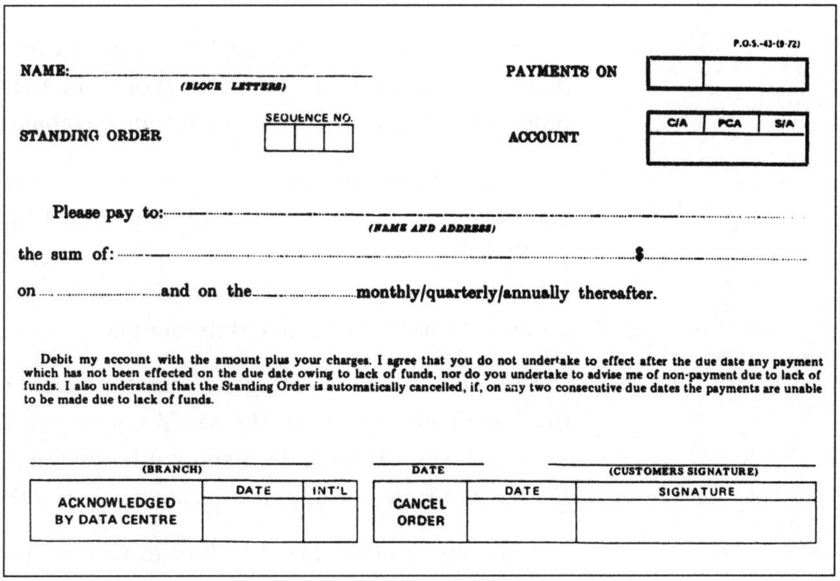

P.O.S.-43-(9-72)

NAME: ______________ (BLOCK LETTERS)

PAYMENTS ON

STANDING ORDER

SEQUENCE NO.

ACCOUNT

C/A	PCA	S/A

Please pay to: ______________ (NAME AND ADDRESS)

the sum of: ______________ $ ______

on ______ and on the ______ monthly/quarterly/annually thereafter.

Debit my account with the amount plus your charges. I agree that you do not undertake to effect after the due date any payment which has not been effected on the due date owing to lack of funds, nor do you undertake to advise me of non-payment due to lack of funds. I also understand that the Standing Order is automatically cancelled, if, on any two consecutive due dates the payments are unable to be made due to lack of funds.

(BRANCH) | DATE | (CUSTOMERS SIGNATURE)

ACKNOWLEDGED BY DATA CENTRE	DATE	INT'L

CANCEL ORDER	DATE	SIGNATURE

Fig. 11.5 Standing order form.

PAYMENT BY DIRECT DEBIT

Many suppliers now use the direct debit facility, by which **they** instruct the customer's bank to transfer money from the customer's account to their own. The customer completes a **direct debit authority** giving their account number, bank branch name and code and, in some cases, the dates for the debits to be paid, e.g. the first day of each month. They sign the form and send it to the supplier to complete with their account number, and bank branch name and code. The supplier then sends the form to the customer's bank as their authority to collect payments.

On the due date the supplier sends to its bank a list of all debits that are due to it and the total amount to be credited to its account. This list is usually provided on diskette, which the bank uses to process the transactions to their branches or to other banks. An advice of the debit is sent to the customer's bank and to the customer. When the customer's branch receives the advice, the account will automatically be debited with the correct amount. The customer can cancel a direct debit authority at any time.

PAYMENT BY CREDIT CARD

Creditworthy people may apply for a credit card, which enables them to buy goods and services on credit in shops, hotels, restaurants and by mail order. Pre-requisites are a minimum annual income and a good credit rating.

The credit card has a magnetic strip, which contains the holder's details including name, credit card account number, start date, expiry date and credit limit, i.e. the maximum amount the card holder may owe at any time. When ordering by telephone or on the Internet, the details that are **printed** on the card have to be given to the supplier.

The amounts due are charged by the suppliers to the bank or company that issued the credit card. The bank/company sends a monthly statement to the card holder showing the amount due and the deadline for payment. Interest is charged on any amount outstanding at the due date.

A Royal Bank of Trinidad and Tobago Visa credit card holder can use the card to purchase goods on credit or to secure cash advances, i.e. borrow money, up to the maximum limit agreed with the Visa officers. Interest is charged on the monthly balance. Repayment is on the balance or by direct debit of monthly payments with an option for cash payments.

PAYMENT BY SWITCH CARD

A Switch card enables a customer to pay for goods in hotels, restaurants and shops without writing a cheque. The seller swipes the card through a machine, which is connected to a computer. The details of the customer's bank account are 'read off' the magnetic strip on the card, the amount of money to be paid is keyed in by the sales clerk and the customer's account is debited with the amount.

PAYMENT BY MONEY ORDER

An inland money order can be bought at a Post Office on presentation of a completed request form. It can be used to send any sum of money not exceeding $500 to a specified person. Payment is made at the Post Office stated on the money order. An issuing fee is charged on money orders, which may be crossed in the same way as cheques so that they can only be paid into the payee's bank account.

PAYMENT BY POSTAL ORDER

In Trinidad and Tobago, British postal orders for amounts of $1 and $2 can be bought at Post Offices for making payments overseas. If a postal order is needed for an amount between the standard denominations, up to two stamps can be stuck on the order to make up the amount. The name of the payee and the Post Office where the order is to be cashed must be written in the spaces provided. If the Post Office nearest the payee is not known, write the town or district where the payee lives, which enables them to cash the order at any Post Office in the place named.

The counterfoil, provided with every postal order, should be completed with the name of the payee, the date, the office of payment and the amount. Keep the counterfoil with a copy of the covering letter.

Postal orders may be crossed in the same way as cheques. Crossed postal orders can only be paid into a bank. An 'open' (uncrossed) postal order may be cashed at a Post Office. Before payment is made, the payee must sign their name in the space provided. This is a form of receipt for the Post Office.

Non-British postal orders are available in other territories in the Caribbean.

PAYMENT BY DOCUMENTARY CREDIT

When goods are bought and sold overseas, i.e. imported and exported, arrangements have to be made to pay for them. If the parties to the transaction do not know each other, the buyer will be wary of paying for the goods before he receives them and the seller will be reluctant to despatch the goods before he has received payment. **Documentary credit**, arranged through a bank, overcomes this problem.

The seller invoices the buyer, who arranges for their bankers to withdraw the required amount of money from their account upon presentation of the original **bill of lading**. Proof of despatch is provided by the seller taking the bill of lading (see Chapter 10, page 289) to his bankers. The bill of lading is exchanged for the money, and both parties are satisfied that they cannot be cheated.

Documentary credit is subject to exchange control regulations, as is any form of payment to overseas countries from most islands in the Caribbean.

PAYMENT BY ELECTRONIC TRANSFER

A computerised system of transferring funds internationally is provided by two organisations:

- SWIFT (Society for World Wide Inter-Bank Financial Telecommunications)
- Moneygram, operated by American Express within a country and internationally.

SWIFT and Moneygram transfer funds electronically, so bank accounts are debited and credited rapidly.

The client instructs their bank to make a payment to a supplier. The bank enters the transaction on to its computer with appropriate instructions for transmission, using SWIFT software. The client's account is debited and, within a short time, perhaps half an hour (depending on transmission availability), the transaction is recorded on the computer in the foreign country. The Moneygram service operates in a similar way.

PAYMENT BY TRAVELLERS' CHEQUES

When people are abroad on business they need to be able to pay either in the currency of the country or by a means that will enable the supplier, e.g. hotel or shop, to obtain payment in their own currency. Banks sell travellers' cheques and foreign currency to customers who are going abroad either on holiday or on business. The customer's account is debited for the equivalent amount in the home currency plus a commission.

Travellers' cheques are issued in US$ and CA$ in denominations of $5, $10, $20, $50 and $100; GB£ sterling cheques are also available. When receiving the travellers' cheques the customer signs each one in front of the cashier. A slip listing the denominations and numbers of the cheques is given to the customer. This slip should be kept separate from the cheques so that if they are lost, the details can be reported to the bank. This must be done immediately so that cashing by any unauthorised person can be stopped and the amount of the lost cheques refunded to the owner.

To cash the cheques the owner has to take them to a bank or bureau de change. Each cheque must be countersigned and dated in front of the cashier. Some form of identification, e.g. a passport, is required. Travellers' cheques can also be given in payment at hotels and shops. Some hotels will also cash cheques but at a lower rate of exchange than the bank or bureau de change.

Travellers' cheques are valid until death as long as they are not dated.

WITHDRAWING MONEY FROM A BANK ACCOUNT

Money can be withdrawn from a bank in three ways:

1. by cheque
2. by debit card
3. by LINX card.

WITHDRAWING CASH BY CHEQUE

When you need cash you have to 'pay yourself' by writing an **open cheque**, which has to be presented for payment at the branch of the bank (drawee) printed on the cheque. The payee line can be completed either with your own name or 'Cash'.

If the cheque has a pre-printed crossing this can be opened by writing 'please pay cash' along the crossing and signing the instruction in full, not initials. The cheque must also be endorsed (signed on the reverse) by the drawer. In some islands, e.g. Jamaica, a crossed cheque cannot be 'opened'. In such a case the cheques would be printed without a crossing, though businesses would ask for printed crossed cheques.

WITHDRAWING MONEY BY DEBIT CARD

By using a special bank debit card, customers can obtain cash at any time of the day or night up to a specified daily maximum, from **cash points** located in the outside wall of some banks. Each customer has a personal identity number (PIN), which they should keep secret. Without the PIN number no other person can obtain money even if the card is stolen.

The steps taken to obtain money from the cash point are as follows.

1. Insert the bank card where indicated, ensuring that the position of the magnetic strip is correct.
2. Key in the PIN.
3. Key in the instructions, i.e. requesting cash, cash slip and/or statement.
4. Key in the amount of cash required.
5. Remove the bank card when instructed to do so.
6. Remove the money.
7. Remove the cash slip and/or statement.

WITHDRAWING MONEY BY LINX CARD

LINX card holders can withdraw cash at any cash point, not necessarily at a branch of their own bank. In Jamaica this service is called JETS. LINX cards can also be used to pay for goods and services.

PAYING MONEY INTO AN ACCOUNT

There are two ways of paying money into an account:

1. by the account holder, or their representative, taking cash and/or cheques with a paying-in slip to their own bank or a branch of their own bank
2. by an account holder instructing their bank to transfer funds from their account to another person's or business's account by credit transfer (see page 322).

PAYING-IN SLIPS

These were explained on page 315. In the course of trading, businesses receive cash and cheques. A detailed listing has to be entered on the paying-in slip.

The paying-in slip has a section to list cash and a section to list cheques. The money must be counted carefully by denomination. The number of coins or notes of each denomination are entered and their value. The total value of cash is entered. The value of each cheque is listed and the total entered under the cash total. The totals of cash and cheques are added and the final total inserted. Each bank's paying-in slips may be in a slightly different format but all require the same information.

The paying-in slip, cash and cheques are then taken to the account holder's own bank or to a branch of the bank, from where the funds will be transferred electronically (see page 326).

ACTIVITY 11.2 Draw a paying-in slip (see Fig. 11.1).

Pay the cash and cheques listed below into your business bank account: 123654 for The Blouse Shop, at Any Bank Limited, Any Town.

- 13 $20 notes; 7 $5 notes; coins – total value $11.00.
- Cheques from BCC Ltd for $578.43; Gerald de Vautier for $60.89; PJ Restaurants Ltd for $1698.34; and De la Ware Florists for $24.70.

Enter the amounts and total the cash, cheques and final total.

USING THE NIGHT SAFE

Certain types of business, e.g. shops, may wish to pay money into their accounts after the banks have closed in order to avoid having large sums of money on their premises overnight or at weekends. They can use the bank's night safe, located in an outside wall of the bank.

The bank issues an account holder with a pouch in which to lock the cash and cheques with a paying-in slip. The pouch is placed in the night safe tray, which is opened with a key provided by the bank. The pouch falls into the safe when the tray is closed.

There are two different types of pouch issued by banks. Each type is dealt with differently when they are retrieved from the night safe by bank staff.

Procedure 1

On the day after pouches have been placed in the night safe the bank staff remove the pouches. They are opened by two members of staff who check the contents against the paying-in slips enclosed by the account holders. The duplicate slips are receipted and placed back in the relevant pouches. The pouches are then available for collection by the customers during banking hours.

At Citibank (Trinidad and Tobago) Ltd this facility is referred to as 'Non-stop banking'. The safe is cleared twice a day so that customers' deposits can be checked and credited to their accounts immediately.

Procedure 2

Bank staff do not open the pouches when they have been removed from the night safe, but hold them until the customers call to collect them during normal banking hours. They may then, if they wish, pay the contents into their accounts or take them away again. There are only two keys to these pouches – one held by the customer and the other kept in the bank's vault in an envelope sealed by the customer for use in case the original is lost.

Banks make an annual charge for each pouch issued. Fig. 11.6 shows a night safe being used.

Fig. 11.6 Night safe being used.

BANK STATEMENTS

Although businesses keep a record of payments and receipts (and individuals should do the same), it is important to receive a statement from the bank at regular intervals. The balance on the statement will seldom be the same as the account holder's record. This is because the statement does not include transactions that have taken place since the last entry on it but have been included in the account holder's own record. It is possible that since the last entry on the statement:

- the account holder may have written some cheques that have not yet been debited to the account
- some cheques paid into the account may not have been credited
- bank charges may have been debited to the account but the account holder may not yet have included them in their own record
- the account holder may have forgotten to enter standing orders and direct debits that have been deducted from the account.

The account holder checks that their record is correct by preparing a **bank reconciliation statement**. The procedure for this is set out below.

1. Check the payments on the bank statement with the cheque counterfoils or copy slip (see page 319).
2. Check the receipts on the bank statement with the paying-in slip counterfoils or copies.
3. List the cheques drawn that have not yet been presented for payment. Add them to the account holder's balance on their record.
4. List any receipts paid directly into the bank that do not appear in the account holder's record, and add them to the balance.
5. List cash and cheques that have been paid into the bank but have not yet been credited to the account holder. Deduct them from the balance.
6. List any standing orders, etc. that have not been entered into the account holder's own record, and deduct them from the balance.
7. Cross-check the new balance in the account holder's record with the bank statement balance. The two figures should match. If they do, update the record with those details in the bank statement not shown in the record.
8. If the balances do not match, first establish the difference and whether it is a plus or minus on the account holder's balance. Then check every figure carefully. It is easy to misread a figure or to have a slightly different figure in the account holder's record. Eventually the error will be found and the difference will be eliminated.

A bank reconciliation statement is shown in Fig. 11.7.

```
BANK RECONCILIATION STATEMENT

Balance in cash book                                          $4867.34

Add cheques not paid by bank          $42.09
                                      350.00
                                        9.50
                                      125.95                    527.54
                                                               5394.88

Deduct cheques received by
bank but not paid                    $150.00
                                     428.59                     578.59

Balance as bank statement                                     54816.29
at 31.5.02
```

Fig. 11.7 Bank reconciliation statement.

Note: 'Cheques not paid by bank' are cheques the account holder has paid to a payee who has not yet paid them into their account or they are still in the cheque clearing process. 'Cheques received by the bank but not paid' are cheques that the account holder has received and paid into their account but they have not yet been credited to their account, i.e. they are still being cleared.

ACTIVITY 11.3 Prepare a statement reconciling the balance in your own record and the bank statement on page 333.

Record of receipts and payments

Receipts		Amount $	Payments	Cheque no.	Amount $
30.3.02	Balance	2345.67	8.4.02	481	116.85
12.4.02		1470.00		482	121.00
24.4.02		242.00	12.4.01	483	875.00
30.4.02		989.17	17.4.02	484	116.85
			22.4.02	485	1000.00
			25.4.02	486	750.65
				487	145.50
			29.4.02	488	659.22
			30.4.02	Balance	1261.77
		$5046.84			**$5046.84**

(continued)

ACTIVITY 11.3 **Bank statement**
(continued)

	Cheque no.	Debit	Credit	Balance
30.3.02				2345.67
11.4.02	482	121.00		2224.67
15.4.02	481	116.85		2107.82
16.4.02			1470.00	3577.82
22.4.02	484	116.85		3460.97
23.4.02	483	875.00		2585.97
29.4.02	485	1000.00		1585.97
			242.00	1827.97
30.4.02	487	145.50		1682.47

THE BANKS' CLEARING SYSTEM

The cheques presented to banks for payment have to be **cleared**, i.e. the drawer's account has to be debited and the payee's account has to be credited. The clearing system is now automated, i.e. operated by computer, and is known as the **Bankers' Automated Clearing System** or **BACS**.

To explain the system of clearing cheques we will use an example of a cheque drawn on the Royal Bank of Trinidad and Tobago Limited (where the drawer has an account) in favour of a payee with an account at the Republic Bank Limited. The procedures are illustrated diagrammatically in Fig. 11.8. For countries other than Trinidad and Tobago, substitute the names of appropriate commercial and central banks.

1. The payee presents the cheque at his branch to be credited to his account.
2. The cheque is sent with all the other cheques paid in that day to the clearing department at the Republic Bank Limited processing centre.
3. Each bank has its own branch clearing system, so cheques drawn on branches of the Republic Bank Limited are sorted from the whole batch and the amounts processed by the bank's own clearing system, by which the drawers' accounts are debited.
4. The clearing department lists all the cheques that were received that day and also makes a microfilm record of the cheques.
5. The cheques drawn on branches of each of the other banks are listed. The cheque drawn on the Royal Bank of Trinidad and Tobago will be included in the list with others received from that bank.

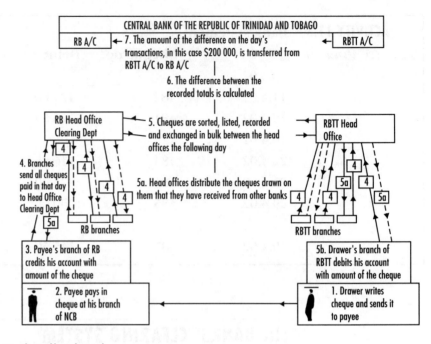

Fig. 11.8 Bank cheque clearing system.

6. When all the cheques have been listed at the Republic Bank Limited processing centre, the amounts owed by each bank to it are totalled.
7. The same process is operated at each bank. The Republic Bank Limited will owe money to the Royal Bank of Trinidad and Tobago because some Republic Bank's account holders will have drawn cheques in favour of payees with accounts at the Royal Bank.
8. The amounts owed by the various banks to each other are processed through the Central Bank of Trinidad and Tobago, where each of the banks holds accounts. There are no transfers of cash unless the amount is very large. The various banks make electronic transfers to the Central Bank, which in turn credits and debits each of the accounts held by the banks.

Clearing a cheque takes five days. 'Special clearing' can be arranged for a cheque over a certain amount by payment of a fee. This enables the bank branch to get credit on the same day as the cheque is presented.

BORROWING MONEY

There are times when an account holder needs to borrow money. There are two ways of borrowing from a bank: overdrafts and loans.

OVERDRAFTS

When an account holder wishes to draw a cheque for a greater amount than the credit held in their account, they must arrange to overdraw. A maximum amount that may be overdrawn is agreed. Each day the account is balanced and, depending on the cheques drawn and presented for payment, the account may be overdrawn some days and not others. Interest is charged on the amount overdrawn each day that there is a debit balance.

LOANS

There are many types of loan available, including:

- personal loan to buy domestic goods or a motor car, say
- industrial loan to a business to buy plant and machinery, for example
- bridging loan to finance the purchase of a new house until the old one is sold.

Interest is charged on all loans, and repayment is usually on the basis of regular instalments over a pre-determined period. The amount of each instalment takes account of interest charges.

A service charge may also be levied. For example, in Trinidad and Tobago, in addition to the interest on a bridging loan, a commitment fee of between 1.5 and 2 per cent is collected from the customer when funds are drawn.

DEVELOPMENT OF BANKING SERVICES

Bank account holders have always been able to obtain advice on insurance, income tax, investment, trusts and wills. Most banks have a trust department, which deals with wills and can act as executor of a will on the person's death.

The banking world has now become much more commercial and is moving into financial areas other than banking. To achieve this the trend is to provide **personal banking centres**, which will provide all the services an individual may need in addition to current banking and credit facilities.

These services will eventually include insurance, mortgages (currently provided only by merchant banks), mortgage packages consisting of a loan, property insurance and mortgage life assurance, stockbroking including financial planning, wealth management and portfolio management carried out by staff with a Certificate in Financial Planning.

Telephone banking will advance from enabling customers to obtain information on credit card account balances, to simple transfer of funds, Internet, mortgage facilities and e-commerce, possibly with e-brand managers who would deal with specific service providers (see Chapter 3, page 55). Development of these services will take time and e-commerce facilities overseas will not be possible as long as there are exchange control regulations.

There will be specific units established for corporate lending (i.e. lending to companies). Most companies need to borrow money from time to time for development and, sometimes, to carry them over a downturn in trade.

The banks will need an ongoing programme of staff training to deal with the new services as they develop.

PRACTICE QUESTIONS

1. List and briefly explain three types of bank account.
2. Explain how money is paid into a bank account.
3. Anyone who has a cheque book has a responsibility to keep it safe. List the precautions you should take to ensure its safety and the security of your bank account.
4. What is the difference between:
   a. cheque and bank draft
   b. standing order and direct debit
   c. credit card and Switch card
   d. money order and postal order?
5. Explain payment by:
   a. documentary credit
   b. electronic transfer
   c. travellers' cheques.
6. What details must be written on a cheque when making a payment?
7. a. What is the significance of a crossed cheque?
   b. Illustrate and explain five types of cheque crossing.
8. Explain the procedure for paying cash or cheque(s) into a bank account.
9. Explain the following: stale-dated cheque; post-dated cheque; dishonoured cheque.

10. You send a cheque to a local company in payment of an invoice. A week later the company secretary telephones you to ask why you have not paid. As the company has not received the cheque you assume that it has been lost in the post or mislaid in the company's office. What would you do?

11. Explain the procedure for withdrawing money from a bank cash point using a debit card.

12. Explain the procedure for arranging to pay by:
    a. direct debit
    b. standing order.
    Give examples of the types of debt you might pay by each method.

13. What is a:
    a. PIN number
    b. LINX card
    c. paying-in slip
    d. bank statement?

14. Most banks now issue only crossed cheques for security reasons. What do you have to do when you want to 'cash a cheque'?

15. There are two ways in which a night safe can be used. Explain both procedures.

16. Explain the difference between a bank loan and a bank overdraft.

17. a. When is a bank reconciliation statement prepared and what is its purpose?
    b. You have just received your organisation's bank statement made up to 30 April. It shows a credit balance of $1620.72. The balance in the cash book was $1594.68 on that date. When the previous bank statement (made up to 31 March) was received, the credit balance at the bank was $1692.70 as against the cash book balance of $1893.20. What possible reasons are there for these differences?

18. What services do banks offer their customers in addition to facilities for making payments and withdrawing cash?

19. The Trinidad Brick Manufacturing Company has a demand deposit account at the Royal Bank of Trinidad and Tobago (Park Street, Port-of-Spain branch). The company has obtained a private loan from Thomas & Wyatt.
    The company is to repay the loan (with interest) in 24 monthly instalments of $480, due on the 15th day of each calendar month. It wishes to arrange for payments to be made from its demand deposit account by standing order.

a. What details must the company fill in on a standing order form?

b. What are the advantages of paying by standing order rather than by cheque for: the company; the lenders?

20. The morning post contains the following remittances.

Sender	Method of payment	Amount $
I Brown Ltd	postal order	154.62
J Smith	cheque	535.50
P Ramsay & Co.	cheque	445.60
LJ Plastics Ltd	cheque	1150.00
Elite Dresses	postal order	94.48
Modern Materials Ltd	cheque	2041.00

The following payments are made in cash at the main office.

Paid by	Amount paid $
Lily and Rose Flowers	Three $100 notes, two 10 cent coins, one 5 cent coin
J Drood	Three $20 notes, two $10 notes; eight 10 cent coins
S Singer	One $100 note, four $20 notes, six 10 cent coins

Prepare a paying-in slip for all the monies to be paid into the bank. You work for Island Designs Limited. Its account number is 6278918 at the National Commercial Bank (JA) Limited, Matilda's Corner Branch, Code no. 37-077.

SHORT ANSWER QUESTIONS

1. When you wish to open a bank account you must provide names of ....

2. The drawer of a cheque is the person who .... it.

3. A cheque dated ahead of time is a .... cheque.

4. If you amend a cheque you must .... or .... the amendment.

5. R/D means ....

Choose the most appropriate ending for each of the following sentences.

6. A Switch card is used to:
a. buy goods in a shop without writing a cheque
b. buy goods on credit
c. obtain cash from an automatic teller machine
d. pay regular accounts over the telephone.

7. Documentary credit is used to:
   a. pay for very expensive goods
   b. pay for goods bought from within the Caribbean
   c. pay for goods bought from overseas
   d. send money to someone living abroad.

8. Moneygram is a computerised system for transferring funds:
   a. within your own territory
   b. within the Caribbean
   c. to North America
   d. internationally.

9. When you withdraw money from the bank by cheque you must:
   a. write 'pay cash' on the back
   b. make the cheque payable to yourself or to 'cash'
   c. ensure that the cheque is crossed
   d. make the cheque payable to 'cash'.

10. BACS stands for:
   a. Business Accounts Clearing System
   b. Bankers' Automated Clearing System
   c. Banker's Automated Cash Service
   d. Banker's Automated Clearing Service.

EXAMINATION QUESTIONS

1.
   a. You are based at the offices of the Spa Health & Fitness Club, 22–32 Queen's Avenue, London NE2 7SP. The club is owned and managed by Mr Joseph Patten.

   The club has an account at the Northeast Bank, Baker Street, London branch; current account no. 476234; bank sort code 35-67-20.

   In the safe this morning were the cash takings from the bar and restaurant from yesterday. These consist of four £20 notes; five £10 notes; six £5 notes; nineteen £1 coins; five 50 pence coins and 65 pence in coppers. These must be paid into the bank today, together with the remittances received in the post this morning, which are listed in the 'Remittances Book', as shown in Fig. 11.9. Complete the paying-in slip in Fig. 11.10.

REMITTANCES BOOK

Date	Remitter's name	Method of payment	Amount	Details	Signature
Today	J Burns	cheque	£250	Subscription	
Today	N Patel	postal order	£25	Invoice 741	Margaret Evans
Today	G Webb	cash	£50 note	Booking deposit (registered)	
Today	D Da Costa	cheque	£250	Subscription	

Fig. 11.9 Remittances book.

Date	**NORTHEAST BANK** **Current Account Credit** **COMPLETE IN BLOCK LETTERS PLEASE**	£50 Notes	
		£20 Notes	
		£10 Notes	
Account holding branch		£5 Notes	
Bank sort code		£1 Note/Coin	
Account in name of		S & I Notes	
Account number		50p	
Cashier's stamp and initials	Paid in by:	20p	
		Silver	
		Bronze	
		Total cash	
		Cheques POs etc. see over	
		£	

NORTHEAST BANK		
Please list cheques/POs etc. Name	£	P
Total cheques carried over		

Fig. 11.10 Forms for completion.

b. State THREE methods by which members could pay their annual subscriptions, other than by cash or cheque.

(Pitman Office Procedures Level 2 1998 Pt 1)

CHAPTER 12

BUSINESS RECORDS

OBJECTIVES When you have studied this chapter you should have acquired the knowledge and understanding to be able to:

1. explain the purpose of keeping records
2. list the records kept in the functions related to finance, sales, production and personnel
3. explain the key details included in each of the records
4. explain the different bases on which employees are paid
5. calculate a simple wage/salary statement
6. briefly explain income tax and National Insurance
7. prepare a cash requisition sheet
8. explain the reasons for monitoring stock and methods of stocktaking
9. explain the legal difference between buying goods on credit and on hire purchase
10. identify the particular points that make buying by mail order different from other methods of buying
11. keep an imprest petty cash account with analysis columns
12. prepare different formats for the visual presentation of statistics
13. identify the most appropriate format in particular circumstances.

It is important to understand why records are kept and to know what records are needed in business. The documents discussed in previous and subsequent chapters are a vital part of the records system as they provide the evidence to support the records. In this chapter we cover the purpose of records and explain the records needed for controlling business activities.

PURPOSE OF RECORDS

There are two main purposes for keeping records – statutory requirements and control.

1. Records required to be maintained by law include financial and related records and personnel records.
2. Records needed for control include:
   - the amount of money being received and spent, the amounts owed to creditors and by debtors (see Chapter 10)
   - the amount and value of stock being held, when orders need to be placed, which orders are received and which are outstanding
   - the number of staff on the payroll, their qualifications, training and progress in the organisation
   - the progress and cost of work, any delays and the reasons for them
   - the peaks and troughs of sales, the products/services that do and do not sell well, and the relationship of sales to production
   - customers' accounts with debit balances overdue, the number of customers who do not pay on time and the credit rating of new customers.

The types of record listed below are explained in this chapter:

- personnel
- salaries and wages
- factory
- stock
- credit sales
- petty cash.

Some methods, and their uses, of presenting statistical information will also be explained.

PERSONNEL

Personnel records must be treated as *strictly confidential*. They must be kept in locked cabinets and only certain people should be allowed access to them. In most organisations no one is allowed to remove a personnel file from the personnel department. If it is essential to send a file to another office, a strict procedure must be followed to ensure that only the authorised person sees the file. Such a situation might arise if, for example, the managing director of the organisation wishes to see a personnel file.

For each employee there is a personnel record, which consists of a file holding various documents. This record can either be on hard copy and/or on computer. Documents may include:

- employee's original application
- interview report and test results
- letter of appointment and/or contract of employment
- forms/notes/letters relating to employment in the organisation
- appraisal or personal development review reports
- training
- absence and lateness
- disciplinary occurrences and grievances
- accident reports.

EMPLOYEE'S ORIGINAL APPLICATION

The application form (see Fig. 16.5) that the employee completed when applying for his first job with the organisation normally contains the information listed below:

- name (first name(s) and surname), address, sex, date of birth, marital status
- education – schools, colleges, university attended (with dates)
- qualifications – educational (from school, college and university), technical (for skills and crafts) and professional (for accounting, engineering, medical, etc.)
- employment history (the names of previous employers, titles of jobs held, duties involved, salary/wage, reason for leaving each job)
- further training, e.g. evening classes and training courses attended.

INTERVIEW REPORT AND TEST RESULTS

When an applicant for a vacancy is interviewed, a report should be written by the interviewer(s) and attached to the application form.

Applicants for jobs may be asked to undergo a test. The result of the test should also be attached to the application form.

The interview report and test results provide evidence of the reasons why an applicant was, or was not, accepted for a particular vacancy.

LETTER OF APPOINTMENT AND/OR CONTRACT OF EMPLOYMENT

Some organisations write a letter of appointment containing all the details of the contract. Other organisations write a letter with a minimum of detail and later issue a contract of employment. When an employee starts work, full details of their conditions of service should be confirmed even though they would have been given this information at their interview.

The information given may include some or all of the following details:

- job title and duties (usually provided in a job description - see Chapter 2, pages 37-8)
- salary scale, starting salary, salary review dates and increments
- period of probation
- hours of work
- holiday entitlement (statutory and leave)
- length of notice to be given on termination of employment by employer and by employee, during probation and after confirmation in post
- disciplinary and grievance procedures (often included in a staff handbook).

FORMS/NOTES/LETTERS RELATING TO EMPLOYMENT IN THE ORGANISATION

When an employee starts work in an organisation, they are usually required to complete certain forms. These may include such information as next of kin, names and dates of birth of children, and bank account branch and account numbers. In government departments and in organisations working in secret areas, e.g. computer research, new employees have to sign an oath of loyalty or secrecy.

Thereafter, details of any changes are recorded. Such changes may include:

- promotion
- job transfer
- location transfer, e.g. from one branch of an organisation to another
- increase in responsibility within a job
- increase in salary or change of salary scale.

APPRAISAL OR PERSONAL DEVELOPMENT REVIEW

Many organisations have an annual or bi-annual appraisal scheme, nowadays often referred to as a personal development review (PDR). Each employee's performance during the previous period, effective use of training given, further training needed to improve skills and/or acquire and develop new skills and, in some cases, promotion prospects are discussed by the employee with their supervisor or manager.

Often the employee is asked to complete a form before the discussion. The manager adds comments to the form, usually after the discussion, and both sign the completed form. The employee has the right not to sign the form if they disagree with the manager's comments.

This appraisal/PDR form is a very important record. In some organisations the employee's salary increase will be based on their previous year's performance.

TRAINING

When a new employee starts work they should receive induction training (see Chapter 16, page 502). A record of the training given, both on and off the job, should be completed and, ideally, signed by the employee as well as the supervisor/manager.

When an employee has been confirmed in a position they may be offered further training. This may include courses of half a day, one day or more. The courses may be in-house, i.e. arranged by the company, or external, i.e. arranged by a training organisation. The employee would attend an external course at a venue away from their organisation. An in-house course may be conducted either on site or at an external venue.

Many organisations require a report to be written by every employee who attends an in-house or external training course. Often they are asked to complete an **evaluation form**, which will indicate what benefit they gained from the course. These completed forms may be stored in a course file rather than a personal file. However, a record of training courses attended by an employee should be kept on their personal file.

ABSENCE AND LATENESS

A record of each employee's absence through sickness, on holiday or on a training course must be kept. In some cases, wages are deducted for lateness and/or absence. Also a check must be kept on how many days of their holiday entitlement an employee has taken and how many remain. Many organisations do not allow employees to 'carry over' leave not taken in one year to the next year, except in exceptional circumstances.

If an employee is frequently on sick leave, it may be that their employment may be terminated. An organisation hires a person to do a job and if they are unable to attend work they cannot expect to retain their job. If an employee is genuinely sick, has had an accident or has to have an operation, evidence in the form of a medical certificate is required, usually after three days. Medical certificates must be filed on the employee's personal file.

If an employee has an accident at work a form must be completed (see page 348). A copy of the form must be filed on the employee's personal file as it is possible that there will be a claim for compensation or the employee will be entitled to injury benefit.

DISCIPLINARY OCCURRENCES AND GRIEVANCES

Sometimes people transgress the rules and disciplinary action is taken against them. This means that they may receive warnings about their behaviour – for example, if they refuse to follow their supervisor's instructions. If their behaviour does not improve they may eventually lose their job.

An employee who does not do their job properly, e.g. they are constantly making mistakes or not meeting deadlines, can be disciplined. They should be given additional training if necessary and encouraged to improve, but if they do not they must expect to be fired.

It is very important that every action taken in a disciplinary case is recorded. Notes made and signed by a manager should also be signed by the employee. This proves that the employee agrees that the notes are accurate.

An employee may have a grievance at some time in their employment. For example, they may think they are being asked to do all the menial tasks while their colleagues do all the interesting work. Or they may object to being asked to do regular overtime. The procedure for dealing with a grievance is generally for the employee to talk first to their supervisor or manager. If they do not get satisfaction, they can talk to a more senior manager and then, if they still do not get satisfaction, they can talk to the personnel manager.

Details of the grievance, how it was dealt with and what the outcome was, must be recorded on the employee's personal file.

ACCIDENT REPORT

If any employee has an accident, however minor, they should report it to their supervisor/manager. An employee who slips on a wet floor and sprains an ankle, may not think it is important, but later it may get worse and result in several days off work.

A report must be completed and sent to the health and safety officer and/or the personnel department. The organisation's insurance company has to be notified of all accidents in case a claim is made against the organisation. The information that is normally required in an accident report includes:

- the name of the injured person
- the date and time of the accident
- the place where the accident occurred
- details of the accident including the injury, however slight
- the name(s) of witness(es), if any
- any first aid, medical or hospital treatment received by the injured person
- the name of the person who reported the accident, with time and date.

All organisations should have a first-aid box so that basic treatment can be given. Ideally there should be one or more people trained in first aid in the organisation.

An **accident report form** is shown in Fig. 12.1.

ACTIVITY 12.1 The Caribbean Yacht Company manufactures small yachts at Port Antonio, Jamaica. At 1015 on Monday 21 May 2002 John Jackson was painting the hull of a yacht in dry dock. He was standing on a ladder propped against the vessel. In reaching too far to his right, he over-balanced and fell to the bottom of the dry dock, breaking his leg. He shouted to his mate, Ben Lara, who decided not to try to move John, and called an ambulance immediately. John was soon on his way to hospital. Ben then reported the accident to his manager.

Draw up a form, as shown in Fig. 12.1, and complete it with the details above.

DEPARTMENTAL RECORDS

Some individual records, including those listed below, are summarised in the personnel department. These include:

- numbers of people recruited
- numbers and categories of people who leave (known as **labour turnover**)
- training needs, extracted from completed appraisal forms
- numbers and frequency of training courses conducted
- numbers of employees who have attended various training courses

```
THE P-O-S ENGINEERING COMPANY
ACCIDENT REPORT FORM

This form is to be completed for every accident that occurs within the company buildings or grounds. When
completed send it to the personnel manager within 24 hours of the accident occurring.

Employee involved in accident

Surname ................................... First name ........................................... Title ............

Department .................................................................. Employee reference .................................

Date of accident ..................... Time ..................... Location ................................

Was the accident reported immediately? ..........................................................................................

If so, who reported it? .....................................................................................................................

To whom was the accident reported? ...............................................................................................

Details of accident ...........................................................................................................................

.......................................................................................................................................................

.......................................................................................................................................................

.......................................................................................................................................................

Nature of injury ...............................................................................................................................

.......................................................................................................................................................

Was first aid given? ................................. How soon after the accident? ...................................

Who gave first aid? ................................................. Was s/he qualified? ....................................

Was injured person taken to hospital? ............................................ At what time? ..........................

Witness (if any) name and address ..................................................................................................

.......................................................................................................................................................

Signature of person who completed this form ..................................................................................

Date ........................................
```

Fig. 12.1 Accident report form.

- sickness absence
- details of accidents that occur without any injury to an employee and those that do result in injury.

These summaries provide valuable information on which policies and procedures can be reviewed.

The number of people who are recruited to and who leave the organisation during a year may indicate, for example, that unsuitable people are being recruited, that conditions of employment are not competitive with other organisations or that supervision is poor. This results in high labour turnover, which is costly and also demotivates employees.

Training needs for individuals can be summarised in order to identify priorities and organise courses needed by the greatest number of employees. This also indicates which employees are due for further training for promotion, updating on computer software, and which departments encourage staff to attend courses. At the end of the year the number of training courses conducted and the numbers of employees who attended during the year can be compared with the training needs identified at the beginning of the year.

Sickness absence records enable the personnel department to see whether there are certain departments where sickness is more prevalent than the average. This might indicate a high level of stress, or poor working conditions, or some other problem that should be investigated.

An accident in which an employee sustains an injury has to be reported individually to an organisation's insurance company. In addition, an annual summary of accidents has to be provided.

SALARIES AND WAGES

Employees may be paid by the hour, the day, the week or the month. This means that their remuneration is calculated on the basis of an hourly, daily, weekly or monthly rate. Casual workers, i.e. people who are not permanent employees, on construction sites or in dockyards, say, are examples of hourly- or daily-paid employees. Temporary staff who work for agencies are also paid an hourly rate. In factories, workers may be paid a **piece rate**, which means that they are paid according to the number of articles they produce. Otherwise they are paid **time rate** according to the number of hours they work. Permanent employees are paid weekly or monthly rates. Actual payment is nearly always made weekly or monthly, either in cash, by cheque or into a bank account (see Chapter 11, pages 318 and 322).

PIECE RATE

A piece rate is used as a form of motivation to encourage employees to produce more, which means they will be paid more. However, the articles produced have to be of an acceptable standard. Waste articles are not paid for.

At the end of the week employees complete job cards or piece work tickets by filling in the number of articles, or pieces, they have completed. The cards are initialled or signed by the supervisor and sent to the salaries and wages department, where the employees' pay is calculated.

TIME RATE

A time rate is usually an hourly rate, which means that if an employee is absent from work he is not paid, although in some organisations a certain number of days' sickness is paid to all employees. Lateness is usually calculated in 15-minute blocks, so anyone who is 5 minutes late loses 15 minutes' pay. This is known as 'losing a quarter'.

The standard time rate is paid for a certain number of hours in a day. Additional hours are counted as **overtime** and paid at a higher rate.

Most organisations pay time and a half for overtime hours worked Monday to Saturday inclusive, and double time on Sunday.

Each employee paid by time rate has a number that is written on their **time card** (see Fig. 12.15). At the beginning of each week the time cards are placed in a rack next to a special clock called a **time clock**. When employees arrive for work they each take their card from the rack and put it into the machine attached to the clock. The machine stamps the time on the card. When the employees leave, they repeat the procedure.

An employee's stamped time card provides a record of lateness, absence and attendance. At the end of each week the time cards are sent to the salaries and wages department for the wages due to each employee to be calculated in accordance with the number of hours worked. The number of hours to be paid at standard rate and the number of hours to be paid at time and a half and/or double rates are multiplied by the appropriate rates.

COMMISSION

Commission is paid to many sales people to encourage them to make more sales. They may be paid a basic weekly or monthly salary, for which they have to sell a minimum number or a certain value of items. Additional sales then earn commission, e.g. 5 per cent of the selling price. Some organisations recruit part-time sales staff, who are paid solely on what they sell. Details of the number of items sold and their value is sent to the salaries and wages department so that the amount to be paid can be calculated.

GROSS PAY

This is the total amount of money earned by an employee in a week or a month. From this amount certain deductions are made.

Deductions from gross pay

Employees are required by law to have certain deductions made from their gross pay. In addition, they may make voluntary deductions.

Statutory deductions are:

- income tax
- health surcharge
- National Insurance (NI)
- National Housing Trust (in Jamaica).

Voluntary deductions may include:

- pension scheme
- sports or social club
- savings account.

All deductions are subtracted from an employee's gross pay. The employer then pays the total amounts of statutory deduction subtracted from the gross pay of all employees to the appropriate government departments. Voluntary deductions are paid to the insurance company or to the trustees that run the pension scheme, the sports/social club and the bank that runs the savings account scheme. After deductions from gross pay the employee receives **net pay**.

INCOME TAX

Income tax is generally deducted on a **PAYE** (Pay As You Earn) system in Caribbean territories. This means that everyone pays a proportion of their yearly tax liability each time they are paid, either weekly or monthly. All employers have to keep precise records of gross salaries and wages, all deductions and net pay.

All businesses are obliged to keep proper accounts of all transactions. These accounts must be audited annually to ensure that the profits, whether paid to shareholders of companies or taken by sole traders as earnings, are assessed for income tax liability.

The allowances – i.e. income that is allowed tax free – and the rates of tax are set each year by the government. The increase or decrease depends on the state of national finances and the amount of money needed for services.

Allowances

Allowances in Trinidad and Tobago include a personal allowance, to which everyone is entitled, a mortgage for people buying a house and/or tertiary education for children up to a combined maximum, and an annuity or pension to which contributions are being paid. These allowances are deducted from the gross pay, the amount left being **taxable pay**. For the year 2001 these allowances were:

personal allowance	TT$ 25 000
mortgage/tertiary education	18 000
annuity/pension	12 000
maximum total allowances	55 000

This means that people entitled to claim all the allowances start paying income tax on a gross salary of $55 000.01. The allowances are reviewed annually.

A certain percentage (currently 28 per cent) is charged on the first $50 000 of taxable pay and a higher percentage (currently 35 per cent) on amounts of $50 000.01 and over.

Calculating tax payable

This is the responsibility of employers, who receive the necessary documents on 1 January each year. These documents are:

- tax deduction form TD1
- tax tables (PAYE).

A **tax deduction form TD1** is kept by the employer for each employee. Every week or month, depending on how frequently the employee is paid, details of gross pay, taxable pay, deductions and net pay are entered on the payslip.

The tax tables are 'ready reckoners' for calculating the amount of free or non-taxable pay of the employee, which is deducted from the gross pay, and the amount of tax due on the taxable pay.

At the end of each tax year, **TD4 certificates** are completed by the employer. Each employee must be given two copies of the certificate on or before the last day of February each year following the year in which the tax was deducted. A TD4 certificate must be given by the employer to an employee who leaves their employment during the year.

During the year the employer pays the employees' income tax and health surcharge (see below) deductions to the Board of Inland Revenue. A **PAYE tax deduction remittance form** (see Fig. 12.2) must be completed and sent to the Board with the deductions to be paid. One payment for all the employees' deductions is made.

Every taxpayer should have a file number allocated by the Board of Inland Revenue. An employee starting a new job, who does not have a file number, applies for a number to be allocated by completing **form P10** (see Fig. 12.3). This is sent to the Board of Inland Revenue attached to the letter offering employment. The employee must quote this number in all future contact with the Board.

Each year the employee receives from the Board of Inland Revenue a personal income tax return, **employee's declaration of emolument and deductions form 1A** (see Fig. 12.4) to be completed and returned with the TD4 certificate (tax return).

The employee must also complete a TD1:

- on the day they take up new employment
- within seven days if there is a change in personal circumstances
- if required by the Board of Inland Revenue to do so.

On form TD1, the employee states the claims to be made, e.g.:

- deduction for interest on a loan in respect of an owner-occupied property or children's tertiary education
- approved pension fund or deferred annuity, which means that the pension fund money will be invested when the employee retires to provide a pension instead of receiving a lump sum
- National Insurance premium (70 per cent maximum).

Health surcharge deductions

These are paid in Trinidad and Tobago by the employer to the Board of Inland Revenue. This is effectively an additional tax. It is calculated on a weekly basis from Monday to Sunday. The amount payable for each employee is based on salary as follows:

Salary –				
Weekly	$0.01 to $109.99	NSD	$4.80 per week
	$110.00 to $9999.00		$8.25 per week
Monthly	$0.01 to $469.99		$4.80 per week
	$470.00 to $9999.00		$8.25 per week

INSTRUCTIONS TO EMPLOYERS

1. Complete one form each month (rubber stamp may be used to show name and address) and attach to your remittance preferably by cheque made payable to the Board of Inland Revenue.

2. The tax deducted or withheld each month must be remitted by the 15th day of the following month. Failure to remit will incur a penalty of 50 per cent or $40.00 whichever is greater, plus interest at the rate of 15 per cent per annum thereafter.

3. If you discontinue business you must within the following week make a final remittance and make returns in respect of all employees. (*See* notes to employers)

4. The Board of Inland Revenue *will* notify you if the amount of your *cumulative total* does not agree with its records.

5. Any deductions which you are specifically instructed by the Board of Inland Revenue to make from the Emoluments of your employees through Garnishee Orders or Deduction Orders on Government Departments in respect of their tax arrears should not be included in the Remittance Form. They should be listed separately on a particular remittance form provided for the purpose.

Note:—This Receipt is valid only for the amount registered by the Receipting Machine of the Board of Inland Revenue.

G.P., Tn./To.—L 377—75,000— /95

GOVERNMENT OF THE REPUBLIC OF TRINIDAD AND TOBAGO
BOARD OF INLAND REVENUE

P.A.Y.E. TAX DEDUCTION REMITTANCE

P.A.Y.E. File Number	DEDUCTION PERIOD		B.I.R. File Number
	MONTH	YEAR	

Business Name of Employer (Block Letters)

Address ....

TAX ALREADY REMITTED	TAX NOW REMITTED	CUMULATIVE TOTAL

Penalty ....

Interest at 15% ....

Interest from .... to ....

BOARD OF INLAND REVENUE COPY

RECEIPT No.	DATE	AMOUNT

Fig 12.2 Form TD4 PAYE tax deduction remittance.

I.T. Form P—10/84

APPLICATION FOR INDIVIDUAL INCOME TAX FILE NUMBER

(Please See Instructions Overleaf)

PLEASE PRINT

RESERVED FOR FILE NUMBER

1.	FULL NAME (First Name)	(Middle Name—if none draw line)		(Surname)	
2.	Other names by which known				
3.	Date of Birth		4. Sex:	Male ☐	Female ☐
5.	Present Mailing Address				
6.	Occupation				
7.	Name and Address of Present Employer				
8.	If self employed: *(a)* Business Name *(b)* Nature of Business		*(c)* Business Address		
9.	Identification Document:	N.I.S. Number	I.D. Card Number	Passport Number	
10.	Have you ever filed an Income Tax Return: ☐ No ☐ Yes File Number		*(If yes, state mailing address on last return filed)*		
11.	Reason for now applying for File Number				
12.	Date		13. Signature		
	FOR OFFICIAL USE ONLY				

Fig. 12.3 Application for individual income tax file number, Form P10.

Payment to the last day of the month must be remitted by the 15th of the next month with a completed **health surcharge deduction remittance form C-3L** (see Fig. 12.5). Late payment penalties are a fine of 100 per cent of the amount due plus 20 per cent per annum interest calculated on a daily basis.

NATIONAL INSURANCE

The National Insurance Scheme (NIS) is a contributory scheme that provides cash benefits in most territories for old age, invalidity, employment injury and death. Benefits are financed by contributions from all categories of workers and employers. The rates of contribution vary from one territory to another and can be obtained from a local Social Security Office.

Jamaica

The NIS provides a comprehensive range of benefits to insured persons and their dependants in accordance with the provision of the National

Form T.D.—1

REPUBLIC OF TRINIDAD AND TOBAGO
BOARD OF INLAND REVENUE

EMPLOYEE'S DECLARATION OF EMOLUMENTS AND DEDUCTIONS

Any person who makes a false declaration is liable on summary conviction to a fine or imprisonment or to both such fine and imprisonment.

(Please read Notes overleaf before completing this form)

USE BLOCK CAPITALS

B.I.R. File Number............................

I.D. Card Number ....

Surname..

Other Names... Date of Birth............................

Home Address..

Name of Spouse residing with me...

Date of Marriage.................... Was Marriage Registered?................ Spouse's B.I.R. No. ....

Current Emolument Income

Income from Salary, Wages or Pension: (including taxable allowances and benefits in kind)

Name and Address of Employers	Rate of Pay Weekly/ Fortnightly/ Monthly	Annual Amount
....		
....	$....................	$....................
....		
....	$....................	$....................
....		
....	$....................	$....................
Total Emolument Income		$....................

CERTIFICATION

I HEREBY CERTIFY that the information given in this Declaration filed with

*..is
TRUE AND CORRECT.

Date.................................... Signature...
                                                    Employee

---

*Insert name of Employer or Board of Inland Revenue as appropriate.

Fig. 12.4 *Employee's declaration of emoluments and deduction, Form 1A.*

Insurance Scheme Act (Revised Laws of Jamaica, 1973). Contributions are payable in respect of working persons between the ages of 18 and 65 for women, and 70 for men.

Under the scheme, employers and employees must pay combined flat-rate and wage-related contributions as shown in Table 12.1. These contributions are deducted at the same time as PAYE income tax and the

INSTRUCTIONS TO EMPLOYERS

1. Complete one form each month (rubber stamp may be used to show name and address) and attach to your remittance cash/certified cheque made payable to the Board of Inland Revenue.

2. The Health Surcharge deducted or withheld each month must be remitted by the 15th day of the following month. Failure to remit will incur an additional payment of 50 per cent, plus interest at the rate of 15 per cent per annum thereafter.

3. If you discontinue business you must within the following week make a final remittance and make returns in respect of all employees.

4. The Board of Inland Revenue *will* notify you if the amount of your *cumulative total* does not agree with its records.

5. Any deductions which you are specifically instructed by the Board of Inland Revenue to make from the Emoluments of your employees through Garnishee Orders or Deduction Orders on Government Departments in respect of their Health Surcharge arrears should not be included in this Remittance Form. They should be listed separately on a particular remittance form provided for the purpose.

6. Mailed payments should be sent to Board of Inland Revenue, Trinidad House, Port-of-Spain, on or before the due date and made by certified cheques payable to the Board of Inland Revenue. Other payments may be made at any Inland Revenue Office from Monday to Friday between 8.00 a.m. to 3.00 p.m.

Note:—This Receipt is valid only for the amount registered by the Receipting Machine of the Inland Revenue.

G.P., Tr./To.—O 142—200,000— /98   I.T. Form C–3L

BOARD OF INLAND REVENUE COPY

RECEIPT No.	DATE	AMOUNT

Fold Here

RECEIPT No.	DATE	AMOUNT

GOVERNMENT OF THE REPUBLIC OF
TRINIDAD AND TOBAGO
BOARD OF INLAND REVENUE

HEALTH SURCHARGE DEDUCTION REMITTANCE

P.A.Y.E. File Number	DEDUCTION PERIOD		I.R. File Number
	MONTH	YEAR	

Business Name of Employer (*Block Letters*) ....

Address ....

Health Surcharge Already Remitted	Health Surcharge Now Remitted	Cumulative Total

Additional Payment ....

Interest ....

Interest from .... to ....

....
Cashier's Signature

Fig 12.5 Health surcharge deducation remittance, Form 3-GL.

National Housing Trust (see page 363). The weekly flat-rate contributions are as shown in Table 12.1.

Table 12.1 *Weekly flat-rate contributions*

Category	Insured person (cents)	Employer (cents)
1. a. Domestic worker	10	20
b. JDF members	10	20
c. All other insured persons	15	15
2. Self-employed persons	30	
3. Voluntary contributors	40	nil

The level of wage-related contributions is 5 per cent of the insurable wage between $10 and $150 per week, split equally between employer and employee in the case of category 1 c and 5 per cent for category 2 (self-employed persons).

Each employer completes and sends to the Ministry of Social Security a registration form R1, giving details of the establishment. A registration number is allocated by the Ministry.

Each individual insured person completes a registration form R2, giving full name, date of birth, sex and marital status. The completed form is sent to the local Social Security Office where a registration number is issued, to be used on all the insured person's NIS documents throughout the period of contributions to the scheme.

The employer must have a deduction card C2 for each employee. On pay day, this card is completed by matching the salary of the employee with the similar amount shown in the Social Security Office contribution tables C49, and entering the amount deducted in the column provided. Payment of all the contributions must be remitted by the employer to the collector of taxes with completed form C3 by the 14th of the following month.

An employer must pay a contribution for each whole or part week during which the person is employed. Contributions are not paid if an employee is receiving any of the benefits listed below, except disablement pension benefits under employment injury.

Several benefits, payable by the Ministry of Social Security, carry contribution conditions, with the exception of employment injury for which there only needs to be a contract of service, written or oral. These are:

- old age
- invalidity

- survivors
- employment injury – disablement pension, part medical fees, assistance with spectacles, dentures, artificial limbs, crutches, etc.
- funeral grant
- maternity allowance for domestic workers
- maternity grant to businesses employing more than 75 per cent women.

In some territories the rates for **voluntary contributions** are based on the earnings class into which the applicant contributed, but in Jamaica there is a flat-rate contribution of 40 c per week. (A voluntary contributor is an insured person who has made at least 52 contributions to the scheme and is not liable to contribute as an insured person because they may not be working or have gone abroad.)

A list of documents relating to the NIS in Jamaica is shown in Table 12.2.

Table 12.2 *NIS documents*

social security deduction card	C2
National Insurance remittance card	C3
employer's annual return: declaration and certificate	C4
Social Security leaving certificate for insured employee	C5
Social Security certificate of pay and contributions deducted	C7
contribution tables	C49
employer's registration form	R1
insured person's registration form	R2

Instructions on how to complete the documents are obtainable from any local Society Security Office.

Trinidad and Tobago

The NIS provides a comprehensive range of benefits to all working persons between the ages of 16 and 65 in accordance with the National Insurance Act Chapter 32.:01 (Act 35 of 1971). In addition, persons above or below the insurable age who may suffer injury in the course of their work are entitled to benefits.

Employers and employees must pay combined contributions in the ratio of two-thirds and one third respectively. Total weekly contributions are calculated in 12 classes ranging from $8.79 in Class 1 for people earning between $80.00 and $129.99 per week to $68.04 in Class 12 for people earning over $810.00 per week. The rates of contributions for employers and employees are shown in Fig. 12.6. These rates are reviewed annually.

NIS Level	WEEKLY EARNINGS		MONTHLY EARNINGS		NIS DEDUCTIONS		
	From	To	From	To	Employee	Employer	Total
1	80.00	129.99	347.00	562.99	2.93	5.86	8.79
2	130.00	179.99	563.00	799.99	4.33	8.66	12.99
3	180.00	229.99	780.00	996.99	5.75	11.50	17.25
4	230.00	289.99	997.00	1256.99	7.28	14.56	21.84
5	290.00	359.99	1257.00	1559.99	9.10	18.20	27.30
6	360.00	429.99	1560.00	1862.99	11.07	22.14	33.21
7	430.00	499.99	1863.00	2166.99	13.02	26.04	39.06
8	500.00	569.99	2197.00	2469.99	14.98	29.96	44.94
9	570.00	649.99	2470.00	2816.99	17.08	34.16	51.24
10	650.00	729.99	2817.00	3162.99	19.32	38.64	57.96
11	730.00	809.99	3163.00	3509.99	21.57	43.14	64.71
12	810.00	999 999.99	3510.00	999 999.99	22.68	45.36	68.04

Fig. 12.6 Trinidad and Tobago NIS table.

An employer must pay a contribution for each whole or part week during which the person is employed. A contribution of $1.00 per week is payable by the employer for an unpaid apprentice. For employees under 16 or over 65 years of age, a Class Z contribution, ranging from $0.60 to $4.62, has to be paid. Contributions are not paid if an employee is receiving from the National Insurance Board either sickness benefit, maternity benefit or employment injury benefit.

The employer is responsible for paying all contributions by the direct method of payment (DMP) system. This means that payment is made directly to the Board, accompanied by a completed **summary of National Insurance contributions due/in arrears form NI 187** (see Fig. 12.7) and cash or a cheque. Payment must be paid by the 15th of the month following the month for which it is due. Late payment is penalised by a fine of 25 per cent of the amount due plus 15 per cent per annum interest calculated daily. A summary of payments for all employees must be submitted on **statement of contributions paid/due form NI 184** (see Fig. 12.8) to the National Insurance Board.

There are seven benefits payable under the system:

1. sickness
2. invalidity
3. maternity
4. survivors

THE NATIONAL INSURANCE BOARD   NI 1 8 7

SUMMARY OF NATIONAL INSURANCE CONTRIBUTIONS DUE/IN ARREARS

(Prepare in Duplicate)

SECTION "A" - EMPLOYER INFORMATION

EMPLOYER'S TRADE NAME :

ADDRESS :

TELEPHONE NO:

CONTRIBUTIONS DUE BEFORE MAY 03, 1999: [YYYY MM DD] TO 1999 05 02

CONTRIBUTIONS DUE FROM MAY 03, 1999: 1999 08 01 TO 1999 08 31

TOTAL NUMBER OF EMPLOYEES FOR THE LATER PERIOD [   ] AND UNPAID APPRENTICES [0   ]

FOR OFFICIAL USE
L.O. CODE

EMPLOYERS REG.NO:

SECTION "B" - VALUE OF CONTRIBUTIONS PAYABLE

	$	c
ARREARS PAYMENT DUE (before May 03, 1999)		
CONTRIBUTIONS PAYABLE THIS PERIOD (after May 03, 1999)		
PENALTY		
INTEREST		
TOTAL PAYMENT DUE		
AMOUNT PAID		
DIFFERENCE		

SECTION "C" - METHOD OF PAYMENT

(1) HOW PAID	(2) AMOUNT	
	$	c
$ 100 X		
20 X		
10 X		
5 X		
1 X		
SILVER		
COPPER		
CHEQUE		
TOTAL		

CHEQUE NUMBER

List additional cheque numbers and values overleaf

SECTION "D" - CERTIFICATE OF DECLARANT

I/we solemnly and sincerely declare that the information given is a correct reflection of contributions due and payable for all insured persons for the period stated.

NAME:

SIGNATURE :

POSITION:

DATE: 1999 09 15

SECTION "E" - FOR OFFICIAL USE

[ ] NI 184 RECEIVED   [ ] DISKETTE RECEIVED

AMOUNT RECEIVED $ _____   RECEIPT NO. _____   _____
SIGNATURE OF CASHIER

Fig. 12.7 Summary of National Insurance contributions due/in arrears, Form NI 187.

THE NATIONAL INSURANCE BOARD
STATEMENT OF CONTRIBUTIONS PAID/DUE

NI 184

EMPLOYER'S TRADE NAME: _____ EMPLOYER'S REGISTRATION NUMBER: ☐☐☐☐☐☐ LOCAL OFFICE CODE: ☐☐

ADDRESS: _____

CONTRIBUTION PERIOD FROM: |1|9|9|9|1|0|0|1| TO |1|9|9|9|1|0|3|1| No. of Weeks in Period: |0|4|
YYYY MM DD   YYYY MM DD

1. NATIONAL INSURANCE NUMBER	2. NAME OF EMPLOYED PERSON OR UNPAID APPRENTICE (SURNAME / FIRST NAME)	3. DATE OF BIRTH (YYYY/MM/DD)	4. DATE EMPLOYED LAST DATE WORKED (YYYY/MM/DD)	5. SALARY FOR PERIOD $	6. VALUE OF CONTRIBUTION DUE WEEKLY					7. TOTAL VALUE OF CONTRIBUTIONS $
					WK1 $	WK2 $	WK3 $	WK4 $	WK5 $	B/F

TOTAL NO. OF EMPLOYEES: ☐   TOTAL VALUE OF CONTRIBUTIONS: 0.00

1. The correct National Insurance Number for each employed person must be shown in column 1. It is an offence not to do so
2. Where new employees are hired add particulars including N.I. Number (if known), Date of Birth, and date employed. Attach completed NI 4 if National Isurance number is not known. For separated employees state last date worked.
3. Salary information must be included in column 5 for each employee.

WARNING! THE LAW NOW IMPOSES A PENALTY FOR THE LATE SUBMISSION OF THIS INFORMATION AND FOR INCORRECT OR INCOMPLETE INFORMATION

4. Record value of contribution per week in column 6.
5. Submit this form with your payment and completed NI 187 by the last working day of the month reported on.
6. No contributions are due when Sickness, Maternity, Employment Injury or Invalidity Benefits payable
7. The board will accept this information on diskette.

SIGNATURE OF EMPLOYER _____   ☐☐☐☐ ☐☐ ☐☐
                                      YYYY MM DD

Fig 12.8 Statement of contributions paid/due, Form NI 184.

5. funeral grant
6. employment injury
7. retirement.

Certain contribution conditions have to be met to enable an insured person to become eligible to receive benefits. In the case of employment injury benefit, where the contribution for insured persons or unpaid apprentices is payable wholly by the employer, there is no contribution condition. The contribution conditions for other benefits are listed below.

- Sickness and maternity – 10 out of 13 contributions must have been paid.
- Invalidity – the invalid should have been in receipt of 26 weeks of sickness benefit.
- Survivors – 10 contributions must have been paid.
- Retirement – 1 contribution for a retirement **grant**; a minimum of 750 contributions for a **retirement pension**.

A first-time employer has to register with the National Insurance Board by completing **application to register as an employer form NI 1** (see Fig. 12.9) and submitting it to the nearest National Insurance office.

A first-time employee has to apply for registration on **application to register as an employed person form NI 4** (see Fig. 12.10). The employer has to complete **application for registration form NI 3** (see Fig. 12.11), which lists all the applicants for registration. The completed NI 3 and NI 4 forms must be submitted to the nearest National Insurance office.

National Insurance forms may be submitted to the National Insurance Board either on hard copy or on diskette.

NATIONAL HOUSING TRUST

In Jamaica employers contribute 3 per cent and employees 2 per cent of gross pay to the National Housing Trust scheme. On the National Insurance deduction card C2, there is a column headed 'National Housing Trust'. The employee's 2 per cent deduction from gross salary should be entered in this column. For further details about this scheme consult the National Housing Trust Office.

PAYROLL

The list of employees' names, personnel/employee numbers and details of hours worked, gross pay, deductions and net pay, is known as the payroll.

THE NATIONAL INSURANCE BOARD
THE NATIONAL INSURANCE REGISTRATION REGULATIONS
APPLICATION TO REGISTER AS AN EMPLOYER

NI 1

Please Read these Instructions Carefully before Completing

1. Please type or Complete in Block Letters and Submit to the Nearest National Insurance Office.
2. The Form must be Signed by the Managing Director/Partner/Owner/Company Secretary.

FOR OFFICIAL USE
LOCAL OFFICE NO.:

EMPLOYER REGISTRATION NO.:

1. NAME OF BUSINESS OR COMPANY

2. ADDRESS OF BUSINESS OR COMPANY (State exact address e.g. Mile Mark, Light Pole Number)

(STREET)

(CITY/DISTRICT/COUNTY)

TELEPHONE NUMBERS: FAX NUMBER:

3. MAILING ADDRESS OF BUSINESS OR COMPANY

(STREET)

(CITY/DISTRICT/COUNTY)

e-MAIL ADDRESS OF BUSINESS OR COMPANY

4. COMPANY BOARD OF INLAND REVENUE NUMBER:
5. COMPANY REGISTRATION NUMBER:
6. COMPANY DATE OF REGISTRATION
YYYY MM DD

7. NAME AND HOME ADDRESS OF OWNERS/PARTNERS/DIRECTORS
(Use separate sheet for additional Owners/partners/directors)
WARNING! THE BOARD MUST BE NOTIFIED PROMPTLY OF ANY CHANGES

NAME AND TITLE	HOME ADDRESS	TELEPHONE NUMBER	DATE OF OWNERSHIP/ DIRECTORSHIP/ PARTNERSHIP YYYY MM DD	SALARIED? YES NO

(a)

Fig. 12.9 Application to register as an employer, Form NI 1 (a) front; (b) reverse.

2/NI 1

8. ADDRESS OF REGISTERED OFFICE (Where Applicable)

9. NATURE OF BUSINESS (Type of Industry)

10. NUMBER OF:
    a) EMPLOYED PERSONS
    b) PAID APPRENTICE
    c) UNPAID APPRENTICE
    d) TOTAL

11. DATE FIRST EMPLOYEE WAS HIRED:
    YYYY MM DD

NOTE: AN UNPAID APPRENTICE IS ANYONE IN TRAINING FOR WHICH REMUNERATION OF LESS THAN $80.00 PER WEEK IS EARNED.

12. STATE ADDRESS WHERE PAY RECORDS ARE KEPT:
    (STREET)
    (CITY/DISTRICT/COUNTY)

13. STATE ADDRESS WHERE PERSONNEL RECORDS ARE KEPT:
    (STREET)
    (CITY/DISTRICT/COUNTY)

14. DO YOU HAVE BRANCHES OF THIS BUSINESS IN OTHER LOCATIONS? ☐ YES ☐ NO

If "YES", please list the name and address of each branch and the location where its pay and personnel records are kept.

FOR OFFICIAL USE

NAME	ADDRESS	LOCATION OF RECORDS	REGISTRATION NO.

15.
COMPANY STAMP (If Any)

I /WE SOLEMNLY AND SINCERELY DECLARE THAT THE INFORMATION GIVEN IS CORRECT.

_____
AUTHORISED SIGNATURE

_____
NAME IN BLOCK LETTERS

DATE:
YYYY MM DD

_____
OFFICE HELD BY SIGNATORY

5/99

(b)

THE NATIONAL INSURANCE BOARD
THE NATIONAL INSURANCE REGISTRATION REGULATIONS
APPLICATION TO REGISTER AS AN EMPLOYED PERSON
(Other than Self-employed) OR Apprentice)

NI 4

INSTRUCTIONS

1. Please TYPE or complete in BLOCK LETTERS.
2. Employers must register employed persons and apprentices within 14 days of employment. Late registration could result in a fine.
3. The law requires that you furnish your employer with the personal particulars necessary to complete this form.
4. All questions must be answered: If you do not know your Father's name or Mother's maiden name, the words "not known" must be inserted on the respective lines.
5. Proper recording of your National Insurance Contributions and prompt and accurate settlement of your claims cannot be achieved if you do not provide the information required on this form.
6. Read the Declaration at the back carefully and sign in the space provided.

ALL INFORMATION MUST BE VERIFIED BY YOUR EMPLOYER

FOR OFFICIAL USE
LOCAL OFFICE NO.:

NATIONAL INSURANCE NO.:

1. Surname: _____ First Name: _____
   Middle Name: _____

2. Name at birth if different from above: (Changed by Deed Poll, Marriage)
   Surname: _____ First Name: _____

3. Other names by which known:
   Surname: _____ First Name: _____

4. Are you an apprentice? ☐ Yes ☐ No

5. Sex: ☐ Male ☐ Female

6. Home Address: _____
   STREET
   _____
   CITY/DISTRICT/COUNTY

7. Date of Birth: | YYYY | MM | DD |

8. Place of Birth: _____
   STREET
   _____
   CITY/DISTRICT/COUNTY

9. Multiple Birth? ☐ Yes ☐ No
   If "Yes", please state name of siblings
   Surname: _____ Other Name(s): _____
   Surname: _____ Other Name(s): _____

10. Any Family members with same name? ☐ Yes ☐ No
    If "Yes", Please state relationship and Date of Birth:
    Relationship: _____ Date of Birth: | YYYY | MM | DD |
    Relationship: _____ Date of Birth: | YYYY | MM | DD |

(a)

Fig. 12.10 Application to register as an employed person, Form NI 4 (a) front; (b) reverse.

2/NI4

11. Father's Name:

Surname: ☐☐☐☐☐☐☐☐☐☐☐☐☐☐ First Name: ☐☐☐☐☐☐☐☐☐☐☐☐☐☐

12. Mother's Maiden Name: ☐☐☐☐☐☐☐☐☐☐☐☐☐☐

13a. Valid Identification Document (One Only):
☐ Electoral Identification Card ☐ Passport ☐ Driver's Permit

13b. Expiry Date: ☐☐☐☐ ☐☐ ☐☐
YYYY MM DD

ID Number: ☐☐☐☐☐☐☐☐☐☐☐☐☐☐

14. Marital Status: ☐ Single ☐ Married ☐ Separated ☐ Widowed ☐ Divorced ☐ Common Law

15. If Marital Status is Common Law, please give particulars of Common Law Spouse:

Name of Common Law Spouse:

Surname: ☐☐☐☐☐☐☐☐☐☐☐☐☐☐ First Name: ☐☐☐☐☐☐☐☐☐☐☐☐☐☐

16. Business Name of Employer: ☐☐☐☐☐☐☐☐☐☐☐☐☐☐☐☐☐☐☐☐☐☐☐☐

17. Address of Employer: ☐☐☐☐☐☐☐☐☐☐☐☐☐☐☐☐☐☐☐☐☐☐☐☐
STREET
☐☐☐☐☐☐☐☐☐☐☐☐☐☐☐☐☐☐☐☐☐☐☐☐
CITY/DISTRICT/COUNTY

18. Occupation: ☐☐☐☐☐☐☐☐☐☐☐☐

19. Pay Frequency: ☐ Weekly ☐ Fortnightly ☐ Monthly   Amount $ ☐☐☐☐

20. First Date of Employment: ☐☐☐☐ ☐☐ ☐☐
YYYY MM DD

21. Have you been previously registered? ☐ Yes ☐ No   If "Yes", state N.I. Number: ☐☐☐☐☐☐☐☐

22. Are you currently employed elsewhere? ☐ Yes ☐ No

If "Yes", state Business Name and Address of Other Employer:

Business Name of Employer: ☐☐☐☐☐☐☐☐☐☐☐☐☐☐☐☐☐☐☐☐☐☐☐☐

Address of Employer: ☐☐☐☐☐☐☐☐☐☐☐☐☐☐☐☐☐☐☐☐☐☐☐☐
STREET
☐☐☐☐☐☐☐☐☐☐☐☐☐☐☐☐☐☐☐☐☐☐☐☐
CITY/DISTRICT/COUNTY

CERTIFICATE OF DECLARANT

I solemnly and sincerely declare that I am the applicant named herein and that the particulars set out in this application are true. I make this declaration conscientiously believing same to be true and I am aware that if there is any statement in this declaration which is false in fact or which I know or believe to be false or do not believe to be true, I am liable to legal process.

Declared this _____ day of _____ 19 ____

_____   _____
Signature or Mark of Declarant   Signature or Witness to Mark

Was information Verified by Employer? ☐ Yes ☐ No

COMPANY STAMP

_____   _____
EMPLOYER'S SIGNATURE   DESIGNATION

5/99

(b)

THE NATIONAL INSURANCE BOARD
APPLICATION FOR REGISTRATION
LIST OF EMPLOYED PERSONS (OTHER THAN SELF-EMPLOYED PERSONS) AND UNPAID APPRENTICES

NI 3

Please Read These Instructions Carefully Before Completing

1. Please type or complete in Block Letters.
2. Prepare in Duplicate and submit to the nearest National Insurance office. Additional sheets should be used where necessary.
3. State classification code as either "A" or "B" in column Two (2).
4. Each employee must complete a Form NI 4 - "Application to Register as an Employed Person".

NAME OF BUSINESS OR COMPANY:

EMP. REG. NO.

ADDRESS OF BUSINESS OR COMPANY:

TELEPHONE NO.

1	2	3			4
DATE OF EMPLOYMENT	CLASSIFICATION CODE	FULL NAME AND ADDRESS OF EMPLOYED PERSON AND UNPAID APPRENTICE			(FOR OFFICIAL USE)
YYYY | MM | DD		(A) SURNAME	OTHER NAME(S)	(B) ADDRESS	NATIONAL INSURANCE NUMBER

P.T.O.

(a)

Fig. 12.11 Application for registration, Form NI 3 (a) front; (b) reverse.

2/NI 3

1	2	3		4
DATE OF EMPLOYMENT	CLASSIFICATION CODE	FULL NAME AND ADDRESS OF EMPLOYED PERSON AND UNPAID APPRENTICE		(FOR OFFICIAL USE)
		(A)	(B)	NATIONAL INSURANCE NUMBER
YYYY | MM | DD		SURNAME OTHER NAME(S)	ADDRESS	

DATE: [YYYY MM DD]

SIGNATURE OF EMPLOYER OR AUTHORISED AGENT

COMPANY STAMP (If Any)

(FOR OFFICIAL USE)

NAME   SIGNATURE   DATE

RECEIVED BY: _____   _____   [YYYY MM DD]

29.01.92

(b)

In a small business the payroll may be kept in a book. Any size of business with a PC can have payroll software, which enables the calculations to be made much more quickly. In a large organisation the payroll is run on the mainframe computer (see Chapter 3). A section of a payroll is shown in Fig. 12.12.

PAYROLL
Period 1–31 July 2002

Name	Employee number	Basic salary $	Overtime		Total gross pay $	Deductions						Net pay $
			Hours	Pay $		PAYE $	NIS $	Pension $	Union dues $	Social club $	Other dues $	
Ali M	3456	3100.00	Nil	Nil	3100.00	265.26	77.28	100.00	55.00	150.00	–	2452.46
Graham J	3672	2900.00	5	100.00	3000.00	240.26	77.28	100.00	55.00	100.00	75.00	2352.46
Lee P	2974	3500.00	10	225.00	3725.00	440.40	90.72	100.00	55.00	–	–	3038.88
Smith T	3187	3600.00	Nil	Nil	3600.00	405.40	90.72	100.00	55.00	120.00	80.00	2748.88
TOTALS		13100.00	15	0325.00	13425.00	1351.32	336.00	400.00	220.00	370.00	155.00	10592.68

Fig. 12.12 Section of a payroll.

PAY ADVICE

Each employee receives a pay advice or a **pay slip**. If payment is by cash or cheque the slip will be enclosed in the same envelope. If payment is made direct to the employee's bank account, the pay slip will be on its own. The pay advice should show:

- how the gross pay is made up
- statutory and voluntary deductions
- net pay.

In most organisations, pay slips are produced from computer. A specimen is shown in Fig. 12.13.

CASH REQUISITION

The employer has to cash a cheque to obtain money with which to pay the wages of employees who are paid in cash. The money will be needed in a variety of denominations so that each pay packet can be made up with the exact amount of money for each employee. A requisition is made up itemising the denominations needed for each pay pack. Each column is then totalled so that the amount of each denomination required can be supplied by the bank. A typical cash requisition is shown in Fig. 12.14 on page 372.

12: BUSINESS RECORDS ■ 371

PAY ADVICE		Date 29 June 2002
Name: P Lee		Employee number 2974
Month no. 6	Period 01.06.02 – 30.06.02	Tax Code no. – –
	$	$
Basic Salary	3500.00	
Overtime: 10 hours @ $22.50 per hour	225.00	
Total Gross Pay	3725.00	
Less Pension	100.00	
Taxable gross pay		3625.00
Deductions: Income tax	179.66	
National Insurance	90.72	
Social club	100.00	
Savings	300.00	670.38
		$2954.62

Fig. 12.13 Pay advice for staff paid monthly.

ACTIVITY 12.2 Listed below are the wages to be paid to six employees. Use these figures to draw up a cash requisition sheet as shown in Fig. 12.14. Next work out the amount of each wage to be paid in the various notes and coinage. Finally total each column, add up the total across the page and check that it is the same as the total of the wages for the six employees.

John O'Leary	$3850.00
Mustapha Peters	3008.40
Jean Bisson	3124.00
Paul Mercury	3200.10
John Diaz	3460.70
Cynthia Chang	3470.10

CASH REQUISITION   Date 29 June 2002

Wages $	$100	$20	$10	$5	$1	25c	10c	5c	1c
0000.00									
0000.00									
0000.00									
0000.00									
TOTAL									

CASH SUMMARY

Notes	$100 ×	$
	20 ×	
	10 ×	
	5 ×	
	1 ×	
Coins	25c ×	
	10c ×	
	5c ×	
	1c ×	
TOTAL		$

Compiled by: ....
Initials
Checked by: ....
Initials

Fig. 12.14 Cash requisition.

ACTIVITY 12.3

a. Copy out the clock card shown in Fig. 12.15.
b. Complete the clock card in accordance with the information given below.
c. Calculate the total gross pay.

Robert Lai Fook's normal working week is 40 hours, i.e. 8 hours per day. He is paid a standard rate of $18.00 per hour. When he works overtime during the working week and on Saturday he is paid time and a half. When he works on a Sunday he is paid double time.

He clocks in every weekday morning at 0800 and clocks out at 1230 for lunch. He clocks in again at 1330. His finishing time varies.

He clocks out on Monday and Tuesday at 1700
       Wednesday 1800
       Thursday 1730
       Friday   1700

On Saturday he works from 0730 to 1300.
On Sunday he works from 0830 to 1230.

CLOCK CARD						
Week ending 00.00.00			Name			
			Employee no.			

	MORNING		AFTERNOON		HOURS	
	In	Out	In	Out	Basic	Overtime
Monday	0000	0000	0000	0000		
Tuesday						
Wednesday						
Thursday						
Friday						
Saturday						
Sunday						
TOTAL						

Basic time ..... hours @ $ 0000.00
Overtime ..... hours @ $ 0000.00
Overtime ..... hours @ $ 0000.00
TOTAL $

Fig. 12.15 Clock card.

FACTORY

Administration underpins all of an organisation's activities. The factory where goods are produced is no exception. The records in a factory office are intended to ensure that activities are kept on schedule, that work is done according to specification and that costs are monitored. Factory records include:

- planning schedule
- job cards
- cost cards
- cost schedules
- production order
- progress advice
- transport destination call schedule.

PLANNING SCHEDULE

So that people and machines can be used most effectively, it is essential to plan the work that each person will do and the machines that will be used.

Also machines have to be 'out of action' at times for maintenance. Planning charts (see pages 393–6) are used to show what is to be done, when, over what period of time. On the same charts the actual achievements can be shown so that it is easy to see when work is ahead of, on or behind schedule. Actual production is usually summarised from progress advice or job cards (see below).

JOB CARDS

A job card is completed for each piece of work undertaken by an employee or group of employees. A job may be a single item, a batch of goods or undertaking a service. When a mechanic comes to your office to service a copier, they complete a job card on which the details of work done, materials or parts used and time taken are recorded. It is usual for the job card to be signed by the quality controller or inspector, or the customer.

COST CARDS

The cost of producing each item or providing a service may be recorded separately or may be included on the job card. The items costed are:

- labour (the employee's time)
- materials, which may include 'bought in' parts, i.e. completed parts to be assembled into the product.

A combined job/cost card is shown in Fig. 12.16.

COST SCHEDULE

A cost schedule is a list of all the materials and parts used in a product, and the time taken for each operation involved in its production. Every detail is costed. An overhead charge may be added. This is usually a percentage of the cost and covers such expenditure as rent, rates, air conditioning, lighting, water, etc. These expenses cannot be allocated to an individual item so the total cost of these expenses is divided on a proportional basis, the more expensive items bearing a larger share of the overheads.

JOB CARD

Job no. 241

Date 10.6.02

Job description 10 BLOUSES Model 168 Size 16

Authorised by P Waters

Materials	Quantity	Unit cost $	Cost $	Total $
Cotton voile	25 yds	12.00	300.00	
Shoulder pads	10 pr	3.00	30.00	
Buttons	50	0.40	20.00	
				350.00

Labour

Name	Hours	Cost per hour $	Cost $	
Pat	1½	8.00	12.00	
Esther	4	7.00	28.00	
Samantha	4	7.00	28.00	68.00
			Sub-total	418.00
Overheads @ 30%				125.40
			TOTAL	543.40

Date started .... Date finished ....

Inspection

Signature .... Date ....

Completion of costs

Signature .... Date ....

Fig. 12.16 Combined job/cost card.

ACTIVITY 12.4 The Trinidad Lighting Company produces table lamps and lampshades. Look at the table below. First, add together the cost of materials and labour, and insert the total for each lamp model. Then calculate 30 per cent of the total and insert the amount in the 'Overheads' column. Finally, add the 'Total' and 'Overheads' columns to find the total cost of each lamp model.

Lamp model number	Materials	Labour	Total	Overheads at 30%	Total cost
A 45609	$ 45.00	$ 105.00	$	$	$
A 47825	48.50	151.50			
B 24581	58.90	81.10			
B 24762	103.70	168.40			
D 47079	29.35	48.15			

PRODUCTION ORDER

Many factories produce goods that require items to be issued from stores before they can be made. In the example in Fig. 12.17, the items required are materials for umbrellas. The cloth is stored in bales and the cord on rolls, and the required amounts for a particular job are cut off as needed. The frames and handles are ready-made bought-in parts.

The production order is an authorisation to the storeman, signed by the works manager or production controller, to issue the items required. The person doing the job in the workshop would take the signed order to the stores to obtain the materials needed.

The production order ensures that:

- jobs are not duplicated,
- existing stock has been checked, to confirm the need to produce more,
- there is no fraud, i.e. employees do not produce things for themselves or to sell cheaply to their friends.

PROGRESS ADVICE

In large organisations there is usually a production control section consisting of 'production controllers' or 'progress chasers' whose job it is to check the progress of goods being manufactured. In a small factory this task

PRODUCTION ORDER		No. 06482
Job start date: 15.8.02		
No of items required: 100 MODEL 45B		
Parts required		
Code	Description	
CL 862	Blue nylon (30 ins ea)	
CO 128	Blue cord (18 ins ea)	
FR 060	Frames model 10	
H 241	Blue handles	
Signature: L Eades	Date: 12.8.02	

Fig. 12.17 Production order.

may be done by a quality controller. A progress advice form is completed and sent to the works manager who compares the details with the planning chart. He can see at a glance whether production is ahead of, on or behind schedule. If it is behind schedule it may affect other planned production. The sales department may have to be notified as it may mean that customers' orders cannot be delivered when promised.

TRANSPORT DESTINATION CALL SCHEDULE

This form is included in this chapter because transport is often under the control of the works manager. Working out the delivery route may be left to the van/lorry driver; sometimes it is done by the despatch clerk. The schedule lists the consignments in the sequence in which they will be delivered. The route is planned to be economical of time, keeping the cost of petrol and driver's time to a minimum.

STOCK

'Stock' is the word used to cover any articles, items, goods or materials kept in a stock room, storeroom, store or stores, ready for use when needed. Stock may be for internal use, e.g. stationery, or it may be kept to replenish shelves, etc. in a retail shop or department store, or it may be kept to send to customers who order directly from a mail-order company.

Factories usually have two stores, one for the raw materials and parts needed to make the product, the other for storing the finished products that will be sent to wholesalers, retailers or direct to customers.

STOCK RECORDS

Records of stock may be kept on cards, on sheets or on computer. For the purpose of explaining the information contained in a stock record we will look at the example of a stock record card (also called a stock control card).

The following details are normally recorded at the top of the card.

- The stock item code and description. Each item of stock is given a code, which may consist of figures or a combination of letter(s) and figures. This code is used in catalogues to identify the item, for ordering and selling, and for financial records.
- The store reference – in some organisations the store reference is different from the catalogue reference.
- The store location reference, which may be a shelf number, a bin number or a bay number. A bin number is used for items that are kept in containers and the bay number is a section of the stores. In some cases the location reference may consist of the bay and shelf or bin number.
- The maximum, re-order and minimum levels – maximum level is the quantity of stock that should not be exceeded; re-order level is the quantity at which an order for replacement stock should be placed; minimum level is the 'danger signal' that should generate urgent contact with the suppliers. These levels are set on the basis of expected usage or sales, delivery times and cost. The levels may vary at different times of the year for 'seasonal' stock, i.e. items that sell better at certain times of the year.

- The unit, which means how the goods are sold – e.g. individually, in boxes of a certain number or in bales. Cloth is normally sold to retailers in bales of so many yards or metres.

Below the items explained above are some or all of the following columns.

- Date – to record when goods are received or issued.
- Receipts – quantity and goods received note number (see Chapter 10).
- Issues – quantity, requisition number (see Chapter 10), and department or staff member to whom the item(s) was/were issued.
- Balance – the quantity in store after the quantity received has been added to the previous balance or the quantity issued has been deducted. It is important to check the balance against the re-order level every time stock is issued.
- On order – date ordered, quantity, order number and date received.

In some organisations the cost and/or sales value of the items in stock is shown in a column beside the balance. A simple stock card is shown in Fig. 12.18.

Standard Stapling Machines Ref.: X4094 Unit: item						Maximum: 10 Re-order: 5 Minimum: 2
Date	Reqn no.	Issues	Department	Inv no.	Receipts	Balance
1.7.02						8
5.7.02	089	1	Reception			7
8.7.02	142	2	Sales			5
19.7.02	098	1	Chairman			4
24.7.02				9078	5	9
31.7.02	126	1	Accounts			8

Fig. 12.18 Stock record card.

Most stock consists of consumable items such as stationery, spares for repairs and parts for manufacturing. There are also non-consumable items, e.g. office furniture and equipment. The record of these 'capital expenditure' items or **assets** is called an **inventory**.

The details recorded for each item are:

- inventory number, in sequence as each item is added to the list
- name of the item

- model number and/or serial number
- description of the item
- cost of the item
- name of the supplier
- date purchased
- location of item.

It is important to keep an inventory for insurance purposes and for annual depreciation of assets, i.e. reduction in value, for accounts purposes.

> **ACTIVITY 12.5** Draw up a copy of the stock record card shown in Fig. 12.18. This card is for pens, code 14894. The maximum, re-order and minimum levels are 100, 40 and 20 respectively. The opening balance is 46. Insert these details and the stock movements listed below. Complete all the columns.
>
> | | | |
> |---|---|---|
> | 1.7.02 | Issued | 12 pens to training department |
> | 2.7.02 | Issued | 2 pens to mailing room |
> | 4.7.01 | Issued | 2 pens to stock room |
> | 4.7.02 | Issued | 3 pens to reception |
> | 5.7.01 | Received | 60 pens Inv. No. 465 |
> | 5.7.01 | Issued | 50 pens to sales department |
>
> What is the closing balance?
> After which transaction(s) would you indicate the need to re-order?

STOCK CONTROL

It is essential that there is always enough stock in store to issue when needed. The term 'out of stock' means that a particular item is not available. It is most likely on order unless it is unobtainable for any reason. It is equally important that there is not too large a quantity of an item in store because the money spent in paying for the items cannot be used for anything else. Also if stock is held for too long it may deteriorate.

There are various methods of controlling stock to avoid wastage, pilfering and loss through deterioration or damage, including:

- keeping strictly to the maximum, re-order and minimum levels
- ensuring that the correct documents for ordering and issuing stock are completed and authorised

- recording receipts and issues either immediately or in accordance with a pre-determined time schedule, e.g. daily
- checking goods received carefully for damage, shortages, items not ordered, etc.
- storing goods in the correct place and marking them clearly so that they can always be found
- storing goods such as ink and copy cartridges in a dark place
- issuing goods on the FIFO (first in, first out) principle, i.e. the oldest goods are issued first, which means that goods received must be stored behind or under the remaining stock
- ensuring that cupboards/storeroom doors are kept locked to avoid pilfering
- ensuring that stocktaking is carried out regularly (see below).

STOCKTAKING

There are two methods of stocktaking: **continuous stocktaking** or perpetual inventory, and **annual stocktaking** or inventory.

Continuous stocktaking means that staff trained as stocktakers or stock auditors, visit each branch of an organisation and check physical stock against stock records. Not all the stock is checked at each visit; the items to be checked are chosen randomly. Continuous stocktaking helps to minimise pilfering and loss of stock through incorrect storage and/or careless handling.

Annual stocktaking has to be carried out for the end-of-year financial accounts required by law. The value of the stock held at this time, called **closing stock**, is calculated and included in the organisation's balance sheet. The balance sheet shows the financial situation of the company, i.e. the value of what it owns and money owed to it (assets), and money owed by it (liabilities).

Annual stocktaking is done by auditors. All limited and public limited companies must appoint auditors whose job it is to check all the accounts, including the documents (invoices, etc.) and certify that they are accurate. Small businesses usually have an accountant who can certify that the accounts are correct for income tax purposes.

CREDIT SALES

Nearly all businesses and many individual customers buy goods on credit. We have discussed in Chapters 10 and 11 the ways in which businesses buy and sell goods. Individual customers can buy goods on credit, by hire purchase and by mail order.

CREDIT RATING

Customers who wish to buy on credit must have an acceptable **credit rating**; this means that the customer's past financial history is good, i.e. they do not have large debts outstanding, they meet their regular payment obligations on time and have no record of fraud. A person's company's credit rating can be obtained from a **credit reference bureau** where appropriate information has been obtained from banks and traders. Some companies offering credit apply direct to a customer's bank and/or to other traders for a **credit reference**.

After examining the information obtained, the company decides whether to allow credit to the customer and, if so, how much.

BUYING GOODS ON CREDIT

Many companies now offer customers credit either free or at very low interest. Repayment is usually by regular monthly payments, referred to as **instalments**, over a period of one, two or three years. In some cases, repayments do not start for a year after the date of purchase. If interest is charged, this is calculated into the instalments.

If the customer defaults on the repayments, the goods cannot be reclaimed by the seller since the goods have been sold and are owned by the customer.

BUYING GOODS ON HIRE PURCHASE

Many companies sell expensive goods, e.g. furniture and electrical equipment such as refrigerators, on hire purchase. This means that the customer 'hires' the goods, paying a hire charge at regular intervals over an agreed period. At the end of the period the customer is given the option to buy the goods for a small charge, usually another month's payment, which has been included in the **hire purchase agreement**.

The customer has the use of the article from the first payment but legally the goods are still owned by the seller. This means that if the customer stops paying the monthly hire charge, the seller can reclaim the goods, although there are legal safeguards for the customer. Most hire purchase sales are arranged by the seller through a finance company.

In Jamaica, goods sold under a hire purchase agreement have a stated price, including interest and service charges. When the agreed number of payments has been received, the goods automatically become the customer's property.

Complete and accurate records about every hire purchase transaction must be kept. Each customer's record must include:

- the number of the hire purchase agreement
- the details of the goods
- the hire price
- the amount of the monthly hire charge and the number of payments to be made
- the date when each payment is due
- the receipt of each payment made by the customer
- the date of any letter(s) reminding the customer of an overdue payment.

The customer must be given adequate time to respond before action is taken against them. The seller would rather obtain payment than reclaim the goods.

MAIL ORDER

Mail order is becoming more and more popular as people lead busier lives. It is also useful for people who live away from towns where the larger stores are located. Goods can be ordered by post, telephone, fax, e-mail and on the Internet.

There are many companies that sell by mail order only. Other companies, e.g. department stores, have a mail-order department, which may sell some of the goods sold in the store but also some goods not available in the store.

Mail-order firms advertise their goods in magazines and newspapers, and/or produce illustrated catalogues. Some companies advertise on the Internet by having a website, which shows the items available in colour and enables customers to order electronically.

Because mail-order customers cannot see the item they are ordering, goods have to be sent on approval in the first instance. Customers are allowed a certain number of days in which to decide whether they wish to keep the goods. If they decide to keep the items, they pay for them either:

- on the invoice enclosed in the package, or
- on receiving an invoice after a pre-determined period, to be paid by a certain date, or

- by returning a form agreeing to pay by instalments, which can be arranged by standing order or direct debit (preferred by sellers) or by cheque.

If customers do not wish to keep the goods, they return them by the service used by the seller, usually post, courier or haulier, depending on the size and weight of the goods.

Some mail-order companies appoint **agents**, usually reliable customers, to sell to their friends and order in bulk. The agents are not employed by the company but are given a discount on the goods they order for themselves and their friends.

A mail-order company must keep detailed and accurate records of the goods that have been sent on approval or sold, and on the instalments that are paid by customers. Many customers pay weekly instalments over a long period, so records must always be up to date (customers are not pleased to receive reminders about overdue instalments that they have paid).

PETTY CASH

The paying out of money for small items bought for cash is often the duty of a junior member of staff. The term **petty cash** is used because the amounts are small. Petty cash may be kept in a general office or by a secretary for a manager. It is used for items such as local travel expenses (bus/train fares, taxis), postage, stationery and office refreshments.

> **ACTIVITY 12.6** Consider the small items that members of staff may have to buy themselves and for which they are later reimbursed (paid back). Make a list of such items.

The petty cash must be kept securely in a locked cash box, which should be stored in a locked drawer or cupboard. When paying out petty cash, the box should be open only while the cash is being taken out of the box. The box itself should be locked away as soon as the payment has been completed.

When any item is bought, a receipt should be obtained. The person reclaiming the cash should complete a **petty cash voucher** (see Fig. 12.19).

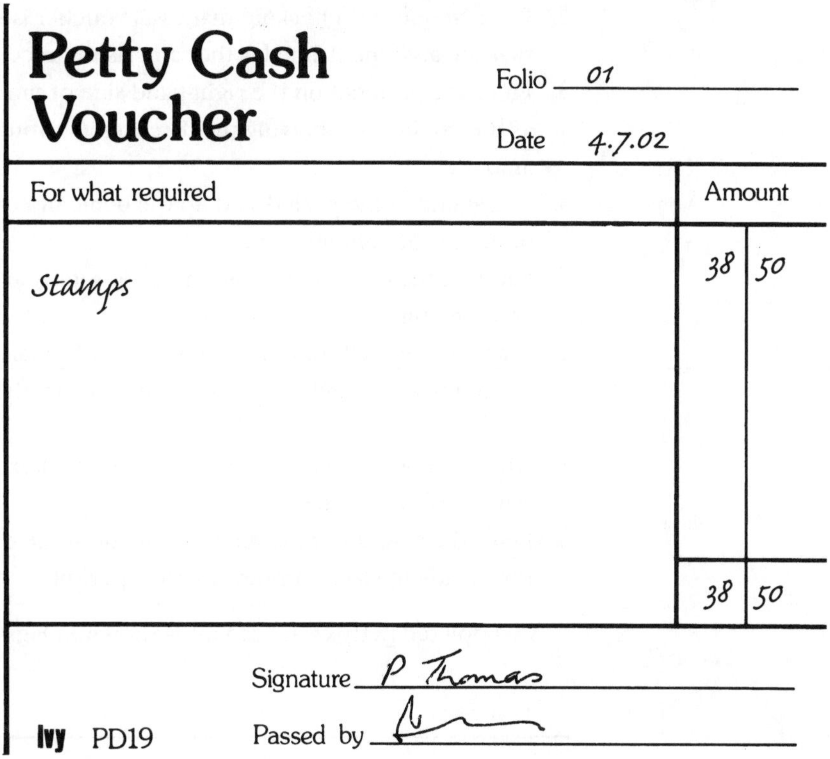

Petty Cash Voucher

Folio __01__

Date __4.7.02__

For what required	Amount	
Stamps	38	50
	38	50

Signature __P Thomas__

Passed by __[signature]__

Ivy   PD19

Fig. 12.19 Petty cash voucher.

Notice that it is signed by the person to be reimbursed and another person, usually a manager or supervisor.

The petty cashier must record the payment in a **petty cash book** or on computer, to be printed out at the end of the period. The vouchers must be kept safely in date order. The auditors will check the petty cash book and vouchers at the end of the financial year.

The most common way of recording petty cash transactions is by the **imprest** system. This means that the petty cashier receives a set amount of money to start the petty cash, pays out as necessary, adds up what has been spent over the period, balances the account, requests and receives repayment of the amount spent, and has the original amount to start the new period.

The process is carried out in the steps listed below.

1. Receive the imprest, which has been decided as adequate for a specific period, and record it as a receipt on the left-hand side of the petty cash book, known as the debit side. The entry must include the date, cash received and the amount.

2. Pay as requested, checking that each voucher is completed correctly and that the amount claimed is the same as the receipt/total of receipts.
3. Enter the payment on the right-hand side of the petty cash book, known as the credit side, showing the date, item(s), voucher number and amount.
4. At the end of the period, add up the debit and credit columns, and write in the credit column total.
5. Subtract the credit total from the debit total and write the balance in the credit column.
6. Write in the totals of both columns – both totals should be the amount of the imprest – and write the balance below the total in the debit column.
7. Give the book, or a printout from the computer, to the cashier, who will reimburse to you the amount spent.
8. Enter the amount of the reimbursement in the debit column. You are now ready to start your new imprest period.

A completed petty cash account is shown in Fig. 12.20.

Date	Description	Amount $	Date	Description	V no.	Amount $
01.07.02	Cash received	400.00	4.07.02	Stamps	01	38.50
			8.07.02	Parcel	02	10.35
			10.07.02	Stationery	03	42.70
			11.07.02	Taxi fare	04	16.00
			18.07.02	Coffee, tea	05	8.20
			22.07.02	Book	06	21.50
			25.07.02	Cleaning	07	75.00
						212.25
			31.07.02	Balance		187.75
		400.00				400.00
31.07.02	Balance	187.75				
1.08.02	Cash received	212.25				

Fig. 12.20 Petty cash account.

Most organisations need an **analysis** petty cash account. This means that the amount of each payment is written in an analysis column as well as in the credit column. Each analysis column is headed with the type of expenditure, such as those listed on page 384, and those you thought of for Activity 12.6.

At the end of the imprest period the analysis columns are totalled individually. The totals are written in beside the credit column total. The analysis totals should be added up to check that they come to the same amount as the credit column total.

The completed petty cash account shown in Fig. 12.20 is shown as an analysis account in Fig. 12.21.

Date	Description	Amount $	Date	Description	V no.	Amount $	Office expenses $	Postage staty $	Publications $	Travel $
01.07.02	Cash received	400.00	4.07.02	Stamps	01	38.50		38.50		
			8.07.02	Parcel	02	10.35		10.35		
			10.07.02	Stationery	03	42.70		42.70		
			11.07.02	Taxi fare	04	16.00				16.00
			18.07.02	Coffee, tea	05	8.20	8.20			
			22.07.02	Book	06	21.50			21.50	
			25.07.02	Cleaning	07	75.00	75.00			
						212.25	83.20	91.55	21.50	16.00
			31.10.00	Balance		187.75				
		400.00				400.00				
31.07.02	Balance	187.75								
01.08.02	Cash received	212.25								

Fig. 12.21 Petty cash analysis account.

ACTIVITY 12.7 Draw up a petty cash sheet with five analysis columns headed 'Travel', 'Stationery' ('Staty' for short), 'Books', 'Postage', 'Sundries'. You have been allocated an imprest of 420.00 per month. Enter receipt of this amount; then enter the following payments. (Note: V no. is 'voucher number'.)

01.08.02	Taxi to printer	V no. 001	$18.00
05.08.02	Paper clips	002	6.30
07.08.02	Reference book	003	8.20
14.08.02	Coffee, milk, sugar	004	14.00
23.08.02	Parcel post	005	13.80
26.08.01	Glue and labels	006	27.50

Balance the account and show reimbursement of the amount spent.

PRESENTATION OF STATISTICS

There are various ways of presenting numerical (or statistical) data. The most common is typed tables (see page 389). Data presented in this format is usually kept in files for reference as needed. However, figures are needed for many reasons as well as for simple reference.

If you want to know how many students are booked on a communications training course you either retrieve the bookings file for that course and look at the record of nominations received or retrieve the file on computer; this could be called 'direct reference'. However, if you wanted to know how many students had attended the last six communications courses, it would be easier if you could look at one document rather than six. Moving a stage further, if you want to compare the bookings over a year for each of six different courses, each course having been conducted five times, you do not want to have to retrieve 30 pieces of paper. Visual presentation of statistics can overcome this problem and serve many other useful purposes.

PURPOSES OF VISUAL PRESENTATION

Various **formats** can be used to present statistics in a way that enables you to see at a glance the information you need. These formats can be used to:

- determine a trend or trends
- compare different items, e.g. sales of various products
- determine progress, e.g. of a project
- show proportions in relation to a whole, e.g. the amount of expenditure on different items in the budget
- provide a pictorial image of numbers, e.g. representing a certain number of houses sold by a drawing of a house
- show allocation of holidays, dates of meetings, room bookings, etc.

FORMATS

Statistical data can be presented in the following ways:

- tables
- line graphs
- multi-line graphs
- vertical bar graphs
- horizontal bar charts

- charts
- pie charts
- pictograms
- picture charts.

Each of these formats is explained and illustrated on the pages that follow.

Tables

Tables are set in columns, each column clearly headed and each line identified on the left (see Fig. 12.22, which shows the number of units sold by representatives over a three-month period.

Representative	January Units	February Units	March Units
Arkwright	78	157	75
Barnes	312	501	301
Bartholemew	255	454	250
Beavers	237	566	325
Bell	59	120	75
Clive	346	406	300
Dent	45	98	53

Fig. 12.22 Table of numerical data.

Line graphs

Line graphs consist of:

- a vertical line or axis on the left that has a scale, which increases upwards; this is the variable scale because it represents data that may be changeable over a period of time
- a horizontal line or axis, which has a fixed scale, e.g. months or years.

The line graph in Fig. 12.23 shows the amount of profit made by a small business over four years. It is easier to see the trend from a graph than from a table.

To draw a line graph you draw the vertical and horizontal axes on a sheet of graph or squared paper. The big squares on graph paper are divided into 10 little squares across and 10 down. To **plot** the graph you take the first

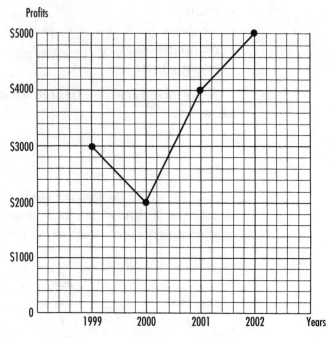

Fig. 12.23 Line graph.

item profit of $3000 in 1999. You move your pencil up to 3000 and across to 1999 and make a dot. The next year profits were $2000. You repeat the plotting and then join the two dots with a straight line.

ACTIVITY 12.8 Draw a line graph on graph or squared paper. On the vertical axis write in 10, 20, 30, 40 and 50. On the horizontal axis write in the months of the year (just the initial letters will do). Enter the two figures given in the paragraph above. Then complete the graph for the year as follows:

March	27	August	38
April	36	September	14
May	20	October	22
June	19	November	36
July	42	December	48

Multi-line graphs

These are the same as line graphs but consist of two or more lines that enable a comparison to be made. Fig. 12.24 shows three lines, each one

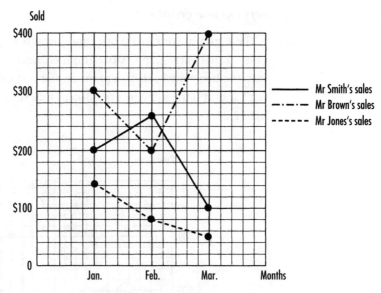

Fig. 12.24 Multi-line graph.

different in order to represent different items. Plotting is done in the same way as for a single-line graph.

ACTIVITY 12.9 Here are three sets of statistical data representing the value of sales made by three different representatives – Peter, Mary and Tom – from 1997 to 2001. Their manager wants to compare their performance over that period. The sales figures range from $200 to $4500.

a. Draw a vertical axis marked in $000s from 1 to 5 and the horizontal axis marked in years from 1997 to 2001; then plot the sales of each of the representatives and draw in three different types of line.

Year	Peter	Mary	Tom
1997	$2300	$3400	$3200
1998	3000	4100	4000
1999	2800	4500	3800
2000	3200	4200	3900
2001	2600	3500	3800

b. Look at your graph and think how you might comment on the performance of each of the sales representatives.

Vertical bar graphs

These graphs (or charts) offer another way of presenting data instead of a line or multi-line graph. A bar graph is drawn vertically with a 'pillar' from the horizontal axis to a point on the vertical axis. Fig. 12.25 shows as a bar graph the same information as that shown as a line graph in Fig. 12.23.

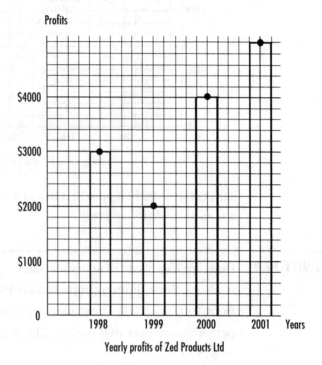

Fig. 12.25 Bar graph (vertical).

Horizontal bar charts

These present the information with the pillars sideways. In the example in Fig. 12.26, there are three different sets of data in each set of columns. It is not easy to identify trends with this kind of chart, but it is easier to see individual comparison. In Fig. 12.26 the sales performance of Brown, Smith and Jones in relation to each other is clear. It also shows that the trend of each perons's achievement bears no relation to that of the other two.

Charts

Charts can be used for a wide range of purposes. They are commonly used to control the progress of projects or tasks such as arranging an event.

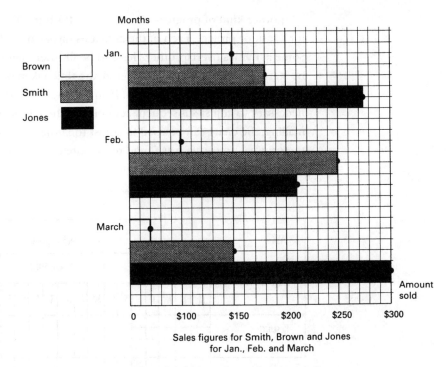

Fig. 12.26 Bar chart (horizontal).

Fig. 12.27 is an example of a **progress chart** for the arrangements to be made for inviting people to an event. It is easy to see at a glance whether everyone who has been sent an invitation has replied, whether they need hotel accommodation and, if so, whether it has been reserved and the guest notified. At a glance it can be seen what is outstanding so that follow-up action can be taken as appropriate. If anyone telephones with a query relating to the task an instant answer can be given.

Name	Invitations sent	Accepted	Declined	Hotel requested	Hotel reserved	Hotel details sent
Miss Benson	8.7.02	10.7.02		✓	11.7.02	15.7.02
Miss Carter	8.7.02	17.7.02				
Mlle Dupont	8.7.02	15.7.02		✓	17.7.02	19.7.02
Mrs Worrall	9.7.02	10.7.02		✓	11.7.02	15.7.02
Frau Wurot	9.7.02		✓			
Mme Lebrun	11.7.02	16.7.02		✓	17.7.02	19.7.02

Fig. 12.27 Progress chart.

Another kind of progress chart is a **Gantt chart**. This shows the timescale for a task or project. Each of the activities involved is allocated a timespan. Some activities overlap, others have to be finished before the next one can be started. As each task is completed, the time taken is inserted on the chart so that any variation can be seen. If an activity is overdue it may be necessary to adjust subsequent activities. If the task is repetitive, e.g. a mailing, the chart can be used to adjust the timescale for the next mailing if the original timescale was found to be unrealistic. A Gantt chart is illustrated in Fig. 12.28.

TASK	Week beginning																				
Report on wage increases	13 May 2002							20 May 2002							27 May 2002						
	M	T	W	T	F	S	S	M	T	W	T	F	S	S	M	T	W	T	F	S	S
Research																					
Outline report																					
Photographs																					
Draft report																					
Edit																					
Print																					

Key ——————— Allocated time
    - - - - - - - - Actual time

Fig. 12.28 Gantt chart.

An example of a **holiday chart** is shown in Fig. 12.29. It is very important that the staff in any one section or department do not take their holidays at the same time or overlap too much. A chart enables control of holiday dates to be kept easily. If, for example, Jane Greene asked for her holiday from 16–23 May, it can be seen that she will clash with Fred Parkins, who has already booked his holiday for that week. Therefore Jane will have to decide on an alternative time.

Week beginning:	January				February				March				April				May				June				July				August			
	6	13	20	27	3	10	17	24	3	10	17	24	31	7	14	21	28	5	12	19	26	2	9	16	23	30	7	14	21	28	4	11	18	25
Jardine C				|–––|–––|																											
Lara D							–––	–––											–––															
Manson E															–––													–––	–––					
Peters B		–––							–––	–––																								
Smith R							–––							–––	–––						–––													
Thomas W																										–––	–––							–––	–––

Fig 12.29 Holiday chart.

There is a great variety of printed charts available from stationery suppliers in A1 and A3 sizes. They may be on laminated paper or on boards, which can be used continuously. All have spaces at the top and side for headings to be inserted. Coloured markers can be placed on the board in holes, slots or channels, or held on magnetically or by other methods of adhesion. The markers can be added, taken off or moved about to show changes in the situation from day to day, or from hour to hour if necessary. These charts are often referred to as **visual control boards**.

Pie charts

Pie charts are commonly seen in company literature or other documents generally distributed to the public. For example, a charity wanting to show the sources of its income and the proportion from each source can do so very well with a pie chart, as shown in Fig. 12.30. Each 'slice' of the pie is in proportion to the whole.

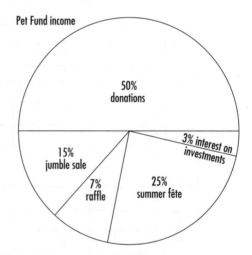

Fig. 12.30 Pie chart.

ACTIVITY 12.10 Draw a pie chart showing the following proportions of a workforce by sex and age. The total number of employees is 1000.

Age	Male	Female
16–20	50 (5 per cent)	200
21–50	200 (20 per cent)	450 (45 per cent)
50+	50	50

PICTOGRAMS

Pictograms are made up of symbols representing a certain number of items. In Fig. 12.31 each 'sun' represents 5 days of sunshine enjoyed in a particular resort. Each line represents a different month. This would be useful for a company selling pension schemes to include in a brochure to show how attractive this resorts in terms of the weather.

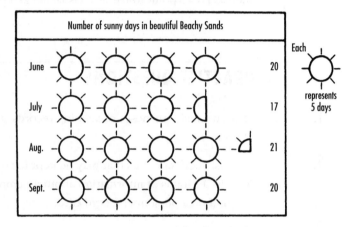

Fig. 12.31 Pictogram.

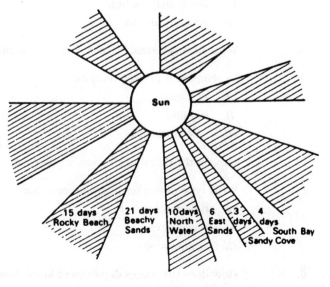

Fig. 12.32 Picture chart.

PICTURE CHARTS

These can be an effective way of representing a few statistics on a poster, in advertisements and in magazines. The amount of sunshine in different areas is shown in the picture chart in Fig. 12.32.

The graphs, charts, etc. explained in this chapter provide a very good way of explaining statistical information in a report or presentation. They can be produced on a computer using graphics software, and reproduced on an overhead projector transparency or presented on a computerised system such as Powerpoint to use as a visual aid at a presentation.

PRACTICE QUESTIONS

1. State two main purposes of keeping records, giving two examples of each.

2. *a.* List six documents that may be kept for personnel records.
   b. List 12 items of information about an employee you would expect to find on a personnel record card.

3. Explain the following:
   i. letter of appointment
   ii. contract of employment
   iii. appraisal report
   iv. disciplinary action
   v. accident report.

4. What details should be included in an accident report?

5. Explain the following records:
   i. sickness
   ii. training
   iii. labour turnover.

6. Explain the difference between piece rate and time rate.

7. What type of worker might be paid on:
   i. time rates
   ii. piece rates
   iii. commission?

8. How does the wages department know how much to pay people who work additional hours (overtime) to their normal working hours?

9. Explain the following terms:
  i. gross pay
  ii. net pay
  iii. deductions
  iv. PAYE
  v. National Insurance.

10. Give three examples of statutory deductions and three examples of voluntary deductions.

11. Every year all employees have to inform the Inland Revenue of their income. What form is used for this purpose?

12. What tax-free allowance is everyone entitled to claim in your territory?

13. The National Insurance that is deducted from employees' salaries enables the government to pay various benefits. State six such benefits.

14. What is a:
  i. time card
  ii. pay slip
  iii. payroll
  iv. cash requisition?

15. List and explain three types of factory record.

16.
  a. What details are recorded on stock records?
  b. State six ways in which stock wastage can be controlled.
  c. What are maximum, re-order and minimum levels?

17. Draw a stock record card for A4 ruled pads and enter the following details.

Maximum stock: 500   Minimum stock: 50   Re-order level: 150

2.5.02   Balance in stock 260
3.5.02   Issued 40 pads to purchasing department
8.5.02   Issued 60 pads to sales department
17.5.02 Issued 30 pads to administration department
20.5.02 Issued 50 pads to training department
23.5.02 Issued 10 pads to transport department
27.5.02 Received 400 pads from Super Stationers Ltd
28.5.02 Issued 20 pads to information processing department

18.
  a. Why is stocktaking necessary?
  b. Explain two methods of stocktaking.

19.
  a. What is meant by the term 'credit rating'?
  b. Why is it necessary for a supplier to obtain a credit reference for a new customer?

20. What is the difference between buying goods on credit and buying on hire purchase?

21. The head of the department in which you work has asked you to set up a petty cash system. Decide what system you would recommend and explain how it is operated. Include details and diagrams of the records and documents that have to be kept.

22. Explain the following terms:
  i. mail order
  ii. goods sent on approval
  iii. option to buy
  iv. instalments.

23. You work for the transport manager of a large manufacturing company in the Caribbean. There are about 50 sales representatives throughout the islands, each of whom is provided with a car. Your manager asks you to start a card index system to record details of the representatives' cars, the mileage each covers, repairs and maintenance, and any other relevant details.
  a. What type or types of equipment would you consider?
  b. Draft an index card on which to record the information.
  c. Draft a form to be completed weekly by each sales representative.
  d. Write a memorandum for the transport manager to sign, enclosing the form you have drafted and explaining the new system to the sales representatives.

24.
  a. Copy the blank chart on page 401 and use it as the basis for a Gantt chart. The tasks are scheduled as follows, assuming that 1 is a Monday:

   Task 1   1–5 and 8–9
   2   8–12 and 15
   3   11–12 and 15
   4   15–19 and 22

   Enter the tasks by a straight line across the scheduled dates.

  b. The tasks actually took:

   Task 1   2–5 and 8–10
   2   9–12 and 15–16

3   15-17
4   17-20 and 22

Enter the time the tasks actually took in a different colour if possible.

Task	1	2	3	4	5	6	7	8	9	10	11	12	13	14	15	16	17	18	19	20	21	22
1																						
2																						
3																						
4																						

c. How many days' overtime has been worked and what rate of overtime would be paid?

25. Explain the following:
  i. axis
  ii. visual control board
  iii. multi-line graph
  iv. pie chart
  v. vertical bar chart.

26. Design a line graph to show the yearly expenditure of the Well-Made Products Company on stationery. Plot these figures on the graph:

1997 – $3500
1998 – $2000
1999 – $3000
2000 – $4000
2001 – $4500.

27. You are employed as assistant to the chief clerk of a department that consists of the head of department, chief clerk, three assistant clerks, a secretary who works mainly for the head of department, and one typist.

The chief clerk asks you to draw up a holiday rota chart and to indicate on it the holiday arrangements that the staff in the department would like. Each person is allowed four weeks' holiday but may take only two weeks consecutively. The rota will then be discussed if there are any problems. The holiday periods the staff would like are as follows:

Week beginning × number of weeks

Head of department – 13 May × 1   10 Jun × 2   21 Oct × 1
Chief clerk   – 18 Mar × 2   7 Oct × 2
Assistant clerk 1*   – 22–28 Mar × 1   22 Jul × 2   21 Oct × 1

Week beginning:	March				April				May				June				July				August				September				October		
	4	11	18	25	1	8	15	22	29	6	13	20	27	3	10	17	24	1	8	15	22	29	5	12	19	26	2	9	16	23	30	7	14	21	28
Head of dept																																			
Chief clerk																																			
Asst clerk 1																																			
Asst clerk 2																																			
Asst clerk 3																																			
Secretary																																			
Typist 1																																			

Assistant clerk 2*	–	1–8 Apr × 1	3 Jun × 1	12 Aug × 2
Assistant clerk 3	–	6 May × 1	15 Jul × 2	9 Sep × 1
Secretary	–	11 Mar × 2	20 May × 1	23 Sep × 1
Typist	–	20–26 Mar × 1	8 Jul × 2	14 Oct × 1

*A day is included in lieu of Good Friday/Easter Monday

    a. Copy the chart on page 402 and block in the periods when each employee would like to be away on leave.

    b. What problems become evident from the chart?

28. Figures of sales for the preceding year were as follows:

June 2001	$48 000	December 2001	$90 000
July 2001	42 000	January 2002	86 000
August 2001	47 000	February 2002	82 000
September 2001	52 000	March 2002	87 000
October 2001	53 000	April 2002	92 000
November 2001	60 000	May 2002	100 000

Prepare a bar graph showing this information.

29. Prepare a pie chart to show the percentage of revenue derived from six different products.

Product	**Percentage**
Fruit and vegetables	10
Dairy foods	15
Tinned and bottled groceries	20
Wines and spirits	25
Bakery	20
Fresh meat and fish	10

30. Briefly describe a:
    i. pictogram
    ii. Gantt chart
    iii. horizontal bar chart
    iv. multi-line graph.

SHORT ANSWER QUESTIONS

1. People who are paid some of their salary on the basis of how many products they sell are said to work ....

2. At the end of each financial year an employer must complete a/an .... for each employee.

3. An employee's absence and lateness are recorded on their ....

4. National Insurance is a .... deduction made from an employee's wages.

5. The list of employees' names and the calculations of their individual pay is known as a/an ....

Choose the most appropriate ending for each of the following sentences.

6. The pay advice:
   a. instructs the employee to collect their wages
   b. provides the employee with details of the salary payment
   c. informs the employee how much money has been paid into the bank by way of salary
   d. is a list of money required to pay wages in cash.

7. A job card:
   a. instructs the production unit to produce goods ordered by a customer or required for stock
   b. contains details of the work done in the factory
   c. lists the jobs for the day
   d. gives details of the manufacturing process.

8. The works manager must be kept informed of the work being done in the factory. He receives each day:
   a. a production checklist
   b. a list of jobs completed
   c. a progress advice
   d. a list of work in progress.

9. When stock reaches a pre-determined minimum level it is time to:
   a. place an order
   b. chase an order that has been placed some time before
   c. check stock
   d. issue only when stock is needed very urgently.

10. When people buy goods on hire purchase they:
    a. own it immediately
    b. share ownership with the shop/store from which they bought it
    c. do not own it until they have paid all the instalments
    d. have an option to buy, which is covered by the last instalment.

EXAMINATION QUESTIONS

1. Cash must be kept .... within an office.

2. The .... is the set amount of money that should be in the petty cash box at the start of each week or month.

(Pitman Office Procedures Level 1 1998 Pt 1A)

3. Name THREE pieces of information recorded on a stock control card.

   a. ....
   b. ....
   c. ....

(Pitman Office Procedures Level 1 1998 Pt 1B)

4. A .... is set to reduce the loss of stock through deterioration.

5. Travel, postage and sundries are examples of petty cash .... columns.

(Pitman Office Procedures Level 1 1999 Pt 1A)

6. Name THREE printed headings on a petty cash voucher, excluding the description of goods.

   a. ....
   b. ....
   c. ....

(Pitman Office Procedures Level 1 1999 Pt 1B)

7.   a. Stationery is very expensive and must be stored and controlled carefully.

   i. Outline the steps that could be taken to ensure the *issue* of stationery stock is carefully supervised.

   ii. State eight rules to be followed regarding the *storage* of stationery.

   b. What type of stock is entered on an inventory?

(Pitman Office Procedures Level 1 1999 Pt 2B)

8. Using the data below, draw up a line graph to show the sales position in Harare in the three years shown.

Sales figures for Harare

	1995	1996	1997
Pen/pencil sets	2500	3000	1250
Pen sets	3000	2500	4000
Pencil sets	–	1000	2000
Gift sets	250	250	3000

(Pitman Office Procedures Level 2 1998 Pt 1)

9.   a. Draw up a stock card for A4 white bond paper and record the following entries.

   - The reference number is ES124 and the item is supplied in reams. On 1 January there were 40 reams in stock. The maximum level is 50 reams and the minimum level 10 reams; the re-order level is 20 reams.

- During the first two weeks of January the following stock movements took place.
    - On 5 January, 5 reams were issued to the Purchasing Department on requisition number 285. On 8 January the Sales Department collected 10 packs on requisition 148 and on 9 January Accounts were issued with 5 reams on requisition 122. On 10 January 30 reams were received on Invoice Z452. The appropriate balances must be shown.
    b. What information is needed to set a re-order level?
    c. When compiling an inventory of *non*-consumable stock what information would be recorded?

(Pitman Office Procedures Level 2 1998 Pt 2)

CHAPTER 13

MEETINGS

OBJECTIVES When you have studied this chapter you should have acquired the knowledge and understanding to be able to:

1. explain the purposes of informal and formal meetings
2. arrange a meeting from given information
3. prepare the documentation for a meeting from given information
4. attend a meeting to take notes of relevant discussion
5. draft minutes for the chairperson's approval.

In business, meetings are held frequently for many different reasons. They may be held, for example, by people:

- within a department or group within an organisation
- from different departments or groups within an organisation
- from many different organisations, one of which has organised the meeting
- who are members of professional bodies.

PURPOSES OF MEETINGS

Meetings are held when a discussion is needed. Possible purposes include:

- to exchange views and perhaps update colleagues on current situations
- to consult people in order to seek their opinions and views before making a decision on policy or action

- to negotiate, e.g. prices for products, deadlines for completion of work, terms and conditions of a contract, staff pay and conditions (usually with trades union representatives
- to give instructions (brief) a number of people at the same time so that they all receive the same information
- to report progress on action previously agreed
- to report problems and try to find possible solutions acceptable to all or the majority
- to obtain information, e.g. for planning
- to encourage motivation of individuals and develop more effective team working.

TYPES OF MEETING

There are two main types of meeting: informal and formal. The former may or may not have been officially notified in writing; it may have been called verbally and it may or may not be conducted in accordance with standard meeting procedures. If it has been called, for example, by a manager, to discuss a particular problem, there is unlikely to be an agenda. Notes of such a meeting may be made by one of the staff attending the meeting or by a member of the support staff called in to take notes. It is unlikely that formal minutes would be required. A record of the main points discussed and any decision taken or actions agreed written up in note form would be adequate.

The formal meeting has to be conducted according to certain rules, depending on the type of organisation involved. Minutes or, occasionally, a report of the proceedings will be required. (Notes are explained on page 427, minutes and reports in Table 13.2.) There are various types of formal meeting, some of them statutory (which means that, by law, they must be held).

STATUTORY MEETINGS

These include annual general and extraordinary general meetings, meetings of boards of directors of companies, and committees of officers and appointed/elected members of professional and voluntary organisations.

ANNUAL GENERAL MEETINGS

AGMs are held by public limited and private limited companies, incorporated groups such as professional institutions, e.g. Institute of

Management, any organisation that is financed by its members or the public. The company chairman and directors of the board should attend, and the shareholders have the right to attend. They have responsibility for voting directors on or off the board, approving (or not) financial matters and accepting (or not) the chairperson's report on the previous year's activities and the directors' recommendations for future activities. For non-profit-making organisations, the officers and appointed committee members should attend and all members are entitled to attend. If any member is unable to attend, the rules may allow them to appoint a **proxy** to vote on their behalf.

EXTRAORDINARY GENERAL MEETINGS

EGMs are called when a 'one-off' situation arises where the approval of the shareholders or membership is required, for example when a change to the Memorandum and Articles of Association of a company or the constitution of an organisation is required.

BOARD MEETINGS

Board meetings must be held at regular intervals as stated in a company's Memorandum and Articles of Association. The directors are concerned with agreeing policy, setting objectives for the company, approving budgets and appointment of top management.

COMMITTEE MEETINGS

Committee meetings are required by the constitution of an organisation, including voluntary organisations. The chairperson, officers and appointed members should attend. Their role is similar to that of a board of directors.

There are various kinds of committee set up for specific purposes. A **policy** committee has responsibility for developing, reviewing and revising policies. An executive committee deals with the day-to-day affairs of an organisation. An **advisory** committee may have to discuss various aspects of the organisation's affairs and make recommendations to the board, a main committee or, sometimes, to a government department.

A **standing** committee is one that is set up by a local authority independently of statutory requirements. Such committees continue though the membership may change. Members are usually appointed.

SUB-COMMITTEES

These are set up by a main committee. A sub-commitee may have responsibility for a particular aspect of the main committee's work, e.g. finance, event planning, membership approval. The sub-committee chairperson reports on their work at main committee meetings.

'AD HOC' COMMITTEES

These are set up by a committee to consider a specific, usually non-recurring, situation such as discussing a proposed change of policy. The ad hoc committee chairperson would report to the main committee their decision or recommendations.

DEPARTMENTAL MEETINGS

These may be formal or informal. They are likely to be chaired by the head of the department or the deputy head, and usually deal with matters related to the work of the department.

ARRANGING A MEETING

It is usually quite difficult to find a time that is convenient for all the members of a group. For this reason it is advisable to plan meetings as far ahead as is practicable and reasonable.

When asked to arrange a meeting, start by asking who are the key people. You also need to know the chairperson's preferred date, time and venue (place) for the meeting.

You may have to work manually or you may have the facility on your computer to organise the meeting electronically. If you do not have this computer facility, prepare a grid (as shown in Fig. 13.1a) and then contact each key person in turn, noting the times each one is free on each of the possible dates (see Fig. 13.1b). When everyone has been contacted you should be able to isolate a time when all of them and a meeting room (if you have to reserve one) are available. You can then contact other members of the group to tell them the time, date and venue that has been arranged. Any non-key members who are not available may wish to send a substitute in their place.

(a)

NAME	MONDAY		TUESDAY		WEDNESDAY		THURSDAY		FRIDAY	
	am	pm	am	pm	am	pm	am	pm	am	pm

(b)

NAME	MONDAY		TUESDAY		WEDNESDAY		THURSDAY		FRIDAY	
	am	pm	am	pm	am	pm	am	pm	am	pm
Beckham	x	3–4	9–12	x			x	2–3.30	x	2–3.30
Grundy		x	10–12	2–4	11–12			x	x	x
Le Mare	10–12	2–4	9–11	2–4.30				3–5	10–12	x
Keating	10–11	x	9–11.30		9–12.30	x	x	x	9–12	x

Key

Blank square — completely free
Cross — not free at all
Times — when available

Fig. 13.1 (a) Blank meeting grid; (b) completed meeting grid.

ACTIVITY 13.1 Your manager asks you to arrange a meeting for either Tuesday, Thursday or Friday next week. The meeting will take approximately 1 hour. He wishes five of his staff to attend: Adele, Gerald, Harold, Jasmin and Trevor. You find out when they are free as shown below.

Draw a grid as shown in Fig. 13.1a, complete it for the five staff and identify a time when the meeting could be held.

Adele is free on	Tuesday	1400–1600
	Thursday	0800–1100 and 1530–1700
	Friday	1200–1630
Gerald is free on	Tuesday	1330–1500
	Thursday	1000–1200
	Friday	0830–1130 and 1400–1630

(continued)

ACTIVITY 13.1
(continued)

Harold is free on	Tuesday	1430-1530
	Thursday	1100-1300
	Friday	1000-1130 and 1330-1530
Jasmin is free on	Tuesday	1500-1700
	Thursday	1130-1230 and 1400-1630
	Friday	1430-1600
Trevor is free on	Tuesday	0800-1130 and 1400-1600
	Thursday	1400-1700
	Friday	0800-1100 and 1330-1530

A checklist should be used when a more formal meeting is being arranged. The example shown in Fig. 13.2 can be adapted to your own particular way of arranging meetings. It is advisable to have a file (this can be any suitable folder) for each meeting being organised. At the front, keep a copy of the checklist and tick off each activity as it is completed. This reminds you of how far you have progressed with the arrangements, enables anyone else to see the stage reached if you are not available and provides proof of what has been done.

CHECKLIST FOR ARRANGING A MEETING

Planning the meeting   Check

1. Open file
2. Check room available; if not alternative dates
3. Check members available
4. Confirm time and date
5. Check minutes of previous meeting already distributed
6. List papers required for meeting
    (a) to be distributed before meeting
    (b) to be distributed at meeting

Preparing for the meeting

7. Reserve room
8. Duplicate notice/notice with request for agenda items/notice with agenda
9. Duplicate papers already available.
10. Distribute notice (see 8 above) previous minutes (if not already distributed) and papers available.
11. Check travel and hotel requirements of individuals

Fig. 13.2 (continued).

12. Make travel/transport reservations
13. Make hotel reservations
14. Notice for the press (general meetings)
15. Request material for papers/draft papers (give submission date)
16. Prepare draft papers for approval
17. Invite editors (general meetings)
18. Prepare/order name cards
19. Get draft papers approved
20. Duplicate papers
21. Prepare visual aids
22. Distribute papers
23. Order printed notice indicating venue location
24. Arrange for stand for venue location notice
25. Check supplies — pens/pencils, copy paper, lined paper
26. Arrange transport for supplies if venue outside organisation
27. Prepare seating plan
28. Arrange photographer (general meetings)

The day before the meeting

29. Check accommodation
30. Arrange refreshments
31. Copy of previous minutes in the minute file/book
32. Prepare attendance book/sheet
33. Prepare supplies — pens/pencils, paper, spare copies (agenda, minutes, papers), papers for distribution
34. Check reference books, files required; standing orders
35. Inform security officers/commissionaire/receptionist of time, place of meeting, names of members
36. Prepare notice of venue location (if not printed)
37. Sort papers into order; flag documents in files
38. Prepare executive's 'meeting preparation sheet'
39. Prepare chairperson's agenda/meeting brief
40. Pack books, papers, etc. for transport if venue outside organisation

The day of the meeting

41. Set up notice of venue location
42. Re-check refreshment arrangements
43. Check room — sufficient chairs, glasses, water, gavel, air conditioning, ventilation (ashtrays if smoking allowed)
44. Prepare table —
    Each place — Name card, paper, pen/pencil, agenda, discussion papers

    In addition

    Chairperson — Meeting brief, documents relating to agenda items
    Committee Secretary — Minute file/book, letters and messages of apology, appropriate reference books/ documents/files

Fig. 13.2 Checklist for arranging a meeting (continued overleaf).

		Check
The day of the meeting		
In addition		
Note-taker	— Attendance book, copy of minutes, shorthand/ A4 pad, pens/pencils	

45. Make arrangements with telephone operator for messages to be taken . . . .
46. Remind executive of meeting . . . .
47. Be in attendance in the room 10/15 minutes before meeting to greet members . . . .

During the meeting

48. Ensure that all members sign attendance book . . . .
49. Take notes . . . .
50. Make separate notes of specific details for executive . . . .
51. Be prepared to find documents on files . . . .

After the meeting

52. Collect papers, minute file/book, attendance book, files, reference books, pens/pencils, unused paper and return to correct places . . . .
53. Tidy room, close windows, turn off heating/air conditioning . . . .
54. File spare copies of documents . . . .
55. Enter date of next meeting in diaries . . . .
56. Enter preparation dates in work schedule . . . .
57. Draft minutes for approval . . . .
58. Copy minutes . . . .
59. Distribute minutes . . . .
60. Insert copy of minutes in minute file/book . . . .
61. Index minutes . . . .
62. Check ACTION points . . . .
   (a) those you can deal with e.g. correspondence . . . .
   (b) those your executive must deal with . . . .
63. Deal with your ACTION points . . . .
64. Follow up your executive's and members' ACTION points to ensure deadlines met . . . .

Fig. 13.2 (continued).

DOCUMENTS

A variety of documents is used for meetings, especially more formal meetings. The most commonly used documents and their uses are listed in Table 13.1.

A **notice of meeting** should be sent to members well in advance of the meeting unless the date has been agreed at the previous meeting. Examples of notices for a committee meeting and an annual general meeting are shown in Figs 13.3a and 13.3b.

Table 13.1 *Frequently used documents and their uses*

Document	Use
Notice of meeting	To inform members of the time, date and venue of the meeting (see Fig. 13.3)
Agenda	To inform members of the topics to be discussed (see Fig. 13.4)
Supplementary papers	To provide background information on one or more topics on the agenda as a briefing to members before the meeting
Working papers	To provide information and proposals that will form the basis for discussion
Chairperson's agenda (or briefing)	To provide the chairperson with up-to-date details relevant to each agenda item (see Fig. 13.5)
Minutes of previous meeting	To provide a record of the business transacted at the previous meeting, for the approval of members and signature by the chairperson
Action sheet	To provide a summary of action points agreed at the meeting (see Fig. 13.9)

NATIONAL ASSOCIATION OF TRADERS

PO Box 661
BRIDGETOWN

14 June 2002

To: All Members of the Advisory Committee for Recruitment of Technical Inspectors

NOTICE OF MEETING

A meeting of the Committee is to be held at 1400 hours on Thursday 27 June 2002 in the Conference Room at Trading House, High Road, Bridgetown.

The agenda and papers for the meeting will be distributed on 21 June 2002.

MK Small
National General Secretary

(a)

Fig. 13.3 (a) Notice of a committee meeting (continued overleaf).

(b)

WEST INDIES LIGHTING COMPANY LIMITED

NOTICE IS HEREBY GIVEN that the Annual General Meeting of the West Indies Lighting Company Limited will be held at the Company's Head Office, 14 Main Street, Port-of-Spain at 1130 hours on Friday 19 July 2002.

AB Davidson
Secretary

(c)

WEST INDIES LIGHTING COMPANY LIMITED

To: Departmental Managers   15 May 2002

A meeting of all Departmental Managers is to be held in the Chairman's Office at 1030 hours on Monday 27 May 2002 to discuss the 2002/03 budget.

Will you please submit, on the form below, items for discussion by Wednesday 22 May 2002.

....

To: BD Johns
      Company Secretary

Will you please include the following item(s) on the agenda for the meeting to be held at 1030 hours on Monday 27 May 2002

_____
_____
_____
_____
_____

Signed: _____   Date: _____

Fig. 13.3 (continued) (b) notice of an annual general meeting; (c) notice of meeting requesting items for the agenda.

A notice of meeting may be varied in the following ways:

- the notice may be combined with the agenda
- the date when the agenda and other papers will be sent out may not be stated
- members may be asked to submit items for the agenda (see Fig. 13.3c).

The name of the committee secretary should appear on the notice either by signature or printed (as shown in Fig. 13.3a). (There may not be a formal committee secretary position; the person responsible for organising the meeting is fulfilling this role.)

An **agenda** for a committee meeting is shown in Fig. 13.4a. This document may be compiled by the chairperson and/or the committee secretary. The agenda should reach the members at least a week before a meeting. An agenda for an annual general meeting is shown in Fig. 13.4b. This must be published at least 14 days before the meeting.

NATIONAL ASSOCIATION OF TRADERS

PO Box 661
BRIDGETOWN

21 June 2002

To: All Members of the Advisory Committee for Recruitment of Technical Inspectors

AGENDA

The agenda for the meeting of the Committee to be held at 1400 on Thursday 27 June 2002 in the Conference Room at Trading House, High Road, Bridgetown is as follows.

1. Apologies for absence
2. Minutes of the meeting held on Thursday 25 April 2002
3. Matters arising from the minutes
   31/02   Mr Nelson's report on discussion with Ministry of Education
4. Traders for which inspectors are required
5. Qualifications of inspectors
6. Dates for action
7. Any other business

MK Small
National General Secretary

(a)

WEST INDIES LIGHTING COMPANY LIMITED

ANNUAL GENERAL MEETING

AGENDA

1. Minutes of the Annual General Meeting held on 14 September 2001.
2. Matters Arising from the Minutes.
3. Chairman's Report for the year ended 30 June 2002.
4. Financial Accounts for the year ended 30 June 2002.
5. Election of two directors on the retirement of Mr JD Hanson and Mrs ET Waters. Mrs Waters is willing to stand for re-election.
6. Formation of a subsidiary company for the expansion of wholesale trade.

AB Davidson
Secretary

(b)

Fig. 13.4 (a) Agenda for a committee meeting; (b) agenda for an annual general meeting.

Supplementary papers are often lengthy documents. It is important that they be distributed in sufficient time before the meeting to enable the members to read the papers and, if necessary, to undertake any relevant research for their own contributions to the discussion. Supplementary papers may be in the form of reports in which recommendations are presented for approval by the committee.

Working papers may either be draft documents or background information for discussion prior to documents being drafted. Working papers will ultimately become formal documents approved by the committee.

A **chairperson's agenda** should be prepared as close to the time of the meeting as practicable to ensure that the details are up to date and complete. Each agenda item is supplemented with details that will help the chairperson conduct the meeting in a professional manner. A specimen chairperson's agenda is shown in Fig. 13.5.

NATIONAL ASSOCIATION OF TRADERS

ADVISORY COMMITTEE FOR RECRUITMENT OF TECHNICAL INSPECTORS

Meeting at 1400 hours on Thursday 27 June 2002

CHAIRPERSON'S AGENDA

1. Apologies	
2. Minutes of previous meeting	
3. Matters arising from the minutes	46/02 Mr Nelson to report on his discussion with the Ministry of Education
4. Traders for which inspectors are required	Ministry of Education suggest inspectors for groups of traders rather than individual traders
5. Qualifications of inspectors	Mr Nelson to report on his discussions with Ministry of Education. Ministry of Labour suggest City & Guilds Final Certificate (see correspondence)
6. Dates	Secretary suggests Advertisements: 5.7.02 Receipt of applications: 19.7.02 Selection test: 26.7.02 Invitation for interview: 5.8.02 Interviewing panels: 12.8.02 Offer of appointment: 19.8.02 Appointment effective: 1.10.03
7. Any other business	

Fig. 13.5 Chairperson's agenda.

The **minutes of the previous meeting** should have been distributed within a short time of the meeting having taken place. There are committees that meet so frequently that the minutes are distributed with the agenda for the next meeting. On the other hand, some meetings are annual. The minutes may be distributed within a few weeks of the meeting but a second copy may be sent with the agenda for the next year. This is wasteful and to overcome the problem of some members losing their copy, a few extra copies can be available at the next meeting.

Various formats for the presentation of minutes are shown in Fig. 13.9.

ACTIVITY 13.2 Your manager asks you to prepare a notice and agenda (to be combined) for a meeting to be held at 1000 on the first day of next month. The group is the Health and Safety Working Party and the notice is to be addressed to 'All members of the Working Party'. The meeting will be held in Meeting Room 3 on the 4th floor of City House.

The agenda items are Apologies, Minutes of the meeting held on (first day of last month), Matters arising (minute no. 16/00 Budget, and minute no. 20/00 Transport), Fire extinguisher training, Safety representative nominations, Any other business.

MINUTE FILE

Usually the second item on the agenda, after 'Apologies', is 'Minutes of the meeting held on [date]'. When the minutes of the previous meeting are approved by the committee they should be signed by the chairperson in the presence of the members. This is then the legal record of the business transacted at that meeting. The signed minutes are kept in a file, which must be stored safely.

Certain security measures can be taken to ensure that the documents are not tampered with or lost. It is not difficult to remove a page from a file and replace it with a revised page, easily produced on a computer. To avoid this possibility it is advisable for the chairperson to initial each page. For additional security, the pages of the minutes for a particular committee can be numbered sequentially, as in a book. This ensures that a complete set of minutes cannot be removed from the file without this being noticed.

It is useful to have an index in the minute file (see page 433).

COMMITTEE FILES

People who attend the meetings of a particular committee normally keep a file specifically for the documents relating to those meetings. These would include notices, agendas, minutes, reports, supplementary and working papers. If the papers are too voluminous, separate files can be maintained, one for agendas and minutes, another for supplementary papers (which can be quite bulky). References in agendas and/or minutes to previous minutes and/or supplementary papers should be indicated by 'flagging', i.e. affixing an index tab with a note of its significance to the appropriate page.

PRESENTATIONS

Preparing for a presentation may involve ordering equipment, e.g. overhead projector or computerised equipment such as laptop, projector and screen for Powerpoint (see Chapter 3, page 60), slide projector, or video and TV. Visual aids such as transparencies may be required. Videos or film slides may have to be obtained. Handouts, either text or copies of transparencies or Powerpoint 'pages', may be needed.

You may be called upon to set up the equipment and/or to show a presenter how to use it.

OVERHEAD PROJECTORS

The transparency is placed 'right way up' on the glass top of the projector. The light inside the box projects the image through a lens and on to the mirror at the top of the arm. The image is then reflected from the mirror on to the screen. Transparencies can be handwritten with marker pens, produced on an office copier from a handwritten, typed or printed master, printed on a laser printer from a diskette or disk, or printed on a graphics printer in colour.

The overhead projector must be cleaned regularly to ensure that the glass and mirrors are free from marks or dust, which can be reflected on the screen. It is also essential to have a spare bulb available and some blank transparency sheets.

SLIDE PROJECTOR

Slide projectors are used to show coloured transparency photographs. The films to be shown are arranged in the correct sequence in a box or carousel attached to the projector. Each slide is moved into position by remote control, which enables the presenter to talk to the audience and operate the projector at the same time.

MEETING ROOM

The meeting room must be prepared either the night before the meeting or on the day of the meeting, well before the members arrive. A perfectly prepared meeting room indicates a professional approach. A checklist for preparing a meeting room is given in Fig. 13.6.

It is essential that all equipment is set up, its position checked so that all members will have a clear view, is tested and ready to use well before the meeting. If anything is wrong there is then still time to put it right.

CHECKLIST FOR PREPARING A MEETING ROOM

Environment

Windows and curtains, ventilation, air conditioning
Cleanliness and tidiness – carpet, furniture, no dirty crockery, no dying plants or flowers, no stacks of paper or equipment 'dumped' on shelves or tables

Furniture

Table(s) correctly positioned
Sufficient chairs, correctly positioned
Side table(s) for refreshments, papers

Supplies

Writing/blotting pads, writing paper, pens, pencils
Papers – agenda, minutes, working papers, etc.
Reference books, files, etc.
Name cards (useful if the number of members exceeds about eight)
Water jugs and glasses
Ashtrays or 'No Smoking' notices
Wastepaper bin
Telephone(s) near to chairperson if needed for making calls: the telephones should be rerouted to avoid incoming calls disrupting the meeting

Directions/information

Location of meeting room on direction board (usually in reception)
'Meeting in Progress' sign on door/outside room to avoid interruptions
Instructions to telephone operator not to call extension

Fig. 13.6 Checklist for preparing a meeting room.

TELECONFERENCING

When people who live long distances apart need to meet, it is possible to hold the meeting either as an audioconference or a videoconference.

An **audioconference** is a group of people who can be linked together via their direct-line or mobile telephones. The subscriber who arranges the conference call books time with the national telecommunications company, which allocates a conference number. The people involved are informed of the time, date and telephone number before the meeting. They also receive all the necessary documentation by post, fax or e-mail. Each person calls the conference number at the given time and they introduce themselves as they join the group. They should also identify themselves when they speak during the meeting. The subscriber who arranges the meeting usually acts as chairperson.

In-house audioconferences consist of extension users who can take part from their own workstations. One external subscriber can also be involved.

A **videoconference** works on the same principle, but because video cameras and monitors are required there are small groups of people at up to three specific locations. The participants can see each other on the monitors and can also see documents shown on the screens. Each person in each group has a microphone so that everyone can be heard clearly.

The *advantages* of audio- and videoconferences over face-to-face meetings are:

- the participants save travel time and are less tired as a result
- meetings can be held with people worldwide
- saves the cost of travel, accommodation, meals, etc.
- saves the cost of arranging and hiring accommodation
- the chairperson and the members prepare more carefully
- a tape recording can be arranged to provide a permanent record
- participants tend to be more concise than they would be face to face.

Particular advantages of videoconferences are:

- body language visible to the participants
- documents can be displayed on the screen
- a permanent record is automatically available.

The *disadvantages* of teleconferences are:

- it may be difficult to find a mutually convenient time, especially if some of the participants are overseas
- there is no body language visible in audioconferences
- one or more of the participants may have telephone equipment or line problems, which could cause them to miss some vital information
- the chairperson may have more difficulty in managing the meeting because of lack of eye contact.

Particular disadvantages of videoconferences are:

- the equipment is expensive to buy
- hiring a videoconference studio is expensive (but still cheaper than paying air fares and accommodation costs)
- some people do not feel comfortable when they know they are being recorded on video.

STRUCTURE OF FORMAL COMMITTEES

Formal committees consist of a chairperson and members. They may be appointed or elected either as individuals or as representatives of official organisations by the members of the organisation, e.g. the shareholders of a company or the members of the voluntary organisation.

The rules under which a committee is formed often include a clause that allows the co-option of one or more members. This means that the committee members themselves may, by agreement, appoint another person to join them in their discussions. **Co-opted members** have no voting rights and may be required for a specific purpose and therefore a limited time.

It is common to have **ex-officio members** on formal committees. Usually an ex-officio member is on the committee by virtue of an executive function, e.g. a college principal would be an ex-officio member of a board of governors and a company secretary an ex-officio member of a company's board of directors. Ex-officio members have no voting rights.

Usually the rules include the need for a meeting to be attended by a **quorum**. This is the number or percentage of members who must be present at a meeting for the decisions taken to be legal. Ex-officio members cannot be counted for the purpose of forming a quorum.

PROCEDURE

A meeting should be conducted by a chairperson, or a discussion leader in an informal meeting. 'Officers' of the committee should also be present. Some committees have a rule, which states that each member is expected to attend a minimum number of meetings in a year. This ensures that decisions are taken by most of the committee members.

If the chairperson is absent from the meeting, the vice-chairperson, if there is one, **takes the chair**, or the members nominate one of their number to act as chairperson. This person is then said to be 'in the chair'.

The meeting is declared open by the chairperson at the time appointed for the meeting to start, provided that a quorum of members is present. If a quorum is not present the chairperson may wait until sufficient members are in attendance and then open the meeting, or the meeting may be postponed, i.e. put off, until another date.

General rules for the conduct of formal meetings are as follows.

1. The topics for discussion must be dealt with in the order in which they appear on the agenda unless the committee agrees otherwise. The agreement to change the order of items must be minuted.
2. Minutes of the previous meeting are 'taken as read' if they have been distributed to members sufficiently in advance of the meeting. If not, they should be read aloud by the secretary.
3. If approved by the committee, the minutes should be signed by the chairperson as 'an accurate record of the proceedings'. Any amendments agreed by the committee must be recorded in the current minutes and the previous minutes are signed 'subject to amendment of minute no. ....'.
4. A **motion** must be proposed and seconded, and a vote must be taken. The chairperson must state how the members voted, i.e. 'the motion was carried (or rejected) unanimously' (everyone for/against), 'majority of x to x' (for/against) or 'x in favour/against with x abstentions'. If the motion is carried, the outcome is a **resolution**.
5. If an **amendment** to a motion is proposed and seconded, the amendment must be voted on before the motion; if the amendment is carried, the committee will then vote on the **amended motion**.
6. A member may propose a **rider** to the resolution. This adds a point to the resolution but *must not change it.*
7. If a member considers that there is an irregularity in the proceedings, i.e. the rules are not being followed, the chairperson's attention is drawn to

the **point of order**. The chairperson should immediately give a decision so that the proceedings can continue.
8. If the members consider that the chairperson is not conducting the meeting in accordance with the rules, a motion of 'no confidence in the chair' can be put to the vote. If passed, the chairperson would have to give way to a member elected to be in the chair.

PREPARING TO TAKE NOTES AT A MEETING

The person who is to take notes at the meeting should be given adequate notice so that there is time for preparation. This will involve:

- reading the agenda and the minutes of the last two meetings
- 'back tracking' the matters arising to the point where the topics were first raised so as to understand the background to the latest situation
- checking whether there has been any correspondence relevant to any of the agenda items
- reading the relevant section of any document referred to in the agenda
- reading supplementary and/or working papers
- discussing with the chairperson the objective(s) of the meeting if these are not known/understood and the objective(s) of each agenda item – this is a crucial pre-requisite to effective note-taking during the meeting (see below).

TAKING NOTES AT A MEETING

It is useful to have a notepad ruled in half lengthwise. Use either the right- or left-hand side of the page, depending on whether you write with your right or left hand, and in the blank half insert notes such as 'A' for action, 'priority', 'remind chairperson'. Fig. 13.7 illustrates a note-taking sheet.

If possible, the note-taker should sit next to the chairperson. This makes it easier to discreetly raise queries or clarify points that are not clear.

The extent of note-taking depends on whether the record of the meeting is to be in the form of notes, minutes or a report. It is important to know this beforehand.

Note-taking demands great concentration and involves a number of skills. The most important are:

- listening – *active* listening with intense concentration

A Request Bldg Inspector 2.3 PJ	Extension to property, Highfield Foundations completed. Digging out for drains in progress. Completion expected 1 March. Schedule for phases of bldg to be discussed – original schedule upset by bad weather.
A Arrange client discussion RT PRIORITY	
A Follow up end March. RT	Leaking roof, Lymm Church. Temporary cover in place. Estimate for full repair £45,000. Agreement of Church Council awaited.
A Arrange delivery of hire equipment to site 11.3.02 PJ	Sandstone cleaning, County Hall Estimate accepted. Work to start 14.3.02. Hire equipment arranged.

Fig. 13.7 A ruled page for note-taking.

- comparing what is being said with the objective of the agenda item
- deciding whether what is being said is, or may be, relevant to that objective; if it is not, ignore it
- extracting relevant key points from what is being said, ignoring all repetition
- mentally summarising the key point
- recording the key point in own words.

A chairperson may summarise during and after discussion of each item on the agenda. Record the summary – it will be a great help when drafting the minutes.

There are specific details that the note-taker must record. These are as follows. Points 1 and 2 are illustrated in Fig. 13.8.

1. Motions, amendments and riders must be recorded verbatim, i.e. word for word as spoken, with the names of proposers and seconders.
2. The number of members voting for and against a motion, amendment or rider, and the number of abstentions.
3. Concise details of action agreed, names of people concerned, deadlines for completion or review, and reporting procedures.

> Mr J Hall proposed that:
>
> the Committee should recommend to the Chief Executive the purchase of a new staff car at a price not exceeding $100 000.
>
> Mr BD Parker seconded the motion, which was carried unanimously.

Fig. 13.8 A motion proposed, seconded and carried.

If a note-taker is in doubt about a decision or action point, it is wise to clarify such points with the chairperson discreetly and tactfully at the time, unless there will be an opportunity to do so later.

The question of recording a meeting is often raised. If the meeting is to be a long one, a recording is very valuable as back-up. The note-taker should still make notes because it is very time-consuming to listen to several hours of recorded tape, and the exercise of making notes still has to be carried out. Some people do not like to be recorded but there should be no objection if they are assured that as soon as the minutes have been agreed as an accurate record of the proceedings, the tape will be wiped clean.

DRAFTING THE RECORD OF THE MEETING

Some of the notes taken during the meeting will have been points that might be relevant to the objective of the agenda item. Some of those points will no longer be valid once the final outcome is known. Before starting to draft the minutes, mark with a highlighter pen the key points in your notes that should be included in the minutes. This will only take a few minutes and the drafting can then be done more quickly.

NOTES OF A MEETING

Notes may vary from a stark statement of 'action points agreed', to a very brief summary in note form of major points of discussion and action points.

MINUTES OF A MEETING

The minutes should consist of the following:

- heading – name of group/committee and time, date and venue of meeting
- members present, usually best in alphabetical order

- people in attendance – people who have certain expertise and are invited to attend usually for specific agenda items only; they may not vote
- apologies from members who informed the chairperson that they would be unable to attend the meeting
- observers – who may neither take part in the discussion nor vote
- minutes of topics discussed.

Each individual minute has a structure and may consist of the following parts:

1. number and title, which must clearly identify the topic
2. subject matter – the facts or situation to be discussed, presented by the chairperson or a member of the group who is responsible for the matter; any constraints stated, such as legal or financial, should also be included
3. key facts of the discussion, including any precedents and/or processes by which a decision is reached
4. action points – what is to be done, who is to do it, deadline and, if necessary, reporting procedure
5. agreement/decision/resolution – the definitive statement of what was decided by the meeting, e.g. recommendations. (An agreement usually refers to an informal decision; a decision is an outcome reached without a vote; while a resolution is the outcome of a vote.)

Minutes are intended to provide an **accurate** record of the business transacted at the meeting. As minutes are a legal document they can be, and sometimes are, used as evidence in a court of law or at a legally constituted tribunal. Accuracy is therefore of paramount importance. The composition of the minutes must therefore be clear, concise and to the point. It is not the role of the note-taker to 'interpret' what was said, but to *record* it. The meaning intended by the speaker must be conveyed.

There is a trend towards writing an informal record of a meeting. This is perfectly acceptable as notes when the meeting is informal. For a formal meeting it is better to write in the professionally accepted manner.

Write in the third person (not using 'I', 'we' or 'you') and in the past tense. You are writing about what happened in the meeting, which has now passed, not about the events. Therefore, if a member speaks in the present tense, the point will be recorded in the past tense. If spoken in the past tense, the record will be in the past perfect.

Example of speech: I am in the process of completing the project report
Recorded as: Mr X was in the …

Example of speech: I have completed the project report
Recorded as: Mr X had completed …

Use plain language using simple words, short sentences, careful punctuation and correct grammar.

Avoid ambiguous words, or phrases that are open to interpretation, e.g. reasonable, considerable, short, long, as soon as possible, matter of urgency.

Avoid colloquial expressions and the phraseology of the spoken word, which is usually unnecessarily long, e.g. 'at this moment in time' (now), 'over the top' (exaggerated).

Avoid 'said that', 'stated that', 'thought that', 'considered that', etc.

NATIONAL ASSOCIATION OF TRADERS

MINUTES OF THE MEETING OF THE ADVISORY COMMITTEE FOR RECRUITMENT OF TECHNICAL INSPECTORS HELD AT 1400 HOURS ON THURSDAY 27 JUNE 2002 IN THE CONFERENCE ROOM AT TRADING HOUSE, HIGH ROAD, BRIDGETOWN

Present: Mr PJ Dunn   Chairman
          Mr CT Cooper
          Miss F Edwards
          Mr P Nelson
          Mrs ST Stanley
          Mr ED Watts
          Mr PS Wells

Apologies for absence were received from Mr TH Henley

36/02   MINUTES OF PREVIOUS MEETING

The minutes of the meeting held on 25 April 2002, having been distributed, were taken as read and unanimously approved.

37/02   MATTERS ARISING

31/02   Mr P Nelson reported that he had had discussions with senior officials of the Ministry of Education. Although willing to allow technical inspectors access to technical training institutions, there had at first been strong feeling against schools participating in the scheme. It had been pointed out that technical inspectors could assist schools to achieve realistic practical standards, which would benefit those students who wished to enter industry direct. Eventually agreement had been reached that all schools and institutions under the Ministry's jurisdiction should participate in the scheme.

IT WAS AGREED that the Permanent Secretary, Ministry of Education, should be asked to confirm his decision in writing.

38/02   TRADES FOR WHICH INSPECTORS REQUIRED

A list of trades, attached as Appendix I, was handed to members. There was divergence of information …

(a)

Fig. 13.9 (a) Minutes without an action column (continued overleaf).

> **NATIONAL ASSOCIATION OF TRADERS**
>
> MINUTES OF THE MEETING OF THE ADVISORY COMMITTEE FOR RECRUITMENT OF TECHNICAL INSPECTORS HELD AT 1400 HOURS ON THURSDAY 27 JUNE 2002 IN THE CONFERENCE ROOM AT TRADING HOUSE, HIGH ROAD, BRIDGETOWN
>
> Present: Mr PJ Dunn   Chairman
>   Mr CT Cooper
>   Miss F Edwards
>   Mr P Nelson
>   Mrs ST Stanley
>   Mr ED Watts
>   Mr PS Wells
>
> Apologies for absence were received from Mr TH Henley
>
> | | | | ACTION |
> |---|---|---|---|
> | 36/02 | MINUTES OF PREVIOUS MEETING | The minutes of the meeting held on 25 April 2002, having been distributed, were taken as read and unanimously approved. | |
> | 37/02 | MATTERS ARISING | 31/02 Mr P Nelson reported that he had had discussions with senior officials of the Ministry of Education. Although willing to allow technical inspectors access to technical training institutions, there had at first been strong feeling against schools participating in the scheme. It had been pointed out that technical inspectors could assist schools to achieve realistic practical standards, which would benefit those students who wished to enter industry direct. Eventually agreement had been reached that all schools and institutions under the Ministry's jurisdiction should participate in the scheme. | |
> | | | IT WAS AGREED that the Permanent Secretary, Ministry of Education, should be asked to confirm his decision in writing. | Chairman |
> | 38/02 | TRADES FOR WHICH INSPECTORS REQUIRED | A list of trades, attached as Appendix I, was handed to members. There was divergence of information ... | |

(b)

Fig. 13.9 (continued) (b) minutes with an action column.

The name of a member who wishes 'to go on record' must be given with a summary of the point(s) made. Otherwise it is not usually necessary to give names of who said what. Decisions are the outcome of discussion among the members, all of whom have equal responsibility for the decision, whether or not they agree with it.

Specimen minutes (without) and (with) an action column are shown in Figs 13.9a and 13.9b respectively.

NUMBERING MINUTES

There is a variety of ways of numbering minutes. Some form of numbering is essential for ease of reference. A few methods are given below.

1. Numbering consecutively from the date of the first meeting, continuing indefinitely. The year may be added for quicker reference.

116	Date of next meeting	or	116/00
117	Minutes of previous meeting		117/01
118	Final dividend		118/01

2. Minutes may start at 1 at the first meeting of each year. The year is then included in the minute number.

    1/00
    2/00
    ...
    68/00

    1/01
    2/01 etc.

3. The meeting is numbered and the minutes are numbered from 1 for each meeting. This method is particularly appropriate for progress meetings when the agenda follows the same format for every meeting.

    Meeting held on 16 May 2000   (6th meeting)

6/1	Minutes of meeting held on 27 April 2000
6/2	Review of action points
6/3	Financial report

    ...

    6/10   Date of next meeting

    Meeting held on 23 June 2000   (7th meeting)

7/1	Minutes of previous meeting
7/2	Review of action points
7/3	Financial report
	... etc.

PRESENTATION OF MINUTES

There are various methods of presenting minutes. There may be a house style that has to be followed. If not, there is a tendency to follow what has been done before. If the layout can be improved for easier reading and subsequent reference, the following points may usefully be borne in mind.

An 'Action' column on the right-hand side of the page is useful as a means of enabling committee members to see immediately what action is required of them. Names in the Action column may be highlighted on each individual copy as an additional aid to fast reference. Two simple but clear formats are shown in Figs 13.9a and 13.9b.

PREPARING AN 'ACTION SHEET'

It is not always possible to produce and distribute the minutes within a short time after the meeting. In such cases it is useful to prepare an 'Action sheet', which can be sent out immediately. This lists the individual members who agreed to undertake one or more tasks, the action to be taken, the deadline for completion and the reporting procedure.

Even when minutes are distributed soon after a meeting, an action sheet provides quick reference and may therefore be added to the minutes as an appendix. It is also useful for the person who has to follow up on actions before the next meeting. The chairperson can use it as an *aide-mémoire* at the next meeting when reviewing the progress of actions.

Action sheets are presented in different formats. Fig. 13.10 shows one form of presentation. The details can be arranged in the order of the items on the agenda if preferred.

ACTION SHEET

The following actions were agreed at the Residents Committee Meeting held on Tuesday 5 November 2002.

Name	Min. Ref.	Action	Deadline
Mr PR Mills	28/02	Letter to City Council	13.04.02
	30/02	Quotation for new roof	Next meeting
Miss S Peters	27/02	Sub-committee to arrange fund-raising events	29.05.02
Mrs D Saunders	29/02	List of signatures for submission to City Council	23.04.02

Fig. 13.10 Action sheet.

INDEXING MINUTES

It is often necessary to refer to minutes of previous meetings to check decisions regarding action to be taken, the precise wording of a recommendation, etc.

Numbering minutes consecutively throughout the year or throughout the life of the body enables the minute titles to be indexed alphabetically, which facilitates reference. This means that a topic discussed at more than one meeting must be minuted under the same title each time. Also titles must give a concise and accurate indication of the topic.

Indexing can be done on the computer but if that facility is not available, it can be written in a book or typed on cards, loose-leaf pages or strip index to be inserted in a folder. The disadvantage of a book is that the titles cannot be written in alphabetical order under the index letter. The disadvantage of cards is that one card can get lost and it is not so easy to take a box, drawer or rotary file of cards to a meeting (see Chapter 7, page 198). Loose-leaf sheets can be produced by word processing and are easily updated. Strip index provides the flexibility of cards for inserting new titles with the relative ease of movement from office to meeting room.

The title of each minute is followed by the minute number and the date of the meeting at which it was discussed. Example:

| Stores | 123 | 14.3.98 | 157 | 23.8.99 | 189 | 24.10.02 |

By referring to the index, all the decisions taken in relation to the topic can be traced easily and quickly.

ROLE OF THE CHAIRPERSON

The chairperson's role in a meeting is to control the discussion and guide the members. This is done by:

- stating the matter to be discussed
- giving any additional information available (usually presented on the chairperson's agenda (see page 418)
- indicating what is required of members, e.g. a recommendation or a decision on action to be taken
- ensuring that points raised are relevant

- ensuring that all members are given an opportunity to express their views
- summarising the discussion
- putting motions to the vote
- declaring the decision of the meeting.

ROLE OF THE 'COMMITTEE' SECRETARY

Formal committees may have an appointed 'Committee Secretary' who has responsibility for all aspects of committee administration. The administration for less formal committees (or groups) may be undertaken by a clerk, secretary or technical assistant.

The secretary's role is administrative. They must ensure that the chairperson and members have all relevant documents in adequate time to prepare for the meeting. All the statutory documents required and any other documents, such as correspondence, to which reference might be made during discussions should be available at the meeting. The secretary is expected to fulfil his/her role by:

- preparing the agenda in consultation with the chairperson
- receiving and obtaining approval for supplementary papers
- distributing the agenda and other documents in good time for members to prepare for the meeting
- ensuring that the meeting room is properly prepared and that all necessary books, files and documents are available
- ensuring that the attendance book/sheet is signed by the people who attend the meeting
- reading the minutes of the previous meeting(s) if they have not been distributed before the meeting
- ensuring that the chairperson signs the minutes of the previous meeting; these minutes are then a legal record of the meeting
- producing relevant correspondence and documents as required during the meeting
- making notes of the discussion
- noting all details of actions agreed (see page 426)
- noting motions/decisions/resolutions verbatim with the names of proposers and seconders, and the method and results of voting
- ensuring that the rules governing the conduct of meetings are followed.

ROLE OF A MEMBER

A member of a meeting is expected to make a positive contribution to the discussions by:

- studying the agenda, minutes of the previous meeting and supplementary papers before the meeting
- considering a point of view, obtaining relevant information and deciding what to say and how to say it
- listening carefully to and considering objectively other members' contributions
- explaining their point of view coherently, concisely, clearly and logically
- following the chairperson's directives
- offering to take action when appropriate
- noting action to be taken, details of deadlines, people to whom reference should be made, relevant documents, etc.
- ensuring that action is taken in accordance with the details agreed
- reading minutes as soon as they are received to check details of action to be taken
- informing the secretary of any discrepancies or inaccuracies in the minutes.

COMMITTEE TERMS

Table 13.2 gives you a list of useful committee terms to refer to.

Table 13.2 *Committee terms*

abstain/abstention	Not voting either for or against a motion. See also 'nem. con.' and 'nem. dis.'.
ad hoc committee	A group of people appointed to deal with a specific matter.
agenda	A list of items to be discussed at a meeting, with sufficient detail to indicate the purpose of the discussion.
adjourned by consent	The unfinished business of a meeting will be discussed at another meeting by agreement with those present.
adjourned 'sine die'	The unfinished business of a meeting will be discussed at a further meeting for which a date will be arranged later.
amendment	A change proposed to a motion.

(continued)

Table 13.2 *(continued)*

annual general meeting (AGM)	A meeting of all members or shareholders of an organisation, held annually.
attendance book/sheet	The book/sheet that must be signed by each member present at a meeting.
ballot	Written vote with provision for preserving the secrecy of each individual's vote.
casting vote	An additional vote, usually held by the chairperson, to enable a decision to be taken in the case of an equal number of votes being given both for or against a motion.
co-opted member	People invited by committee members to join the committee.
ex officio/ex-officio member	A person who attends meetings by virtue of the office they hold, e.g. a principal attending a meeting of school governors.
extraordinary general meeting (EGM)	A meeting of all members or shareholders of an organisation to discuss some matter of importance for which the consent of all or the majority is needed.
go into committee	Division of members at a meeting into groups, each group to undertake discussion of specified subjects.
go into division	Physical division of members for voting purposes.
in attendance	A person who is not a committee member, invited to attend and participate in the discussion at a meeting.
in the chair	A person other than the chairperson fulfilling the role.
lie on the table	A matter is said to 'lie on the table' when no action can be taken on it.
majority	The greater number of members either for or against a motion.
memorandum	A document setting out information to enable the committee to make a policy decision.
Memorandum and articles of association	The legal documents setting out the objectives of a company and the rules by which it must conduct its affairs.
minute book or file	A book/file containing the signed copies of minutes of meetings held.
minute of narration	A summary of key points raised in discussion before a decision is taken on a particular item of business.
minutes of resolution	A summary of all the resolutions passed; the resolutions, motions and amendments must be recorded verbatim; the names of proposers and seconders must be included.
minutes	A summary of the proceedings of a meeting.
motion	A proposal that certain action be taken.
nem. con./nem. dis. (nemine contradicente/ nemine dissentiente)	The passing of a resolution without opposing votes but with some members abstaining.

(continued)

Table 13.2 *(continued)*

notice	A notification to members of the time, date and place of a meeting. It may include the purpose.
point of order	A question from a committee member, or a suggestion that a certain procedure is irregular, or that a statement is inaccurate.
poll	A count of votes, for and against a motion, from lists of signatures.
postpone	Put off to a later date.
proceedings	The business discussed, main points of discussion, decisions and resolutions taken during a meeting.
proposer	The person who recommends a particular decision be taken by formally stating 'I move that ...'.
proxy	A person authorised by a member to vote on his/her behalf.
putting the question	Chairperson putting a motion to the vote.
quorum	The minimum number of members necessary for the business of a committee to be conducted. The quorum is stated in the committee's terms of reference.
report	Full details of the business and discussion of a meeting *or* information presented to a committee outlining what has been done prior to the meeting.
resolution	Definitive decision on a motion made by a majority vote of members.
rider	An addition to a resolution.
seconder	A person who supports the proposer of a motion.
standing committee	A permanent committee established to deal with a specific subject, e.g. education in local government.
standing orders	Rules governing the conduct of meetings.
statutory meeting	A meeting required by law.
sub-committee	A small number of people appointed by a main committee to undertake certain specific work on its behalf.
terms of reference	Work to be done by a committee.
unanimous	The agreement (or rejection) of all members present.
verbatim	Recorded word for word, exactly as spoken.

PRACTICE QUESTIONS

1. Give five possible reasons for holding a meeting.
2. What information do you need from your manager in order to arrange a meeting?
3. What is the difference between an annual general meeting and an extraordinary general meeting?

4. What is meant by:
   i. statutory meeting
   ii. sub-committee
   iii. 'ad hoc' committee?

5. Your executive, Mr James Ross, has asked you to arrange a meeting with three of his staff – Mr Peter Johnson, Mr Michael Short and Mr Peter Smith. The meeting will probably last for about two hours. It cannot be held before next Tuesday because information needed for the meeting will not be available until Monday afternoon. It must not be later than Thursday because the matters to be discussed must be settled before Mr Ross leaves for New York on Friday.

Copies of the diaries of Mr Ross and his staff for the relevant three days are shown in Fig. 13.11. Decide the possible times available for a meeting and suggest which would be the best if there is a choice.

JAMES ROSS

Tuesday	Wednesday	Thursday
1230 Lunch a Booth (Hilton Hotel) 1630 J R Lang	0930 Langden mtg 1200 Dinner (W's b'day)	1030 Mrs Aitken ? Lunch (Les James)

PETER JOHNSON

Tuesday	Wednesday	Thursday
1130 IMA mtg (Sheraton)	1100 Mansfield 1530 Tel Ghana Adrian	0900 Johnson + Peters (French Cleaners Ltd) 1100 Maitland

Fig. 13.11 Diaries

MICHAEL SHORT

Tuesday	Wednesday	Thursday
0900 Peter Smith discuss Poolside	? Poolside	
1400 Poolside Co		1600/1630 Jack Strange (from Mexico) Dinner

PETER SMITH

Tuesday	Wednesday	Thursday
0900 Mike S - Poolside Co		0930 Franks & Co (14 Peter Street 3rd floor)
1400 Poolside Co	1800 ICSA C'tee mtg (office)	

Fig. 13.11 (continued).

Mr Ross is not usually in the office until just before 0930. He has no set time for leaving and often works late. Prepare a grid, using as an example the blank grid shown in Fig. 13.1a to enable you to identify the times when all the staff are available.

6. You are asked to arrange a meeting of office supervisors for a week next Wednesday. The meeting is to be held in Conference Room 1 at 1030. The items to be discussed are: salary increases, grievance procedures, safety and punctuality. Write or type a combined notice of meeting and agenda to be distributed to all office supervisors in the organisation.

7. You are asked to attend a meeting to be held next day in order to take notes and draft the minutes. How would you prepare for this task?

8. Explain the following terms:
   i. annual general meeting
   ii. ballot

iii. standing orders
   iv. minutes
   v. minute file
   vi. action sheet
   vii. working papers
   viii. quorum
   ix. ex-officio member
   x. committee secretary.

9. You have been asked to prepare a conference room ready for a meeting. Make a list of what is involved in this task.

10. Prepare a notice of a meeting requesting items for the agenda. The meeting of all trades union representatives is to be held at 1400 next Friday in Meeting Room 3 on the 4th floor of Trade Union House.

11. List five points that are the responsibility of:
    i. the chairperson
    ii. the committee secretary
    iii. the members.

12. What is the difference between the chairperson of a meeting 'taking the chair' and being 'in the chair'?

13. List five key skills that are needed for note-taking at a meeting.

14. Explain the following terms:
    i. proxy
    ii. notice of a meeting
    iii. co-opted member
    iv. chairperson's agenda
    v. formal meeting
    vi. action column
    vii. terms of reference
    viii. minute index
    ix. chairperson
    x. motion.

15. Describe each of the following including its uses:
    i. an action sheet
    ii. a minute index.

16. a. State three advantages and three disadvantages of teleconferencing.
    b. State three particular advantages and three particular disadvantages of videoconferencing.

SHORT ANSWER QUESTIONS

1. Formal minutes should be written in the ……… ……… and the ……… ……… .
2. When several people have a discussion on the telephone they use a/an ……… service.
3. The first item on an agenda is usually ……… .
4. The minimum number of people who must be present in order to hold a formal committee meeting is a/an ……… .
5. Motions must be recorded ……… .

Choose the most appropriate ending for each of the following sentences.

6. Supplementary papers are:
   a. extra copies of minutes
   b. working papers
   c. papers giving information about the topics to be discussed
   d. a list of items to be discussed.

7. The action sheet provides a summary of the:
   a. discussion at a meeting
   b. decisions taken
   c. action points agreed
   d. chairperson's notes.

8. The chairperson's agenda:
   a. helps them to control the meeting
   b. lists the people who will be present at the meeting
   c. provides confidential information
   d. provides up-to-date information on the agenda topics.

9. Minutes are a:
   a. verbatim record of a meeting
   b. record of decisions taken and how they were reached
   c. brief record of the member's comments
   d. record of action points.

10. When taking notes at a meeting, the note-taker should:
    a. write down a summary of the key points of the discussion and decisions taken
    b. take down everything that is said
    c. listen and then write down as many of the comments as possible
    d. write down decisions and action points only.

EXAMINATION QUESTIONS

1.
   a. Outline reasons for holding informal meetings.
   b. State the requirements for formal meetings to be valid.
   c. Define the following terms connected with meetings:
      i. rider
      ii. casting vote
      iii. point of order
      iv. verbatim.

   (Pitman Office Procedures Level 2 1998 Pt 2)

CHAPTER 14

TRAVEL ARRANGEMENTS

OBJECTIVES When you have studied this chapter you should have acquired the knowledge and understanding to be able to:

1. deal effectively with a request for travel arrangements to be made
2. obtain all relevant information before making arrangements
3. use checklists to ensure that no detail is forgotten
4. advise the traveller on the documentation needed for different modes of transport
5. advise the traveller on different methods of payment for travel and hotels
6. make arrangements for the transport of equipment
7. schedule an itinerary with appointments for meetings etc.
8. prepare a pack for the traveller
9. agree with the traveller what work to deal with while they are away
10. use sources of information on all aspects of travel.

Organisations vary in the ways in which arrangements are made for their staff to travel. It may be the responsibility of the traveller, an assistant, a travel department within the organisation or an external travel agent. Most companies have procedures for arranging travel and it is very important that these are followed to ensure that there are no difficulties created, either for the organisation, for the person making the arrangements or the traveller.

HANDLING A REQUEST

The objective of making business travel arrangements is to ensure that the traveller is able to fulfil the purpose(s) of the journey. Unless a similar trip has been made by the traveller previously, a lot of information has to be obtained about means of travel, accommodation, documents, money and methods of payment, carriage of equipment and materials, and insurance.

The starting point must be the traveller's needs and wishes. When you are asked to arrange travel there are certain details you need to know. In general terms this means asking:

- the purpose of the journey
- who is responsible for each aspect of the arrangements – travel, meetings, preparation of presentations, etc.
- the traveller's needs and preferences
- the travel requirements, i.e. places to be visited, for how long, etc.
- equipment needed (if any)
- arrangements for carrying on the traveller's work while away.

Next look at each of the key areas in turn, finding out from the traveller their requirements and preferences. Other sources will also be needed.

TRAVEL

Check with the traveller:

- places to be visited, the sequence in which they are to be visited and the number of days required in each location
- dates of travel (allow for time differences, time to recover from journey, dates of staff, public, religious holidays/festivals, factory shutdown periods)
- numbers travelling, separately and/or together for all or part of the journey
- preferred airline/car hire firm/coach service and class of travel
- whether non-changeable tickets would be acceptable to save cost
- travel insurance required
- point(s) of departure and arrival – by air, hire car, train, ferry, coach
- stopovers required
- special arrangements needed for people with disabilities if travelling with others
- catering facilities required, e.g. special diet

- accommodation needed at points of departure and destination, e.g. near airport or in the centre of city/town
- transport facilities to/from points of departure/arrival to be arranged or to be dealt with by organisation to be visited
- identification for being met on arrival
- business/first-class or executive lounge facilities required at airports.

Specific information that may be needed is listed below. This information is available from travel agents, airline/car hire/ferry/coach/train companies. Before contacting them prepare a rough itinerary list of places to be visited and the number of days in each. In order to be familiar with the place names and their locations it is worth looking them up on a map. It may be necessary/desirable to change the sequence of the visits. Timetables can also be useful when discussing possible flights etc.

By air:

- classes of travel available
- flight departure and arrival times
- airports and terminal numbers
- check-in arrangements – times and places, first/business/club class, electronic, collection of tickets by pre-arrangement
- baggage allowance – weight, size, number of pieces.

By car:

- types of car available, including power steering, automatic, air conditioning, etc.
- pick-up and return points (check charge for return at point different from pick-up)
- charges.

By ferry:

- routes and classes of travel
- types of berth – single/double for single/multiple occupancy
- times – departure/arrival, earliest boarding/latest disembarking
- dock (location) and dock gate number
- check-in arrangements (time and place)
- bar/dining facilities on board
- duty-free shopping.

By coach:

- stations (location) – departure and destination
- routes
- times – departure/arrival, earliest boarding and disembarkation

- facilities on board – toilet, refreshments
- type of seating, e.g. reclining for overnight travel.

By train:

- stations (location) – departure and destination
- routes and classes of travel
- overnight sleeping berths – single/double
- departure and arrival times
- buffet/dining car
- non-smoking seats, berths
- seats pre-bookable in carriage/compartment/dining car.

ACCOMMODATION

Check with the traveller:

1. type of accommodation – hotel including class, e.g. 4-star, guesthouse, self-catering, single/double/family room, suite, non-smoking
2. facilities required – private bath/shower, tea/coffee making, minibar, trouser press, hairdrier
3. ground floor or upper floor
4. good view
5. quiet room away from kitchen, ballroom, etc.
6. facilities for people with disabilities, including lifts wide enough for wheelchairs
7. location – near airport/centre of town/places to be visited
8. leisure facilities, e.g. swimming pool, squash courts, golf course, gymnasium
9. likely time of arrival.

Information on hotels and other accommodation can be found in hotel guides – national, international and for specific countries (sometimes available from the country's tourist office). Check with the hotel:

10. location
11. types of room available, e.g. non-smoking, with facilities for those with disabilities
12. earliest and latest check-in times
13. whether room can be held until late/all night on credit card guarantee
14. whether special dietary requirements can be provided, e.g. diabetic, coeliac (gluten/wheat-free), vegetarian
15. restaurant facilities, whether tables can be reserved, room service

16. leisure facilities available
17. deposit required/cancellation period without charge.

DOCUMENTS

Check with the traveller:

1. what travel documents are already held and whether they are valid for the period of intended travel
2. what health vaccinations/inoculations have been administered and whether they are still valid
3. whether an international driving licence is held and is still valid.

Specific information that may be needed is listed below.

Check:

- passport (application forms are available locally – you will need to find out where)
- health – BCG (tuberculosis), lifetime cover
    TAB 1–3 years' cover
    cholera 6 months' cover
    smallpox 3 years' cover
    yellow fever 10 years
    } arrangements have to be made with a doctor or health clinic
- international driving licence (valid for one year), obtainable from motoring organisations
- visa required for any of countries to be visited*
- permits for travel within certain countries, e.g. China*
- work permits*
- permits to take photographs*
- permits to import equipment and re-export, i.e. take in equipment and bring it out again.*

For all except the health documents, one or two photographs are required with a fee.

MONEY AND METHODS OF PAYMENT

Check with the traveller:

1. how hotel bills are to be paid, i.e. by them or by an account sent direct to the organisation

---

*Application forms and information on what is required are obtainable from the appropriate embassy, high commission or consulate.

2. what credit cards they have and whether they are valid for the dates of the intended travel
3. how much money is required in foreign currency
4. how much money is required in travellers' cheques and what kind of cheques, e.g. American dollars, pounds sterling.

Specific information that may be needed is listed below.

Check:

- what credit cards are accepted by the airlines and hotels
- whether a credit card company will issue new cards before the departure date if the existing card(s) expire during the travel period
- what rates of exchange are in force (these may change)
- how much notice the bank needs to supply foreign currency and travellers' cheques
- exchange control regulations (home country and destination).

CARRIAGE OF EQUIPMENT AND MATERIALS

Check with the traveller:

1. equipment needed (have a checklist to tick off)
2. when and where equipment required
3. whether equipment should be insured for travel and abroad
4. whether equipment/materials are to be brought back to home country.

Specific information that may be needed is listed below.

Check:

- whether any of the equipment to be taken can be damaged by scanning at airports, e.g. films, compact discs etc.
- appropriate method of transporting to destination, e.g. by courier, air freight, train, road service
- security in transit
- whether equipment can be taken as excess baggage and whether airline will guarantee its arrival at same time as passenger loading/unloading facilities at destination
- restrictions on any particular equipment at destination
- censorship regulations on films and publications at destination
- electricity at destination – voltage and current (AC/DC)

- documentation required for import into and export out of foreign country and re-importation into home country
- cost of insurance in transit and abroad.

INSURANCE

Check with the traveller:

1. what cover is needed – personal accident, medical, loss of baggage, travel delays, equipment.

   Specific information that may be needed is listed below.

Check:

- insurance brokers/companies, banks, travel agents, etc. that offer appropriate insurance
- cover included in the various policies available, e.g. personal accident, loss of baggage/money/credit cards, cancellation of travel through death of close relations or personal illness
- the premium charged for the period required.

GENERAL INFORMATION

Depending on the country/countries to be visited, it may be necessary to obtain additional information:

- health precautions recommended, e.g. anti-malaria treatment, safety of drinking water (take water-purification tablets), medical hygiene (take first-aid kit with hypodermic needles)
- business and social customs including protocol and any other special requirements/regulations (especially in countries of different cultures and/or religions)
- suitable clothing (business and social according to weather and custom – temperature variations day and night can be substantial and, in some countries, women may be expected to conform to local custom)
- lingua franca (commonly used language in the country of destination) – whether phrase book needed
- medical/dental facilities, fees, reciprocal arrangements with home country, existing medical/dental insurance policy valid for overseas
- local hours of work, holidays

- local facilities for banks, shopping (including medication)
- electricity voltage and type of current (AC/DC) for domestic appliances
- mobile telephone – whether compatible with network in countries to be visited, if not ask hotel to arrange hire.

SCHEDULING APPOINTMENTS

Companies to be visited have to be notified of the traveller's itinerary, the people they would like to meet, topics to be discussed, meetings that would be beneficial. The traveller may not always know whom they need to see and will leave it to their contact to organise meetings.

When scheduling appointments allow time for travel, security/reception procedures on arrival at each organisation, meetings/interviews, breaks for keying in/writing/dictating notes. Always allow contingency time during the day so that a traffic hold-up or a late start to an appointment can be 'made up' later.

Ensure that the people being visited know what they are expected to prepare, and that the traveller, too, knows what they have to prepare.

If arrangements are to be made by people at the destination, constant contact must be maintained before the traveller starts the trip. Any changes to times, topics for discussion and the documentation needed must be notified.

There may be social arrangements, e.g. drinks parties, dinners. The traveller should have some free time for consultation with fellow travellers or colleagues at head office. A schedule should be prepared and appointments entered immediately they are made. Indicate the purpose of each appointment and also free time.

A specimen appointment schedule is shown in Fig. 14.1.

ITINERARY

Having obtained most of the information you need you can now prepare a draft itinerary. This should include:

- dates
- travel from/to

APPOINTMENT SCHEDULE – KUALA LUMPUR

Miss Janice Boyd and Mr Michael Aspinall

Monday 15 July 2002

0815	Meeting with Senior Managers of Malaysian Airlines to discuss requirements for upgrading computer system
	Lunch at Malaysian Airlines
	Contact Mr James Riddell at Head Office
	Prepare outline for report to client

Tuesday 16 July 2002

0815	Conducted tour of Computer Department
	Meet key staff individually to discuss current problems
1415	Conducted tour of all areas using computer systems
	Discuss with staff their ideas for upgrading the system
Evening	Free

Wednesday 17 July 2002

1100	Meeting with Singapore Airport Director and Head of Computer Systems to determine benefits gained from their latest computer upgrade
	Tour of computer room and Malaysian Airline check-in desks

Fig. 14.1 An appointments schedule.

- flight numbers, train identification (if any), ferry name (if any), car hire firm's name
- reporting locations (airport terminals, train station, ferry dock, car hire pick-up/delivery points)
- departure and arrival times and locations
- accommodation.

An example of an itinerary is shown in Fig. 14.2.

It may be possible to make provisional reservations (flights, hotels, etc.) pending the approval of the traveller(s). In any case, submit the draft itinerary to the traveller(s), indicating any important points such as why any of their stated requirements have not been accommodated. It may be that the traveller(s) will ask you to make some further enquiries. When they are happy with the itinerary, you will be able to make reservations.

ITINERARY FOR MR PR LANE

Thursday 18 July 2002

1530	hours	Leave office – company car
1600	hours	Check-in at Piarco Airport
1700	hours	Depart Flight BW 000 (BWIA)
2100	hours	Arrive Norman Manley Airport, Jamaica
		Taxi from airport to Super Hotel, Kingston
2200	hours	ETA* Super Hotel (Refreshments ordered)
		(Confirmation letter attached)

Sunday 21 July 2002

1030	hours	Taxi from Super Hotel to Norman Manley Airport
1100	hours	Check-in at airport
1200	hours	Depart Flight BW 000 (BWIA)
1545	hours	Arrive Miami Airport, Miami
		Coach to city terminal
		Taxi to Waldorf Hotel
1730	hours	ETA* Waldorf Hotel

*ETA = estimated time of arrival

Fig. 14.2 Itinerary.

RESERVATIONS

TRAVEL

- Give all the details necessary for the airline, train company, etc. to provide the travel facilities required by the traveller.
- Always state the day as well as the date.
- Check the details you obtained previously relating to cost, times, facilities, locations, etc.

HOTELS

- Give all the details of the traveller's requirements including day and date of arrival and 'departing on [day and date]', and state the number of nights.
- State if arrival will be late, i.e. after 1800.
- Make reservations for meals as appropriate.

Some hotels will ask for confirmation, others will not, particularly if the reservation is made through a group booking centre. Some hotels offer to confirm to the client; it is always wise to confirm, and this can be done by letter, fax, telex or e-mail. A specimen letter confirming a reservation is shown in Fig. 14.3.

---

17 May 2002

The Manager
Super Hotel Group Ltd
PO Box 48
KINGSTON
JAMAICA

Dear Sir

RESERVATION: Mr PR Lane

I confirm my telephone reservation of one single air-conditioned room with private bath at the Kingston Super Hotel for three nights from Thursday 18 July to the morning of Sunday 21 July 2002.

Mr Lane will arrive in Kingston on flight BW 000 from Port-of-Spain. Estimated time of arrival is 2100 hours so he should arrive at the hotel at about 2200 hours. Will you please arrange for refreshments to be available for Mr Lane when he arrives?

Mr Lane will pay the account by American Express credit card.

Yours faithfully

DE Frank
Travel Clerk

Fig. 14.3 Letter confirming hotel reservation.

CHECKING DOCUMENTS

When documents are received it is essential that they be checked very carefully. Ensure that the details listed are correct, as outlined in Table 14.1.

Table 14.1 *Document checklist*

Passport	spelling of first name and surname, address, validity (number of years/expiry date), photograph
Visa	dates, length of stay
Travellers' cheques	variety of denomination, total, currency
Insurance policies	dates, risks covered, name of policy-holder
Hotel reservations	dates of arrival and departure (number of nights), type of room, meal reservations, car parking
Car reservations	type of car, dates for pick-up and return, number of days, cost and what it includes
Travel tickets	dates, points of departure, destinations, check-in and departure times, cost

ELECTRONIC AIRLINE BOOKING

Many airlines now make reservations electronically. This means that the passenger does not have a conventional air ticket. The reservation is filed in the computer. On arrival at the airport the passenger goes to the designated check-in desk shown on the indicator. A step-by-step guide is given on each check-in machine for accessing the reservation, giving personal identification and receiving a ticket/boarding card (see Fig. 14.4). The passenger then takes the boarding card to a check-in desk for checking in baggage.

TRAVEL PACK

All the travel documents should be placed in a folder with the itinerary, in the sequence in which they will be required. It is useful to prepare a list of the documents (in addition to the itinerary). Travel documents should be

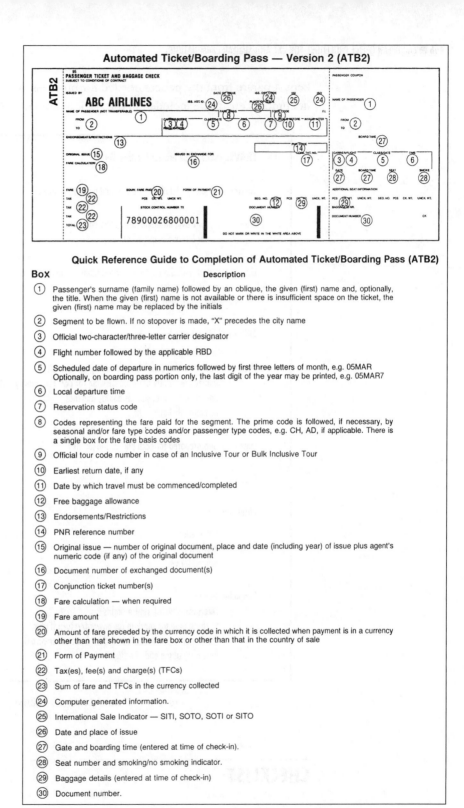

Fig. 14.4 *Automated air ticket/boarding pass with a description of each detail.*

kept separate from the papers needed for business. A checklist of documents etc. to be included in the pack is shown in Fig. 14.5.

TRAVEL PACK to be provided to traveller(s)

Confirmed itinerary (detailed document and pocket summary)

Documents   for travel including tickets and vouchers
            for interviews and meetings

List of all contacts including national representative in each location,
            name and address
            telephone, telex and fax numbers

Airline and airport telephone numbers

Maps   how to reach venue from motorway/airport, etc.
        immediate vicinity of venue showing car park(s), railway station(s)
        and other facilities such as banks, churches
        recognisable landmarks

Luggage labels prepared for each part of the journey

Business cards

Writing paper
        letterheads
        drafting
        printed forms

Reminder note to
        reconfirm onward/return flights
        to check time for check-in for onward/return flights
        (reminder to put watch/travel clock back or forward if
        necessary at the end of a flight)

Fig. 14.5 Travel pack checklist.

CHECKLIST

Arranging travel can be a mammoth task. It is essential to have a working checklist affixed to the inside front cover of the file for the trip. A sample checklist is shown in Fig. 14.6.

TRAVEL ARRANGEMENTS CHECKLIST

Itinerary

Establish – departure date
　　　　　　return date

Reservations – car/taxi (to/from departure and arrival points)
　　　　　　train – class
　　　　　　　　　seat – smoking/non-smoking/restaurant;
　　　　　　　　　　　facing/back to engine;
　　　　　　　　　　　window/corridor
　　　　　　bus/coach – seat – smoking/non-smoking
　　　　　　flight – class
　　　　　　　　　seat – smoking/non-smoking
　　　　　　　　　　　window/aisle
　　　　　　　　　　　preferred location in cabin
　　　　　　ship – class
　　　　　　　　　berth – single/double
　　　　　　　　　　　deck

Confirm reservations

VIP lounge at airport

Tickets

Unaccompanied baggage – estimated weight

Car hire – class/type of car
　　　　　manual/automatic
　　　　　air conditioning
　　　　　power steering
　　　　　documents required
　　　　　international driving licence

Finance

Travellers' cheques – amount
　　　　　　　　US dollars/Canadian dollar/sterling, etc.
　　　　　　　　denominations

Currency – local
　　　　　foreign

Credit cards – valid
　　　　　acceptable at hotels

Fig. 14.6 Travel arrangements checklist (continued overleaf).

Hotels

Reservations – later/early-morning arrival

                type of room – single/double/twin

                      with/without bath/shower

            meal on arrival

Diets catered for

Facilities for those with disabilities

Sports facilities

Entertainment

Conference/meetings facilities

Payment

Insurance

All risks (baggage)

Car

Life/personal accident

Medical

Documents

Passport including visas

Health – cholera (valid for 6 months)

       TAB (valid for 1–3 years depending on country)

       yellow fever (valid for 10 years)

Tickets

Reminder to reconfirm onward/return flights

Confirmation letters of hotel reservations/hotel vouchers

Excess baggage vouchers

Driving licence – national

              international

Fig. 14.6 (continued).

IN THE ABSENCE OF THE TRAVELLER

It is important to have a means of communication between you and the traveller(s). You will have a copy of the itinerary so it will be easy to contact them if necessary by telephone (at the hotel), by mobile phone, fax or e-mail. (The latter is convenient if there is a big time difference between the countries.)

BEFORE DEPARTURE

You need to agree with the traveller:

- what they expect to occur during their absence
- what they wish to be contacted about
- how correspondence should be dealt with, i.e. what to pass to someone else for action, what to acknowledge and keep for traveller's return
- what appointments can be made for after traveller's return
- any tasks they would like done while they are away in readiness for their return.

DURING ABSENCE

Make a note of:

- people who telephone and say they will call, or ask for the traveller to call when they return
- correspondence passed to others for action
- important correspondence dealt with
- appointments made subject to confirmation
- tasks done
- any important decisions taken or problems solved.

Keep files of documents for action in priority order:

- documents for information
- reading material.

Before the traveller returns, check that all documents are sorted and arranged in appropriate files, and that urgent notes and papers are in a file on top of the pile.

AFTER RETURN

Draw the traveller's attention to any particularly urgent and/or important matters that need immediate action or about which they should be informed.

SOURCES OF INFORMATION

Various sources of information, including reference books under the heading of 'Travel', are given in Chapter 15 (see pages 470 and 474).

ACTIVITY 14.1 You are secretary to Miss Margaret Williams, Permanent Secretary, Ministry of Education, in Trinidad and Tobago. She is to visit Barbados, Jamaica and St Lucia. She will leave Trinidad on Monday morning in three weeks' time and is prepared to give up five working days to the tour if necessary. The order in which the islands are visited is flexible but the minimum time possible should be spent travelling.

The purpose of the tour is to visit chief education officers (CEOs) in the islands. She hopes to visit secondary schools where business studies are available and a technical college in each island. Miss Williams wishes to find out as much as possible about these facilities as she is hoping to extend the facilities in Trinidad. She has already spoken to the chief education officers by telephone.

Miss Williams would also like to meet representatives of employers from various types and sizes of business. She would like to know their expectations of young people trained for employment. The local Chambers of Commerce would be able to arrange this. She would let them know when she would be available after hearing from the CEOs.

a. Arrange the itinerary including suggested flights and hotels.
b. Prepare a draft letter to be sent to each of the chief education officers.

(continued)

ACTIVITY 14.1 *(continued)*	c. Prepare a draft letter to be sent to the directors of the Chambers of Commerce (see Appendix 4).
	d. Assume you have telephoned the hotels and made provisional bookings. Prepare a draft fax confirming the reservation at each hotel.

PRACTICE QUESTIONS

1. You are asked to book hotel accommodation for a manager. What information do you need before you can make a reservation?

2. You need a passport to travel abroad. How will you obtain one?

3. Why is it important to inform a hotel if you expect to arrive late?

4. You are asked to collect air tickets from a travel agent.
   a. What information should you be given before you go?
   b. What points should you check before you leave the travel agent?

5. Your manager is to attend two Caricom meetings next month. The first meeting is in Barbados, starting on the first Monday of the month, and will last for three full working days. The second meeting is to be in Jamaica and will start on Thursday afternoon of the same week. It will continue until the following Tuesday afternoon.
   Prepare an itinerary for your executive giving all dates and times of departure, and arrival times of flights, as well as flight numbers. A BWIA West Indies Airways Limited route map is shown in Fig. 14.7.

6. Referring to the itinerary you prepared for question 5, write an e-mail to the travel agent asking them to make all the necessary reservations. The travel agent is the Business Tour Company, e-mail address: businesstourtrinidad@wow.net.

7. Your executive is travelling to New York to attend a sales conference and has requested you to reconfirm his return flight on BWIA West Indies Airways Limited. What details will you check?

8. You have made a telephone reservation for Mr John Levine to stay at the Excelsior Hotel in Georgetown, Guyana, for five nights (Monday to Friday inclusive) of the second week of next month.

Fig. 14.7 BWIA route map.

    a. Refer to the appropriate timetables and select suitable flights to and from Guyana.
    b. Write a letter to the Excelsior Hotel confirming your telephone reservation. Include all relevant details. Mr Levine will pay his account by credit card.
    c. Prepare an itinerary for Mr Levine's trip.

9. Your manager is to travel to New York and London and asks you whether he needs visas. How would you find out and what steps will you take if he does?

10. What kind of travellers' cheques would you buy if you were travelling to:
   a. Barbados
   b. London
   c. Toronto
   d. Buenos Aires
   e. Kuala Lumpur?

SHORT ANSWER QUESTIONS

1. Many airlines have three classes of travel. These are ...., ... and ....

2. When travelling outside your own country you must have a/an ....

3. Before you are allowed into some countries you must have a/an ....

4. When making appointments for a manager who is away, these should be ....

5. The best source of information on flights is a/an .... or a/an ....

Choose the most appropriate ending for each of the following sentences.

6. When a manager is away, incoming mail should be:
   a. kept unopened in a file for their return
   b. opened and sorted according to priority and filed for their return
   c. opened and put on the appropriate file
   d. opened and dealt with if possible or acknowledged before being sorted and put in a file for their return.

7. Airlines automatically insure their passengers for:
   a. illness during a flight
   b. loss of baggage
   c. travel delays
   d. personal accident.

8. When arranging appointments for a business trip you should:
   a. keep them as short as possible
   b. pack them into as short a time as possible to leave the traveller some free time
   c. allow contingency time during each day in case of unforeseen delays
   d. keep mealtimes as short as possible.

9. When a hotel reservation is made by telephone it:
   a. does not need to be confirmed
   b. should be confirmed by letter, fax or e-mail

c. should be confirmed by the hotel
d. can be checked a day or two before the traveller's arrival date.

10. When a manager returns from a business trip you should welcome them back and then:
   a. ask if they had a good time
   b. tell them there are some e-mail messages in their mailbox
   c. draw their attention to matters that need immediate or very urgent action
   d. tell them what has been going on in the office.

EXAMINATION QUESTIONS

1. Scribesworld Ltd is a company distributing speciality writing equipment. Its head office is in London with branch offices in several continents.

BRANCH OFFICES	RECOMMENDED HOTELS
GPO BOX 6450 SYDNEY NSW 2001 AUSTRALIA Fax 08-345 0908 Tel. 08-345 0907	Brighton Beech SYDNEY NSW 2002 AUSTRALIA 08-717 4910 08-717 4909
Cockspur House Nile Street BRIDGETOWN BARBADOS Fax 02-253 5871 Tel. 02-253 5879	Sunshine Rockley New Road CHRISTCHURCH BARBADOS 02-274 1109 02-274 1009
186 Jalan Raja Chulan 50200 KUALA LUMPUR MALAYSIA Fax 03-261 1411 Tel. 03-261 1410	KASSIM 8 Jalan Sultan 50050 KUALA LUMPUR, MALAYSIA 03-270 6645 03-270 6600
14 Churchill Road HARARE ZIMBABWE Fax 09-304 9808 Tel. 09-304 9908	Warren Park HARARE ZIMBABWE 09-780 1008 09-780 1000

Fig. 14.8 (a) Branch offices list.

```
┌─────────────────────────────────────────────────────────────────┐
│                                                                 │
│   SCRIBESWORLD LTD                         SCRIBES HOUSE        │
│   Tel. 0207 710 5000                       10 Chester Street    │
│   Fax 0207 710 5005                        LONDON W3 3DG        │
│   ─────────────────────────────────────────────────────────     │
│                                                                 │
│   FACSIMILE TO                                                  │
│   .............................................................│
│   FAX NO. .....................................................│
│   COPY TO .....................................................│
│   FAX NO. .....................................................│
│   FROM ........................................................│
│   DATE .................................... NO. OF PAGES ......│
│   ─────────────────────────────────────────────────────────     │
│                                                                 │
│                                                                 │
│                                                                 │
│                                                                 │
│                                                                 │
│                                                                 │
│   SIGNATURE ...................................................│
│                                                  END OF MESSAGE │
└─────────────────────────────────────────────────────────────────┘
```

Fig. 14.8 (b) Facsimile form.

You are personal assistant to Mr John Land, general manager at head office. Two weeks from today Mr Land is to visit the Harare branch, where he will be provided with a car and a chauffeur. A hotel suite has provisionally been booked for four nights by the Harare office.

a. Using the data in Fig. 14.8a and the form in Fig. 14.8b, prepare a fax direct to the hotel, copy to Harare branch, confirming Mr Land's reservation for his stay in Harare. His flight arrives at 2030 hours local time. Ask the hotel to hold the suite until his arrival. Include exact dates of Mr Land's booking. His return flight leaves on the morning of the fifth day. Also ask them to confirm that secretarial services are available.

    b. Apart from tickets, make a list of any THREE health or travel documents Mr Land might require, and briefly state the purpose of each.

(Pitman Office Procedures Level 2 1998 Pt 1)

2.   *a.* State the actions that could be taken to ensure the smooth running of an office during the absence of the manager on a business trip.
    b. List the main items to be included on a business trip itinerary.
    c. What factors should be taken into account when constructing an itinerary regarding the times between appointments?

(Pitman Office Procedures Level 2 1998 Pt 2)

CHAPTER 15

SOURCES OF INFORMATION

OBJECTIVES When you have studied this chapter you should have acquired the knowledge and understanding to be able to:

1. consider a wide range of sources as starting points for research
2. use reference books in a systematic and effective way
3. use a dictionary to solve both spoken and written language queries
4. take a structured approach to a research task.

The world is full of information. The problem is finding the facts that are needed from day to day in business. In this chapter, we will consider:

- sources that provide information for business activities
- the kinds of information that can be obtained from each source
- reference books
- how to use reference books
- how to use a dictionary
- the best approach to the process of research.

SOURCES OF INFORMATION

The list below gives a range of sources for many kinds of information:

- banks
- Chambers of Commerce

- companies and corporations
- company records
- employers' organisations and trades unions
- foreign consulates, high commissions and embassies
- government ministries and departments
- the Internet
- libraries
- maps
- newspapers and newspaper offices
- non-governmental organisations (NGOs)
- Post Offices
- professional institutes
- reference books
- telecommunications companies
- travel agents, airlines, airports, overseas tourist boards
- United Nations agencies
- Viewdata.

TYPES OF INFORMATION FROM EACH SOURCE

Only a brief résumé of information available from each source can be given here but the list in Table 15.1 should provide a guide as to what can be found at each source.

Table 15.1 *Types of information and their sources*

Source	Information
Banks	Exchange rates for foreign currencies
	Interest rates
	Types of bank account, credit/borrowing facilities available
	Services available to customers, e.g. insurance
Chambers of Commerce	Ownership of companies, directors' names, addresses and telephone numbers, subsidiary companies
Companies and corporations	Financial situation from annual reports
	Products and/or services
	Special events, e.g. promotions, sales, new product launches
Employers' organisations	Trade figures
	Effects of legislation on business

(continued)

Table 15.1 *(continued)*

Source	Information
Employers' organisations	Market potential at home and abroad
	(A list of employers' organisations throughout the Caribbean is given in Appendix 3 Part 2)
Foreign consulates, high commissions and embassies	Business opportunities
	General information about the country
	Health requirements, i.e. vaccinations, etc.
	Travel difficulties, restrictions
	Visa requirements
Government ministries, departments	Legal requirements, i.e. regulations, related to affairs dealt with by the particular ministry or department
	Publications explaining what kind of affairs are dealt with, where contact can be made and, in some cases, who to contact
The Internet	Almost any and every kind of information covering local, national and international affairs (see Chapter 3, pages 55–8)
Libraries	The British Council and the United States Information Service have a wide range of information
	Most libraries have reference books (see page 471) and newspapers (see below)
Maps	World atlases which, depending on the publisher, include maps of population, climate, habitats of animals, health, wealth and transport networks
	National maps for regions or areas of the country
	Street maps for the main towns in regions or areas, and for local area towns and villages
Newspapers and newspaper offices	News articles and editorial columns, articles for particular sectors of the community, e.g. women and professionals, financial news including stock market dealings, sports
	Some newspaper offices provide a library service of articles etc. published – in the Caribbean, the *Trinidad Guardian*, *Trinidad Express Newspaper*, *Daily Gleaner* (Jamaica) and *The Advocate* (Barbados) provide this service; in the UK, there is *The Times* and the *Daily Telegraph*
Non-governmental organisations (NGOs)	Information related to the organisation's function, e.g. training; NGOs may be established in parallel with government ministries or departments to meet the objectives of government initiatives
Post Office	*Post Office Guide* and leaflets on individual services

(continued)

Table 15.1 *(continued)*

Source	Information
Professional organisations and journals	Institutes and associations whose members belong to a specific profession, e.g. accountants, attorneys, engineers, personnel, provide information to their members on relevant matters of law, best practice, and examination requirements and studies; they also publish a journal, usually monthly, which contains a great deal of information related to the particular profession
Records of own company	Annual reports from previous years Brochures and/or catalogues Files and records held in various departments and/or the central filing department Leaflets and booklets explaining the company's development, future plans and products/services
Reference books	See page 471 where the various kinds of relevant reference books are listed
Telecommunications companies	The telephone directory gives details of services and products available and their costs, and lists subscribers' telephone, telex and fax numbers *Yellow Pages* lists business subscribers' telephone, telex and fax numbers; advertisements are charged for Leaflets and booklets explaining particular services and products, and how to use them
Travel agents, airlines, airports, overseas tourist boards	Brochures and information on travel (by air and sea), accommodation internationally, including the Caribbean Flights, costs, arrival and departure times of aircraft, accommodation, air timetables Arrival and departure times of flights, taxi and courtesy bus services, facilities in the airport Travel, accommodation, holiday routes, leisure facilities, sports, etc. in specific areas, visa and health regulations brochures, maps and accommodation guides
Trades unions	Legal rights of employees Services provided to trades union members
United Nations agencies	Funding available for projects Educational materials International law relating to individual agency's operations, e.g. World Health and International Labour Organizations

(continued)

Table 15.1 *(continued)*

Source	Information
Viewdata	Teletext on television channels provides news, travel information, weather reports and information of many other kinds
	Videotex – advertisements on screen, usually seen in public places such as Post Offices or airports

REFERENCE BOOKS

We will look at reference books under specific categories and, after that, we will examine how to use them. The categories are:

- Caribbean information
- Dictionaries
- English language
- General information
- People
- Travel.

CARIBBEAN INFORMATION

- *Caribbean Year Book* contains details of who's who in the Caribbean.
- *Caribbean Yellow Pages* published by Caribbean Publishing Co. Ltd (1980) lists names and addresses of manufacturers, exporters/importers and distributors.
- *Cote Ce, Cote La* (see under Dictionaries).
- *Official Gazette* published weekly in all islands, contains information about government decrees and amendments to existing legislation, vacancies in the public service, promotion and termination of appointment of civil servants, and other official information emanating from government.
- *Ninety Most Prominent Women in Trinidad and Tobago*, published by Inprint Caribbean Ltd.
- *Regional Telephone Directory* lists companies covering territories in the north, south and east Caribbean.
- *Trinidad and Tobago Export Directory* published by TIDCO annually.
- *Who's Who and Handbook of Trinidad and Tobago* – Business 2001–2, contains details of people of note in Trinidad and Tobago.

- *Who's Who in the Caribbean* contains details of people of note in the whole region.

DICTIONARIES

- All written languages have a dictionary and there are many dictionaries available for **international languages** such as English, French, German, Spanish, etc.
- **Subject** dictionaries contain the terminology used in many hundreds of specialist areas such as agriculture, computers, economics, finance, legal terms, management, needlework, science and technology, etc.
- *Cote Ce, Cote La* by Jon Mendes is a dictionary of local Caribbean sayings (1996).
- *Dent Dictionary of Abbreviations* by John Paxton, published by JM Dent & Sons Limited, ISBN 0-460-86129-8, provides a fuller list of abbreviations than the general dictionaries or reference books.
- *The Wordsworth Dictionary of Difficult Words* by Robert H Hill, published by Wordsworth Editions Ltd, ISBN 1-85326-308-7, gives the meanings of unusual words.
- *The Past Times Book of Cliches* by Betty Kirkpatrick, published by Bloomsbury Publishing plc, ISBN 0-7475-2030-5, is a dictionary in which many phrases that are used daily but not in their literal sense, are explained.
- *The Past Times Book of Slang* by Rosalind Fergusson, published by Routledge. The catalogue reference can be obtained from the Library of Congress.
- *New Era Pocket Shorthand Dictionary*, ISBN 0-58-229890-3, and *Pitman 2000 Pocket Shorthand Dictionary*, ISBN 0-58-228722-7, published by Pitman Publishing. Valuable for checking spelling as they give both root words and their full derivatives, e.g. 'benefit' and 'benefiting', which most dictionaries do not.

ENGLISH LANGUAGE

- *New Fowler's Modern English Usage* by RW Burchfield, 4th edition (1998), published by Oxford University Press, ISBN 0-19-860263-4.
- *The King's English* by HW and FG Fowler, 3rd edition (1977), published by Oxford University Press, ISBN 0-19-881330-9.

- *Thesaurus of English Words and Phrases* by Roget, Peter and Kirkpatrick, published by Penguin Books, ISBN 0-14-027736-6, provides synonyms for the various meanings of each word.
- *Usage and Abusage: A Modern Guide to Good English* published by Penguin Books, ISBN 0-14-051442-2.

ACTIVITY 15.1 Obtain any of the English language books listed above or any English grammar book. Read each of the following sentences, find out why they are incorrect and note down your answer.

1. When you have read the letter please reply to myself.
2. Their not going out again today.
3. The girl which went out is on holiday.
4. The number of accidents are rising.
5. Every one of the group were keen to go to work.
6. Mary gave the dog it's food.
7. This is the man who I saw in the shop yesterday.
8. The most bigger of the boys is a football player.
9. Me and you are playing together in the championship.
10. I have not given him no books.
11. Due to the bus being late I missed the flight.
12. She was not illegible to vote as she was not old enough.

GENERAL INFORMATION

- *Kelly's Directories* published annually are for businesses, listing products alphabetically with the names of businesses that provide each product listed under its heading.
- *Pears Cyclopaedia* published annually by Penguin Books, ISBN 0-14-029749-9, gives information under headings – the wider world (Events, Prominent people, Local and central government, Law, International organisations); general (Dictionary, Foreign phrases, Business dictionary and Legal notes); home and personal (Medical dictionary, First-aid hints, Cookery, Gardening, Sports, Domestic pets).
- *Whitaker's Almanack* published annually by TSL, ISBN 0-11-702261-6, contains statistics and information on every country in the world, e.g. government officials' names, imports/exports, revenue, population, language, production, industry.

- *The Statesman's Year Book* published annually by Macmillan, ISBN 0-333-77566-X, is divided into four parts: Part I statistics for commodities and information about international organisations, e.g. UNO, NATO; Part II Commonwealth countries; Part III USA; and Part IV other countries. These list information under the headings: Types of government, Area and population, Education, Justice, Finance, Defence, Production, Commerce, Communications, Money and banking, Weights and measures, Diplomatic representatives, Books of reference which provide additional information.
- *Titles and Forms of Address* by Graham Walters, published by Black, ISBN 0-71-364647-0.
- *Debrett's Correct Form* by Patrick Montague-Smith, 3rd edition (1999), published by Headline Book Publishing plc, ISBN 0-74-722330-0. Forms of address for titled people and others, including those in official positions in Great Britain; advice on protocol and etiquette for formal business and social occasions; a section relating to the USA and other countries.

PEOPLE

Most of the books listed below are published in the United Kingdom but the information in them is of international use:

- Air Force, Army and Navy lists
- *Crockford's Clerical Directory* (lists the clergy)
- *Debrett's Peerage and Titles of Courtesy*
- dentists' register
- *Directory of Directors*
- *International Who's Who*
- law list (barristers and solicitors)
- register of nurses
- *Who's Who in America*
- *Who's Who in the Caribbean* (see also under Caribbean)
- *Who's Who in the Commonwealth*
- *Who's Who in the World 2002*
- *Who was Who* (prominent people who have died).

TRAVEL

- *ABC Passenger and Shipping Guide*, Lloyds International List, gives details of shipping lines and agents.
- *OAG Flight Guide* published monthly, gives flight information and costs for airlines throughout the world.
- Hotel and accommodation guides, national and international.

There are also many specialist reference books. The titles indicate the types of office in which they are used. Some examples are listed below:

- *Annual Abstract of Statistics*
- *Banker's Almanack and Year Book*
- *Hansard* (official report of proceedings in the Parliament of Trinidad and Tobago)
- *Insurance Blue Book*
- *Municipal Year Book*
- *Stock Exchange Year Book.*

HOW TO USE A REFERENCE BOOK

Most reference books have a 'contents' page at or close to the front. Look at this and identify the chapter or section heading which suggests that it contains the information you want. If what you want is a little unusual, your first try may not be successful but try other headings before you give up.

Some reference books, e.g. those dealing with language, have an index at the back. An index is much more detailed than a contents page and is arranged alphabetically. Look carefully and if you cannot find what you want, think of other words that might lead you to the correct information. For example, if you are looking for anything to do with filing, you may find it under 'storage and retrieval', rather than the word 'filing' itself.

When you find some useful information make a note of where you found it so that you will be able to find it without 'hunting around' in future. It is useful to keep an alphabetical 'information book' in which you note each item of information under its topic heading.

ACTIVITY 15.2 Go to a reference library and choose any reference book on a topic that interests you. Look at the contents list, choose a chapter and see what facts you can find that you did not know. Also look in the index for information you would like to find.

HOW TO USE A DICTIONARY

You look in a dictionary when you need to know something about a word, including its:

- spelling
- pronunciation
- meaning
- part of speech
- plural form of a noun
- past tense or participle of a verb
- derivation.

SPELLING

Sometimes it is difficult to find the word you want if you do not know the first one or two letters. Most words begin with the letter that represents the sound. You need to learn the possible starting letters of eight sounds. Table 15.2 will help you with this.

Table 15.2 *Spelling guidelines*

Sound	Possible spelling	Example
f	f, ph	fat, physical
g	g, gh	got, ghost
j	j, g	jam, giant
k	k, c, ch	kiosk, car, character
kw	qu	quick
n	n, gn, kn, pn	new, gnome, knife, pneumonia
s	s, c, ps, sc	sit, cell, psychology, science
sh	sh, ch	shade, charade
zer	zer, xer	zero, xerography

Some words beginning with 'h' are pronounced without it, e.g.:

- 'heir' pronounced 'air'
- 'honest' pronounced 'onest'.

Homophones can cause difficulty. These are words that sound the same but are spelt differently, depending on their meanings or parts of speech. For example:

- principle – meaning a rule (noun)
- principal – meaning head teacher (noun) or most important (adjective)

- practice – a noun, e.g. the doctor has a busy practice
- practise – a verb, e.g. you must practise every day.

There are many homophones and care must be taken to differentiate them by spelling.

There are also words that sound similar but are spelt differently, as well as having different meanings. For example:

- affect – a verb, e.g. the new rules will affect all the children
- effect – a noun, e.g. the new rules will have an adverse effect on all staff.

PRONUNCIATION

You need to look in the information pages of a dictionary to find out how pronunciation is indicated in that particular edition. Some publishers place a mark before the syllable to be stressed, others after, and yet others place the mark above it. Examples:

benefit	'benefit, ben'efit or benefit	(stress on first syllable)
interment	in'terment, inter'ment or interment	(stress on second syllable)
weekday	'weekday, week'day or weekday	(stress on first syllable)
weekend	week'end, weekend' or weekend	(stress on last syllable).

As there is sometimes more than one way of dividing words into syllables, the marks are generally placed to indicate clearly the exact letters to be stressed. Examples are: cool'ly, i.e. there are two 'l's to be pronounced; but wooll'en, i.e. only one 'l' to be pronounced.

The actual sounds are shown in many dictionaries in phonetic spelling in brackets. As there are many different ways of writing phonetics you need to look in the front pages of the dictionary to find out how the different sounds are represented in that particular publication.

MEANING

The meaning of each word is explained immediately after it. Often there are several meanings, though the differences are slight. If the meanings are quite different they are usually listed separately for each meaning and marked 1, 2, 3, etc. If the differences are slight the meanings all follow the word but are numbered. Example:

sealer 1 a person or thing that seals. 2 (formerly in Britain and currently in the USA) an official who examines the accuracy of weights and measures. 3 a coating of paint, varnish, etc. applied to a surface to prevent the absorption of subsequent coats.

sealer a person or ship occupied in hunting seals.

The variety of meanings can be confusing. If you are looking up a word that you have seen in a report or a book, find the meaning that seems to fit the context of the rest of the sentence.

PARTS OF SPEECH

There are eight parts of speech indicated in a dictionary, as shown in Table 15.3.

Table 15.3 *Parts of speech*

noun	n.	pronoun	pron.
verb – transitive	v. or vb. (tr.)	preposition	prep.
verb – intransitive	v. or vb. (intr.)	conjunction	conj.
adjective	a. or adj.	interjection	int. or interj.
adverb	adv.		

A transitive verb has an object, an intransitive verb does not. For example:

- the verb 'hit' is transitive because you always have to hit *something*, e.g. I shall hit the ball very hard
- the verb 'live' is intransitive because you cannot live anything, e.g. I live here.

Words that have two or more parts of speech are followed by all the relevant abbreviations, e.g.: n. and v. Words that exist only in plural form, e.g. 'hives' meaning a skin eruption, are followed by 'n. pl.' (noun plural). A colloquial form of a word is followed by (colloq.). There may also be an indication that the colloquial form of a word can be made plural by adding 's', e.g. hippo (colloq.: pl.s.). This means that 'hippo' is a colloquial version of hippopotamus but 'hippo' can be made plural in its own right.

PLURAL FORM OF A NOUN

Most nouns are made plural by adding 's'. This is not usually indicated except as explained for colloquial words. There are exceptions, and in these cases the plural ending is given in brackets.

For example:

- bureau n. (pl. -eaux)
- datum n. (pl. -ta)
- syllabus n. (pl. -buses or -bi).

Datum is rarely used, 'data' being the common form of the word. In this case the two words are given as separate entries in the dictionary.

PAST TENSE OR PARTICIPLE OF A VERB

Past tenses and participles of verbs are generally formed by adding -ed to the verb, e.g. start, started; jump, jumped. When the verb is irregular – e.g. go, went, gone; have, had; is, was, been – the full words are shown. For example: go v.i (past went; p.p. gone). The abbreviation p.p. stands for 'past participle'.

DERIVATION

Many English words are derived from other languages including French, German, Greek and Latin. The abbreviations for these are F or Fr., G or Ger., Gk, Lat. This information is generally given at the end of the explanation(s) of the word.

ACTIVITY 15.3 Obtain a good English dictionary and find the answers to the following questions.

1. Correct the spelling errors in these words and phrases:
   - *i.* proffered – favoured
   - *ii.* the increase will effect them
   - *iii.* in the process of been updated
   - *iv.* seperate
   - *v.* benefitting
   - *vi.* admissable.

2. Find the spelling of the words that sound as follows:
   - *i.* farinx
   - *ii.* kronic
   - *iii.* sikotic
   - *iv.* jenteel
   - *v.* gurkin
   - *vi.* nash
   - *vii.* kwit
   - *viii.* nuckle
   - *ix.* seeling.

3. Explain the difference in meaning between:
   - *i.* brake and break
   - *ii.* formerly and formally
   - *iii.* ascent and assent
   - *iv.* desert and dessert
   - *v.* faint and feint
   - *vi.* passed and past.

(continued)

> **ACTIVITY 15.3**
> *(continued)*
>
> 4. Find out the meaning of and how to pronounce the following words:
>   - *i.* integral
>   - *ii.* superfluous
>   - *iii.* supernumerary
>   - *iv.* spherical
>   - *v.* antipathy.
>
> 5. What part or parts of speech are the following:
>   - *i.* but
>   - *ii.* shout
>   - *iii.* superlative
>   - *iv.* superimpose
>   - *v.* until
>   - *vi.* themselves
>   - *vii.* damn
>   - *viii.* integrate
>   - *ix.* torn.

THE BEST APPROACH TO THE PROCESS OF RESEARCH

When you need to find a source of reference it is important to do it as systematically as possible in order to avoid wasting time. Ideally, think of possible sources – places, people, books, etc. and make a list. Then decide the most likely source and start there.

Unfortunately likely sources do not always come to mind readily. In that case think of any possible source that might point you in the right direction. Do not forget the nearby sources such as files and other records. There could be someone in your office or in the organisation who might have the information you are seeking or know where to find it. Ask around. People are generally helpful but it is important to 'help yourself' as much as possible. Perseverance is the key to research.

PRACTICE QUESTIONS

1. Explain the meanings of the following words and phrases:
   - *i.* English usage
   - *ii.* synonyms
   - *iii.* antonyms
   - *iv.* derivation
   - *v.* the peerage
   - *vi.* proverbs
   - *vii.* similes
   - *viii.* visas
   - *ix.* meterological records
   - *x.* pronunciation.

2. Refer to one of the books on English usage, or a dictionary, for the following information:
   - *i.* the difference between 'stationary' and 'stationery'
   - *ii.* whether 'grey' may also be spelt 'gray'

iii. the plural of 'wharf'
iv. the pronunciation and meaning of 'diphthong'
v. the meaning of the prefix 'super'.

3. Refer to appropriate reference books to find out:
i. whether 'dining room' should be hyphenated
ii. the past tense of 'occur'
iii. the difference in meaning between 'principal' and 'principle'
iv. the meaning of the printer's correct sign #
v. the salutation of a letter to a President
vi. how to display an agenda
vii. how a diaeresis should be typed.

4. Refer to the *Statesman's Year Book* (there should be a copy in your local reference library) and find the following information:
i. the name of the President of the Federal Reserve Bank of the USA
ii. the national flag of Mexico
iii. the headquarters and the name of the Secretary General of Caricom
iv. the functions of the World Health Organization.

5. In which reference books would you look for the following information?
a. Details of the head of state in your territory.
b. The cost of sending a letter by airmail to India.
c. How to address a bishop.
d. Present vacancies in the public services.
e. A list of the shipping agents represented locally, including their telephone numbers.

6. List and outline the uses of any five reference books you would expect to find in an office.

7. Use a dictionary to answer the following questions.
a. Write out the following words, putting in the accents to show where the stress falls: daughter, incomprehensible, proficient, enchant, representative, queen-cake, self-love, semi-final.
b. Look up and note down the plural forms of: memorandum, medium, appendix, analysis, helix, hetaera, hiatus.
c. Find the past tense and past participles of: learn, sleep, steal, stand, run, fly, think.

8. State three types of information you may get from each of the following:
- banks
- travel agents
- libraries
- newspapers
- Chambers of Commerce

- embassies, high commissions, consulates
- employers' organisations
- the Internet
- business organisations, e.g. companies
- trades unions.

9. What information would you find in a world atlas? What other kind of maps/atlases are there and what information can you get from them?

10. Obtain a reference book that gives forms of address. Find out how you would address the following people in a letter:
    i. the Prime Minister
    ii. the local vicar
    iii. a Member of Parliament
    iv. the Chief Justice
    v. an archbishop.

SHORT ANSWER QUESTIONS

1. If you wanted to know the exchange rate of a currency you would contact a/an ....

2. If you wanted to know about travel restrictions in Russia you would contact the ....

3. The Internet holds a wide range of information on ...., ... and .... affairs.

4. The British Council and United States Information Service have excellent .... in many countries.

5. To know the arrival time of a flight you could contact the .... or ....

6. Write the following parts of speech in full and give an example of each: prep., conj., vb. tr., n., adv., inter., pron., vb. intr.

7. The key to successful research is ....

8. 'To eat humble pie' is an example of a ....

9. 'Golly!' is a .... word.

10. Write abbreviations for the following words: insurance, meeting, conference, about, committee.

CHAPTER 16

OBTAINING EMPLOYMENT

OBJECTIVES When you have studied this chapter you should have acquired the knowledge and understanding to be able to:

1. identify the various starting points for seeking a job
2. prepare a well-structured curriculum vitae
3. complete an application form correctly
4. prepare effectively for an interview
5. reply correctly to an invitation to interview and to a job offer
6. prepare for your first day at work in a new job
7. write a letter of resignation if/when the need arises
8. think about how you will work in a team environment.

There will be various times in your life, starting with when you leave school, when you wish to find employment or change your job. This is a very important matter, because you spend nearly a quarter of your life at work. You need to work to live, but you also need to be in a job that is right for you. You need to think carefully about what you are capable of doing now, in accordance with your qualifications, and what you hope to achieve in the future. This will lead you to think about the type of organisation that would provide you with the right working environment as well as opportunities for progress.

WHERE TO START LOOKING

There are several starting points for job-seekers. These include:

- advertisements in newspapers and magazines
- advertisements on radio and television
- employment agencies
- friends already in work whose employers need additional staff
- casual applications to organisations you think may have vacancies
- Ministry of Labour and Co-operatives website.

Advertisements can be found at the employment exchange, in shop windows and on noticeboards for staff such as bar attendants, gas station attendants, stores clerks and domestic workers.

ADVERTISEMENTS

The amount of information in a job advertisement varies from minimal to very detailed. Ideally an advertisement should tell you:

- briefly about the organisation
- the job title and key duties of the job
- qualifications and experience needed
- how to contact the company – telephone, letter or e-mail
- whom to contact
- telephone number/postal address/e-mail address.

Read the advertisement very carefully. If you think you need more information in order to decide whether to apply for the job you should telephone to ask for more details. For example, you might wish to know where the organisation is located, whether your qualifications are adequate, what the job involves (if duties are not given in the advertisement) or what salary scale applies (if you are wanting to change your job).

Check carefully how you should apply. Possible methods include:

- send a cv (curriculum vitae)
- write giving details of your education, experience and outside interests
- telephone for an application form.

A **curriculum vitae** should present a profile of you. It should include:

- your name
- date of birth

- address
- schools attended, with dates
- examinations passed (or awaiting results if leaving school)
- work experience (part- or full-time)
- special skills
- leisure interests, e.g. sports
- any other information relevant to the job.

A typical cv is illustrated in Fig. 16.1.

CURRICULUM VITAE

Name: Miss Susan Harvey

Address: 43 North Hill Road
KINGSTON
JAMAICA

Telephone No.: Kingston 6431

Date of birth: 16 August 1984

Education: Montego School from 1991 to 2000
Kingston College from 2000 to 2002

Examinations:

Year	Qualification	Subject	Grade
2001	General Proficiency CXC	English	1
		Maths	2
		History	2
		Literature	1
		Spanish	2
2002	GCE 'O' level	Biology	B

Work experience while at school

Helping in local grocery shop on Saturdays and during holidays

Work experience while at college

Three weeks' secretarial work at St Ann's Bay Insurance Company arranged by college
Summer holiday work as receptionist in Hotel Splendide, Montego Bay
Saturday work in local dress shop

Interests/hobbies

Music (as member of north Hill Musical Society, and piano playing), swimming, tennis

Date available for work: August 2002

References:

Mr H Enright Mrs F Wright
Principal St Ann's Bay Insurance Company
Kingston College 4 High Street
KINGSTON ST ANN'S BAY

Fig. 16.1 Curriculum vitae.

A cv should be accompanied by a covering letter (see Fig. 16.2).

> 'Sea View'
> Orinoco Way
> SAN FERNANDO
> Trinidad
>
> 19 July 2002
>
> The Albright Metal Company Ltd
> 113 Main Street
> PORT-OF-SPAIN
>
> Dear Sirs
>
> I have just seen your advertisement for a junior typist in the accounts office in today's *Post & Advertiser* and would like to apply for the position.
>
> I have recently finished a one-year National course at Merrick Road College and could come for an interview at any time suitable for you.
>
> I enclose details of my qualifications and experience.
>
> Yours faithfully
>
>
> Jennifer Adams (Miss)
>
> ENC

Fig. 16.2 Covering letter for curriculum vitae.

If the advertisement states 'Write giving details', you can apply either by sending a cv with a covering letter or by writing a letter that sets out your details. Letters and cvs may be typed or handwritten unless the advertisement states 'in your own handwriting'.

When the instruction is '**Telephone for an application form**', be ready to state the vacancy you wish to apply for (the organisation may have several vacancies), give your name (spell your surname if necessary) and postal address. Some organisations give a telephone answering machine number, so be prepared to give the information clearly and concisely.

EMPLOYMENT AGENCIES

Employment agencies act as agents for employers. They also find employment for job-seekers. An agency has recruitment consultants who interview job-seekers and select appropriate people to be interviewed by the employer.

An employer wishing to use an agency's services may contact a recruitment consultant and give details of the vacancy for which they wish to recruit. The recruitment consultant checks records to see if there is anyone suitable already registered as a job-seeker. If there is no one suitable, the agency advertises. It is important to check how to apply but usually it is in order to visit the agency to find out more about the job.

If you are looking for a job you can go to an agency and be registered. The recruitment consultant takes notes of your details (as in a cv) and finds out from you the sort of job you hope to find. It is a good idea to take your cv with you because this ensures that all the details are included and are accurate. The recruitment consultant may be able to tell you of a vacancy immediately. If not, you will be contacted when a suitable vacancy occurs.

When you are notified of a vacancy you decide whether you want to attend an interview at the organisation. If so, an appointment will be made for you. Your cv will be sent to the organisation by the agency.

The employer pays the agency, and the agency charges those seeking employment a registration fee. In addition they may offer to prepare a cv for you and for this they would be entitled to make a charge, but check how much it would cost before agreeing to the work being done.

Many organisations have a policy of advertising vacancies internally before advertising externally, so that existing employees can apply. This provides opportunities for employees to apply for a job that would give promotion. Sometimes, employees like to change jobs because they are not happy in their existing jobs or because they would like to broaden their experience.

FRIENDS

Some organisations employ friends of existing employees.

CASUAL APPLICATIONS

If there are particular organisations that you would like to work in you may write to them, asking if there are any vacancies for which you might be qualified to apply. Some employers keep a file of casual applications to which they refer when a vacancy arises. Write a letter (see Fig. 16.3) and enclose your cv. Do not be disappointed if you do not receive a reply. Many employers get hundreds of casual letters and can reply only to those that are of interest to them.

---

43 North Hill Road
KINGSTON

22 July 2002

Johnson and Williams Ltd
17 Bell street
KINGSTON

Dear Sirs

I have just finished a two-year course at Kingston College and am looking for a secretarial position. I enclose my curriculum vitae.

I have not yet received the results of my examinations at college but I have given the grades I achieved in my mock examinations to give you some idea of what my results might be.

I am particularly interested in the accounts side of the business as maths has always been one of my favourite subjects and I have helped my father with his accounts for his business for the last six months. However, I am anxious to gain experience in the business world and would welcome any position where I could increase my knowledge and skills.

I am working temporarily in the afternoons in a supermarket but would be available for interview any morning. If the mornings are not possible I am sure I could arrange to have time off in the afternoon to come for an interview.

Yours faithfully

Susan Harvey (Miss)

Fig. 16.3 Unsolicited application.

MINISTRY OF LABOUR AND CO-OPERATIVES (MOLC) WEBSITE

The MOLC website provides a range of services to members of the public. It holds information on occupational data, job vacancies, education and training programmes, labour laws and trends specific to individual industries. The National Employment Service (NES) maintains a database that enables vacancies and applicants to be matched.

Individual job-seekers can:

- search on-line for job vacancies
- post their credentials on-line for review by employers with vacancies
- print a personalised résumé and job reference list.

Employers can:

- post job vacancies that can be reviewed by people looking for jobs
- search on-line for prospective employees
- request the Ministry to provide a list of qualified applicants.

The privacy of job-seekers and employers is an important factor in the scheme. Access to the NES is possible from a personal computer or through kiosks located in sub-offices.

The MOLC website address is http://www.labour.gov.tt.

ACTIVITY 16.1 Study the cv shown in Fig. 16.1. Write a cv for yourself, including the details listed on page 485.

APPLYING FOR A JOB

COVERING LETTERS

Earlier we said that a cv should be accompanied by a covering letter. This would also be necessary if you had telephoned for an application form. You would write a brief letter enclosing the completed form (see Fig. 16.4).

APPLICATION FORMS

It is usual to complete an application at some stage in the recruitment process. This is usually as a first step but if a cv has been requested, the applicant who is offered and has accepted the job may be asked to complete an application form for the organisation's personnel records.

```
                                              43 North Hill Road
                                              KINGSTON

                                              30 July 2002


Miss Susan Williams
Personnel Manager
Johnson and Williams Ltd
17 Bell Street
KINGSTON


Dear Miss Williams

Thank you for your letter of 25 July 2002 and application form. I have
completed the application form, which is enclosed. If you decide to
interview me I can be available at any time.

Yours sincerely


Susan Harvey (Miss)

ENC
```

Fig. 16.4 Covering letter for completed application form.

Each employer's application form may be a little different from others. Generally, similar information to that given on a cv is required. There may be additional details such as any criminal convictions, driving licence and state of health.

An application form is designed with sections for each type of information: personal details, education, experience, etc. A specimen application form is shown in Fig. 16.5.

Before completing the form, it may be useful to make a photocopy and complete it so as to ensure that you complete the original perfectly. It is very important to read the form carefully. In particular, note any special instructions such as 'Use block capitals', 'Write in black', etc.

FORM 2903 (12/82)

THE ROYAL BANK OF TRINIDAD AND TOBAGO LIMITED
APPLICANTS QUESTIONNAIRE

SURNAME ____________ GIVEN NAMES ____________ Male ☐ Female ☐

ADDRESS ____________

____________ TELEPHONE NO. ________

DATE OF BIRTH | COUNTRY OF BIRTH | NATIONALITY | MARITAL STATUS

N.B. Original Birth Certificate or Passport must be provided.

TYPE OF EMPLOYMENT FULL-TIME ☐ PART-TIME ☐ TEMPORARY: No. of months available ________

When are you available to begin work? ____________

EDUCATION

Secondary School, Secretarial, Business or Technical School, University. (Supporting Original Certificates must be provided).

SCHOOL	SUBJECTS PASSED AND QUALIFICATIONS OR LEVELS ATTAINED

Knowledge of: ☐ Typing.......w.p.m. ☐ Shorthand........approx. w.p.m. ☐ Dictaphone

What was your favourite subject(s) at school? ____________

Why? ____________

What Subject(s) did like least like at school? ____________

Why? ____________

Did you prefer working: (i) with a group ☐ (ii) on your own ☐? Give reasons for your preference ________

What were your extra curricular interests or activities? ____________

To what extent were you absent or late at school (i) Sometimes ☐ (ii) Often ☐ (iii) Never ☐

Comment: ____________

Do you wish to further your education? Yes ☐ No ☐ If yes, please indicate when and in which areas of study.

EMPLOYMENY HISTORY:

Have you ever worked before Yes No ☐ If yes, please complete the following

NAME AND ADDRESS OF EMPLOYER	DATE OF EMPLOYMENT FROM	TO	TYPE OF JOB	SALARY

What did you like most about your job(s)? ____________

What did you like least about your job(s)? ____________

What is/was your reason(s) for leaving? ____________

May we contact your present and/or previous employer? Yes ☐ No ☐ If no, please explain: ________

If your employment was not continuous, please indictae your activities in the interim period(s). ________

GENERAL INFORMATION

What influenced you to apply to this Bank? Tick where appropriate:

Advertisement ☐ Relative or Friend ☐ Employee ☐ Teacher ☐ Lectures by Bank Personnel ☐

Brochure ☐ Formerly an employee of R.B.T.T. ☐ Previous experience with another bank ☐

other ☐ (Please specify) ____________

Do you intend to make banking your career? Yes ☐ No ☐ If yes, what are your career objectives? ________

If no, how long do you wish to work in the Bank? Tick where appropriate:

(i) Approx. 1 Year ☐ (ii) 2–5 years ☐ (iii) Over 5 years ☐ (iv) Other ☐ (Please specify)

What factor(s) might cause you to alter these plans? ____________

Fig. 16.5 Application form (continued overleaf).

What factors would urge you to do your best at a job? ______

What might cause you to do less than your best at a job? ______

Have you any dependants, e.g. children, etc? Yes ☐ No ☐ If yes, what arrangements have you made for their care?

How do you relate to other members of your family, including your parents? ______

What are your hobbies? ______

What qualities do you admire most in your friends? ______

Describe your personality. For example, are you shy and reserved, friendly and outgoing, etc? ______

What type of work do you think is best suited to your personality, education and, if any, previous job experience? (Please be as explicit as possible). ______

In your opinion, what is the attitude of people towards discipline and work today? ______

Have you ever been convicted of a criminal offence involving dishonesty or breach of trust (including, but not limited to Robbery, Embezzlement, Forgery, Perjury, etc.) for which you have not recieved a pardon? Yes ☐ No ☐

Indicate Geographic Preferences

Anywhere in Trinidad & Tobago ☐ Anywhere in Trinidad excluding Tobago ☐ North Trinidad ☐

South Trinidad ☐ East Trinidad ☐ Central ☐ Other ☐ (Specify)

What role do you feel The Royal Bank of Trinidad and Tobago Limited has to play in the future of Trinidad and Tobago?

HEALTH RECORD

	YES	NO
1. Have you ever had any serious disease or injury?	☐	☐
2. Have you ever been refused employment on medical grounds?	☐	☐
3. Have you ever given up employment on the advice of a physician?	☐	☐
4. Have you ever been expelled from school or lost a job for using alcohol or because of non-medical drug usage	☐	☐
5. Are you currently on a programme of prescribed drugs or medication	☐	☐
6. Are you aware of any current health condition or disability that could affect performance on the job and/or attendance record or otherwise impose limitations on your ability to perform satisfactory?	☐	☐

7. When did you last have a chest x-ray? ....

What were the results ....

8. Are you currently under treatment of a physician? ☐ ☐

Have you ever suffered from, or were you told you had any of the following conditions. Answer "Yes" or "No"

Heart Trouble	Prolonged Fever ....
High Blood Pressure	Tuberculosis ....
Hernia or Rupture	Nervous Trouble or Breakdown ....
Persistent Cough	Asthma or Hay Fever ....
Pleurisy	Kidney Trouble ....
Sugar in Urine	Stomach Pain or Ulcer ....
Arthritis	Cancer or Tumour ....
Rheumatism	Venereal Disease ....
Epilepsy or Fits	

Have any of your family suffered from any of the following conditions?

Diabetes	Tuberculosis ....
Cancer	Insanity ....

Date ....

....
Signature of applicant

Fig. 16.5 (continued).

Be sure to include details of any Saturday and/or holiday jobs you have had, and any other information about yourself that would indicate special skills that might be useful in a work situation. (For example, you may be involved in voluntary work of some kind.)

Most forms have a section headed 'Referees'. A referee is a person to whom your prospective employer can write asking for an opinion of your ability and character. A prospective employer would not normally write to your current employer until they decide to offer you a job. They may, however, write to a past employer and/or a person who knows you outside work, either before inviting you for interview or before offering you employment.

A **reference** is a confidential document that is kept by the employer on a personal file. It is not intended to be seen by the person about whom the reference has been written. You may have a **testimonial** from a previous employer. This is addressed 'To whom it may concern' and gives similar information to that given in a reference. This usually includes details of attendance, ability, and personal attributes such as conscientious working, good leadership skills and reliability.

You may be asked to give the names and addresses of two or three people who can give a prospective employer an opinion of your ability and character. If you are a school-leaver you would give the name of your school principal and the name of someone who knows you. You would also give the name of any Saturday or holiday job employer. If you are already in work it is usual to give the name of your current employer and one past employer, as well as someone who knows you outside work.

Before you give a person's name as a referee, you must ask their permission to do so. When doing this, check that you know their correct title, the correct spelling of their name, any honours and/or academic qualifications that should follow their name (see Chapter 5, page 121) and their full postal address.

When you have completed the photocopy check that you have given all the information required, that all dates are correct and there are no spelling errors. Then complete the original and check it very carefully. The person who receives your application will gain an impression from the presentation of your form. Never complete it with a drink nearby – coffee stains do not create a good impression! Write legibly and neatly.

Be quite sure that all the information you have given on the application form is correct. If you are employed and it is later found out by the employer that you have given incorrect information, you can be dismissed immediately.

> **ACTIVITY 16.2** Obtain an application form and study it carefully. Complete it with your own details. Then ask a tutor, parent or friend to read it and tell you whether they think you have given all the information required and their impression of it. Would a prospective employer be favourably impressed?

If you are asked for copies of certificates and/or testimonials, send photocopies and take the originals with you to the interview. Never send originals by post because, if lost, they cannot be replaced.

Some employers ask for a photograph. A passport photograph is adequate and should be attached firmly to the form in the space provided.

FOLLOWING UP AN APPLICATION

Employers have different ways of dealing with applications for employment. Some acknowledge all letters/cvs/application forms as they are received. Others wait until they have shortlisted people for interview (see below) and then invite those chosen either by telephone or letter. They then acknowledge those not chosen and explain that they have not been shortlisted. Some employers do not acknowledge any but those chosen for interview, which is very discourteous.

It is in order to follow up an application about 10 to 14 days after the closing date for applications. You would ask whether applicants have been selected for interview yet.

Some advertisements, or letters enclosing application forms, invite the applicant to visit the organisation informally. It would normally be someone in the personnel department who would meet you for an informal chat and show you the department where the vacancy is. Never ignore this invitation. It is an opportunity to ask questions, see whether you would like the working environment, whether the people seem friendly and whether the job is what you would like. It also impresses the employer very favourably if you take the trouble to make an informal visit.

INTERVIEWS

When an employer receives applications, they compare them with a job description (see Chapter 2, pages 37-8) and person specification, which sets out the skills etc. needed, to determine how closely they match requirements. If your application has most of the employer's requirements in terms of qualifications, experience, etc., you will be shortlisted for interview. That means that you will receive a telephone call or a letter inviting you to attend for an interview.

You will be told where and when the interview is to be held. If you are invited by telephone, be sure to write down the details immediately. If you are not sure of the location ask for directions. You should also be told whom to report to on arrival (this person may not be the interviewer).

You may be told who will conduct the interview. It may be the personnel officer and/or a manager in the department where the vacancy is to be filled. You may see the personnel officer first and then the manager, or both together. When there is more than one person interviewing it is known as a **panel interview**. Applicants for civil service posts are always interviewed by a panel of at least three, sometimes more, interviewers.

If you are to be tested you should be told what the test will be, how long it will take and what, if anything, to bring with you.

If you are invited to interview by letter you should reply, by telephone or letter, confirming that you will be able to attend at the time and on the date stated. If you are not able to attend on that time and/or date, telephone to explain and say that you would very much like to have an interview if an alternative time/date could be arranged. This is usually possible. Be sure to thank the person you speak to for accommodating you.

A letter inviting an applicant for interview is shown in Fig. 16.6. A letter confirming attendance is shown in Fig. 16.7.

An interview is a very important step in the process of obtaining employment. Many people have not been offered a job they were very well qualified for because they performed poorly at their interview.

PREPARATION

The secret of a successful interview is **preparation**. You must be as well prepared as the interviewer.

The first step is to find out as much as you can about the organisation. What type of organisation is it? What does it make/sell/provide services for? How big is the company – or how small? Is it the headquarters of a large company with a lot of branches all over the country, or the world? Is it a company with many subsidiaries in different parts of the world? Is it a small specialist company?

> The Albright Metal Company Ltd
> 113 Main Street
> PORT-OF-SPAIN
>
> Tel. 662 2389
> Fax 662 1479
> e-mail albright@www.com
>
> 26 July 2002
>
> Miss Jennifer Adams
> 'Sea View'
> Orinoco Way
> SAN FERNANDO
>
> Dear Miss Adams
>
> **VACANCY FOR JUNIOR TYPIST**
>
> Thank you for your application for this post.
>
> I am pleased to inform you that you have been shortlisted for interview at 1000 on Friday 2 August. Please report to the main reception and ask for me.
>
> Will you please telephone me on 662 2324 to let me know whether the time and date are convenient. If not an alternative time and/or date can be arranged.
>
> Please bring with you to the interview your National course project file.
>
> Yours sincerely
>
> Courtenay Murray

Fig. 16.6 Letter inviting applicant for interview.

Think about the questions you could be asked. Almost certainly these will relate to:

- your good and not-so-good subjects – which were most challenging or stimulating, which you most disliked, why you were not good in certain subjects
- your strengths and limitations – what particular skills or personal attributes you have that are positive (strengths) and negative (limitations)
- your ambitions – why you chose to answer the advertisement for this particular company, what you hope to achieve in the next two or three years.

> 'Sea View'
> Orinoco Way
> SAN FERNANDO
> Trinidad
>
> 28 July 2002
>
> Ms Courtenay Murray
> The Albright Metal Company Ltd
> 113 Main Street
> PORT-OF-SPAIN
>
> Dear Ms Murray
>
> **VACANCY FOR JUNIOR TYPIST**
>
> Thank you for your letter of 26 July 2002 offering me an interview.
>
> I shall be pleased to attend at 1000 on Friday 2 August and look forward to meeting you.
>
> Yours sincerely
>
> Jennifer Adams (Miss)

Fig. 16.7 Letter confirming attendance at interview.

Be prepared to give reasons for your answers. A good interviewer will ask in-depth questions to find out what you really want (or do not want).

Next, decide what you will need to know in order to make a decision as to whether to accept the job if it is offered. Most people would want to know the following:

- what the job involves – you should be given a job description
- conditions of service – hours of work, holiday entitlement, overtime requirements and pay, pension scheme, union representation required/advised/allowed, notice required to terminate employment
- salary – scale, starting point for the job, increase on satisfactory completion of probation (see page 502), frequency of reviews, frequency of payment (weekly or monthly), method of payment (cash, cheque, paid into a bank account)

- career progression – training opportunities, career prospects (promotion). Make a note of these and any other points on which you would like information.

If you are a school/college-leaver, gather together the following:

- your last school report
- result slips of examinations passed
- a portfolio of project work done during a course.

ATTENDING THE INTERVIEW

Decide what you will wear – something appropriate, smart and businesslike – you want to look professional.

Find out how long it will take you to get to the interview location. If you plan to travel by car check that you know where you can park if there are no car-parking facilities at the location itself. Allow yourself at least 15 to 20 minutes more than you need in case of problems, such as being caught in a traffic jam. Take the papers you have gathered together and a notepad and pencil/pen.

When you arrive, give your name and state who you are there to see. You may be asked to take a seat in reception from where someone will collect you, be directed to another place to wait, or be directed to the interview room. Be prepared to smile and shake hands when you are greeted. Take a seat where indicated in the interview room; sit upright, well back in the chair.

The interviewer should start by telling you how they will conduct the interview. This means telling you:

- the objectives of the interview – for them to see if you are right for the job, the team and the organisation
- how long the interview will be (approximately)
- the sequence of questioning
- when you may ask questions
- when and where the test (if there is to be one) will take place.

When the interviewer asks questions think carefully about each one and decide what the interviewer wishes to know. Then phrase your answer to show that you have understood the question and know the answer. If you do not know the answer, say so. Never try to bluff; you will be found out.

Towards the end of the interview, the interviewer will give you information about pay, conditions, etc. If the information does not answer all of the questions you wrote on your list, wait until you are invited to ask questions; it is quite in order to use the checklist of questions you prepared – most interviewers are impressed by the fact that an interviewee has prepared well. You should also take the opportunity to ask anything you would like to know about the job, the company and the department you would be working in if offered employment.

During the interview look interested, listen attentively, smile – but not too much. When the interview ends, thank the interviewer, smile and say goodbye courteously.

BEING TESTED

The most common types of tests for office staff are copy/audio-typing, spelling, numeracy, English language and general intelligence.

BEING OFFERED EMPLOYMENT

If your application was good enough to earn you an interview, and if your interview was good enough to make a positive impression on the interviewer(s), you may be offered the job. Some organisations inform applicants immediately or the same day if they have been successful. If you are not certain whether you wish to accept the offer, you can say that you would like a little time to think about it and discuss it with your parents or teachers. Say that you will let them know the next day. Thank them for the offer, even if you think you will not accept it, and be sure to make contact when promised.

Usually the interviewer will say that they have more people to see and will contact you (by telephone/letter). They should also give you an idea of when, e.g. by the end of the week. However you are informed, you will receive a formal 'offer' letter, as shown in Fig. 16.8.

The offer letter should confirm the details discussed at the interview, i.e. job title, conditions of service, salary, increment dates, optional or compulsory pension scheme, notice required to terminate employment, start date, probationary period (see page 502) and training to be given (if any). These details may be given in a **contract**. You will receive two copies of either the offer letter or the contract, one of which you should sign, after checking the details carefully, and return to the company.

EH Turnbull Ltd
11 East Street
BRIDGETOWN

Our ref. FM/245/02   5 August 2002

Miss Nina Allandale
127 Acacia Avenue
BRIDGETOWN
BARBADOS

Dear Miss Allandale

ASSISTANT SECRETARY IN PUBLICITY DEPARTMENT

I refer to your recent interview and am pleased to offer you this position under the terms set out below.

1. The position is permanent, subject to satisfactory completion of six months' probation.
2. The starting salary will be $3000.00 per month to be reviewed at the end of the probationary period and annually thereafter.
3. The hours of work will be 0900 to 1700 Monday to Friday.
4. Your annual holiday entitlement will be 20 days increasing by one day a year after the first two years up to a maximum of 25 days.
5. You will be required to join the company pension scheme on confirmation of appointment at the end of your probabtion.
6. All other conditions of service are set out in the Staff Handbook, a copy of which is enclosed. You are asked to read this carefully and sign the form at the end of the handbook. You should bring this with you, together with income tax and National Insurance documents on your first day.
7. We agreed a start date of Monday 2 September 2002.

I look forward to welcoming you to the Publicity Department, and I wish you a successful and happy time with the company.

Yours sincerely

Michael Maskew
Marketing Manager

ENC

Tel. 482-1234   Fax 482-4321   e-mail turnbull@caribsurf.com

Fig. 16.8 Employer's letter offering employment.

In a small company the procedure may be less formal. You may receive a telephone call or a letter offering you the job with basic details only. In this case you will reply either accepting or rejecting the offer. A letter accepting an offer of appointment is shown in Fig. 16.9. Fig. 16.10 shows a rejection of offer letter.

127 Acacia Avenue
BRIDGETOWN
Barbados

9 August 2002

Mr Michael Maskew
Marketing Manager
EH Turnbull Ltd
11 East Street
BRIDGETOWN

Dear Mr Maskew

Thank you very much for your letter of 5 August offering me the position of assistant secretary in the Publicity Department. I am very glad to accept the position under the terms you set out in your letter.

I look forward to starting work on Monday 2 September and shall report at 9 am.

Yours sincerely

Nina Allandale (Miss)

Fig. 16.9 Letter accepting offer of employment.

3 Upper Way
SAN FERNANDO
Trinidad

25 April 2002

Mr R Lovatt
The Goodhall Trading Company Ltd
114 Old Street
PORT-OF-SPAIN

Dear Mr Lovatt

Thank you very much for your letter of 23 April offering me the position of mailing clerk in your order department.

I am sorry that I am not able to accept your offer of employment. Since attending the interview I have accepted the offer of a position in another company.

Yours sincerely

Ann Frankland (Mrs)

Fig. 16.10 Letter rejecting offer of employment.

If you are not offered employment you will receive a letter thanking you for attending the interview but regretting that you have not been selected. You do not need to acknowledge this letter but if you wish to apply to the company again in six months or so, you could write to the interviewer, mentioning the interview you attended.

STARTING WORK

When you start your new job you will be on **probation**. This is a two-way situation. You are 'on trial' with the employer so that they can make sure that you can do the job, that you fit into the team and that you are right for the company. It is also for you to decide whether you like working in this organisation, whether you feel comfortable with the team once you have settled in and whether the job is what you expected and you feel you can be committed to it. Probation is usually three months, though some companies have a six-month probationary period.

Your first day at work, or in a new job if you have already worked, will be demanding. It is a good idea to have an early night before this important day; think about what you will wear and prepare everything so that you will not be in a rush next morning. You will be in an unfamiliar environment, meet new people, be given a lot of information and be asked many questions.

INDUCTION

Your offer letter will have informed you who to report to and when. This is usually the personnel officer, who will start your induction. This is a process that goes on throughout your probationary period. It may include a formal 'induction course', training in the company's systems and procedures, and any additional skills you need to do the job.

The first stage of your induction is normally with the personnel officer, who will go over the conditions of service with you to ensure that you are familiar with them, and give you an opportunity to ask any questions if you need clarification of any points. This will include:

- disciplinary procedures – what happens if you disobey the company rules or do not meet required standards
- grievance procedures – who you should go to if you have a problem.

You will then probably be taken to meet your manager/supervisor, whom you may have met at the interview. They will introduce you to the people with whom you will be working. There may be one of your colleagues who has agreed to 'look after' you for your first few days. This person would tell you where to find things, take you for breaks/lunch, show you the machines you will use in your job and generally help you to 'find your feet'.

Your manager/supervisor will tell you more about the job, its purpose, what standards are expected of you and who will be your contacts.

If you are to attend an induction course, you will be told when this will take place. It may be for half a day, a whole day or longer. You should be given a programme from which you will see that it is intended to give you more information about the organisation, what it does and who the senior managers are. Senior managers may give short talks about the work of their departments. House rules will be discussed, e.g. how the telephone should be answered, how documents should be presented (layout or house style). You may be asked to join in discussion groups and there may be visits to general services such as the mail room, computer services and reprographics. You will find all this extremely helpful and will also meet other employees who are new to the organisation.

At the end of each day say, with a smile, 'Good evening' to your supervisor and colleagues, and thank the person who has looked after you. You will soon find yourself fitting in if you make the first move to show that you appreciate what is being done for you.

During your probationary period there should be regular reviews. This means that your manager/supervisor and/or a member of the personnel staff will invite you for an informal discussion to find out how you are getting on. They will take this opportunity to tell you how they think you are progressing and you will be able to tell them if you are having any problems. Be sure to prepare for these reviews; they are a valuable means of assessing what progress you are making and, ultimately, whether you want to stay in the job if this is confirmed.

Assuming that, at the end of your probationary period, your employer is happy with your work and the way you have adapted, you will be 'confirmed in the post'. This means that you have completed the probationary period satisfactorily and are now a permanent member of staff. You will receive confirmation in writing and should acknowledge the letter.

APPRAISALS

Many organisations have an appraisal, or personal review, scheme either on an annual or half-yearly basis. It is an opportunity for you and the person you report to, to have a discussion about your progress. You can say how you think you are getting on and can discuss any difficulties you may have with the work. Your reporting officer will tell you how they think you are progressing, make suggestions for improvements and agree with you how such improvements can be achieved. Training needs are discussed and you may be offered an opportunity to attend a course that will help you in your job and possibly enable you to acquire broader experience.

RESIGNING

You may stay with one employer for many years. On the other hand you may wish to leave at some point for any one of a variety of reasons. The normal procedure is:

1. inform your immediate manager/supervisor
2. write a letter to the personnel officer, stating that you are giving the agreed notice of termination of employment
3. though not required, it is courteous to give a reason for leaving
4. the date on which you will be leaving
5. request for a reference if you would like to have one – however, many organisations do not now give references to individual employees.

A specimen resignation letter is shown in Fig. 16.11.

The personnel officer may ask you to attend an exit interview. This is informal and is intended to keep managers informed of the reasons their staff leave. If an employee is leaving because they are unhappy, it is important that their personnel officer knows this and why. It is not always possible for an employee to give reasons to a manager/supervisor, especially if they are the cause of the unhappiness. Equally, if a lot of staff are leaving in order to earn more money, perhaps the company should review its pay scales.

SEX DISCRIMINATION

At the time of writing (early 2002) some Caribbean governments are proposing to enact legislation to stop discrimination on the grounds of sex. In relation to employment this means that a person must not be discriminated against at any stage in the recruitment process or at any time during their employment because they are of a particular sex. As an example, an employer should not discriminate against a woman who applies

37 Bath Road
PORT MORANT
Jamaica

24 July 2002

Mr FJ Dobson
Hills Cameras and Equipment Ltd
12 Marine Road
SPANISH TOWN

Dear Mr Dobson

I have been offered a position at Bellamy's Ltd and have agreed to begin work there on 1 September. I therefore wish to give you a month's notice that I shall be leaving my position as secretary to the Sales Manager, Mr Hargreaves, on 26 August.

I have already informed Mr Hargreaves of my intention to leave.

Yours sincerely

Janet Rogers (Mrs)

Fig. 16.11 Letter of resignation.

for a job as an engineer, provided she is qualified for the job; nor against a man who applies for a job as a secretary. Selection must be based on suitability for the job as set out in the personnel specification.

CAREER DEVELOPMENT

Some people think that they ought to progress up the promotion ladder by right of years of service. However, there is only one way to climb the promotion ladder and that is by hard work. This means taking every opportunity to learn, even if it is not immediately relevant to the job you are doing. If you are asked to do something beyond your job, grab the opportunity. Always ask if you are not sure how to do something. Always keep promises and explain the reason if you are not able to do so.

Also remember that we have to work with other people. Consideration is the key. Consider them and they will consider you. This is what makes for good team work.

Remember that 'Success is a journey, not a destination'; may your journey through your working life be a successful one.

PRACTICE QUESTIONS

1. Name four sources of information on jobs available. Explain how you would use them.

2. **a.** Reply to the following advertisement, which appeared in your local newspaper.

   > ADMINISTRATIVE ASSISTANT for Chief Accountant's office. Write for application form and further information to:
   >
   > Mrs Janet Wimpey, Personnel Officer, National Trading Company Limited Kingston

   b. Write a letter to a person whose name you would like to give as a referee, asking their permission to do so.

3. **a.** Reply to the following advertisement, which appeared in your local newspaper.

   > RECEPTIONIST for large trading company in Port-of-Spain. New office. Good conditions of service. Applications in writing with curriculum vitae to:
   >
   > James Muhammed, Office Services Manager, Caribbean Traders Limited, 68 High Street, Port-of-Spain

   b. What is meant by 'conditions of service'?

4. You have been invited to attend an interview for a post as a general clerk. You have no information about the post or the organisation. Make a checklist of points you will expect to be told or will ask at the interview.

5. You have received a letter offering you the post of senior typist at Gay Fabrics Limited, PO Box 478, Georgetown, Guyana. All details are given in the letter. Write a letter accepting the offer and stating the date on which you will be available to start work.

6. You are employed as a word processor operator at Kingston Traders Limited. You have applied for and been offered a post as a junior secretary at Jamaica Breweries Limited. The salary is considerably higher than that which you are now earning and the job will offer you greater scope for development. Write a letter to your personnel officer resigning your present post.

7. You attended an interview yesterday and were offered the job of junior secretary. You have decided to reject the offer as you think it is very similar

to the job you are doing at present; it would not, therefore, offer you the challenge you seek. Write a letter to Miss Jenny Price, the Recruitment Officer at Perfumes Limited, PO Box 489, Bridgetown, Barbados, rejecting the offer.

8. You have applied for a post as receptionist/typist and have been invited for interview.
   a. How would you prepare for the interview?
   b. How would you dress for the interview?
   c. How would you try to show the interviewer that you should be considered for the job?

9. What do you understand by the terms:
   i. induction
   ii. appraisal?

10. What would you expect to be told on your first day in a new job?

APPENDIX 1

COMMON GRAMMATICAL ERRORS

The errors set out below are commonly found in business documents. Study the errors and always check your letters for grammatical accuracy.

1. **Subject/verb agreement** – Singular nouns always take a singular verb. A few words cause problems, e.g. number, a lot of. For example:
   - There is a large number of people at the meeting.
   - There is a lot of things to do.
   - There are lots of things to do.

2. **Collective nouns** – Words such as 'association', 'company', 'department', 'government' may be used either in the singular or the plural. If you refer to the committee as a group of people it is singular. If you refer to something done by all the members as individuals it is used in the plural. For example:
   - The committee has come to a conclusion.
   - The committee have taken part in the survey (i.e. the committee members have taken part individually).

3. **Adjectives and adverbs** – An adjective qualifies (or describes) a noun, an adverb modifies a verb. For example:
   - The letter looked attractive. 'Attractive' is an adjective describing 'letter'.
   - The letter was displayed attractively. (Attractively is an adverb qualifying the verb 'was displayed'.)

4. **Me/myself** – 'Me' is an objective pronoun, 'myself' is a reflexive subject pronoun. For example:
   - 'Give it to me.' } not 'myself'
   - 'Please send your reply to me.'
   - I will go myself (meaning that I shall not send anyone in my place).

5. **I/me** – 'I' is a subject pronoun, 'me' an object pronoun. For example:
    - He and I will go.
    - Give it to him and me.
6. **Possessive pronoun with the -ing part of a verb**, e.g. 'coming' – use my/your/his/her/our/their, not me/you/he, etc. For example:
    - He will be pleased to hear of my coming.
    - Our leaving will make things difficult.
    - Your knocking on the wall deafens us.
7. **It's and its** – It's is short for 'it is'; its is the possessive pronoun. For example:
    - It's going to be a fine day.
    - Its cover is coming off.
8. **Placing of full stop with quotation marks/brackets** – If the complete sentence is inside quotation marks or brackets the full stop is placed inside the closing quotation mark or bracket. If the sentence within the quotation marks or brackets is not complete the full stop is placed after the closing quotation mark or bracket. For example:
    - 'The manager has taken disciplinary action.'
    - He said 'the manager has taken disciplinary action'.
    - I cannot discuss the matter now. (There are difficulties to be overcome first.)
    - Decisions will be taken later (depending on the outcome of a review).
9. **Due to/owing to/because of** – 'Due to' indicates the cause of a result and should not be used at the beginning of a sentence. The word 'due' is an adjective, even when followed by 'to', and so 'due to' must qualify a noun. For example:
    - It was impossible for me to get there due to the weather. Incorrect. ('It was impossible for me to get there' is not a noun-phrase.)
10. **Either/any** – 'Either' is used for two, 'any' for three or more. For example:
    - You may send either a letter or a fax.
    - You may send any of those documents by fax.
11. **Either/or, neither/nor** – Either/or are positive, neither/nor are negative. For example:
    - I shall send the parcel either today or tomorrow.
    - I have neither money nor materials to do the job.
12. **Like/as** – 'Like' is often used incorrectly in place of 'as'. 'Like' (and 'unlike') are adjectives that can also be used as prepositions. 'As' is a conjunction. For example:
    - It was, like I said, an impossible situation.   Incorrect.
    - It was, as I said, an impossible situation.   Correct.
    - You are not wearing uniform unlike I do.   Incorrect.

- You are not wearing uniform unlike me.   Correct.
13. **Till/until** – At the beginning of a sentence 'until' is preferable.
14. **Try to** – 'Try and' is frequently used with another verb but is incorrect because it is impossible 'to try' and also do something else at the same time. For example:
    - I shall try and come tomorrow.   Incorrect.
    - I shall try to come tomorrow.   Correct.
15. **Who/whom/whose** – These are interrogative pronouns. 'Who' is a subject pronoun, 'whom' an object pronoun and 'whose' a possessive pronoun. For example:
    - Who wrote this letter?
    - Whom did you see?
    - Whose book is this?
16. **Shall** and **will** are used to:
    - indicate future action; for example:
      - I/we shall do some painting this evening.
      - You will think it difficult until you read the instructions.
      - He/she/they will arrange for them to be collected.
    - indicate willingness, strong intention or determination; for example:
      - I will call on my way home.   (willingness)
      - We will get you home tonight.   (determination)
      - You shall finish that before you go.   (compulsion)
      - He shall have a bicycle for his birthday.   (determination, promise)
17. **Should** is used:
    - to express uncertainty when used in the first person; for example:
      - I should be pleased if you would/could see me today. (I should ... is conditional on something else happening.)
      - I should like a drink. (Implies if I may have one/if there is one.)
    - in the second and third person to indicate 'ought to'; for example:
      - You should see the new houses.
      - They should laugh when I tell a joke.
18. **Would** is used to express:
    - uncertainty when used in the second and third person; for example:
      - You would go if you knew how much she wants to see you.
      - He/she/they would want to have a new house if he/she/they knew how much easier it would be to maintain.
    - willingness or desire when used in the first person; for example:
      - I would see you tomorrow but I have to go to London. (I would be willing if I were able.)
      - I would like a new dress but I cannot afford it.

19. **Could** is used in place of 'would be able to' and so is conditional. For example:
    - I could do it if you gave me sufficient time.
    - You could do it but you do not try. (You could do it if you tried.)
20. **Double negative** – Two negatives make a positive. For example:
    - I did not find no errors.   Incorrect   (I did find some errors).
    - I did not find any errors   *or*
    - I found no errors.   Correct.

APPENDIX 2

TIPS ON PUNCTUATION

A **full stop** is always used at the end of a sentence.

A full stop is *not* used:

1.	after an ordinal ending	1st January, 2nd March, 3rd April
2.	in correspondence, when open punctuation is used, i.e. not above or below the body of a letter	
3.	with $ or c	$12 20c
4.	with metric symbols	3 m 125 mm
5.	in a postcode or zipcode	
6.	after Roman numerals	Charles I Form VI Chapter X i ix
7.	after items in a list	The following were elected: Mr David Abbott Miss Mary Geraghty Ms Angela Brown
8.	with 24-hour-clock times	0800–1215

A **comma** is sometimes *essential*; at other times it is optional, rather a matter of personal choice. The modern tendency is only to use commas when they are essential. A comma indicates a pause – if you have to pause to make sense, put a comma at that point. There are, however, certain rules. A comma is used as follows.

1. To separate a list of nouns or adjectives in a sentence but is not used between the last two items if they are linked by the word 'and' or 'or', for example:
   - We have supplies of pens, pencils, biros, crayons.
   - We bought tea, coffee and sugar.
2. Before and after a word/phrase, which is in apposition:
   - The Managing Director, Mr Henry Smith, is abroad.

3. Sometimes, to mark millions and thousands in figures, but these days a space is usually left instead of a comma:
   - 10 600 000 or 10,600,000
   - £98 426.75 or £98,426.75.
4. To separate the two parts when the subject changes within the sentence:
   - The Secretary having read the minutes, the Chairman asked the meeting to accept them as a true and correct record.
5. After 'However', 'Therefore', 'Nevertheless', 'Moreover', 'Indeed', 'Furthermore', at the beginning of a sentence. Commas are placed before and after these words in the middle of a sentence:
   - However, we shall be pleased to send you samples.
   - We shall, however, be pleased to send you samples.
6. To avoid ambiguity:
   - There were bright green curtains in the window. (Colour 'bright green'.)
   - There were bright, green curtains in the window. (The curtains were 'bright' and colour 'green'.)
7. Between adjectives that independently modify a noun:
   - A young, attractive girl entered the room.

Additional information or explanation within a sentence can be enclosed between commas, dashes or brackets. For example:

- His shops, particularly those in city centres, are doing well.
- The directors – all four of them – are middle-aged men.
- The senior staff (almost all men) feel strongly about the rule.

A **semi-colon** is a strong 'slow down' signal, stronger than a comma but not as strong as a full stop. The semi-colon is used:

1. to separate two obviously related clauses in a sentence when the second clause is
   - a conclusion or inference to be drawn from the first, *or*
   - an opposing statement to the first, *or*
   - a qualifying statement beginning with such words as still, otherwise, nevertheless, yet, however, therefore, so, but, *or*
   - an alternative statement.
2. when such items as names and addresses, goods and their prices, persons and their offices, are set out in continuous prose instead of being presented in list form
3. in itemised points, each of which forms a complete sentence.

The **colon** is used:

1. as a mark of introduction; for example, it can introduce a list, a quotation or a summary within a sentence:
   - The course consists of: shorthand, typewriting, English and accounts.

2. to introduce a list or an extract, with or without a hyphen.

A **question mark** is used at the end of a sentence that asks a question. This takes the place of the full stop.

- What is your name?
- Where do you live?
- How old are you?

Note that when the question is put into indirect speech, no question mark is used, e.g. 'He asked me what my name was.'

Note the use of the question mark in the following sentences:

- Who is to make the decision – the sales manager? The advertising manager? The production manager?
- You will finish the report tomorrow, will you not?

A **hyphen** is used in the following instances:

1. in compound words (note that many words that were once hyphenated are now accepted without, e.g. today, tonight, proofreading)
2. at the end of a line to indicate that the word has been divided
3. in compound numbers from twenty-one to ninety-nine when typed in words, and to separate the numerator from the denominator in fractions, e.g. two-thirds
4. to distinguish between words such as recreation and re-creation, recover and re-cover, reform and re-form, recount and re-count, remark and re-mark – for example, 'His remark about having to re-mark all the scripts was not strictly true'
5. in compound titles containing 'ex' 'vice' and 'elect' – for example, 'He is the ex-President of the USA'
6. when a series of hyphenated adjectives has a common basic element that is omitted in all but the last adjective – for example, 'The teams have a 4-, 5- and 8-goal average'.

Note that there are no spaces before or after a hyphen.

A **dash** is longer than the hyphen and used:

1. to represent a form of parenthesis or apposition, giving greater emphasis than if commas or brackets had been used – for example, 'Almost all candidates – 95.2 per cent – passed the examination'
2. to add a thought at the end of a sentence – for example, 'They have offered me a rise – far more than I expected'
3. to represent 'to' as in Trinidad–Tobago, e.g. in 'Trinidad–Tobago flight'.

Note that when typing or keying in, a space is left before and after the dash. In printing, the dash is shown as a long line, usually an 'en' line (The girl – who had blue-grey eyes – has disappeared) or, sometimes, an 'em' line (The girl—who had blue-grey eyes—has disappeared); note that no spaces are used with the latter.

An **apostrophe** usually denotes possession. To find out whether a word is possessive, change the order to include the word 'of', e.g. The man's house – The house of the man. If you can do this, it is possessive.

The apostrophe is used:

1. for a plural or singular word that does not end in 's' or a singular word that ends in 's' – add the apostrophe **and** 's' – for example, the duchess's hat, the girl's dress and the women's shoes were all new
2. for a plural word that ends in 's' – add the apostrophe only – for example, the clerks' returns were late this week
3. to indicate that a letter or letters have been left out – for example,
   - Don't answer the question.
   - Let's have a celebration.
   (note that this form should be used only in speech and informal communications)
4. in expressions of time and distance – for example, the secretary has taken a week's holiday

Note that the apostrophe is used for It's = 'it is' but *not* for the possessive:

- It's not unusual for its engine to stop.
- Its cover is torn.

Inverted commas are used:

1. to indicate quotations – for example, the report concluded: 'There is no justification for spending a million pounds on equipment.'
2. for direct speech – for example, he said 'There is no justification for drug abuse.'
3. for titles – for example, 'The Times', 'The Alpine Murder' by Jason Sand.

Note that in the case of point 3 above, italic text is more usually employed (instead of inverted commas) where this facility is available.

APPENDIX 3

PART 1 COUNTRIES IN THE CARIBBEAN, THEIR CAPITALS, OFFICIAL LANGUAGES AND CURRENCIES

Country	Capital	Official language	Currency
EASTERN CARIBBEAN			
Anguilla	The Valley	English	EC Dollar*
Antigua and Barbuda	St John's	English	EC Dollar*
Bahamas, The	Nassau	English	Bahamian and US Dollar
Barbados	Bridgetown	English	Barbados Dollar
Belize	Belize	English	Belize Dollar
Cuba	Havana	Spanish	Cuban Dollar
Dominica	Rousseau	English	EC Dollar*
Grand Cayman and Cayman Brac	George Town	English	Cayman Dollar
Grenada	St George's	English	EC Dollar*
Guyana	Georgetown	English	Guyana Dollar
Jamaica	Kingston	English	Jamaica Dollar
Montserrat	Plymouth	English	EC Dollar*
Nevis	Charlestown	English	EC Dollar*
St Kitts	Basseterre	English	EC Dollar*
St Lucia	Castries	English	EC Dollar*
St Vincent and The Grenadines	Kingstown	English	EC Dollar*

Country	Capital	Official language	Currency
Surinam	Paramaribo	Surinam-Tongo/ English	Surinam Guilder
Trinidad and Tobago	Port-of-Spain	English	T & T Dollar
Turks and Caicos	Cockburn	English	Jamaica Dollar

NETHERLANDS ANTILLES

Country	Capital	Official language	Currency
Aruba	Oranjestad	English/Dutch	Antillean Guilder
Bonaire	Kralenoijk	English/Dutch	Antillean Guilder
Curaçao	Willemstad	English/Dutch	Antillean Guilder
Guadeloupe	Pointe à Pitre	French	Euro
Martinique	Fort-de-France	French	Euro
Saba	The Bottom	English/Dutch	Antillean Guilder
St Eustatius	Oranjestad	English/Dutch	Antillean Guilder
St Maarten	Philipsburg	English/Dutch	Antillean Guilder
St Martin	Marigot	English/French	Euro and US Dollar

VIRGIN ISLANDS

Country	Capital	Official language	Currency
St Croix	Frederikstad	English	US Dollar
St Thomas	Charlotte Amalie	English	US Dollar

* Eastern Caribbean Dollar

PART 2 COUNTRIES OF THE COMMONWEALTH

Antigua and Barbuda
Australia
Bahamas
Bangladesh
Barbados
Belize
Botswana
Brunei Darussalam
Cameroon
Canada
Cyprus
Dominica
Fiji Islands
The Gambia
Ghana
Great Britain
Grenada
Guyana
India
Jamaica
Kenya
Kiribati
Lesotho
Malawi
Malaysia
Maldives
Malta
Mauritius
Mozambique
Namibia
Nauru
New Zealand
Nigeria
Pakistan
Papua New Guinea
St Kitts and Nevis
St Lucia
St Vincent and the Grenadines
Seychelles
Sierra Leone
Singapore
Solomon Islands
South Africa
Sri Lanka
Swaziland
Tanzania
Tonga
Trinidad and Tobago
Tuvalu
Uganda
Vanuatu
Western Samoa
Zambia
Zimbabwe

APPENDIX 4

PART 1 CARIBBEAN ASSOCIATION OF INDUSTRY AND COMMERCE MEMBERSHIP LISTING

Antigua and Barbuda Chamber of Industry and Commerce Ltd
7 Redcliffe Street
PO Box 774
St John's
Antigua
President: Mr Clarvis Joseph
Exec. Dir.: Mrs Holly Peters
Tel: 268-462-0743
Fax: 268-462-4575

Bahamas Chamber of Commerce
PO Box N-655
Nassau N P
The Bahamas
President: Mr Bismark Coakley
Exec. Dir.: Ms Ruby L Sweeting CCE
Tel: 242-322-2145
Fax: 242-322-4649

Barbados Chamber of Commerce and Industry
1st Floor Nemwil House
Collymore Rock
St Michael

Barbados
President: Mr John Williams
Exec. Dir.: Mr Rolph OW Jordan
Tel: 246-426-2056
Fax: 246-429-2907
E-mail: bdscham@caribsurf.com

Belize Chamber of Commerce and Industry
63 Regent Street
PO Box 291
Belize City
Belize
President: Mr Roger Taylor
Exec. Dir.: Mr Kevin Herrera
Tel: 501-2-73148/70014
Fax: 501-2-74984
E-mail: bcciwu@bt1.net

BVI Hotel & Commerce Association
James Frett Building
Wickham's Cay 1
Roadtown
Tortola
British Virgin Islands
President: Mr Kedrick Malone
Exec. Dir.: Ms Nadine Battle
Tel: 284-494-3514
Fax: 284-494-6179
E-mail: bvihca@caribsurf.com

Cámara de Comercio de la República de Cuba
21 Street A
Vivado
Havana
Cuba
President: Lic. Antonio Carricarte Corona
Sec. Gen.: Sra. Martha Camacho
Tel: 537-303-356
Fax: 537-333-042
E-mail: camara.cenia@inf.cu

Dominica Association of Industry and Commerce
PO Box 85

Fields Lane/All Street
Roseau
Dominica
President: Mr A Burnett Biscombe
Tel: 767-448-2874
Fax: 767-448-6868
E-mail: daic@marpin.dm

Santo Domingo Chamber of Commerce
Arzobispo Nouel 206
Santo Domingo
Dominican Republic
President: St Jose Manuel Armenteros
Sec. Gen.: Sra Milagros Puello
Tel: 809-688-9073
Fax: 809-685-2228
E-mail: camara.sto.dgo@codetel.net.do

Grenada Chamber of Industry and Commerce
PO Box 129
Deco Building, Mt Gay
St George's
Grenada
President: Mr Christopher De Allie
Exec. Dir.: Mr Christopher De Riggs
Tel: 473-440-2937
Fax: 473-440-6627
E-mail: gcic@caribsurf.com

Chambre de Commerce de Point-à-Pitre
BP 64
97152 Pointe-à-Pitre
Guadeloupe
President: Mr Felix Clairville
Sec. Gen.: Mr Claudy Alie
Tel: 590-250-611
Fax: 590-250-606
E-mail: alie@netgua.com.fr

Berbice Chamber of Commerce and Development Association
17–18 Strand
PO Box 18
New Amsterdam

Berbice
Guyana
President: Mr Ramesh Maraj
Tel: 592-3-3324
Fax: 592-3-3597

Georgetown Chamber of Commerce and Industry Inc.
156 Waterloo Street
PO Box 10110
Georgetown
Guyana
President: Mr Maniram Prashad
Exec. Dir.: Mrs Joanie Ousman
Tel: 592-2-55846
Fax: 592-2-63519

Guyana Manufacturers' Association
157 Waterloo Street
Georgetown
Guyana
President: Mr Ronald Webster
Exec. Dir.: Mr Inge Nathoo
Tel: 592-2-74295
Fax: 592-2-55615
E-mail: gma@sdnp.org.gy

Chambre de Commerce et d'Industrie d'Haiti
BP 982
Boulevard Harry Truman
Port-au-Prince
Haiti
President: Mr Maurice La Fortune
Tel: 509-222-0281
Fax: 509-257-0454
E-mail: ccih@compa.net

Jamaica Chamber of Commerce and Industry
7–8 East Parade
Kingston
Jamaica
President: Mr Anthony Chang
Exec. Dir.: Mrs Marcia Bryan
Tel: 876-922-0150
Fax: 876-924-9056
E-mail: jamcham@cwjamaica.com

Montserrat Chamber of Commerce
PO Box 247
Plymouth
Montserrat
President: Mr Bruce Farara
Tel: 664-491-2402
Fax: 664-491-6602

Curaçao Chamber of Industry and Commerce
Kaya Junior Salas No 1
PO Box 10
Curaçao
Netherlands Antilles
President: Mr Herman Behr
Exec. Dir.: Mr Paul R J Comenencia
Tel: 5999-4-611451
Fax: 5999-4-615652
E-mail: management@curacao-chamber.an

St Maarten Chamber of Commerce and Industry
CA Cannegieter Street #11
PO Box 454
Philipsburg
St Maarten
Netherlands Antilles
Exec. Dir.: Dr Joan Arrindell-Van Windt
Tel: 5995-4-23590
Fax: 5995-4-23512

Puerto Rico Manufacturers' Association
Ave. Ponce de León 420
Aptdo. 195477
Hato Rey, PR 00918
San Juan
Puerto Rico 00919-5477
President: Mr William Riefkhol
Tel: 787-759-9445
Fax: 787-756-7670
E-mail: prma@i-lan.com

St Kitts and Nevis Chamber of Commerce
PO Box 332
West Independence Square Street
Basseterre

St Kitts and Nevis
President: Mr Michael Morton
Exec. Dir.: Mrs Wendy Phipps
Tel: 869-465-2980
Fax: 869-465-4490

St Lucia Chamber of Commerce, Industry and Agriculture
PO Box 482
Vide Bouteille
Castries
St Lucia
President: Mr Guy Mayers
Exec. Dir.: Mr Brian Louisy
Tel: 758-452-3165
Fax: 758-453-6907
E-mail: chamber@candw.lc

St Vincent and the Grenadines Chamber of Industry and Commerce
PO Box 134
3rd Floor, Corea's Building
Hillsboro Street
Kingstown
St Vincent and The Grenadines
President: Mr Jeffrey Providence
Exec. Dir.: Mr Leroy Rose
Tel: 784-457-1464
Fax: 784-456-2944
E-mail: svgcic@caribsurf.com

The South Trinidad Chamber of Industry and Commerce Inc.
Suite 313, Cross Crossing Shopping Centre
San Fernando
Trinidad
President: Mr Brian Samlalsingh
Exec. Dir.: Mr Melvin Charles
Tel: 868-657-9077
Fax: 868-652-5613
E-mail: secretariat@southchamber.com

Trinidad and Tobago Chamber of Industry and Commerce Inc.
PO Box 499
Columbus Circle
Westmoorings

Trinidad
President: Mr Raoul John
Exec. Dir.: Ms Joan Ferreira
Tel: 868-637-6966
Fax: 868-637-7425
E-mail: ttcic@trinidad.net

Trinidad and Tobago Manufacturers' Association
122–124 Frederick Street
Port-of-Spain
Trinidad
President: Mr Stuart Dagleish
Exec. Dir.: Mr Anthony Guiseppi
Tel: 868-623-1029
Fax: 868-623-1031
E-mail: ttmagm@opus.co.tt

PART 2 CARIBBEAN CONGRESS OF LABOUR TRADES UNIONS MAILING LIST

Antigua and Barbuda Workers Union
PO Box 940
St John's
Antigua
President: Maurice Christian
Gen. Sec.: Keithlyn Smith
Tel: 1-268-462-0442, 1-268-462-2005
Fax: 1-268-462-5220
E-mail: awu@candw.ag

Antigua and Barbuda
Public Service Association
PO Box 1285
St John's
Antigua
President: James Spencer
Tel: 1-268-461-5821, 1-268-463-6247
Fax: 1-268-461-5821
E-mail: abpsa@candw.ag

Antigua Trades and Labour Union
Emancipation House
PO Box 3
46 North St
St John's
Antigua
President: Wigley George
Gen. Sec.: David Jonas
Tel: 1-268-462-0090
Fax: 1-268-462-4056
E-mail: atandlu@candw.ag

Commonwealth of the Bahamas TU Congress
PO Box CB10992

Congress House
Farrington Rd
Nassau
Bahamas
President: Obie Ferguson Jr
Gen. Sec.: Timothy Moore
Tel: 1-242-394-7400
Fax: 1-242-394-7401

National Congress of Trade Unions
PO Box GT 2887
Nassau
Bahamas
President: Duke Hanna
Gen. Sec.: Kingsley Black
Tel: 1-242-356-7459
Fax: 1-242-356-7457

Barbados Workers Union
Solidarity House
Harmony Hall
St Michael
Barbados
President: Hugh Arthur
Gen. Sec.: LeRoy Trotman
Tel: 1-246-426-3495/6/7, Gen. Sec.: 1-246-436-6079
Fax: 1-246-436-6496
E-mail: bwu@caribsurf.com

Barbados Union of Teachers
Merryhill
PO Box 58
Welches
St Michael
Barbados
President: Undene Whittaker
Gen. Sec.: Herbert Gittens
Tel: 1-246-436-6139, 1-246-427-8510
Fax: 1-246-426-9890
E-mail: but@caribsurf.com

National Union of Public Workers
PO Box 174

Dalkeith Rd
St Michael
Barbados
President: Cecil Drakes
Gen. Sec.: Joseph Goddard
Tel: 1-246-426-4971/0422/1764
Fax: 1-246-436-1795
E-mail: nupwbarbados@sunbeach.net

National Trade Union
Congress of Belize
PO Box 2359
Belize City
Belize
President: Edwardo Melendez
Gen. Sec.: Antonio Gonzalez
Tel: 011-501-271596
Fax: 011-501-272864
E-mail: ntucb@btl.net

Bermuda Public Service Association
#2 Angle St
PO Box HM 763
Hamilton
Bermuda HM 10
President: Betty Christopher
Gen. Sec.: Edward Ball
Tel: 1-441-292-6985, 1-441-292-6484
Fax: 1-441-292-1149
E-mail: beepsa@ibl.bm

Central Trade Unions of Curaçao
Schouwburgweg 44
PO Box 3036
Willemstad
Curaçao
President: Pablo Cova
Gen. Sec.: Wilfred Spencer
Tel: 011-5999-737-0255, 011-5999-736-5059
Fax: 011-5999-737-5250

Dominica Amalgamated Workers Union
PO Box 0137
Rousseau

Commonwealth of Dominica
Gen. Sec.: Fedeline Moulon
Tel: 767-448-3048, 767-448-3626

Dominica Public Service Union
Valley Rd
Windsor Lane
Rousseau
Commonwealth of Dominica
President: Sonia Williams
Gen. Sec.: Thomas Letang
Tel: 1-767-448-2101/2
Fax: 1-767-448-8060
E-mail: dcs@cwdom.dm

Dominica Trade Union
70–71 Queen Mary St
Rousseau
Commonwealth of Dominica
President: Kennedy Pascal
Gen. Sec.: Leo B Nicholas
Tel: 1-767-449-8139
Fax: 1-767-449-9060

Waterfront and Allied Workers Union
Hillsborough St
PO Box 181
Rousseau
Commonwealth of Dominica
President: Kertist Augustus
Tel: 1-767-448-2343, 1-767-448-2497
Fax: 1-767-448-0086
E-mail: wawu@cwdom.dm

Grenada Trade Union Council
PO Box 411
St George's
Grenada
President: Derek Allard
Gen. Sec.: Ray Roberts
Tel: 1-473-440-3733
Fax: 1-473-440-3733
E-mail: gtuc@caribsurf.com

Guyana Trades Union Congress
Critchlow Labour College Complex
Non Pariel Park
Georgetown
Guyana
President: Carvil Duncan
Gen. Sec.: Lincoln Lewis
Tel: 011-5922-261493/259099/268968/261146
Fax: 011-5922-270254

Jamaica Confederation of Trade Unions
1A Hope Boulevard
Kingston 6
Jamaica
President: Hugh Shearer
Gen. Sec.: Lloyd Goodleigh
Tel: 1-876-927-2468
Fax: 1-876-977-4575
E-mail: jctu@cwjamaica.com

Montserrat Allied Workers Union
Plymouth
Montserrat
President: Charles Ryan
Gen. Sec.: Hylroy Bramble
Tel: 1-664-491-5049
Fax: 1-664-491-3599, 1-664-491-2264
E-mail: bramblehl@candw.ag

Caribbean Congress of Labour
PO Box 651
Port-of-Spain
Trinidad
Exec. Dir.: Mr George De Paena

APPENDIX 5

ANSWERS TO ACTIVITIES

Activity 1.1
2. production
3. production
4. finance
5. administration
6. personnel
7. marketing
8. marketing
9. production
10. marketing

Activity 1.2
1. administration or any department
2. production
3. transport
4. public relations
5. personnel
6. production (stores or warehouse)
7. accounts
8. production (stores or warehouse)
9. sales
10. legal

Activity 1.3

```
                          President
                              |
                        Vice-President
                              |
   ┌──────────┬──────────┬────┴─────┬──────────────┬────────────────┐
  Chief     Marketing  Production  Information    Personnel and
Accountant   Manager    Manager    Processing       Training
                                    Manager         Manager
   |           |           |           |         ┌─────┴─────┐
 Credit      Public    Research &    Systems   Recruitment  Trainning
 Control    Relations  Development   Analyst     Officer     Officer
  Clerk      Officer   Supervisor
```

Activity 2.1

Here is an example, taking stapling as the task to be followed.

1. Identify document to be stapled
2. Obtain stapler and staples
3. Take set of sheets to be stapled
4. Check sheets are right way up and page numbers are consecutive
5. 'Knock up' pack, i.e. align pages
6. Insert pack into stapler so that staple will be vertical down the top left-hand side of the paper
7. Depress stapling arm
8. Remove document from stapler
9. Check that staple is properly inserted

If you have chosen another task, check your procedure by doing the task for yourself to ensure that you have not missed any steps.

Activity 2.2

Disadvantages of cellular offices are as follows.

1. Expensive as more space is used for each individual
2. Some people do not like working on their own
3. Difficult and expensive to redesign the offices if the walls are brick-built
4. In a very large building, some offices are in the centre so that they do not get any natural light
5. Additional equipment may be needed to provide individuals with copiers, fax machines, printers, filing cabinets; if the individuals have to go to central machines and filing cabinets, etc., they will spend more time away from their desks

Disadvantages of open-plan offices are as follows.
1. Many people find it difficult to concentrate with noise and movement around them
2. It is difficult to discuss confidential matters because of lack of privacy
3. Not everyone likes the same levels of heating, ventilation and lighting
4. Air conditioning is often a circulating system with inadequate filtering, which means that germs are easily passed to everyone
5. Being near colleagues can create a temptation to chat too much

Disadvantages of landscaped offices are as follows.
1. Almost the same as for open-plan offices, except that some privacy is provided by plants and screens

Activity 2.3

Examples may include the following.

Knowledge
1. The correct way to address people in different relationships, e.g. work, personal friendship, new contacts
2. What upsets people, e.g. emotive words, casual attitude
3. How to help people without being patronising

Skills
4. Communication, especially attentive listening
5. Clear speech
6. Helpful without being interfering
7. Ability not to be intimidated by people's status

Personal qualities
8. Tactful, diplomatic, discreet
9. Considerate
10. Helpful
11. Sympathetic
12. Empathetic
13. Understanding
14. Tolerant
15. Persuasive

Activity 3.1

Action	By
1. Investigate existing methods of preparing project plans	Systems analyst
2. Find out from head of research & development what the computerised system is intended to achieve	Systems analyst

3. Feasibility study to check cost-effectiveness and viability	Systems analyst
4. Design the new system (assuming results of feasibility study are positive)	Systems designer
5. Write the program, and design the database and security features	Programmer
6. Test the program	Programmer
7. Prepare any forms needed	Systems analyst
8. Install the system and test in parallel with existing manual system, i.e. run both manual and computer systems until the computer system is proved to be acceptable	Systems designer and systems analyst

Activity 4.1

		VISITORS' REGISTER			
Date	Name of visitor	Name and address of organisation	Referred to	Time in	Time out
*	Miss K Cassandra	Gentian Publishing Co. Ltd, 18 Buckingham Road, Oxford OX2 5PU England	James Casson Purchasing	0950	
	Mrs V de la Cour	Labour and Co-operatives PO Box 456 POS T&T	Standards mtg	1050	
	Mrs M Kinley	Ace Stationers Ltd 48 Main Street POS T&T	Paul Jones Sales	1055	
	Jamil Passmore	46 High Rise San Fernando T&T	Standards mtg	1055	
	F R Jameson Fmgt	Overseas Promotions 63 Victoria Street Chichester Essex England	Victoria Payne Marketing	1110	
	George Badsey	Personnel Computers Limited 15 Beach Road POS T&T	Emily Peters Personnel	1115	

* Insert today's date

Activity 4.2

This activity is best discussed in small groups. The telephone calls listed will depend on which territory you are in. The people who might use each type of call depends on the size and type of organisation. Did you consider all sizes of business, from sole trader to multinational company?

Activity 4.3

```
                                          URGENT : (YES)/NO

   Message for:    Miss Jane Little
   Time:     10.30 am        Date :   17.2.02

                     WHEN YOU WERE OUT

   Mr    John Downs

   Of:    Computers Incorporated

   Telephone:    (local code) 620451

   Address:


   Message:
        Would you be able and willing to give a presentation to Mr Downs' staff on developments in sea
        navigation computers? The ideal time would be on Tuesday or Wednesday of the second or
        third week of next month.
        Mr Downs would like to hear from you tomorrow if possible please.


   Taken by:       (Your signature)
```

Activity 4.4

'You have reached the voicemail of [your name]. It is [day and date]. I am sorry that I cannot take your call at present. I am in the office today so please leave your name and telephone number, and I will return your call as soon as I am free.'

Or

'You have reached the voicemail of [your name]. It is [day and date]. I am sorry that I am out of the office today. Please leave your name and telephone number, and I will return your call tomorrow. If the matter is urgent please call [name of colleague] on [phone number].'

Or

'You have reached the voicemail of [your name]. I am away from the office until [date]. Please leave your name and telephone number, and a colleague will return your call. If the matter is urgent please call [name of colleague] on [phone number].'

Similar messages can be recorded on an answerphone.

Activity 4.5

What to wear simple clothes, e.g. skirt or tailored trousers (not jeans) and blouse, or dress
skirt not above the knee (you may have to bend down) and not below the calf (you could trip over it or catch your heel in the hem)
not too colourful
simple jewellery, e.g. watch, earrings
comfortable but smart shoes – heels not too high (for safety)

Personal presentation neat, shining, well-groomed hair with no fancy headbands or clips
clothes fresh and crisp
shoes clean
hands clean and nails manicured – avoid bright nail varnish
never wear chipped nail varnish
clear speech, not too fast
pleasant smile, look welcoming

Activity 5.1

1. a week
2. progress
3. weekly/monthly tests
4. weekly/monthly meetings
5. four days
6. three months
7. three (or any other precise number)
8. an amount of $00 (a precise amount)
9. between 4 and 5 per cent (or other number)
10. needed today/tomorrow

Activity 5.2

- some figures – what figures?
- the expenditure – what expenditure; all or specific types, e.g. capital expenditure?
- fitting out – fixtures and fittings? Furniture?
- perhaps we had better have a meeting – what about? When?

I need to know how much we have spent so far on fixtures and fittings in the offices in the new building. Will you please let me have the figures by the end of the week? I suggest we then have a meeting the following Monday to discuss them.

Activity 5.3

MEMORANDUM

To: Mrs Mary James, Training Manager   Date: (Today)

From: [Your name]

Subject: Career development

I would like to discuss with you my career development. In particular I need advice on an appropriate course of study.

May I have an appointment please?

Activity 5.4

[Your address]

[Date]

[Fictitious name]
Head of Business Studies
[Local college name and address]

Dear [name]

EVENING-CLASS COURSES IN SECRETARIAL SUBJECTS

I have recently obtained Pitman certificates in Shorthand, Typewriting and Book-keeping at Level 2 at the Stenotype College. I should now like to continue my studies at evening classes.

Will you please send me details of suitable evening-class courses available from next September?

Yours sincerely
[Your signature]

Activity 5.5

Registered letter

Dated ....

Addressed to ....

From ....

Received in mail room on ....

Received by addressee

Signature .... Date ....

Activity 5.6

[Friend's name] WILL ARRIVE THURSDAY [date] DRIVING FROM LONDON HEATHROW STOP EXPECT ARRIVE [time] STAY THREE DAYS [Your name]

Activity 5.7

Walking through the office last night, I was appalled to see the large amount of spoilt letter headings in the wastepaper baskets. In these times of financial difficulty you will, I am sure, realise the necessity for the greatest economy to be exercised in the use of all materials. With word processing there are no excuses for spoilt work. It is simply a matter of proofreading carefully before printing. To say that you have used spellcheck is not a valid excuse because you know that spellcheck does not pick up all errors.

I hope that I shall not have cause to write in this vein again.

Activity 5.8

Training Today, circulation 6000 companies (to named senior staff), increasing to 10 000.
Regionally targeted series of training journals.
In-depth feature reports on subjects of interest to training staff.
Regular contributions from training companies.
September – 'Training for Efficient Use of Information Technology'.
You submit relevant comments, case studies, articles.
Welcome opportunity for discussion.

Activity 6.1

There is no answer to this activity but it would be useful to check with a fellow student or colleague that you have identified the paper and envelope sizes correctly.

Activity 6.2

Facility	*Example use*
Right-hand margin justification	Leaflets
Interchangeable daisywheels	Italics for quotations
Bold type	Highlight headings
Multilingual characters	Documents in a foreign language
Standard letters	Routine acknowledgements
Shading	Highlight a specific area on a form
Very large print	Documents being sent to visually impaired customer(s)
Pagination	Automatically number the pages of a long report
Shoulder headings	Sub-headings in a report
Right flush	Documents containing columns of figures

Activity 6.3

If you have done this activity as a group it would be useful to check what other members of the group have done.

Activity 7.1
Caribbean Jewellery Co. Ltd
Castries City Council Traffic Dept
Computer Shop, The
Dalton, Dr A
8-hour Cleaning Service
Forde, Lady Margaret
Georgina Dress Shop
Health, Ministry of
Instant Copying Company
Jamaican Rum Company Limited
Le Motte, Peter
Lebrun, Mrs LM
Phelps, Dr Adrian
Port-of-Spain Trading Co. Ltd
Sahara Gift Shop
St Mary's Episcopal Church
Social Security, Department of
TEC Computer Software
Tree Felling Company
Wilkins, Miss Jane

Activity 7.2

Dando, Deirdre	D5		Hadley, Hamish	H3
Dark, Leo	D2		Hamilton, Lady M	H2
De la Tour, Victor	D3		Hawkes, Marilyn	H5
Deveril, Jeffrey	D6		Healey, David	H4
Drax, James	D4		Hendrie, Michael	H1
Driscoll, Peter	D1		Hope, Denise	H6

Activity 7.3

10 806	11 800	16 343
10 923	12 151	16 828
10 994	12 943	17 447
11 009	13 414	18 622
11 010	14 116	18 991
11 100	15 347	19 000

Activity 7.4

Support staff training	16.1
Supervisory training	16.2
Management development	16.4
Health and safety training	16.3
Graduate training	16.6
Apprentice training	16.5

Activity 7.5

OUT

SUBSTITUTION NOTE

On loan to :	Mildred Yates
Date :	31 May 2002
Document :	Report
Title :	'Design of New Water Pump'
Date :	February 2002
From :	Water Engineering Company Port-of-Spain Trinidad and Tobago

Activity 7.6

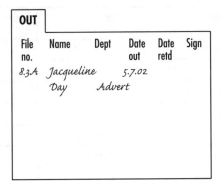

OUT					
File no.	Name	Dept	Date out	Date retd	Sign
8.3.A	Jacqueline Day	Advert	5.7.02		

OUT					
File no.	Name	Dept	Date out	Date retd	Sign
16.4	Doris Arkwright	Accts	8.7.02		

OUT					
File no.	Name	Dept	Date out	Date retd	Sign
38.2	Arthur Jansen	Sales	11.7.02		

OUT					
File no.	Name	Dept	Date out	Date retd	Sign
4.11	Gerald Graham	Engg	16.7.02		

Name	*Due for return*
Jacqueline Day	12.7.02
Doris Arkwright	15.7.02
Arthur Jansen	18.7.02
Gerald Graham	23.7.02

Activity 7.7

Files to archive:

- correspondence (semi-active last year)
- employee records (semi-active for 12 years)
- projects (semi-active for 3 years).

Files to semi-active:

- correspondence
- employee records (employees who left during year before last)
- completed projects.

Activity 8.1

Date received*	Date of letter**	Sender	Subject	Sent to	File no.	Remarks
		John Abraham	Complaint	Customer Services		
		Frederick Lara & Co.	Invoice – Consultancy	Accounts		
		Miss Candida Thompson	Request for vacancy	Personnel		
		Mrs Celeste Franks	Request for product inform	Sales		
		Caribbean Manufacturing Ltd	Catalogue	Purchasing		
		Gerald Barker	Statement of account	Accounts		
		Mr Tina Forde	Brochure – training	Personnel		
		J Tippett & Son	Samples	Purchasing		

* Insert today's date
** Calculate the date of each letter from the information given

Activity 9.1

It would be useful for students to check each others' findings here. The answers may vary from one territory to another so cannot be given here.

Activity 9.2

It would be useful to type up your list and keep it to hand.

Activity 10.1

> [Company name and address]
>
> [Date]
>
> [Name and address of stationery supplier]
>
> Dear Sirs
>
> **ENQUIRY**
>
> Will you please let me know whether you can supply the items listed below. If so, please give prices, delivery charge and delivery time from receipt of order.
>
> - 50 blue wallet folders
> - 10 reams 80 gsm white copy paper
> - 100 plastic slip files with white strip
> - 1 four-hole punch
>
> Yours faithfully
>
> [Your signature]
>
> [Your name printed]
> [Your position]

Activity 10.2

Ensure that you give all the details required to complete the order form.

Activity 10.3

Check the points to be included in the delivery note. No prices are given.

Activity 11.1

No. *001*.	**ANY BANK LIMITED** Any Town	10-10-10
[*Today*] 20 *02*		..[*Today*].... 20 *02* No .*001*
In favour of *Jacob Abraham*	Pay to the order of ...... *Jacob Abraham*	$.. *149–87*...
....	the sum of ..... *One hundred and forty nine / 87c* .... dollars	
....	A/C Payee only	.... [*your signature*] ....
$ *149–87*.	010101 987654321	

Activity 11.2

```
ANY BANK LIMITED
Any Town
            Date  ..[Today's]...      Cheques         Details      Cash incl. coin
         ┌──────────────┐         578 │ 43         67 × 1          67 │ 00
         │ Depositor's  │          60 │ 89          7 × 5          35 │ 00
         │ initials [Yours] │                         × 10
         └──────────────┘         1698│ 34         13 × 20        260 │ 00
         ┌──────────────┐          24 │ 70            ×100
         │ Teller's     │                           COIN            11 │ 00
         │ initials     │                           TOTAL          373 │ 00
         └──────────────┘                 2362│ 36  CHQS          2362 │ 36
Credit account of                                   SUB-
   The Blouse Shop                 Cash received    TOTAL         2735 │ 36
         ┌──────────────┐                           LESS
         │ Account no. 123654 │                     EXCH
         └──────────────┘         Signature         NET
                                                    TOTAL         2735 │ 36

         989878767
```

Activity 11.3

Balance – cash book			1261.77
Add cheques not paid	486	750.65	
	488	659.22	1409.87
			2671.64
Deduct payments not received			989.17
Balance – statement			$1682.47

Activity 12.1

THE P–O–S ENGINEERING COMPANY
ACCIDENT REPORT FORM

This form is to be completed for every accident that occurs within the company buildings or grounds. When completed send it to the personnel manager within 24 hours of the accident occurring.

Employee involved in accident

Surname ..... *JACKSON* ..... First name ..... *JOHN* ..... Title *MR*

Department ..... *Maintenance* ..... Employee reference *078*

Date of accident ..... *21.5.02* ..... Time ..... *1015* ..... Location ..... *DRY DOCK*

Was the accident reported immediately? ..... *No, not until Mr Jackson taken to hospital*

If so, who reported it? ..... *BEN LARA*

To whom was the accident reported? ..... *MANAGER*

Details of accident ..... *John Jackson was standing on a ladder propped against the vessel which he was painting. In reaching too far to the right he overbalanced and fell to the bottom of the dry dock.*

Nature of injury ..... *Broken leg*
Ben Lara decided it was best not to move Mr Jackson until the ambulance arrived.

Was first aid given? ..... *No* ..... How soon after the accident? .....

Who gave first aid? ..... Was s/he qualified? .....

Was injured person taken to hospital? ..... *Yes* ..... At what time? *Shortly after accident*

Witness (if any) name and address .....

Signature of person who completed this form ..... *[Your signature]*

Date *21.5.02*

Activity 12.2

CASH REQUISITION   Date 29 June 2002

Wages $	$100	$20	$10	$5	$1	25c	10c	5c	1c
3850.00	38	2	1						
3008.40	30			1	3		4		
3124.00	31	1			4				
3200.10	32						1		
3460.70	34	3				2	2		
3470.10	34	3	1				1		
TOTAL	199	9	2	1	7	2	8		

CASH SUMMARY

Notes	$100 × 199	$19900	–	
	20 × 9	180	–	
	10 × 2	20	–	
	5 × 1	5	–	
	1 × 7	7	–	
Coins	25C × 2	–	50	
	10C × 8	–	80	
	5C ×			
	1C ×			
TOTAL		$20113	30	

Compiled by: ....
                 Initials
Checked by: ....
                 Initials

Activity 12.3

	MORNING		AFTERNOON		HOURS	
CLOCK CARD Name: *RL Fook* Week ending: Employee no. *001*						
	In	Out	In	Out	Basic	Overtime
Monday	0800	1230	1330	1700	8.00	
Tuesday	0800	1230	1330	1700	8.00	
Wednesday	0800	1230	1330	1800	8.00	1.00
Thursday	0800	1230	1330	1730	8.00	0.30
Friday	0800	1230	1330	1700	8.00	
Saturday	0730	1300				5.30
Sunday	0830	1230				4.00
TOTAL					40.00	11.00

Basic time	40	hours @ $ 18.00	720.00
Overtime	7	hours @ $ 27.00	189.00
Overtime	4	hours @ $ 36.00	144.00
TOTAL			$1053.00

Activity 12.4

Lamp model number	Materials	Labour	Total	Overheads at 30 per cent	Total cost
	$	$	$	$	$
A 45609	45.00	105.00	150.00	45.00	195.00
A 47825	48.50	151.50	200.00	60.00	260.00
B 24581	58.90	81.10	140.00	42.00	182.00
B 24762	103.70	168.40	272.10	81.61	353.73
D 47079	29.35	48.15	77.50	23.25	100.75

Activity 12.5

Pens
Code: 14894
Unit: item

Maximum: 100
Re-order: 40
Minimum: 20

Date	Reqn no.	Issues	Department	Inv no.	Receipts	Balance
1.7.02						46
1.7.02	024	12	training			34
2.7.02	089	2	mail room			32
4.7.02	079	2	stock room			30
4.7.02	093	3	reception			27
5.7.02			received	047	60	87
5.7.02	088	50	sales			37

The closing balance is 37.

Re-order after the first and last transactions.

Activity 12.6
Here are some examples:
- dictionary
- refreshments for department
- meal when travelling
- special item, e.g. paper needed for a particular job
- special pens, markers, etc.

Activity 12.7

Date	Description	Amount		Date	Description	V no.	Amount	Travel	Staty	Books	Postage	Sundries
		$					$	$	$	$	$	$
01.08.02	Cash received	420.00		1.08.02	Taxi to printer	001	18.00	18.00				
				5.08.02	Paper clips	002	6.30		6.30			
				7.08.02	Reference book	003	8.20			8.20		
				14.08.02	Coffee, milk, sugar	004	14.00					14.00
				23.08.02	Parcel post	005	13.80				13.80	
				26.08.01	Glue, labels	006	27.50		27.50			
							87.80	18.00	33.80	8.20	13.80	14.00
		400.00		31.10.00	Balance		332.20					
							420.00					
31.08.02	Balance	87.80										
1.08.02	Cash received	332.20										

Activity 12.8

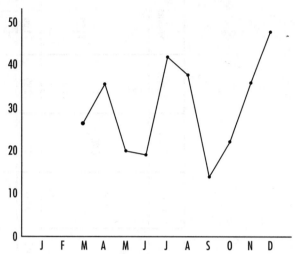

Activity 12.9

(a) You may wish to discuss your thoughts with your colleagues or tutor, if you have one.

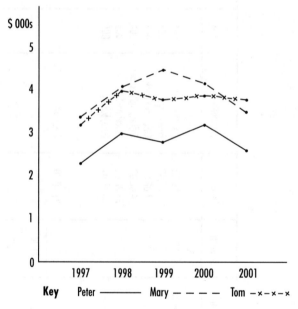

(b) You may wish to discuss your thoughts with your colleagues or tutor, if you have one.

Activity 12.10

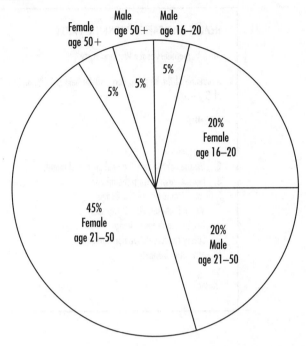

Activity 13.1

NAME	TUESDAY		THURSDAY		FRIDAY	
	am	pm	am	pm	am	pm
ADELE	X	1400-1600	0800-1100	1530-1700	X	1200-1630
GERALD	X	1330-1500	1000-1200	X	0830-1130	1400-1630
HAROLD	X	1430-1530	1100-1300	X	1000-1130	1330-1530
JASMIN	X	1500-1700	1130-1230	1400-1630	X	1430-1600
TREVOR	0800-1130	1400-1600-	X	1400-1700	0800-1100	1330-1530

Only time all available: Friday 1430–1530.

Activity 13.2

HEALTH AND SAFETY WORKING PARTY

To: All members of the Working Party [Date]

A meeting of the Working Party will be held at 1000 on [day] 1 [month] in Meeting Room 3 on the 4th floor of City House.

AGENDA

1. Apologies
2. Minutes of the meeting held on 1 [last month]
3. Matters Arising from the minutes:
    i. Minute no. 16/00 Budget
    ii. Minute no. 20/00 Transport
4. Fire extinguisher training
5. Safety representative nominations
6. Any other business

[Name]

Activity 14.1

a. The sequence of visits will depend on flights available. The best route would be either Trinidad-Jamaica-St Lucia-Barbados-Trinidad, or the reverse.

The itinerary should include date, departure airport, destination, flight number, check-in time, departure time and arrival time.

The name and details of the hotel reserved should be shown after each flight.

b.

DRAFT   Ministry of Education
[Address]
[Date]

[Name]
Chief Education Officer
[Address]

Dear [Name]

I refer to my telephone conversation with you when you kindly agreed to see me and arrange for me to visit secondary schools and a technical college in [island].

I propose to travel to [island] on [date] arriving at [time]. I shall be staying at the [hotel].

As you know, I am keen to find out as much as possible about the facilities for business studies and technical training in other islands. I am hoping to extend these facilities in Trinidad.

I greatly appreciate your willingness to spare time for me and look forward to hearing from you what arrangements you are able to make.

Yours sincerely

Miss Margaret Williams
Permanent Secretary

---

c.

DRAFT   Ministry of Education
[Address]
[Date]

[Name]
[Director]
[Island] Chamber of Commerce
[Address]

Dear [Name]

I hope to visit [island] on [date] to meet the Chief Education Officer to discuss business studies and technical training available in the island. I shall also visit secondary schools and a technical college.

I would very much like to meet some employers to find out from them their expectations of young people trained for employment.

Would you be willing to arrange for me to meet employers from a few companies of various sizes and types? If so, I will let you know when I would be available after the Chief Education Officer has made arrangements for meetings and visits.

Yours sincerely

Miss Margaret Williams
Permanent Secretary

d.

DRAFT Ministry of Education
  [Address]

FACSIMILE   [number]

To: [Hotel]

From: [Your name]

Date:

Subject: CONFIRMATION OF RESERVATION

I confirm the provisional reservation made by telephone as follows:

Miss Margaret Williams
Single room with bath and air conditioning
[No. of nights] from [date] to [date] departing on [date]
Arriving on flight [number] at [time]

Miss Williams will pay the account.

Please confirm this reservation.

Activity 15.1
1. 'Myself' should be 'me' as the object of 'you reply to'.
2. 'Their' should be 'they are' – 'their' is an adjective.
3. 'Which' should be 'who' – 'which' refers to things.
4. 'Are' should be 'is' – subject of the verb is 'the number' (singular).
5. 'Were' should be 'was' – subject of the verb is 'every one' (singular).
6. 'It's' should be 'its' – apostrophe represents a missing letter, i.e. 'it is'.
7. 'Who' should be 'whom' as the object of 'I saw'.
8. 'Most bigger' should be 'biggest' – 'bigger' is of two, 'biggest' of three or more.
9. 'Me' should be 'I' – subject of the verb 'are playing'.
10. 'No' should be 'any' – two negatives make a positive.
11. 'Due to' should be 'because' – a sentence cannot begin with 'due to'.
12. 'Illegible' should be 'eligible' – 'illegible' refers to writing that cannot be read.

Activity 15.2
Discuss the information you found with colleagues or friends.

Activity 15.3
1. *i.* preferred
   ii. affect (verb)

    iii. being (present participle)
    iv. separate
    v. benefiting (stress on first syllable in a multi-syllable word so do not double the consonant before the suffix beginning with a vowel)
    vi. admissible

2.
    i. pharynx
    ii. chronic
    iii. psychotic
    iv. genteel
    v. gherkin
    vi. gnash
    vii. quit
    viii. knuckle
    ix. ceiling/sealing

3.
i.	brake – stop	break – destroy
ii.	formerly – in the past	formally – in accordance with procedure
iii.	ascent – upward slope	assent – agreement
iv.	desert – dry area	dessert – pudding/sweet
v.	faint – dim	feint – mock attack
vi.	passed – went by	past – time gone

4.
    i. essential part of
    ii. unnecessary
    iii. exceeding a proper number (more than needed)
    iv. round in shape
    v. intense dislike

Note: As dictionaries vary in the way they indicate pronunciation it is suggested that you discuss with your colleagues the pronunciation of the words listed.

5.
    i. conjunction
    ii. verb or noun
    iii. adjective
    iv. verb
    v. conjunction
    vi. pronoun
    vii. interjection (slang)
    viii. verb
    ix. past participle of verb 'to tear'

Activity 16.1

When you have written your cv check it against Fig. 16.1 to ensure that you have included all the details needed by a prospective employer.

Activity 16.2

Discuss your completed application form as suggested and make a note of anything that you need to improve when you come to look for a job 'for real'.

APPENDIX 6

SUGGESTED ANSWERS TO QUESTIONS

CHAPTER 1

Practice questions
1.   *i.*   customer services
   ii.   information processing
   iii.   accounts
   iv.   mail room
   v.   administration
   vi.   purchasing
   vii.   personnel
   viii.   public relations
   ix.   research & development
   x.   customer services
2. There is only one person at the top and more in each line until the base line where there are the most staff.
3. The person at the top, e.g. the President.
4. To show the departments in the organisation, and the numbers and types of staff in each department.
5. See pages 9-15.
6.   *i.*   A course arranged for newly recruited employees to explain to them the organisation, its aims and objectives, products, who is who and who does what.
   ii.   A diagram that shows the structure of the organisation.

iii. A person who deals either with one or two specific personnel activities such as manpower planning and recruitment, or the whole range of personnel activities.
iv. Sales of products or services in the home country.
v. Laws that employers have to follow in their dealings with employees.

7. A sole trader owns the business. A partner shares ownership with one or more other partners.
8. The partners.
9. See page 6.
10. A function is carried out in various departments, e.g. certain personnel activities are carried out in all departments. A department is responsible for carrying out specified activities, e.g. sales.
11. See page 8.
12. See page 13.
13. See page 15.

Short answer questions
1. sole trader
2. bankrupt
3. capital
4. Memorandum and Articles of Association
5. Board of Directors, President
6. *c*
7. *b*
8. *b*
9. *b* and *d*
10. *b*

Examination questions
1. see page 15.
2.

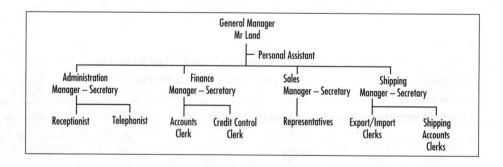

CHAPTER 2

Practice questions

1. You should discuss this question with your tutor and/or colleagues.
2. See pages 35-6.
3. See page 36.
4. *a.* See page 28.
   b. See pages 28-30.
5. See pages 21-2.
6. *i.* Designed to suit the human body
   ii. The angle of a backrest
   iii. Repetitive strain injury caused through continuous use of a particular muscle or ligament
   iv. A device for holding copy in a slightly sloping upright position on the desk
   v. Dark transparent plastic sheet affixed to the top of the VDU and covering the screen to avoid glare
7. See pages 26-7.
8. See page 30.
9. *a.* For use by people with disabilities
   b. No smoking
   c. Fire extinguisher
   d. Water not for drinking
   e. Assembly point
   f. No paper clips (e.g. in shredder)
10. *a.* See page 31.
    b. See page 28.
11. *i.* See page 34.
    ii. See page 33.
    iii. See page 34.

Short answer questions

1. procedures
2. ergonomically
3. guard
4. descriptions
5. closed
6. *a*
7. *d*
8. *d*
9. *c*
10. *c*

Examination questions

1. hazard
2. report
3. write
4. Choose from: calmness, courteous manner, helpful, initiative, commitment.
5. **a.** See page 30 (relevant points).
   b. Never open more than one drawer at a time.
   c. Carry with the heaviest side towards you.
   Ensure that you can see over the load.
   Do not go round corners on the inside in case someone is coming in the opposite direction.
   Do not carry more than you can manage comfortably.
6. Job description

Job title: Administrative Assistant
Responsible to: Administrator
Responsible for: Part-time clerk
Two full-time receptionists
Role: To assist the Administrator with the administration of the club

Duties
a. supervise the incoming mail clerk, ensuring mail is sorted accurately
b. supervise two full-time receptionists, ensuring that the highest standards are maintained in receiving and directing visitors
c. act as relief receptionist when necessary
d. assist the Administrator in the following duties:
   - see page 38, *a* to *f*

7.

Type of accident	Prevention	
Unable to escape in the event of fire	*i.*	Ensure all fire exits are kept clear
Fall causing serious injury	*ii.*	Ensure cabinet drawers/doors and desk drawers are kept closed
	iii.	Wipe up spillages on floor
	iv.	Never stand on a chair to reach a high shelf
	v.	Do not talk to people behind you when going down steps or stairs backwards
	vi.	Do not leave packages in aisles

(continued)

(continued)

Type of accident	Prevention	
Items falling on someone causing shock or injury	*vii.*	Ensure machines and equipment are not left too near the edge of a desk
	viii.	Ensure cupboard shelves are not stacked too full so that things fall out when the door is opened
Cuts	*ix.*	Never leave open scissors, drawing pins, etc. covered with papers on a desk
	x.	Never run a finger down the edge of a sheet of paper

CHAPTER 3

Practice questions

1. A mainframe computer has a large central processing unit and peripheral equipment such as disk drives and printers installed in a computer room with terminals linked to it from offices within the building and from outside.

   A personal computer is a self-contained, stand-alone machine with its own central processing unit, disk drive and printer. It can also be linked to a mainframe to act as a terminal.

2. tape drive
   disk drive
   printer

3.
   - *i.* access the mainframe system from a terminal (or personal computer)
   - *ii.* the code (1 and 0) that can be read by a computer
   - *iii.* programs that enable the computer to carry out various tasks
   - *iv.* a store in the central processing unit where operating programs and information currently being processed are held
   - *v.* a small disc that holds information
   - *vi.* access information on a mainframe and copy it on to a PC's memory
   - *vii.* items such as stationery, disks, printing cartridges
   - *viii.* the device on which a disk is mounted, linked to a central processing unit either on a mainframe or on a PC
   - *ix.* a large volume of information
   - *x.* a code that is unique to an individual and allows that person access to certain information

4. See pages 44-7.
5.
   i. visual display unit - for checking input and recalling information from disk
   ii. keyboard - for keying in new data or updating existing data
   iii. disk drive - for driving the disk that holds the information
   iv. printer - for printing data held on disk on to paper (hard copy)
6. See page 54.
7. *a.* See pages 54-5.
   b. See pages 54-5.
8. *a.* See pages 56-7.
   b. See page 59.
9. See pages 56 and 57.
10. See page 56.
11. See pages 59-60.
12. See page 60.

Short answer questions
1. code
   program
2. work study
   organisation and methods
3. peripherals
4. central processing unit
5. database
6. *b*
7. *a*
8. *c*
9. *c*
10. *d*

Examination questions
1. windows
2. *a.* regular breaks
   b. regular eye tests
   c. ergonomically designed furniture
3. *a.* visual display unit (VDU)
   b. disk drive
   c. printer
4. *Care and maintenance of floppy computer disks*
   In order to avoid corruption of disks the following rules must be adhered to.

i. Never bend the disk
ii. Never write on the cover with ballpoint pen or pencil, use soft felt-tip pen
iii. Do not store near heat
iv. Do not touch visible parts of the disk
v. Identify each disk with a label but do not cover any openings
vi. Have a retention policy, i.e. a pre-determined time for holding each type of information on disk, and delete at the end of that time to avoid filling the disk with unnecessary information
vii. Give each file an easily recognisable identification
viii. Decide on a filing sequence for disks and maintain that sequence
5. mouse
6. program

CHAPTER 4

Practice questions
1. Explain that Mr Liddell is not in the office today and ask if he would like to see Mr Liddell's secretary (if he has one) or another member of staff in the sales department.
2. Say you are very sorry that her product is faulty. Ask if she has spoken to anyone in the customer services department. If not, explain that they are the right people to deal with the matter quickly. Call customer services immediately and ask for the supervisor/manager to come and see the lady.
3. Sign register in case of fire.
   Identification so that anyone the person meets knows them to be a visitor – particularly important if they are in an area where visitors should be accompanied by a member of staff.
4. See page 70.
5. *a.* See page 71, points 1, 2, 3, 4, 5.
   b. See page 71, points 6 and 7, and any changes to points 1 to 5.
6. *a.* See page 71.
   b. See page 71.
7. See pages 73–4 and 78–84.
8. See pages 75–7.
9. See pages 78–9.
10. *a.* See page 82.
    b. Name, day and date, duration of absence, invite caller to leave their name and telephone number, details of when they can expect a return call.
    c. See pages 97–8.

11.   *i.*   direct distance dialling
        ii.   international direct dialling
        iii.   direct dialling in
12. See page 85.
13. See pages 85-6.
14. See pages 88-90.
15. See pages 93-6.
16. See page 91.
17. *a.*   See page 94.
       b.   See pages 94-5.
18. See page 97.
19. See pages 98-9.
20. See pages 100-2.

Short answer questions
1. smile, greet
2. private branch exchange
3. automatic transfer
4. bleeps
5. digital
6. *d*
7. *b*
8. *c*
9. *a*
10. *b*

Examination questions
1. answer-recording machine or voicemail
2. appointments
3. *a.*   Things may be said that on reflection may be better not said
       b.   Neither person has a record of a telephone conversation
       c.   Confidential conversations may be overheard
4. *a.*   To be able to direct visitors to the person who can best help them
       b.   To be able to refer to the details if/when required
       c.   Provide information (brochures, leaflet, pamphlets) about products
          Make appointments for visitors who arrive without them
          Receive deliveries from couriers, etc.
          Arrange collection of letters, packets and parcels
          Arrange taxis for visitors
          Keep reception area tidy
          Check that staff sign in

5. information
6. *a.* See pages 65-8.
   b. See page 69.
7. *a.* People receiving calls do not identify themselves. Ensure that everyone is trained to answer the phone with their name as well as identifying the department.

   Messages often do not get passed on and, when they are, they are not accurate. Provide forms for telephone messages and give a list of the details that must be obtained, i.e. name, organisation and telephone number of caller, whom the message is for, the time and date of call, the key points of the message, all of which should be repeated to the caller.

   Callers are passed from one person to another. Ensure that all staff know what the various departments are responsible for and the key people in each department who can deal with different matters.
   (Any other relevant points would be acceptable.)

   b. Mobile phones are linked to a network of cells throughout the world so that calls can be made from any place to any place – advantageous for people travelling.

   Portable phones (or cordless phones) can be taken around and outside a building up to 100 or 200 metres away from the base unit (depending on the type of phone) – advantageous for people who wish to take the phone from one room to another to avoid having additional instruments.
   (Any other relevant points would be acceptable.)

CHAPTER 5

Practice questions

1. See page 109.
2. *i.* A brief note, often handwritten on a post-it note – very informal
   ii. Normally a typewritten message to another person within the organisation – no company name, address, etc., no opening salutation, no complimentary close
   iii. A very briefly worded message delivered to a person who receives it very quickly, the time depending on the type of telegram
   iv. A message keyed in on a computer transmitted to another computer by machines having an e-mail address
   v. A message typewritten on a telex keyboard and transmitted over a telephone line
3. See 2ii above.
4. Correct grammar, spelling, punctuation

Attractive layout with all parts accurately completed
Concisely worded
Information precise
(Any other relevant points acceptable)

5. See pages 111-12.
6.
   i. now
   ii. about
   iii. (omit)
   iv. acknowledge
   v. give (you)
7. The letter should include your address and the date, the name of the addressee (The Mail Order Bookshop) and its address
   Dear Sirs
   Details must include:
   - title of the book
   - author
   - publisher
   - ISBN number
   - paperback or hardback if you do not know the ISBN number
   - request price including postage.
8. See page 120.
9. See pages 120-1.
10. See page 122.
11. See page 122.
12. See page 122.
13. Dear Mr Bloggs

    Thank you for your letter of [date]. The information given is useful but I need more detail.

    Will you please send me the additional information I asked for in my letter of 15 [last month]. If you think it would be beneficial to have a meeting I shall be pleased to arrange a convenient time and place.

    Yours sincerely

14.
    i. All lines start at the left margin
    ii. A style that everyone in the organisation must follow for a particular document, e.g. letter, report
    iii. Second and subsequent pages of a letter
    iv. Paragraph with all lines starting at the left margin
    v. A copy sent to a person without it being noted on the original
15.
    a. The letter should include your address and the date, the name of the manager (if known), and name and address of the shop

Opening salutation
Heading: Video Recorder
Details must include:

- the model number and identification of the article purchased
- date when purchased
- details of what is wrong with the machine
- enclose copy of receipt
- what action you want the manager to take.

Complimentary close and signature

b. The letter should include the name and address of the shop, and the date, your name and address

Opening salutation
Heading
Details must include:

- thanks for your letter
- apology for the machine not working properly
- action to be taken.

Complimentary close and signature

16. Follow the pattern of previous letters. Give details of poor service and irregular service, e.g. specific dates when service was not given.
17. Dear [name]

    I am honoured by your invitation to present the prizes at your school on speech day. I am delighted to accept.

    Yours sincerely

18. As this is a creative activity it would be useful to ask someone else to look at it and comment. Check that you have included all the details as instructed.
19. See pages 120-2.
20. Company heading

    Date

    Name and address of addressee

    Dear Mr Fletcher

    APPOINTMENT OF STORES SUPERVISOR

    I have pleasure in offering you the post of Stores Supervisor, starting on Monday 1 July 2002.

    Points i, ii and iii can be written in paragraph form amending slightly as necessary.

Will you please inform me by [date] whether you wish to accept the offer.

Yours sincerely
[Signature]

[Name]
Personnel Officer

21. See pages 126-7.
22. See page 128.
23.

STATIONERY ORDER		
Name .... Department		
Date		
Quantity	Items required	(Stores use only) Item code no.
Issued by		
Received by .... Date		

24. PEACOCK NEW YORK ORDER 4581 [Date] NOT RECEIVED STOP URGENTLY REQUIRED STOP PLEASE ADVISE DELIVERY DATE ISLAND TRADERS KINGSTON
25. See page 135.
26. See page 139.
27. See pages 139-40.
28. See page 140.

29. See page 141.
30. See page 142.
31.

| | Faster motoring ⌒means longer br/eaking distances are needed. At 80 miles an hour on a dry road with tyres, car and driver in tip-t/ṗ condition, it takes 300 feet to stop completely. This is equiv/ȧlent to 23 car lengths. If the road is we/ṫ the tyres worn or the driver/ṡ reactions are slow this distance can increase to more than 600 ft. It cannot be stressed to/ strongly#that adequate spacing between ve/ȧc/ḣles on motorways is essential. |

Short answer questions
1. verbose
2. colloquial, slang, commercial jargon (or 'commercialese')
3. military decorations, MC (or other)
4. read the instructions
5. disclaimer
6. *b*
7. *c*
8. *d*
9. *a*
10. *b*

Examination questions
1. ENC., Enc. or enc.
2. envelope
3. *a.* letter
   b. fax
   c. telegram
   (or telex, e-mail)
4. *a.* the addressee usually receives the e-mail as soon as it is transmitted
   b. no envelope or stamps are necessary
   c. saves interrupting people on the telephone

CHAPTER 6

Practice questions
1. See pages 151-4.
2. *i.* See pages 156-7.   *vi.* See pages 154 and 155.
   ii. See page 155.   *vii.* See page 150.
   iii. See page 158.   *viii.* See page 158.
   iv. See page 160.   *ix.* See page 150.
   v. See page 171.   *x.* See page 150.

3. See page 155.
4. See pages 161-2 and 164-5.
5. Memory storage is information held in the machine; storage on diskette/disk is not permanently *in* the machine - the diskette/disk has to be inserted into the disk drive.
6. See page 165.
7.
    i. See page 163.
    ii. See page 161.
    iii. See page 159.
    iv. See page 154.
    v. See page 158.
    vi. See page 156.
    vii. See page 156.
    viii. See page 158.
    ix. See page 150.
    x. See page 154.
8. See page 160.
9.
    i. See page 160.
    ii. See page 156.
    iii. See page 177.
    iv. See page 180.
    v. See page 176.
10. See pages 166-7.
11. See pages 168-70.
12. See page 119 for layout of memorandum and pages 170-1 for instructions.
13. See page 172.
14. See pages 172-3.
15.
    i. offset lithography
    ii. office copier
    iii. copy printer
    iv. computerised image copier/printer
    v. offset lithography (copper plate)
16. See pages 177-80.
17. See pages 179-80.
18.
    i. See pages 172-3.
    ii. See page 180.
    iii. See page 177.
    iv. See page 180.
19. See page 532 Activity 2.1.
20. See pages 181-2.

Short answer questions
1. remote dictation system
2. American quarto
3. grammage
4. pocket
5. impact
6. *c*

7. *d*
8. *b*
9. *c*
10. *d*

Examination questions

1. laser
2. jogger
3. *a.* enlarging/reducing
   b. collating
   c. stapling
4. *a.* check that there is paper in the feedtrays
   b. check that a master or a sheet of copy paper is not jammed
   c. put a notice on the machine and report the fault
5. *a.* to align pages ready for binding
   b. to place the pages one behind the other in sequence
   c. to fasten the pages together in book form
6. reduce
7. audio-typist
8. keep the glass plate clean
   ensure there are no marks on masters
   check the first copy of each run for print density, even density, no 'streaks', copy aligned correctly on the paper

CHAPTER 7

Practice questions

1. See page 189.
2. See page 190.
3. *a.* See pages 191–3.
   b. See page 191.
   c. See page 192.
   d. See page 193.

4.

Type of file	Example of use
i. Manilla folder – card folder with no means of fixing papers	Hold working paper
ii. Ring binder – hard cover with two or four rings	Manuals
iii. Plastic slip file – for one or two sheets only	Papers for individual tasks

(continued)

(continued)

Type of file		Example of use
iv.	Wallet folder – envelope style with gussets at bottom and sides	Project documents
v.	Box file – a hard box with a spring clip inside	Bulky documents such as reports
vi.	Lever arch file – hard cover	A–Z correspondence
vii.	Plastic pocket – opens at top with coloured edge down one side for filing in a ring binder	Covers for individual pages, leaflets, etc. in a presentation file
viii.	Magazine file – an upright box with the top cut away	Magazines, journals

5. *i.* See page 194.
    ii. See page 194.
    iii. See page 194.
    iv. See page 194.
6. See pages 198–9.
7. See pages 199–200.
8. Direct filing is being able to access the file without referring to an index. Filing by name of customer is an example.

    Indirect filing is having to refer to an index in order to locate the file. Filing numerically is an example where an alphabetical index of the names is needed, each name showing the number of the file.
9. BWEE
    Barbados Association of Chemists
    British Council, The
    General Building Society Ltd, The
    Hotel Victoria
    Jamaican Distilleries Ltd
    National Association of Secretaries
    National Council of Labour
    101 Galleries Ltd
    Premier Engineering Co. Ltd, The
    Puerto Rico Chemicals Ltd
    Reliance Telephone Co. Ltd, The
    St Lucia Business Women's Association
    St Luke's Community Centre
    7-Up Bottling Co. Ltd
    Smith, Mrs Janet

Smiths Motor Accessories Ltd
Smythe, Dr JB
T & T Electricity Company, The
T & T Shipping Corporation Ltd

10. See page 205.
11. *i.* See pages 213-14.
    ii. See page 206.
    iii. See page 201.
    iv. See page 194.
    v. See page 212.
    vi. See page 204.
    vii. See pages 214-15.
    viii. See page 204.
    ix. See page 209.
    x. See pages 207-8.
12. Documents awaiting filing - see page 207.
    Pre-sorting - see pages 207-8.
    Preparing documents for filing - see pages 208-9.
    File regularly, daily if possible - see page 210.
13. See pages 211-13.
14. The number of files in the system
    The number of classified files
    The number of files on specialised topics
    What types of documents are filed
    Who needs the files, how often and how quickly
    Who needs to keep files of working papers
    Who will do the filing - are there enough trained people?
    What retention policy is needed
15. *i.* Stock record cards filed in boxes or drawers, alphabetical by name of stock item or numerical if items have numbers
    ii. Confidential staff records filed in folders, locked in drawers or cupboard
    iii. Petty cash vouchers filed in date order in folders or small ring binder
    iv. Plans on microfiche filed in boxes or drawers near microfilm reader
    v. Invoices from suppliers filed in 'Awaiting payment' file until paid, then in date order in 'Purchase accounts' lever arch file
    vi. Catalogues from wholesalers filed in magazine box, dated as received and kept for not more than 12 months
    vii. Minutes of meetings filed in folders or ring binders in date order
    viii. Staff training records filed in individual personnel files
    ix. Sales ledger cards filed in drawers, confidential

    x. Invoices to clients awaiting payment filed in ring binder/lever arch file in numerical order, confidential
16. a/b See pages 222-3.
17. To enable the recipient to identify the relevant file immediately.
18. ***a.*** See pages 216 and 220.
    b. See pages 217-18.
19. ***a.*** See pages 219-20.
    b. See page 216.
20. ***a.*** See page 221.
    b. See page 221.

Short answer questions
1. suspension pocket folders, lateral
2. shallow drawers, cabinets, wavy dividers
3. differentiate
4. daily
5. it is needed
6. *d*
7. *c*
8. *b*
9. *b*
10. *a*

Examination questions
1. microfilm
2. geographical
3. information
4. fireproof cabinet
5. ***a.*** microfiche
    b. filmstrips in jacket
    c. on spool
6. ***a.*** Vertical filing cabinet contains two, three, four or five drawers.
    Advantage - easy to store and retrieve documents
    Disadvantage - space needed for opening the drawers
    b. Lateral filing cabinet contains shelves or racks with suspension pockets hanging from them.
    Advantage - more files stored in the same space as a vertical cabinet
    Disadvantage - not so easy to store and retrieve files
    c. Points to include:
- drawings, maps, etc. should be kept flat
- vertical and lateral filing space is not adequate for this.

    Horizontal filing, i.e. shallow-drawer cabinets are suitable.

7. alphabetical
8. bring-forward (diary or tickler also acceptable)
9. microcopy
10. *a.* St Smith's Hospital
    b. Smith, J
    c. Smith Hotel, The
11. *a.* New files are added on so that space does not have to be saved for possible new files among existing files.
    b. It is obvious when a file is missing because there will be a number (or numbers) missing.
    c. Each topic heading can be numbered and subsidiary files can be given a sub-division number, e.g. Printers 16, Dot matrix 16.1, Laser 16.2, etc.
12. Files get too big
    Cabinet drawers/shelves get jammed with files
    Very old correspondence that is never referred to is held in active files
    There is far more material than necessary to search through when looking for a particular document.
13. *a.* See pages 202-3.
    b. *i.* See pages 213-14.
        ii. legal requirements
        audit requirements
        possibility of documents being needed as evidence in a court of law*
        possible need for future reference, e.g. for comparison purposes
    c. *i.* See page 204.
        ii. See page 212.
14. • Documents should be 'marked off' for filing to ensure that no document is filed until action has been taken on it.
    • Documents awaiting filing should be kept in a tray or concertina file, so that no document gets lost.
    • Filing should be done on a regular basis – daily in a centralised filing section – to ensure that records are kept up to date.
    • Documents should be pre-sorted into groups and then each group of documents can be sorted into sequence so that they can be inserted into the files in the same sequence as the files are arranged.

---

*Generally microcopy and photocopies are accepted in a court of law, provided it is/they are a standard part of an organisation's systems and procedures.

- Before filing, documents should be checked to see that attachments are with the document, pages of the document are fastened together so that no pages get lost.
- Pins should be removed as they are dangerous.
- Paper clips should be removed as other documents are likely to get caught up in them.
- Documents should be punched centrally so that all pages are aligned neatly in their files.
- New files should be opened only if needed to keep files to a minimum.
- When a file gets full (about 150 pages) a continuation file should be opened to avoid having 'bulky' files, which are difficult to handle.
- Files should be 'spring cleaned' at least once a year and files moved from active to semi-active, from semi-active to non-active, and archived as appropriate to make files in use more accessible.

CHAPTER 8

Practice questions
1. See pages 231-5.
2. See page 231.
3. See page 233.
4. See page 235.
5. *a.* See Fig. 8.4 on page 232.
   b. See page 232.
6. See pages 236-7.
7. See pages 237-8.
8. See page 242.
9. *a* and *b* See pages 238-41.
10. *Post Office Guide* and leaflet about particular services.

Short answer questions
1. faced, tapped
2. remittance book
3. C4, C5, DL
4. without an envelope
5. classified
6. *c*
7. *d*
8. *c*

Examination questions
1. sender
2. see pages 236-7.

3. folding
4. slit envelopes
5. *a.* amount of credit used
   b. amount of credit remaining
   c. date changed (daily)

CHAPTER 9

Practice questions
1. See page 251.
2. See page 251.
3. See page 252.
4. See page 257.
5. See pages 257-8.
6.   *i.*   See pages 258-9.
     ii.   See pages 259-60.
     iii.   See page 262.
     iv.   See page 260.
     v.   See page 263.
     vi.   See pages 263-4.
     vii.   See page 260.
     viii.   See page 261.
     ix.   See page 262.
     x.   See page 264.
7.   *i.*   See page 259.
     ii.   See page 260.
8.   *a.*   See page 260.
     b.   See page 262.
9. See page 260.
10. TTPost Courier Service, see page 263.
11.   *i.*   See pages 264-5.
      ii.   See pages 264 and 240-1.
12. See page 265.
13. See page 266.

Short answer questions
1. town
2. red
3. postage
4. customs declaration form
5. poste restante
6. *b*

7. c
8. d
9. a

Examination question
1. registered

CHAPTER 10

Practice questions
1.   *i.*   See page 271.
    ii.   See page 277.
    iii.   See page 300.
    iv.   See pages 283-4.
    v.   See page 281.
    vi.   See page 287.
    vii.   See page 273.
    viii.   See page 289.
    ix.   See page 299.
    x.   See pages 276-7.
2. You should have prepared the following sets of documents:
   - order
   - consignment, delivery or despatch note (depending on method of delivery)
   - goods received note
   - invoice
   - statement with remittance slip.

   Look at Figs 10.6, 10.8, 10.9 10.10 and 10.11 to check that you have included all necessary details.
3. *a.*   Mr PK Kyer
   b.   Excellent Trading Co. Ltd
   c.   A/c4/F/91
   d.   1 August 2002
   e. $250.00
   f. $480.00
   g. $125.00 and $355.00
   h. $730.00
   i.   The full amount must be paid
4. See pages 299-300.
5. *a.*   *i.*   Trade discount is deducted from the cost price of goods sold. Cash discount is deducted from the total amount due for payment within a stated time.

a. ii. The amount of trade discount affects the purchase price and therefore the profit margin of the purchaser when they re-sell. The availability and offer of cash discount has a similar effect but there is also the question of having to pay within a shorter period than may be the case if there is no cash discount.

b.

```
Received from   Mr. P. Thomas                    Date [Today's]
the sum of      eighty dollars
                                                 ┌─────────┐
                                                 │ $80 =   │
                                                 └─────────┘
for   secondhand filing cabinet

                                                 Signed: [Your signature]
```

6. See pages 274–89 (summary page 272).
7. ***a.*** over-charge, items charged not delivered, items returned as incorrect, item damaged, returnable empties
   b.

YKK Co. Ltd
14 Nook Avenue
KINGSTON
JAMAICA

CREDIT NOTE No. 248   Date: [Today's]

Alanson & Co.
13 Long Street
ST VINCENT

Your order no.   0000   Account no. 00000
Our order no.   0000

Quantity	Description	Unit price J$	Cost J$
3	Ace word processors Damaged	20 100.00	60 300.00
12	Contact typists chairs Wrong model supplied	1 080.00	12 960.00
2	Excel plain paper copiers	5 865.00	11 730.00
TOTAL			J$84 990.00

Goods returned on [10th last month] by T & L Steamship Co. Vessel *Enterprise*

8. a.

```
                              ORDER
┌─────────────────────────────┬──────────────────────┬─────────────────────┐
│ Tel. Townlea 4579           │ Date [ Today's ]     │ Order no. 000       │
├─────────────────────────────┴──────────────────────┴─────────────────────┤
│            A—ONE Equipment Ltd, 2nd Avenue, Kingston, Jamaica            │
├──────────────────────────────────────────────┬───────────────────────────┤
│ CUSTOMER ACCOUNT NO.  A 1069                 │ Our Stock Ref.  E818      │
├──────────────────────────────────────────────┴───────────────────────────┤
│ TO                                                                       │
│      Ideal Stationers Ltd                                                │
│      Barton Road                                                         │
│      KINGSTON                                                            │
│      JAMAICA                                                             │
├──────────────────────────────────────────────────────────────────────────┤
│ Please supply and deliver                                                │
├──────────┬───────────────────────────────────┬───────────────────────────┤
│   Qty    │           Description             │          Price            │
├──────────┼───────────────────────────────────┼───────────────────────────┤
│   50     │ Shorthand notebooks, hard cover   │ J$63.00 each              │
│          │                                   │ (less 10%)                │
│          │                                   │                           │
│  100     │ Special ballpens                  │ J$7.00 for 10             │
│          │                                   │                           │
│   24     │ Pencil erasers                    │ J$252.00 per doz          │
│          │                                   │ (less 10%)                │
│          │                                   │                           │
│ 10 boxes │ Medium-sized paper clips          │ J$42.50 for 10 boxes      │
│          │                                   │ (less 15%)                │
├──────────┴───────────────────────────────────┼───────────────────────────┤
│ NO DELIVERIES ACCEPTED UNLESS AGAINST        │ Signed                    │
│ OUR OFFICIAL ORDER                           │                           │
│ PLEASE QUOTE ORDER NO. AND DATE              │         Purchasing Officer│
└──────────────────────────────────────────────┴───────────────────────────┘
```

b. look in the telephone directory or *Yellow Pages* and ask for catalogues to be supplied

look in files of catalogues

c. delivery time, trade discount, cash discount for prompt payment

9. *a.*

```
The New Style Supply Co. Ltd
GEORGETOWN
GUYANA

STATEMENT OF ACCOUNT                                    Date: 30 April 2002

Mr John Thomson                                         Account no. 0000
16 Acre Street
KINGSTON
JAMAICA
```

Date		Debit J$	Credit J$	Balance J$
1.04.02	Balance			249.75
7.04.02	Invoice no. A3405	217.13		
12.04.02	Credit note S. 514		34.40	
14.04.02	Invoice no. A4271	770.40		
23.04.02	Invoice no. A5413	512.00		
26.04.02	Credit note S.689		60.00	
28.04.02	Cash received		249.75	
30.04.02	Balance due			1405.13

Terms 2.5 per cent discount for payment within 7 days

Note that 20 per cent trade discount has been deducted from the prices quoted on both invoices and credit notes. There would not have been trade discount on returned packing cases (credit note S.689).

b.

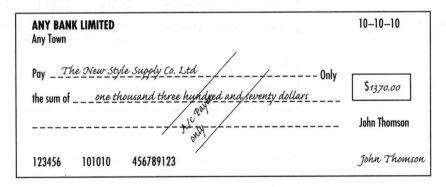

10. distance, number of packages, size of package(s), value of goods
11. *a.* varies from island to island, so you will need to find out for your own area

b. volume of goods, value, fragility/perishability of goods, delivery time, cost

12. a. See pages 290–4.
    b. See page 290.
    c. See pages 289–90.

13.

GAB Jewellery Supply Co. Ltd
PO Box 213
BRIDGETOWN
BARBADOS

INVOICE No. 0000   Date: [Today's]

Goldsmith & Sons
123 Broad Street
BRIDGETOWN
BARBADOS

Your order no.   312/JG   Account no. 0000
Our order no.   0000

Quantity	Description	Unit price B$	Gross cost B$	Discount 33.3 per cent B$	Net cost B$
3 only	Gents' watches	1275.00	3825.00	1275.00	2550.00
10 only	Ladies' watches	950.00	9500.00	3166.66	6333.34
1 only	Lady's gold brooch	1800.00	1800.00	600.00	1200.00
6 pairs	Gold cufflinks	3800.00	11 400.00	3800.00	7600.00
4 only	Gold and diamond rings	4008.00	16 032.00	5344.00	10 688.00
2 only	Gold filigree necklaces	3500.00	7000.00	2333.33	4666.67
3 only	Silver filigree necklaces	800.00	2400.00	800.00	1600.00

TOTAL   34 638.01

Cash discount 2.5 per cent for payment within 30 days

---

14. a. i. Bill of lading, certificate of origin.
       ii. See pages 289–90.
    b. Customs Bill of Sight.
15. requisition
    enquiry
    quotation/estimate/tender
    order

pro-forma invoice
advice note
packing/despatch/delivery/consignment note
invoice
debit note
credit note
statement
cheque

16. *i.* See page 299.
   ii. See page 283.
   iii. See page 280.
   iv. See pages 280–1.
   v. See page 285.
   vi. See page 287.
   vii. See page 288.
   viii. See page 290.
   ix. See page 296.
   x. See page 296.

17. Having only part of an order delivered, the remainder to be sent later. Lack of storage space; not required immediately and may deteriorate if not stored properly.

Short answer questions
1. trade discount
2. debit note
3. air waybill
4. *a.* millimetre
   b. 1
   c. hundredweight
   d. metres
   e. short ton
5. cash discount
6. *c*
7. *d*
8. *a*
9. *b*
10. *d*

Examination questions
1. credit
2. Pro-forma invoice or invoice, statement, receipt.

3.

```
                WOODCRAFT SHEDS LTD
                 WINDSOR SAWMILLS
                    LONDON ROAD
                   WINDSOR WF4 6KP
```

Tel.: 01942 440045   Invoice No.: 54789
Fax: 01942 446753

Order No.: 5419
Order Date: [3 days ago]

Date: [Today's]

Terms: 3% for monthly settlement

Quantity	Description	Item price £	Erection each £	Total price £
1	Feather Edge Shed Apex style size 8' x 6'	259.00	45.00	304.00
2	Heavy-Duty Sheds Pent style size 6' x 4'	305.00	39.00	688.00
1	Super Range Shed Pent Style 8' x 6'	333.00	45.00	378.00

TOTAL goods	1370.00
LESS: 10% trade discount	137.00
NEW TOTAL	1233.00
ADD: sales tax 15%	184.95
TOTAL BALANCE DUE	1417.95

4. advice
5. reply to enquiry/quotation/estimate/tender
6. requisition
   order
   invoice

7. a.

ANALYSIS OF PRICES AND TERMS OF QUOTATIONS FOR PURCHASE OF A DOCUMENT SAFE					
Firm	Price £	Trade discount	Sales tax 15%	Carriage £	ACTUAL PRICE
Link Security	120	Nil	Not inlcuded	Paid	£138.00
S & N Safes	100	10%	Included	£25	£115.00
Reed & Co.	150	15%	Included	Paid	£127.50
Lock & Safe Co.	90	Nil	Not included	£15	£118.50

ANALYSIS OF PRICES AND TERMS OF QUOTATIONS FOR PURCHASE OF A DOCUMENT SAFE					
Firm	Price £	Trade discount	Sales tax 15%	Carriage £	ACTUAL PRICE
S & N Safes	100	(10%) £10.00	Included	£25.00	£115.00
Lock & Safe Co.	90	Nil	£13.50	£15.00	£118.50
Reed & Co.	150	(15%) £22.50	Included	Paid	£127.50
Link Security	120	Nil	£18.00	Paid	£138.00

Note: You might like to check this with your colleagues.

b.

MEMORANDUM

To: [Manager's name]   Date: [Today's]

From: [Your name]

Subject: Purchase of safe

I attach a table analysing the cost of the quotations received from four companies.

All the suppliers can deliver within one week, except for S & N Safes, who have quoted one-month delivery.

8.

Quotation	Cost	Sales tax	Payable	Delivery	Maintenance	Remedial	Guarantee work	Total cost
1 Valid for 1 month	£60 each	£6.00	Monthly statement or 2.5% for payment within 7 days	Usually within 2 working days of signed order	On demand Call-out charge Minimum £25.00 plus hourly rate and materials		Not stated	£66.00 or £64.50 if paid within 7 days
2 Literature enclosed	£64 each	Included	Cash with order	Usually within 2 working days	£10 per year Automatic	Not usually required for reminder separate quotation if needed	1 year 10 years but	£74.00

9.

[Date]

The Sales Manager
[Name of Supplier]
[Address]

Dear Sirs

PEDESTAL DESK AND TYPIST CHAIR

Will you please send details of pedestal desks and typist chairs that you can supply including price, delivery charges if any, and guarantee period.

I also need to know the following details about each item.

Pedestal desk

- size and height of work surface
- non-glare work surface?
- wood or metal
- colours available

Typist chair

- five-star base
- adjustable seat height and tilt
- adjustable backrest height and rake
- seat cover material
- guaranteed non-flammable

Yours faithfully

[Name]
[Title]

CHAPTER 11

Practice questions

1. See page 314.
2. See pages 328-9.
3. See page 317.
4. *a.* See pages 318-22.
   b. See pages 322-4.
   c. See page 324.
   d. See page 325.
5. *a.* See pages 325-6.
   b. See page 326.
   c. See pages 326-7.

6. See page 318.
7. *a.* See page 318.
   b. See page 320.
8. See pages 328-9.
9. See pages 319 and 321-2.
10. See page 321.
11. See pages 327-8.
12. *a.* See pages 323-4.
    b. See pages 322-3.
13. *a.* See pages 327-8.
    b. See page 328.
    c. See pages 315-16 and 329-30.
    d. See pages 330-1.
14. See page 327.
15. See pages 329-30.
16. See page 325.
17. *a.* See page 331.
    b.
    - cheques paid into the bank but not yet credited to the account
    - cheques paid out but not yet debited to the account
    - direct debits and/or standing orders not entered in cash book
    - bank charges not entered in cash book
18. See page 325.
19. *a.* See page 323.
    b. The company does not have to remember to pay on the due date as its account will be debited automatically each month. The lenders do not have to remind the company as their account will be credited automatically with the amount on the due date each month.
20.

NATIONAL COMMERCIAL BANK (JA) LIMITED
Matilda's Corner Branch

Date [Today's]

Depositor's initials [yours]

Teller's initials

Credit Account of
Island Designs Limited

Account no. 6278918

37-077

Cheques		Details	Cash incl. coin	
154	62	× 1		
535	50	× 5		
445	60	2 × 10	20	00
1150	00	7 × 20	140	00
94	48	4 × 100	400	00
2041	00	COIN	1	65
		TOTAL	561	65
4421	20	CHQS	4421	20
Cash received		SUB-TOTAL	4982	85
		LESS EXCH		
Signature		NET TOTAL	4982	85

Short answer questions

1. referees
2. writes
3. post-dated
4. initial, sign
5. refer to drawer
6. *a*
7. *c*
8. *d*
9. *b*
10. *b*

Examination questions

1. ***a.***

Date	NORTHEAST BANK **Current Account Credit** **COMPLETE IN BLOCK LETTERS PLEASE**		£50 Notes	50	00
			£20 Notes	80	00
			£10 Notes	50	00
Account holding branch	BAKER STREET LONDON		£5 Notes	30	00
Bank sort code	3 5 – 6 7 – 2 0		£1 Note/Coin	19	00
Account in name of	SPA HEALTH & FITNESS CLUB		S & 1 Notes		
Account number	4 7 6 2 3 4		50p	2	50
Cashier's stamp and initials	Paid in by: (Your Signature)		20p		
			Silver		
			Bronze	0	65
			Total cash	232	15
			Cheques POs etc. see over	525	00
			£	757	15

NORTHEAST BANK		
Please list cheques/POs etc. Name	£	p
J Burns	250	00
N Patel	25	00
D Da Costa	250	00
Total cheques carried over	525	00

b. direct debit, standing order, credit card

CHAPTER 12

Practice questions

1. See page 342.
2. *a.* See page 343.
   b. See page 343.
3. *i.* See page 344.
   ii. See page 344.
   iii. See pages 344-5.
   iv. See page 346.
   v. See pages 346-7.
4. See page 347.
5. *i.* See pages 345-6.
   ii. See page 345.
   iii. See page 347.
6. See page 349.
7. *i.* workers such as bricklayers
   ii. workers in manufacturing companies
   iii. sales representatives
8. See page 350.
9. *i.* See page 351.
   ii. See page 351.
   iii. See page 351.
   iv. See page 351.
   v. See page 355.
10. See page 351.
11. See page 353.
12. See page 352 (Trinidad & Tobago).
13. See pages 358-9.
14. *i.* See page 349.
    ii. See page 370.
    iii. See page 363.
    iv. See page 370.
15. See pages 373-7.
16. *a.* See pages 378-9.
    b. See pages 380-1.
    c. See page 378.

17.

A4 ruled pads				Maximum: 500 Re-order: 150 Minimum: 50
Date	Issues	Department	Receipts	Balance
2.5.02				260
3.5.02	40	purchasing		220
8.5.02	60	sales		160
17.5.02	30	admin		130
20.5.02	50	training		80
23.5.02	10	transport		70
27.5.02			400	470
28.5.02	20	IP		450

18. *a.* See page 381.
    b. See page 381.
19. *a.* See page 382.
    b. See page 382.
20. See pages 382-3.
21. See pages 384-7.
22. *i.* See pages 383-4.
    ii. See page 383.
    iii. See page 382.
    iv. See page 382.
23. *a.* A5 cards in a box
    b.

CAR – Registration no.
    Make
    CC
    Year of purchase
		NAME OF REPRESENTATIVE			

Date	Mileage	Maintenance		Repairs	
		Date	Mileage	Date	Parts

c.

```
Name ............................................................. Car registration no. ................................................
Week beginning .................................................................
```

Mileage at start of week ....

at end of week ....

Maintenance carried out*

Date.................................

Mileage............................

Any repairs beyond normal maintenance ....

....

Repairs*

Date.................................

Mileage............................

Work done..

....

*Please attach garage job sheet

Signed .... Date ....

d.

MEMORANDUM

To: Sales Representatives   Date [Today's]

From: Transport Manager

Subject: REPRESENTATIVES' CARS

A new system of records on all company cars is being introduced. This will ensure that all cars are serviced regularly and replaced when appropriate.

The information for the records will be provided weekly by you. A form, to be completed at the end of each week, is attached. A completed form should be given to my assistant [Name] every Monday.

Your co-operation in the introduction of this new system will be greatly appreciated.

24. *a* and *b*

Task	1	2	3	4	5	6	7	8	9	10	11	12	13	14	15	16	17	18	19	20	21	22
1																						
2																						
3																						
4																						

    c. Two days; Saturday at time and a half.

25.   *i.* See page 389.
  ii. See page 396.
  iii. See pages 390–1.
  iv. See page 396.
  v. See page 392.

26.

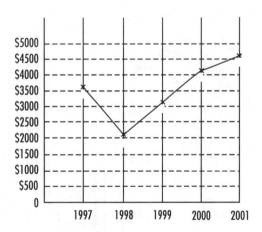

27. *a.*

	March				April				May				June				July				August				September				October			
Week beginning	4	11	18	25	1	8	15	22	29	6	13	20	27	3	10	17	24	1	8	15	22	29	5	12	19	26	2	9	16	23	30	7	14	21	28
Head of Dept																															
Chief Clerk																															
Asst Clerk 1																															
Asst Clerk 2																															
Asst Clerk 3																															
Secretary																															
Typist 1																															

*Asst clerk 1 will take a day before the week in lieu of Good Friday   *Asst clerk 2 will take a day after the week in lieu of Easter Monday

b. Head of department and asst clerk 1 follow chief clerk in October without time for handing over.

Chief clerk and asst clerk 1 are on holiday the same week beginning 25 March.

Asst clerk 2 follows asst clerk 1 in March/April without time for handing over.

Typist's week overlaps secretary's second week in March and also part of asst clerk 1's week.

Typist's fortnight in July overlaps asst clerk 3's first week in July – this may not be important.

28.

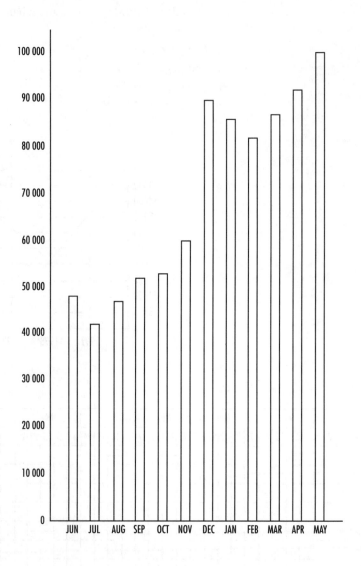

29.

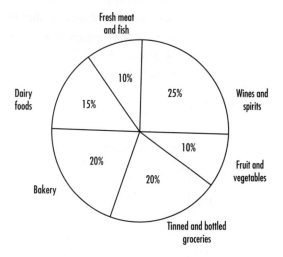

30. *i.* See page 397.
    ii. See page 394.
    iii. See page 392.
    iv. See pages 390-1.

Short answer questions
1. on commission
2. TD4 certificate
3. personal file
4. statutory
5. payroll
6. *b*
7. *a*
8. *c*
9. *b*
10. *d*

Examination questions
1. locked in a box
2. imprest
3. See page 378.
4. maximum level
5. analysis
6. See Fig. 12.19, page 385.
7. *a.* *i.* No stock should be issued without a requisition. The requisition should be signed by the person ordering the stock and authorised by a supervisor or manager. One person should

be in charge of stationery with another person as back-up. The stationery cupboard should be kept locked so that individuals cannot help themselves.

  ii. See pages 380-1.
 b. See page 379.

8.

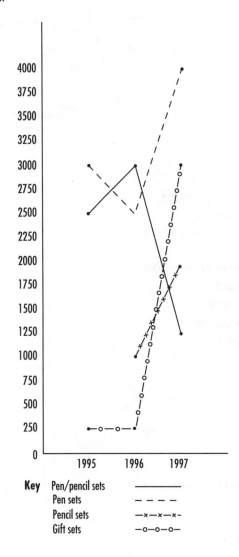

Key	Pen/pencil sets	————
	Pen sets	– – – –
	Pencil sets	—x—x—x—
	Gift sets	—o—o—o—

9. *a.*

A4 white bond paper Ref.: ES124 Unit: ream					Maximum: 50 Re-order: 20 Minimum: 10	
Date	Reqn no.	Issues	Department	Inv no.	Receipts	Balance
1.1.02						40
5.1.02	285	5	purchasing			35
8.1.02	148	10	sales			25
9.1.02	122	5	accounts			20
30.1.02		50		Z452	30	50

    b.   See page 378.
    c.   See pages 379-80.

CHAPTER 13

Practice questions

1. See pages 407-8.
2. Preferred time and day(s) or date(s)
   Who is to chair the meeting
   The people who must be present - key people, and others
   Preferred venue
   Whether notes/minutes of the meeting will be required
   Deadline for sending out the agenda and any papers
   Whether refreshment/lunch will be required
3. See pages 408-9.
4.   *i.*   See page 408.
     ii. See page 410.
     iii. See page 410.
5. Everyone is free on Thursday from 1400-1600.
   Mr Ross's lunch is not certain so presumably he can arrange it to suit.
   Tuesday is not possible because Michael Short and Peter Smith are away all day.
   Wednesday from 1330-1530 would be possible if Mr Short is not at Poolside (again a query).

6.

OFFICE SUPERVISORS' MEETING

To: All Office Supervisors [Date]

A meeting of Office Supervisors is to be held at 10:30 on Wednesday [date] in Conference Room 1.

AGENDA

1   Salary increases
2   Grievance procedures
3   Safety
4   Punctuality

[Name]

---

7. See page 425.

8.
   i. See pages 408–9 and 436.
  ii. See page 436.
 iii. See page 437.
  iv. See pages 428 and 436.
   v. See pages 419 and 436.
  vi. See page 432.
 vii. See pages 415 and 418.
viii. See pages 423 and 437.
  ix. See pages 423 and 436.
   x. See page 434.

9. See page 421.

10.

TRADES UNIQUE COUNCIL

To: All Trades Union Representatives   [Date]

A meeting of all Trade Union Representatives is to be held at 1400 on Friday [date] in Meeting Room 3 on the 4th floor of Trade Union House.

Will you please submit, on the form below, items for discussion by Wednesday [10 days before the meeting].

....

To: BD Johns
        Council Secretary

Will you please include the following item(s) on the agenda for the meeting to be held at 1400 hours on Friday [date]:

Signed: .... Date: ....

---

11.   *i.*   See pages 433–4.
     ii.   See page 434.
    iii.   See page 435.
12. 'Taking the chair' means that the appointed chairperson is conducting the meeting. 'In the chair' means that another member of the group is fulfilling the chairperson's role.
13. See pages 425–6.
14.   *i.*   See pages 409 and 437.
     ii.   See pages 414–16 and 437.
    iii.   See pages 423 and 436.
     iv.   See page 418.
      v.   See page 408.
     vi.   See page 432.
    vii.   See page 437.
   viii.   See page 433.
     ix.   See page 433.
      x.   See pages 424, 426–7 and 436.
15.   *i.*   See pages 432 and 436.
     ii.   See page 433.

16. *a.* See pages 422 and 423.
    b. See pages 422 and 423.

Short answer questions
1. third person, past tense
2. audioconferencing
3. apologies
4. quorum
5. verbatim
6. *c*
7. *c*
8. *d*
9. *b*
10. *a*

Examination questions
1. *a.* See page 408.
   b. See page 424.
   c. *i.* See page 437.
         ii. See page 436.
         iii. See page 437.
         iv. See page 437.

CHAPTER 14

Practice questions
1. See page 446.
2. Methods of obtaining passports vary from territory to territory. (You have to find the answer to this by research.)
3. So that the room will be retained for you, as some hotels re-let rooms if guests do not check in by a certain time.
4. *a.* whose name the ticket is booked in
       dates and destinations of flights
       whether already paid for, or whether the traveller or company is to be invoiced
   b. See page 454.
5. You will need to obtain flight times from airline leaflets or travel agents. If the home island is Barbados the flights will be Jamaica Barbados. (The dates given at the top of page 603 are specimen only.)

ITINERARY – [NAME]						
Date	Time	Flight no.	Destination	Check-in time	Dep. time	Arr. time
6.10.02	0000	(Leave home)	Airport			
6.10.02		00000	Barbados			
10.10.02	0000	(Leave hotel)	Airport			
10.10.02		00000	Jamaica			
15.10.02*	0000	(Leave hotel)	Airport			
15.10.02*		00000	Home island			

* If there is a late afternoon/evening flight; if not, departure would be 16.10.02.

6.

businesstourtrinidad@wow.net [Date]

Will you please make the reservations listed below for [full name].

All flights are to be economy/business/first class.

Date	Flight no.	From	To	Dep. time	Arr. time
6.10.02	0000	(Leave home)	Airport		
6.10.02		00000	Barbados		
10.10.02	0000	(Leave hotel)	Airport		
10.10.02		00000	Jamaica		
15.10.02*	0000	(Leave hotel)	Airport		
15.10.02*		00000	Home island		

* If there is a late afternoon/evening flight; if not, departure would be 16.10.02.

7. Dates of flight, flight number, departure time, OK (flight confirmed), correct name of passenger.
8. *a.* Check the flight details to ensure arrival and departure times are reasonable.

b.

> [Today's date]
>
> Front Office Manager
> Excelsior Hotel
> [Address]
>
> Dear Sir
>
> CONFIRMATION OF RESERVATION
>
> I refer to my telephone conversation when I made the following reservation:
>
> Mr John Levine
> One single room with bath and air conditioning
> Five nights from Monday 8 July 2002 to Friday 12 July, departing on Saturday 13 July
>
> Mr Levine will arrive on Flight 00000 from [home island].
>
> He will settle his account by credit card.
>
> Yours faithfully
>
> [Name]

    c. Refer to question 5 to check that you have included all details in the itinerary.
9. Contact the American Embassy to check whether a visa is needed. If so, find out from your travel agent the procedure for obtaining a visa.
10. **a.** American dollar
    b. Sterling, Euro or American dollar
    c. Canadian or American dollar
    d. American dollar
    e. American dollar

Short answer questions
1. economy, business, first class
2. passport
3. visa
4. subject to confirmation
5. travel agent, airline
6. *d*
7. *b*
8. *c*
9. *b*
10. *c*

Examination questions

1. ***a.***

SCRIBESWORLD LTD
Tel. 0207 710 5000
Fax 0207 710 5005

SCRIBES HOUSE
10 Chester Street
LONDON W3 3DG

FACSIMILE TO

Warren Park Hotel   HARARE   ZIMBABWE

FAX NO. 09-780 1008
COPY TO Branch Office   14 Churchill Road   HARARE   ZIMBABWE
FAX NO. 09-304 9808
FROM   Head Office
DATE   [Today's]   NO. OF PAGES 1

I confirm the provisional reservation made by the Harare branch of Scribesworld Limited, as follows:

Mr John Land, hotel suite for four nights from [day, date] to [day, date], departing on [day, date].

Mr Land's flight arrives at 2030 hours local time. Will you please hold the suite until his arrival?

Will you please confirm this reservation and let me know whether secretarial services are available?

SIGNATURE ....

END OF MESSAGE

---

   b. tetanus – against lockjaw caused by dirt getting into a wound
       typhoid – against disease ingested with food or water
       hepatitis A – against disease caused by contaminated food or drink
       (others include poliomyelitis, smallpox, diphtheria)

2. ***a.*** See page 459.
   b. See pages 450–2.
   c. See page 450.

CHAPTER 15

Practice questions

1.
    i. English words and phrases commonly used and understood
    ii. Word that means the same as another word
    iii. Word that means the opposite of another word
    iv. Word derived from a word in another language, e.g. Latin or French
    v. Aristocracy
    vi. Short, memorable saying
    vii. Saying something is like something else that is different
    viii. Endorsements
    ix. Weather records
    x. The way a word is spoken

2.
    i. Stationary – standing still
    Stationery – paper
    ii. Grey/gray – interchangeable
    iii. Wharves (or wharfs)
    iv. 'Diffthong', two vowel sounds combined to make one syllable, e.g. 'ow' combines the light vowels 'a' and 'oo'
    v. Placed above or over

3.
    i. No
    ii. Occurred
    iii. See page 476.
    iv. Leave a space
    v. Mr President
    vi. A list of topics numbered under the heading 'agenda'
    vii. With mark 'typed over a second of two vowels to indicate that they are pronounced separately', e.g. naive (pronounced ni-eve)

4.
    i. Alan Greenspan
    ii. Green, red and white vertical stripes with an eagle in the centre of the white stripe
    iii. Georgetown, Guyana; Dr Edwin Carrington, Secretary General CARICOM
    iv. Co-ordinating international health activities and helping governments to improve health services

5.
    a. *Statesman's Year Book*
    b. *Post Office Guide* or postal leaflets
    c. *Debretts Correct Form*
    d. *Gazette*
    e. *National Weekly Freighting Directory*

6. See pages 471–5.

7. *a.* Dictionaries vary in indicating stress so your answer will depend on the dictionary you use.
   b. memoranda or memorandums, media or mediums, appendices or appendixes, analyses, helices or helixes, hetaerae, hiatus or hiatuses
   c. learnt or learned, slept, stole, stood, ran, flew, thought
8. See pages 468–71.
9. See page 469.
10. *i.* Dear Prime Minister
    ii. Dear Vicar or Dear Mr X
    iii. Varies depending on country
    iv. Varies depending on country
    v. Your Grace

(Note that the style of address on the envelope and inside address of the letter varies depending on the country.)

Short answer questions
1. bank
2. Russian Embassy
3. local, national, international
4. reference libraries
5. airline, airport
6.

Part of speech	**Example**
preposition	over
conjunction	and
verb transitive	conduct
noun	book
adverb	leisurely
interjection	golly!
pronoun	he
verb intransitive	look

7. perseverance
8. cliché
9. slang
10. insce, mtg, confce, abt, ctee

CHAPTER 16

Practice questions
1. See page 484.

2. *a.*

> [Your address]
>
> [Date]
>
> Mrs Janet Wimpey
> Personnel Officer
> National Trading Company Limited
> KINGSTON
>
> Dear Mrs Wimpey
>
> **ADMINISTRATIVE ASSISTANT**
>
> I refer to your advertisement in [local newspaper]. Will you please send me an application form and further information about the post advertised.
>
> Yours sincerely
>
> [Your signature]
>
> [Name]

b.

> [Your address]
>
> [Date]
>
> [Name and address]
>
> Dear [Name]
>
> I am applying for the post of Administrative Assistant at the National Trading Company Limited. When I complete the application form I shall have to give names of referees. May I give your name please? I should be grateful if you would allow me to do so.
>
> Yours sincerely
>
> [Your signature]
>
> [Name]

3. **a.**

> [Your address]
> [Date]
>
> Mr Hanif Muhammed
> Office Services Manager
> Caribbean Traders Limited
> 68 High Street
> PORT-OF-SPAIN
>
> Dear Mr Muhammed
>
> **RECEPTIONIST**
>
> I refer to your advertisement in [local newspaper] and wish to apply for the post of Receptionist.
>
> I enclose a detailed curriculum vitae, which sets out my experience as a receptionist/telephonist.
>
> Yours sincerely
>
> [Your signature]
>
> [Name]
>
> Enc.

b. See page 497.

4. See pages 497–8.

5.

> [Your address]
> [Date]
>
> [Name]
> The Personnel Manager
> Gay Fabrics Limited
> PO Box 478
> GEORGETOWN
> GUYANA
>
> Dear [Name]
>
> **SENIOR TYPIST**
>
> Thank you for your letter of [date] offering me the post of Senior Typist in your company. I am very pleased to accept the offer.
>
> I shall be available to start work on [date].
>
> Yours sincerely
>
> [Your signature]
>
> [Name]

6.

[Your address]

[Date]

[Name]
Personnel Officer
Kingston Traders Limited

Dear [Name]

NOTICE OF TERMINATION OF EMPLOYMENT

I wish to inform you that I have been offered a post at Jamaica Breweries Limited. I have accepted the offer as the post will give me greater scope for development. Also the salary is considerably higher than my present one. I am therefore giving one month's notice that I shall be leaving the company on [date].

I have enjoyed working at Kingston Traders Limited and appreciate having learned a lot since joining the company.

Yours sincerely,

[Your signature]

[Name]

7.

[Your address]

[Date]

Miss Jenny Price
Recruitment Officer
Perfumes Limited
PO Box 489
BRIDGETOWN
BARBADOS

Dear [name]

JUNIOR SECRETARY – OFFER OF APPOINTMENT

Thank you for giving me the opportunity to attend the interview yesterday and for the offer of this post.

I have given the offer very careful consideration but am sorry that I am unable to accept it. I do not think it is very different from my present job and therefore would not provide the challenge I seek.

Yours sincerely

[Yours signature]

[Name]

8. *a.* See pages 495-8.
   b. See page 498 and give an example, e.g. a suit.
   c. See pages 498-9.
9. *i.* See pages 502-3.
   ii. See pages 503-4.
10. See pages 502-3.

APPENDIX 7

STUDY NOTES

STUDYING

Some students will be studying in school or college with extra work to do as homework; others will study on their own without the benefit of guidance from tutors. If you intend to sit an examination, whichever way you study, the approach must be the same – methodical and carefully planned.

Each person learns in their own way. The following suggestions must be adapted to suit each individual.

1. First read the chapter until you come to an Activity.
2. Read the Activity at least twice, or as many times as necessary until you really understand what you are to do.
3. Make a note of any points you are not sure about and refer to the text to clarify them.
4. When you are reasonably sure that you can do the Activity, go ahead and do it.
5. When you have completed the Activity, refer to the suggested answer in Appendix 5. In many cases you will not have produced exactly what is given in the answer; this does not matter, but check that you have covered all the necessary points. Refer to the text for any points that are not clear to you.

When you have read the chapter and worked through all the Activities, attempt the questions grouped at the end of the chapter. It does not matter whether you do the practice questions or the short answer questions first. Work through them but do not waste time trying to answer questions to which you do not know the answer.

Refer to the relevant text for questions you cannot answer. Use the index to find the sections you need. When you have read the appropriate sections, try to answer the questions.

When you have answered as many questions as you can, refer to the suggested answers in Appendix 6. Refer to the text where this is indicated or when you have given an incorrect answer. Make a note of the points you found difficult with the appropriate page number reference.

On another day revise the points you have listed and then try to work through the examination questions. Leave those you cannot answer. Check the answers of the questions you have attempted, noting any points you need to revise. Read the text relating to the questions you could not answer and then attempt to answer them.

This may seem a slow method but it is better to 'hurry slowly' so that each section you learn is fixed firmly in your mind.

When you revise before your examination, use the notes you have made as the basis for revision. Make sure you have retained the knowledge needed to answer the questions.

Bear in mind that questions in examination papers are not designed for you to show just what you know. You are expected to apply that knowledge to life-like situations. When you are employed you will be doing this most of the time.

PREPARING FOR THE EXAMINATION

Do not leave your revision until a week or two before the examination. Draw up a schedule, allocating a certain amount of time over a period of at least a month to cover all sections, spending more time on those that caused you difficulty when working through the questions. Ideally, practise working through at least two past papers under examination conditions.

THE EXAMINATION

Establish how much time you have to answer each question. If, for example, you have two hours to work through a paper, have to answer six questions that each have the same number of marks and the maximum number of marks is 90, you have an average of 20 minutes per question. However, you will need time at the start of the examination to read through the whole paper. *Never* start to answer a question until you have read the whole paper. You will also need time at the end to read through what you have written and possibly add a point or two, or make an amendment. You also need to check spelling and grammar. It would therefore be wise to spend about 16 or 17 minutes on each question. This will give you about 10 minutes for the first reading of the paper and 10 minutes for checking at the end. If you get stuck, do not spend time puzzling. Move on and come back to that question later. It is better to work through those questions you can answer easily in order to get as many marks as you can.

Listen very carefully to the instructions the invigilator gives. You get no marks for doing the wrong thing, however good it might be.

When you have read through the whole paper, re-read each question before answering it. Ask yourself what the examiner wants you to tell them. Answer the question that is asked, not what you think you would like to write. More students fail examinations through giving the wrong answer than through not knowing the work. Be warned!

When you leave the examination room you will have done your best. Do not waste time thinking what other answers you could have given. You will know what you have achieved when the date for the results arrives.

It is customary to wish people good luck when they are taking an examination. We will not do this here, because we believe that success does not depend on luck; it depends on regular, methodical learning and well-planned revision before the examination, followed by attentive reading and clear thinking during the examination.

May you be successful.

INDEX

Notes: Advice on how to use an index can be found on page 475. Abbreviations used in subheadings in the index are: PO = Post Office; VDU = visual display unit.

abbreviations, dictionary of 472
absences 345-6, 349, 350
accidents
   preventing *see* office(s), safety in
   recording 346, 349
   reporting 30, 346-7, 348, 349
accommodation, travellers 446-7, 451, 453, 454
accounts
   annual 3, 10, 381
   bank *see* banks/banking services
   petty cash 385-7
   statements 287-9
   and stock records 380, 381
accounts department 9-10
   see also salaries and wages
   goods received notes 285
   invoices 286-7
   pro-forma invoices 281
   purpose of records 342
action points/sheets 415, 427, 430, 432
action slips 233, 234
activities
   answers to 531-56
   study guidelines 612
Acts of Parliament
   national insurance 355-6, 359
   safety 30-1
address, forms of 121, 474
addresses
   delivery 299
   e-mail 56
   freepost 263
   letters 121, 122, 250-1
   PO requirements 250-1, 252, 258, 259
   redirected mail 259
   telegraphic 131
addressing machines 239
ad hoc committees 410
administration function 6, 8
administrative assistants 38
administrative tasks 15
advertisements, job 484-6
advertising 11
   mail-order firms 383
   unaddressed material 264-5
   on websites 57, 383

advice of duration and charge (ADC) calls 85
advice notes 281-2
advisory committees 409
aerogrammes 254
after sales service 11
agendas, meetings 415, 416, 417, 418, 424
airmail 159, 253-4
air travel
   booking 445, 451, 454, 455
   information on 470, 474
air waybill 290, 292
alphabetical filing 198-201, 203, 205, 207, 208
   minutes 433
alphabets, telephone 89-90
alpha-numeric filing 201-2, 205
American paper sizes 156
annual accounts 3, 10, 381
annual general meetings (AGMs) 3, 408-9
   agenda for 417
   notice of 416
answering machines 82-3, 99
appearance, personal 102
application forms 343, 486, 489-94
applications, job 484-6, 488, 489-94, 495
appointment, letters of 344
appointments
   making 71-2, 450
   travellers 450, 451
   visitors with 65-8
appointments book 72
appraisals 344-5, 503-4
archiving 214-16
atlases 469
attitudes, personal 100-1
audioconferences 422, 423
audio-dictation 151-3
auditors 381, 385

back-up disks 223-4
balance sheets 10
Bankers' Automated Clearing System (BACS) 333

INDEX

bankruptcy 2
banks/banking services
   account types 314
   balances 331-2
   bank drafts 322
   borrowing money 334-5
   cash points 327-8
   cash withdrawals 327-8
   cheques *see* cheques
   choosing 314-15
   clearing system 333-4
   corporate lending 336
   credit cards 59, 85, 87, 324, 448
   crediting an account 316, 322
   credit (paying-in) slips 315-16, 328-9
   credit references 382
   debit cards 327-8
   demand deposit accounts 314-15
     see also cheques
   deposit (paying-in) slips 315-16, 328-9
   direct debits 323-4
   documentary credit 325-6
   electronic transfers 326
   fixed deposit accounts 314
   information from 468
   LINX cards 328
   loans 335
   for making payments 317-27
   Moneygram service 326
   money orders 325
   night safes 329-30
   'non-stop banking' 330
   opening an account 315
   overdrafts 321, 335
   overdrawn accounts 321-2, 335
   paying-in slips 315-16, 328-9
   paying money in 328-30
   pensions 266
   personal banking centres 335
   reconciliation statements 331, 332
   salaries paid into 370
   savings accounts 265-6, 314
   signature cards 315
   standing orders 322-3
   statements 330-3
   SWIFT 326
   Switch cards 324
   telephone banking 336
   term deposit accounts 314
   travellers' cheques 326-7, 448
Barbados
   capital 516
   Chamber of Commerce and Industry 519-20
   currency 516
   official language 516
   postal authority 268
   safety legislation 30
   telephone services 86
   trades unions 527-8

bar charts 392, 393
bar graphs 392
batch processing 50-1
bill of lading 289-90, 291, 326
bill of sight 296, 298
binding, documents 181-2
bleepers 81
blocked style, letters 123
board meetings 409
boards of directors 3, 409
bomb alerts 31, 32, 91-2
borrowing money 334-5
breaks, from computers 28
bridging loans 335
bring-forward systems 222-3
buildings, security 33
business organisations
   addressing letters to 122
   administration 15
   corporate aims 5
   corporate lending 336
   corporate objectives 5-6
   departments 9-15
   functions 6-9
   information from 468-9
   management 4-6
   meetings *see* meetings
   organisation charts 16-17
   pyramid structure 5
   stocktaking 381
   types of 1-4
business records *see* records
business reply service 263
business transactions
   documents used in *see* commercial documents
   payment *see* payment methods
business units, public limited companies 3-4
buying transactions
   documents used in *see* commercial documents
   Internet 59
   payment *see* payment methods

cables (telegrams) 131-3
call off, meaning 299
car, travel by 445, 454
carbon paper 156
card indexes 194, 198, 433
cardphones 87
cards, PO recommended 252
career development 505
Caribbean, the
   capitals of 516-17
   Chamber of Commerce and Industry members 519-25
   countries of 516-17
   currencies 516-17
   information sources 471-2
   official languages 516-17

postal authorities 267-8
trades unions mailing list 526-30
car parks, security 33
carriage forward/paid 299
cash
   paying into bank 328-9
   petty 384-7
   received in mail 235
   for wages 370
   withdrawing from bank 327-8
cash on delivery 299
cash discount 299
cash points 327-8
catalogues 274, 299
cellphones 80-1, 98-9
cellular offices 22-3, 24
central processing units (CPUs) 48, 49, 50, 51
certificate of insurance 290, 293
certificate of origin 290, 294
chairpersons 424-5, 433-4
chairs 25, 26
Chambers of Commerce 468, 519-25
charts
   business organisation 16-17
   statistical 392-6
checklists
   meeting arrangements 412-14
   meeting rooms 421
   travel arrangements 456-8
   traveller's documents 454
cheque books 316-17, 321
cheques 316-17
   amending 320
   amount to be paid 319
   bank reconciliation statements 331, 332
   books of 316-17, 321
   bouncing 322
   cash withdrawals 327
   clearing 333-4
   copy slips 319
   counterfoils 318, 319
   crossed/crossings 318, 320-1, 327
   dating 319
   dishonoured 321-2
   drawing 318-19
   lost 321
   making payment with 318-22
   pay 370
   payee's name 319
   paying into bank 328-9
   post-dated 319
   R/D (refer to drawer) 322
   received in mail 235
   signatures 315, 319
   stale-dated 319, 320
   stolen 321
   stopping payment of 321
   travellers' 326-7, 448, 454
'chron' (day) files 222

chronological filing 198, 199, 204
circulation slips
  incoming mail 233, 234
  memoranda 119
classified documents
  mailing 237-8
  security 210-11, 343
clearing system, cheques 333-4
clerks, job description 37
coach travel 445-6
coinphones 87
collation, documents 175-6, 239-40
collect calls 85
colour coding
  files 206
  forms 130
colour transparencies 420-1
commercial documents 271-2
  acknowledgement of order 280
  advice notes 281-2
  air waybill 290, 292
  bill of lading 289-90, 291, 326
  bill of sight 296, 298
  certificate of insurance 290, 293
  certificate of origin 290, 294
  consignment notes 283
  credit notes 287
  customs bill of sight 296, 298
  debit notes 287
  delivery notes 283, 284
  despatch notes 283
  enquiries 274-6
  entry ex ship for goods liable to duty 296, 297
  estimates 277, 278-9
  export licence 296
  goods received notes 285
  home trade 273-89
  import licence application 294-6
  invoices 286-7
  orders 278-81
  overseas trade 289-98, 326
  packing notes 283
  processing of order 280-1
  pro-forma invoices 281, 282
  quotations 276-8
  receipts 289
  requisitions 273
  shipping 289-90, 294-6
  statements of account 287-9
  tenders 277, 278-9
  terms used 299-300
  units of measurement 300-1
commercialese 114-15
commission payments 350
committee meetings 409, 410
  agendas 417
  co-opted members 423
  ex-officio members 423
  files 420
  minutes 427-33

  notice of 415
  procedure 424-5
  quorum 423
  secretary's role 434
  structure 423
Commonwealth countries 518
communication
  telephone see telephones/telephone lines
  written see written communication
communications managers 13, 45
companies
  information from 468
  limited see limited companies
company records 470
company secretary 13
company solicitor 13
company's risk 299
computers/computerised systems 43-4
  air tickets 454, 455
  batch processing 50-1
  breaks from 28
  central processing units 48, 49, 50, 51
  consumables 53-4, 154-7
  copiers linked to 172
  corrupted information 60
  databases 53
  data transmission 54-5
  document retrieval 223-4
  document storage 223-4
  eyesight tests 28
  firmware 48
  hacking 59-60
  'hardware' defined 48
  Internet 55-9, 469
  laptops 49, 50, 54, 55, 60
  mail sorting 252
  mainframe 48-9, 54-5, 223-4
  memory 48
  modems 54
  money transfers 326
  networks 54-9
  on-line processing 51
  parallel processing 48-9
  people involved with 44-7
  peripheral equipment 50-2
  personal see personal computers (PCs)
  presentations 60, 398
  printers 51-2, 166-7, 172
  programs 48, 52
  random access 51
  security 33, 53, 59
  serial access 50-1
  servers 49, 55
  software 46, 48, 52, 56, 60, 166
  spellcheckers 140
  telephones 74-8
  terminals 48, 49, 53

  viruses 60
  visual display units 27, 33, 52
  Winchester disks 49, 51
  word processing 166
'concertina' files 207, 208
confidential information
  mail 233, 237, 238
  personnel records 342-3
  security 33, 53, 210, 211, 343
consulates 469
consumables
  computer 53-4, 154-7
  typewriter 154-60
continuation sheets 124-5
continuous stationery 156
contracts of employment 344
conversation guidelines 101-2
co-opted members, meetings 423
co-operatives 4
copiers/copying 168-72
copyholders 27, 160
copy printers 172-3
corporate image 100-2
corporations 4
  information from 468
correction fluid 159, 160
correction papers 159-60
cost
  net 300
  trade 300
cost cards 374, 375
cost, insurance and freight (CIF) 299
cost schedules 374
countries
  Caribbean 516-17
  Commonwealth 518
courier services 70, 235, 243-4, 263-4
courtesy titles 121
credit
  buying goods on 382
  documentary 325-6
credit cards
  e-commerce 59
  making payments with 324
  telephone calls 85, 87
  travellers 448
credit control 281
credit notes 287
credit rating 382
credit sale records 381-4
credit (paying-in) slips 315-16, 328-9
credit worthiness, checking 280-1, 382
cubic measurements 301
currencies
  Caribbean 516-17
  foreign 448
curriculum vitae (cv) 484-6, 487, 489
customer services department 12
customs bill of sight 296, 298
customs declaration forms 254, 255

daisywheel printers
danger (hazard) signs 29, 30
databases 53
data input operators 46
data transmission 54-5
date stamping, mail 231-2
day files 222
debit cards 327-8
debit notes 287
deliveries
　addresses for 299
　charges for 299
　commercial documents 283-5
　date for 299
　method 299
　one-off 300
　part 282, 300
　postal 249-50, 256-62
　receiving 69, 235, 283-4, 285
　time 299
　transport destination call schedule 377-8
delivery notes 283, 284
demand deposit accounts 314-15
　cheques see cheques
departments 9-15
　meetings 410, 416
　records 347-9
deposit accounts 314-15
　cheques see cheques
deposit (paying-in) slips 315-16, 328-9
desk notes 116
desks 25, 26
despatch notes 283
diaries
　appointments in 65, 72
　bring-forward systems 222
　reception 65
dictation
　audio 151-3
　shorthand 151
dictionaries 472, 476-9
digital information 150
direct debits 323-4
directors 3, 5, 409
disciplinary occurrences 346
discount
　cash 299
　trade 300
disk drives 51
disks/diskettes 49, 51, 223-4
distribution lists 118-19
dividends 3
dividers, file 194, 204, 206
documentary credit 325-6
document destruction 220-1
document presentation 150
　binding 181-2
　collation 175-6, 239-40
　fastenings 177-80
　importance 182-3

jogging 176
punching 176-7
trimming 176
document production 150
　continuous stationery 156
　formatting 163-4
　paper sizes 154-6
　paper weight 156-7
　printer supplies 154-9
　recording equipment 151-3
　typewriter supplies 154-60
　typewriting 161-4
　word processing 164-6
　writing see written communications
document reproduction 150
　computer-linked 172
　copiers 168-72
　copy printers 172-3
　microcopying 216-20
　offset lithography 173-5
document retrieval see files/filing
document storage see files/filing
dot-matrix printers 167
downloading information 49
due date 287, 299
duplicating machines 172-3

e-business 59
e-commerce 59
electronic air tickets 454, 455
electronic mail see e-mail
electronic retrieval, files 223-4
electronic sorting, mail 252
electronic storage, files 223-4
electronic transfers, money 326
e-mail 56-7, 138-9
embassies 469
emergency procedures 31, 32, 91
employees
　absences 345-6, 349, 350
　accidents 30, 346-7, 348, 349
　appraisal 344-5, 503-4
　career development 505
　care of 26-8
　holiday charts 394, 395
　induction 502-3
　interpersonal skills 36
　job descriptions 37-8
　lateness 345, 350
　obligations 35-6
　personal belongings 34
　personnel records 342-9
　probationary 502-3
　promotion 505
　recruitment 343-4, 348-9, 484-502, 504-5
　resignation 504
　rights 35-6
　safety 28-32, 34
　salaries 349-73
　sex discrimination 504-5
　termination 345, 346

training 345, 347, 349, 502, 503
wages 349-73
employers' organisations 468-9
employment 483
　application forms 343, 486
　applying for 484-6, 489-94, 504-5
　interviews 343, 494-9, 504
　offers of 499-502
　on probation 502-3
　resigning from 504
　sex discrimination 504-5
　starting 502-3
　termination 345, 346
　tests 343, 499
　where to look for 484-9
employment agencies 487
employment contracts 344
English
　books on 472-3
　good use of 110-15, 476-9, 508-15
enquiries, commercial 274-6
entry ex ship for goods liable to duty 296, 297
envelopes 157
　addressing 250-1, 258
　airmail 159
　internal mail 243
　opening 231, 233
　outgoing mail 236, 237, 238, 240
　PO requirements 250-1, 252-3, 258
　quality 158-9
　sizes 158
　styles 158
　window 159
ergonomic furniture 25
errors and omissions excepted (E & OE) 287, 299
estimates 277, 278-9
evacuation procedures 31, 32
exam preparation 613
exam questions
　answers to 557-611
　study guidelines 612-13
exam technique 613-14
exit interviews 504
ex-officio members 423
exporting 289
　see also overseas trade
　licence for 296
express delivery service 259-60
extraordinary general meetings (EGMs) 409
ex works/warehouse 299
eyesight tests 28

facsimile transmission (fax) 135-8, 235
factory records 373-8
fastenings, paper 177-80
faulty goods 283-4, 285

faxes 135-8, 235
ferry travel 445
file notes 117
files/filing 189
  active 213, 214
  alphabetical 198-201, 203, 205, 207, 208
  alpha-numeric 201-2, 205
  archiving 214-16
  bring-forward systems 222-3
  cabinets 194, 196-7
  central registry 14, 191-2
  'chron' 222
  chronological 198, 199, 204
  classified 210-11, 343
  closed 213, 214
  colour coding 206
  committee 420
  'concertina' 207, 208
  cross-referencing 203, 204
  day 222
  dead 213, 214
  departmental 192
  destruction 220-1
  dividers 194, 204, 206
  document preparation for 207-9
  electronic storage 223-4
  equipment 193-8
  by geographic area 203, 205
  guide cards 194, 204, 206
  horizontal 194, 197
  identifying 204, 206
  importance of 209-10
  indexing 194, 198, 201, 203
  individual 192-3
  lateral 194, 195
  letter sorters 207, 208
  lever arch 194, 195, 197
  locations for 190-3
  microcopying 216-20
  minute files 419
  movement of 211-13
  non-active 213, 214
  numerical 198-9, 201-3, 207
  objects filed 190
  opening continuation 209
  opening new 209
  pending 222, 274, 279
  people involved in 190
  pre-sorting 207-8
  retention policy 213-14
  ring binders 194, 195, 197
  safety 28
  security 33, 210-13, 343, 419
  semi-active 213, 214
  by subject 202-3, 205, 207
  vertical 194, 197
  when to do it 206
  working 221-2
  work-in-progress 222
finance function 6-7
financial year 10

fire emergency procedures 31, 32
firmware 48
fixed deposit accounts 314
'flagging' system, files 420
floppy disks 49, 51, 223-4
folding, paper 236, 237, 240
follow-up systems
  action points 415, 427, 430, 432
  bring-forward 222-3
  pending files 222
  telephone messages 96
foreign currency 448
formatting, documents 163-4
forms 128-30
franked mail 240-2, 264
free on board (fob) 299-300
freepost 263
freight charges 299-300
functions, businesses 6-9
furniture
  meetings 421
  office 25-6

Gantt charts 394
goods received notes 285
government information 469, 471, 473, 488-9
grammar 111, 428-9, 508-11
graphics printers 167
graphs 389-92
grievances, employees 346
gross pay 351
gross price 300
guide cards 194, 204, 206
guillotines 176

hacking, computer 59-60
hard copy 150
  production *see* document production
hard disks 49, 223-4
hardware, definition 48
hazard signs 29, 30
health
  keyboard operators 26-8
  office safety 28-32
  travellers 447, 449
health surcharge 353, 355, 357
high commissions 469
hire purchase 382-3
holding companies 4
holiday charts 394, 395
holiday entitlement 345
home trade, commercial documents 273-89
hotel accommodation 446-7, 451, 453, 454
house style, letters 124

image creation 100-3
imperial measures 301
importing 289

see also overseas trade
licence for 294-6
imprest systems 385-7
income tax 351-3, 354-6
indexes
  how to use 475
  of suppliers 274, 275
  to files 194, 198, 201, 203
  to minutes 433
induction, new employees 502-3
information
  about job vacancies 488-9
  classified 210-11, 343
  confidentiality 33
  corruption 60
  databases 53
  downloading 49
  on PO services 267
  for receptionists 71
  researching 480
  security of 33, 53, 210-11, 343
  sources of 274, 467-80, 488-9
  uploading 49
information processing 43-4
  computer consumables 53-4
  computer equipment 47-52
  databases 53
  data transmission 54-5
  department of 14-15
  function of 6, 8
  networks 54-9
  people involved in 44-7
  security 53
  software 52
information processing manager 44-5
information service providers (ISPs) 55-6
ink cartridges 159, 171
ink duplicating machines 172-3
ink-jet printers 167
instalments, payment 382, 384
insurance
  see also National Insurance Scheme
  certificate of 290, 293
  premiums 300
  travel 449, 454
interest
  on bank accounts 314
  on bank loans 335
international mail 253-4
  express delivery 259
  redirection 259
  reply coupons 262
International Paper Sizes (IPS) 154-6
international reference books 472, 473-4
international trade
  commercial documents 289-98
  payment methods 325-7
Internet 55-9, 469
interpersonal skills 36
interviews 343, 494-9, 504

intranets 54
inventory 379-80, 381
invitations 125-6
  to interview 495, 496, 497
invoices 286-7
  pro-forma 281, 282
itineraries, travel 450-2

Jamaica
  capital 516
  Chamber of Commerce and Industry 522-3
  crossed cheques 327
  currency 516
  hire purchase 383
  JETS 328
  National Housing Trust 363
  National Insurance Scheme 355-6, 358-9, 363
  official language 516
  PO agency services 266
  PO boxes 257
  postage rates 253
  postal authority 268
  private bags 257
  redirected mail 258-9
  registered mail 260
  safety legislation 30-1
  telegram rates 132
  trades unions 530
jargon, commercial 114-15
job advertisements 484-6
job application records 343-4
job cards 374, 375
job descriptions 37-8
job offers 499-502
job resignations 504
job-seeking 484-502, 504-5
joggers 176
journals 470

keyboards 50
  operating 27
  posture for 26-7

label printing 239
labour turnover 347, 349
lading, bill of 289-90, 291, 326
landscaped offices 23, 24
language
  books on 472-3
  good use of 110-15, 476-9, 508-15
languages, Caribbean 516-17
LANs (local area networks) 54
laptop computers 49, 50
  data transmission 54, 55
  presentations 60
laser printers 51, 52, 167
lateness, employees 345, 350
laws
  national insurance 355-6, 359
  safety 30-1

legal department 13
legal documents 130
letters 120-5
  see also mail; Post Office services
  addressing 121, 122, 250-1
  of appointment 344
  classified 237-8
  commercialese 114-15
  continuation sheets 124-5
  day files 222
  delivered to reception 69, 235
  display 123-4, 141
  English used in 110-15
  of enquiry 275, 276
  hotel reservations 453
  house style 124
  incoming 231-6
  job application 486, 488, 489, 490
  job interviews 495, 496, 497
  job offers 499-502
  job resignation 504, 505
  layout 123-4, 141
  outgoing 236-42
  paper size 155, 156
  parts 120-2
  printed headings 120-1
  types 120
letter sorters 207, 208
lever arch files 194, 195, 197
libraries 469
limited companies 3-4
  addressing letters to 122
  statutory meetings 408-9, 416, 417
  stocktaking 381
linear measurements 301
line graphs 389-91
line printers 51-2
LINX cards 328
liquid measures 301
loans, bank 335
local area networks (LANs) 54
'losing a quarter' 350

machines
  safe use of 30
  security 33
magnetic dictation machines 152
magnetic disks 51
magnetic ink character recognition 316
magnetic tapes 50
mail 230
  see also Post Office services
  incoming 69, 231-6, 244-5
  internal 242-3
  methods of sending 243-4
  outgoing 70, 236-42, 245
  recorded 233, 235, 257, 260
  redirected 258-9
  registered 233, 235, 257, 260-1
mail order 383-4
mail room 14, 230, 244-5

mainframe computers 48-9, 54-5, 223-4
management, organisations 4-6
management services staff 47
maps 469
marketing function 6, 7-8
measurement units 300-1
meetings 407
  action points/sheets 415, 427, 430, 432
  agendas 415, 416, 417, 418, 424
  amended motions 424, 426
  annual general 3, 408-9, 416, 417
  arranging 410-14
  board 409
  chairperson 424-5, 433-4
  chairperson's agenda 415, 418
  committee see committee meetings
  committee secretary 434
  co-opted members 423
  departmental 410, 416
  documents for 414-19
  drafting minutes of 427-30
  equipment for 420-1
  ex-officio members 423
  extraordinary general 409
  formal 408-10, 423-5, 427-32, 434
  indexing minutes 433
  informal 408, 410, 428
  informal records 427, 428
  member's role 435
  minute files 419
  minutes 415, 419, 424, 427-33
  motions 424, 426, 427
  note-taking at 425-7
  notice of 414, 415-16
  points of order 425
  presentations 420-1
  procedure 424-5
  purposes 407-8
  quorum 423
  recording 427
  resolutions 424, 426
  riders 424, 426
  rooms for 412, 413, 421
  secretary's role 434
  statutory 408-9, 416, 417
  structure 423
  sub-committee 410
  supplementary papers 415, 418
  teleconferencing 422-3
  terms used in 435-7
  types 408-10
  votes/voting 409, 424, 426, 435, 436
  working papers 415, 418
memoranda 118-20
Memorandum and Articles of Association 3
messages, telephone 89-90, 94-8, 99
methods of payment see payment methods
metric measures 301

microcopying 216-20
microfiche 216, 217, 218, 220
Ministry of Labour and Co-Operatives (MOLC) website 488-9
minutes, meetings 415, 419, 424, 427-32
misconduct 36
mobile telephones 80-1, 98-9
modems 54
money
    and banks *see* banks/banking services
    Caribbean currencies 516-17
Moneygram service 326
money orders 325
motions, meetings 424, 426, 427
multi-line graphs 390-1
multinationals 4

National Employment Service (NES) 489
National Housing Trust 363
National Insurance Scheme (NIS) 355-6, 358-63, 364-9
net cost 300
net pay 351
net price 300
networks, computer 54-9
newspapers 469
night safes 329-30
non-governmental organisations (NGOs) 469
note-taking
    meetings 425-7
    stenotyping 151
numerical data 388-98
numerical filing 198-9, 201-3, 207

obligations
    employees 35
    employers 35, 36
obtaining employment *see* employment
office(s)
    employees *see* employees
    furniture in 25-6
    receiving visitors in 72-3
    safety in 28-32, 34
    security 33
    in traveller's absence 459
    types of 22-4
Official Gazette 471
official telegrams 133
offset lithography 173-5
On Jamaica Government Service (OJGS) telegrams 133
on-line processing 51
open-plan offices 23, 24
operations controllers 46
optical disks 51
orders
    documentation 278-81
    production 376, 377

organisation charts 16-17
organisations
    business *see* business organisations
    meetings *see* meetings
origin, certificate of 290, 294
overdrafts 321, 335
overdue payments 382, 383, 384
overhead projectors 420
overheads 374
overseas mail 253-4
    express delivery 259
    redirection 259
    reply coupons 262
overseas trade
    commercial documents 289-98
    payment methods 325-7
overtime working 350
owner's risk 300

packets
    franking 240
    PO recommendations 252
    receiving 69
    recorded delivery 260
packing notes 283
pagers 81, 82
paper
    fastenings 177-80
    folding 236, 237, 240
    punches 176-7
    shredders 221
    sizes 154-6
    trimming 176
    weight 156-7
parallel processing 48-9
parcels
    air 254
    customs declaration forms 254, 255
    franking 240
    receiving 69
    redirection 259
    TTPost courier service 264
    wrapping 242
parent companies
partnerships 2-3
    addressing letters to 122
passports 447, 454
passwords, computer access 53
pay *see* salaries and wages
Pay As You Earn (PAYE) tax 351, 352-3
paying-in slips
    bank accounts 315-16, 328-9
    statements of account 288, 289
payment, terms of 300
payment methods 313, 317-18
    bank draft 322
    cheque 318-22
    credit card 59, 324, 448
    crediting an account 322
    credit sales 381-4
    direct debit 323-4
    documentary credit 325-6

    electronic transfer 326
    hire purchase 382-3
    mail order 383-4
    Moneygram service 326
    money order 325
    postal order 325
    standing order 322-3
    SWIFT 326
    Switch card 324
    travellers 326-7, 447-8
payroll 363, 370
pay slips 370, 371
pending files 222
    orders 279
    requisitions 274
pensions, collection 266
people, reference books on 474
peripherals, computer 50-2
personal allowances, tax 352
personal appearance 102
personal attitudes 100-1
personal belongings 34
personal computers (PCs) 49, 51
    copier-linked 172
    copy printers 173
    data transmission 54
    document storage 223-4
    presentations 60
    security 53
personal development reviews 344-5, 503-4
personal safety 34
personnel department 10
personnel function 6, 7
personnel records 342-9
petty cash 384-7
phonecards 87
photocopiers *see* copiers
phototelegraph service 132
pictograms 397
picture charts 397, 398
piece rates/work 349-50
pie charts 396
planning schedules 373-4
points of order 425
policy committees 409
postage book 237, 238
postage meter franking machines 240-2, 264
postage rates 253-4
postage stamps 237
postal orders 325
post boxes, private 250, 257
postcards 252
postcodes 251-2
poste restante service 257-8
posting, certificates of 260, 262
Post Office services 248-9
    address format 250-1
    advice of delivery 261
    bulk postage 264
    for businesses 262-5

Post Office services cont.
　business reply service 263
　Caribbean authorities 267-8
　certificates of posting 260, 262
　choosing appropriate 265
　collection 249, 256
　complaints about 267
　courier service 263-4
　delivery 249-50, 256-62
　express delivery 259-60
　franked mail 241, 242, 264
　freepost 263
　information 469
　information about 267
　money orders 325
　overseas mail 253-4, 259
　pensions 266
　postage rates 253-4
　postal orders 325
　post boxes 250, 257
　postcodes 251-2
　poste restante 257-8
　private bags 250, 257
　prohibited goods 254
　recommended envelopes 252-3
　recorded delivery 260
　redirected mail 258-9
　registered delivery 260-1
　reply coupons 262
　savings accounts 265-6
　standards 266
　unaddressed mail 264-5
　zipcodes 251-2
post room 14, 230, 244-5
posture 26-7
practice questions
　answers to 557-611
　study guidelines 612-13
premiums, insurance 300
presentation
　documents 150, 175-83, 239-40
　minutes 431-2
　personal 100-3
　statistics 388-98
presentations 420-1
　computerised 60, 398
presidents, company 3, 5
price lists 277, 300
prices
　gross 300
　net 300
　trade 300
　unit 300
　ways of quoting 277
printers
　computer 51-2, 166-7, 172
　consumables 154-9
　copy 172-3
printing department 14
printing labels 239
print sizes 167
private bags 250, 257

private limited companies 3
　addressing letters to 122
　statutory meetings 408-9, 416, 417
　stocktaking 381
probationary employees 502-3
procedures, definition 22
production control 376-7
production department 12
production function 6, 8
production orders 376, 377
professional organisations 408-9, 470
profit 271
profit and loss accounts 10
pro-forma invoices 281, 282
programmers, computer 46
programs, computer 48, 52
progress advice 376-7
progress charts 393-4
project managers 45, 46
projectors 420-1
promotion 505
pronunciation 477
proofreading 140-2
proxy votes 409
public limited companies 3-4
　addressing letters to 122
　statutory meetings 408-9, 416, 417
　stocktaking 381
public phone boxes 87
public relations department 11
punches, paper 176-7
punctuation 512-15
purchasing transactions
　documents used in *see* commercial
　　documents
　Internet 59
　payment *see* payment methods

quality controllers 377
quorum, meetings 423
quotations 276-8

random access 51
reading written communications 142-3
receipts 289
receiving deliveries 69, 235, 283-4, 285
receiving telephone calls 88-9, 93
receiving visitors 65-73
reception/receptionists 65-72
　image creation 100-3
　job description 37
recorded mail 233, 235, 257, 260
recording equipment 151-3
records 341-2
　credit sales 381-4
　factory 373-8
　management of *see* files/filing
　of meetings *see* minutes
　personnel 342-9
　petty cash 384-7
　presenting data in 388-98

　purpose 342
　salaries and wages 349-73
　stock 378-81
recruitment 343-4, 348-9, 484-502, 504-5
reference books 471-80
references
　credit worthiness 280-1, 382
　employment 493
　to open bank account 315
registered mail 233, 235, 257, 260-1
registers
　incoming mail 232, 233-5
　outgoing mail 236
　visitors 66, 67, 68
reminder systems
　action points 415, 427, 430, 432
　bring-forward 222-3
　telephone messages 96
remittance slips 288, 289
repetitive strain injury (RSI) 26
reply coupons 262
reports 126-7
　interview 343
reprography 168
requisitions 273
　cash 370, 372
research, approach to 480
reservations, travel 452-3, 454
resolutions, meetings 424, 426
retention policy, files 213-14
retrieval, documents *see* files/filing
returnable empties 287
revision, exam 613
ribbons, typewriter/printer 159
riders, to resolutions 424, 426
rights, employees 35-6
ring binders 194, 195, 197
risk
　company's 299
　owner's 300
rotary card indexes 194, 198, 433
routing slips 233, 234

safety 28-32, 34
salaries and wages 349
　cash requisition for 370, 372
　commission payments 350
　gross pay 351
　health surcharge 353, 355, 357
　income tax 351-3, 354-6
　National Housing Trust 363
　National Insurance 355-6, 358-63, 364-9
　net pay 351
　overtime 350
　payroll 363, 370
　pay slips 370, 371
　piece rates/work 349-50
　statutory deductions 351-63
　time rate 349, 350, 373
　voluntary deductions 351

sales department 10-11
sales staff 11
  commission 350
sales transactions
  documents used in *see* commercial documents
  payment *see* payment methods
savings accounts 314
  Post Office 265-6
screens (VDU) 27, 33, 52
search engines 57
secretaries
  committee 434
  job description 38
  receiving visitors 72-3
security 32-4
  at reception 66, 67, 68
  e-business 59
  of files 33, 210-13, 343, 419
  of information 33, 53, 210-11, 343
  minute files 419
selling transactions
  documents used in *see* commercial documents
  Internet 59
  payment *see* payment methods
serial access 50-1
sex discrimination 504-5
shareholders 3, 409
shares 3
ships' radio telephone calls 85
shopping, Internet 59
short answer questions
  answers to 557-611
  study guidelines 612-13
shorthand 151
shredders 221
sickness absence 345-6, 349, 350
sight, bill of 296, 298
slide projectors 420-1
slides, for presentations 60
SMLEs 4
software 46, 48, 52
  for Internet access 56
  for presentations 60
  word-processing 166
sole traders 2
special delivery 233, 235
speech
  parts of 478
  on telephone 101
spelling 111, 140, 141, 472, 476-7
staff *see* employees
stamps, postage 237
standing committees 409
standing orders 322-3
staples 179-80
starting work 502-3
statements
  account 287-9
  bank 330-3
statistics, presentation 388-98

statutory deductions from pay 351-63
statutory meetings 408-9, 416, 417
stenographers 38
stenotyping machines 151
stock control 380-1
stock records 378-81
stocktaking 381
storage, documents *see* files/filing
strip indexes 433
study guidelines 612-13
sub-committee meetings 410
subsidiary companies 4
SWIFT 326
switchboards 73-8, 88-93
Switch cards 324
systems, definition 21
systems analysts 45-6
systems designers 45

tables, numerical data 389
tape drives 50-1
taxes
  on business transactions 300
  income 351-3, 354-6
technical support staff 46-7
telecommunication companies 470
telecommunications department 13-14
teleconferencing 422-3
telegrams 131-3
telephone banking 336
telephones/telephone lines
  ADC calls 85
  alphabets 89-90
  angry callers 100
  answering 88-90, 93-7, 100-2
  answering machines 82-3, 99
  attitude to 101
  billing services 86
  bleepers 81
  bomb alerts 91-2
  calling plus services 86
  cardphones 87
  coinphones 87
  communications managers 13, 45
  connecting calls 93-4
  conversation guidelines 101-2
  credit card calls 85, 87
  data transmission 54-5
  digital systems facilities 74-8, 99-100
  direct-line 79, 93-8
  directories 87, 98, 470, 471
  equipment 73-84, 88-100
  extensions 75, 76, 77, 78-80, 91, 93-8
  file notes 117
  image creation 100-2
  international calls 84-5
  intra-island calls 84
  local calls 84
  making calls 92, 97-8

  messages 89-90, 94-8, 99
  mobile 80-1, 98-9
  number reference lists 91
  operator services 85
  pagers 81, 82
  phone books 87, 98, 470, 471
  public boxes 87
  receiving calls 88-9, 93, 100
  services 84-7
  ships' radio calls 85
  speech on 101
  switchboards 73-8, 88-93
  systems 21-2
  telegram delivery 132
  toll calls 84, 85
  TSTT services 85, 86
  using 88-100
  videophones 84
  voice 101
  voicemail 99
telephonists
  bomb alerts 91-2
  handing over 91
  image creation 100-2
  job description 37
  making calls 92
  receiving calls 88-9
  reference lists 91
  taking messages 89-90
telex delivery, telegrams 132
telexes 134-5, 235
tenders 277, 278-9
term deposit accounts 314
terminals, computer 48, 49, 53
termination of employment 345, 346
testimonials 493
tests, employment 343, 499
text, VDU display 27
time cards/clocks/rates 349, 350, 373
titles (personal) 121, 474
tourist boards 470
trade
  commercial documentation in *see* commercial documents
  Internet 59
  measurement units 300-1
  payment methods *see* payment methods
  terms used in 299-300
trade cost 300
trade discount 300
trade price 300
trades unions 470, 526-30
trading accounts 10
training, employees 345, 347, 349, 502, 503
train travel 446
transactions, documents used in *see* commercial documents
transcription machines 151, 152
transparencies 420-1
transport department 12-13

transport destination call schedule 377-8
travel agents 445, 470
travel arrangements 443
　accommodation 446-7, 451, 453, 454
　appointments schedule 450, 451
　checklists 454, 456-8
　contacting the traveller 459
　country-specific information 449-50
　documents 447, 454, 456
　electronic booking 454
　equipment 448-9
　foreign currency 448
　information sources 470, 474
　insurance 449, 454
　itinerary 450-2
　money 447-8
　payment methods 447-8
　reservations 452-3, 454
　tasks in traveller's absence 459
　traveller's wishes 444-6
　travel pack 454, 456
travellers' cheques 326-7, 448, 454
treasury tags 178
Trinidad and Tobago
　bank clearing system 333-4
　bank loans 335
　capital 517
　Chamber of Commerce and Industry 525
　currency 517
　health surcharge 353, 355, 357
　income tax 352-3, 354-6
　National Insurance Scheme 359-63, 364-9
　'non-stop banking' 330
　official language 517
　postage rates 253
　postal authority 268
　postal orders 325
　recorded delivery 260
　redirected mail 258-9
　safety legislation 31
TSTT services 85, 86
TTPost
　courier service 263-4
　freepost 263
typewriters
　document formatting 163-4
　electronic 161-4
　supplies for 154-60

typewriting
　copyholders 27, 160
　error correction 159-60
typists, job description 38

United Nations agencies, information from 470
unit prices 300
uploading information 49

VDUs 27, 33, 52
videoconferences 422-3
videophones 84
Viewdata 471
viruses, computer 60
visas 447, 454
visible card indexes 194, 198
visitors, receiving 65-73
visitors' register 66, 67, 68
visual aids, presentations 420-1
visual display units (VDUs) 27, 33, 52
visual presentation, data 388-98
voice, on telephone 101
voicemail 99
votes/voting, meetings 409, 424, 426, 435, 436

wages see salaries and wages
WANs (wide area networks) 54-5
waybill, air 290, 292
websites 57-8, 59, 383, 488-9
weights, measurement units 301
wide area networks (WANs) 54-5
Winchester disks 49, 51
word-processing software 166
word processors 164-5
words
　grammar 111, 428-9, 508-11
　spelling 111, 140, 141, 472, 476-7
　using a dictionary 476-9
work see employment
workers see employees
workflow, factories 373-4, 376-7
work-in-progress files 222
works managers 12
World Wide Web (WWW) 57-8, 59
written communications 108-9
　see also document presentation; document production; document reproduction; letters; mail; Post Office services
　advantages 109

agendas 417, 418
choosing types of 139-40
commercialese 114-15
composition 110-16
concise, rules for 111-12
desk notes 116
dictionaries 472, 476-9
disadvantages 109
e-mail 138-9
English used in 110-15, 472-3, 476-9, 508-15
faxes 135-8
file notes 117
forms 128-30
grammar 111, 428-9, 508-11
internal memoranda 118-20
invitations 125-6, 495
jargon 114-15
job applications 484-6, 488, 489-94, 495
job interview invitations 495, 496, 497
job offers 499-502
job resignation 504, 505
legal documents 130
letters see letters
minutes 427-30, 431-2
notices of meeting 414, 415-16
paragraphs 113
planning 116
preciseness 112-13
proofreading 140-2
punctuation 512-15
reading 142-3
reports 126-7
sentences 111, 113
spelling 111, 140, 141, 472, 476-7
storage see files/filing
style 113-15
telegrams 131-3
telexes 134-5
tone 113-15, 141
transmission 130
types 110
vocabulary 111

year end accounts 10

zipcodes 251-2